Italian–English
English–Italian
Dictionary

Italian–English
English–Italian
Dictionary

**GEDDES &
GROSSET**

Published 2007 by Geddes & Grosset,
David Dale House, New Lanark, ML11 9DJ, Scotland

© 1998 Geddes & Grosset

First printed 1998
Reprinted 2000, 2003, 2007

ISBN 978 1 85534 335 1

Printed and bound in Poland

POLSKABOOK

	Abbreviations	**Abbreviazioni**
abbrev	abbreviation	abbreviazione
adj	adjective	aggettivo
adv	adverb	avverbio
agric	agriculture	agricoltura
anat	anatomy	anatomia
art	article	articolo
auto	automobile	automobile
aux	auxiliary	ausiliario
biol	biology	biologia
bot	botany	botanica
chem	chemistry	chimica
com	commerce	commercio
conj	conjunction	congiunzione
culin	culinary term	espressione culinaria
elect	electricity	elettricità
excl	exclamation	esclamazione
econ	economics	scienza economiche
f	feminine noun	sostantivo feminile
fam	colloquial term	espressione familiare
fig	figurative use	uso figurato
geog	geography	geographia
geom	geometry	geometria
gr, gram	grammar	grammatica
interj	interjection	interiezione
inv, invar	invariable	invariabile
law	law term	giurisprudenza
m	masculine noun	sostantivo maschile
mar	marine term	termine marittimo
med	medicine	medicina
mil	military term	termine militare
mus	music	musica
n	noun	sostantivo

num	numeral	numerale
pl	plural	plurale
pol	politics	politica
pron	pronoun	pronome
prep	preposition	preposizione
rel	relative	relativo
relig	religion	religione
sl	slang	gergo
tel	telephone	telefono
univ	university	università
vi	intransitive verb	verbo intransitivo
vr	reflexive verb	verbo riflessivo
vt	transitive verb	verbo transitivo
vulg	vulgar	volgare
zool	zoology	zoologia

Italian–English Dictionary

A

a *prep* to; in; at; on; by; with; for.

abbandonare *vt* to abandon; to leave; to forsake; to desert.

abbandonato *adj* disused; marooned.

abbandono *m* desertion; neglect; retirement; withdrawal; abandon, abandonment; walkout.

abbassare *vt* to dim; to turn down:— *vi* to sink:— *vr* ~**rsi** to abase oneself.

abbastanza *adj* enough; fairly:— *adv* enough; reasonably; relatively.

abbattere *vt* to cull; to fell; to dash (hopes).

abbattimento *m* despondency, dejection.

abbiente *adj* well-to-do.

abbigliamento *m* clothing; dress.

abbindolare *vt* to take in.

abbonamento *m* subscription; season ticket:— *vr* ~**rsi** to subscribe.

abbonato *m* subscriber.

abbondante *adj* abundant; plentiful.

abbondanza *f* abundance; affluence; plenty; fullness.

abbondare *vi* to abound.

abbordare *vt* to accost.

abbreviare *vt* to abbreviate, abridge.

abbreviazione *f* abbreviation.

abile *adj* able, adept, adroit.

abilità *f* ability, aptitude.

abissale *adj* abysmal.

abisso *m* abyss.

abituare *vt* to accustom.

abituato *adj* accustomed.

abolire *vt* to abolish.

abolizione *f* abolition.

abominevole *adj* abominable.

a bordo *adv* aboard.

aborigeno *adj* aboriginal.

abortire *vi* to abort.

aborto *m* abortion.

abrasione *f* abrasion.

abrasivo *adj* abrasive.

abside *f* apse.

abbozzare *vt* to draft.

abbozzo *m* draft, sketch.

abbracciare *vt* to embrace; to hug.

abbraccio *m* cuddle; embrace; hug.

abbronzarsi *vr* to tan.

abbronzato *adj* tanned.

abbronzatura *f* suntan, tan.

abete *m* fir (tree), spruce:— **legno di abete** *m* deal.

abile *adj* artful; deft; skilled, skilful.

abilità *f* ability; knack; skill.

abitabile *adj* habitable, inhabitable.

abitante *m/f* inhabitant.

abitare *vt* to inhabit; (ghost) to haunt:— *vi* to live.

abito *m* dress; gown:— **abito da sera** *m* evening dress.

abituale *adj* habitual; ordinary; routine.

abituato *adj* accustomed.

abnegazione *f* self-sacrifice.

abortire *vi* to abort, miscarry.

aborto *m* abortion, miscarriage.

abrogare *vt* to revoke, repeal.

abrogazione *f* repeal.

abusare *vt* to misuse:—**abusare di** to abuse.

abusivo *adj* unauthorised, unlawful.

abuso *m* abuse, misuse.

acacia *f* acacia.

acaro *m* mite.

accademia *f* academy.

accademico *adj* academic:—*m* academic, academician.

accadere *vt* to befall:—*vi* to befall; to happen; to occur; to pass.

accanto *prep* beside:—**accanto a** next to.

accappatoio *m* bathrobe.

accarezzare *vt* to fondle; to pet; to stroke.

accecare *vt* to blind.

accedere a *vi* to assent to; to attain (office); to adhere (to); to access.

accelerare *vt* to accelerate; to hasten; to precipitate:—*vi* to accelerate.

accendere *vt* to switch on; to turn on; to put on; to light.

accendino *m* cigarette lighter.

accensione *f* ignition:—**chiave dell'accensione** *f* ignition key.

accentato *adj* stressed.

accento *m* accent.

accentuare *vt* to accentuate.

accertare *vt* ascertain.

acceso *adj* on, alight.

accessibile *adj* accessible.

accesso *m* access; fit:—**divieto d'accesso** no entry.

accessori *mpl* fittings; trimmings

accessorio *n* accessory; attachment; fitment.

accettabile *adj* acceptable.

accettare *vt* to accept; to take.

accettazione *f* acceptance; reception.

acciaio *m* steel.

accidente *m* accident.

acclamare *vt* to acclaim.

acclamazione *f* acclaim.

acclimatare *vt* to acclimatise:—*vr* ~**rsi** to acclimatise oneself.

accoglienza *f* acceptance.

accompagnamento *m* accompaniment.

accordo *m* agreement:—**essere d'accordo con** to agree with.

accoccolarsi *vr* to nestle.

accogliere *vt* to welcome.

accollarsi *vr* to shoulder.

accomodante *adj* easy-going.

accompagnare *vt* to accompany.

accompagnato *adj* accompanied.

acconsentire *vi* to consent.

accontentare *vt* to indulge; to humour; to please.

accoppiare *vt* to mate:—*vr* ~**rsi** to copulate; to mate.

accordare *vt* to grant; to tune.

accordo *m* agreement; deal; settlement.

accorgersi *vr* to notice.

accreditare *vt* to credit.

accrescere *vt* to increase:—*vr* ~**rsi** to increase.

accumulare *vt* to accumulate.

accuratezza *f* accuracy.

accurato *adj* accurate; careful.

accusa *f* accusation, charge, prosecution (*law*).

accusare *vt* to accuse; to charge.

accusato *m* accused.

accusatore *m* accuser.

aceto *m* vinegar.

acido *adj* acid; caustic; sour:—*m* acid.

acne *f* acne.

acqua *f* water:—**acqua dolce** fresh water:—**tirare l'acqua** to flush.

acquaio *m* sink.

acquatico *adj* aquatic.

acquazzone *m* cloudburst; downpour; shower.

acquedotto *m* aquaduct.

acquerello *m* watercolour.

acquirente *m/f* purchaser.

acquisire *vt* to acquire.

acquistare *vt* to purchase.

acro *m* acre.

acute *adj* acute.

adatto *adj* appropriate; right; fit; suitable; becoming.

adattare *vt* to suit.

addestramento *m* training.

addestrare *vt* to train; to school.

addetto *m* attaché, employee.

addio *m* farewell; goodbye:—*adj* **d'addio** parting.

additivo *m* additive.

addizionare *vt* to add.

addizione *f* addition.

addolcire *vt* to sweeten.

addolorato *adj* sorrowful; pained.

addome *m* abdomen.

addomesticazione *f* domestication.

addominale *adj* abdominal.

addormentarsi *vr* to fall asleep.

addossarsi *vr* to take on.

adeguatamente *adv* suitably.

adeguato *adj* adequate.

aderire *vi* to adhere.

adesivo *m* adhesive; sticker.

adesso *adv, conj* now.

adolescenza *f* adolescence.

adolescente *m/f* adolescent, teenager.

adorabile *adj* adorable, lovable.

adorare *vt* to adore; to worship.

adorato *adj* beloved.

adottare *vt* to adopt.

adulterare *vt* to adulterate; to doctor.

adultero *adj* adulterous:—*m* adulterer.

adultera *f* adulteress.

adulterio *m* adultery.

adulto *adj* adult:—*m* adult, grown-up.

aereo *adj* aerial.

aeronautica *f* air force.

aeroporto *m* airport.

aerosol *m* aerosol.

affabile *adj* affable, amiable, good-natured.

affamato *adj* hungry; starving, famished.

affare *m* affair; deal; bargain; snip.

affari *mpl* business:—**uomo d'affari** *m* businessman:—**donna d'affari** *f* businesswoman.

affascinante *adj* fascinating; glamorous; intriguing.

affascinare *vt* to fascinate; to captivate, charm; to enthral.

affaticare *vt* to fatigue; to strain.

affermativo *adj* affirmative.

affettare *vt* to slice; to affect.

affettato *adj* affected.

affetto *m* affection; fondness.

affidavit *m inv* affidavit.

affilare *vt* to sharpen.

affilato *adj* sharp.

affiliazione *f* affiliation.

affinché *conj* so that.

affinità *f* affinity.

affittare *vt* to lease; to let; to rent.

affitto *m* rent:—**proprietà in affitto** *f* leasehold:—**contratto d'affitto** *m* tenancy.

affluente *m* tributary.

affogare *vt*, *vi* to drown.

affollare *vt* to crowd; to throng:—*vr* ~**rsi** to cram.

affrancatura *f* postage.

affresco *m* fresco.

affrettare *vt* to quicken:—*vr* ~**rsi** to hurry, make haste.

affrontare *vt* to broach; to confront; to deal with, tackle; to face.

affumicato *adj* smoked.

afoso *adj* close, sultry, muggy.

afrodisiaco *m* aphrodisiac.

agenda *f* diary.

agente *m/f* agent:—**agente immobiliare** *m* estate agent.

agenzia *f* agency:—**agenzia viaggi** *f* travel agency.

agganciare *vt* to hook.

aggettivo *m* adjective.

aggiungere *vt* to add.

agghiacciante *adj* gruesome, spine-chilling.

aggiornare *vt* to update; to write up.

aggiustare *vt* to adjust; to mend, repair.

agglomerato *m* chipboard.

aggravamento *m* aggravation.

aggravare *vt* to aggravate.

aggraziato *adj* graceful.

aggredire *vt* to mug.

aggressione *f* aggression.

aggressivo *adj* aggressive.

aggressore *m* aggressor; attacker.

agile *adj* agile; lithe; nimble.

agilità *f* agility.

agitare *vt* to agitate; to stir; to churn; to flail:—*vr* ~**rsi** to fidget; to dither; to wriggle.

agitato *adj* flustered.

agitazione *f* agitation.

aglio *m* garlic:—**spicchio d'aglio** *m* clove of garlic.

agnello *m* lamb.

ago *m* needle.

agonia *f* agony.

agosto *m* August.

agricolo *adj* agricultural.

agricoltura *f* agriculture, farming.

ahi! *excl* ouch!

AIDS *m* AIDS.

aiuola *f* (garden) border; flower bed.

aiutante *m/f* assistant; help:—**aiutante di campo** aide-de-camp.

aiutare *vt* to assist, aid, help.

aiuto *m* aid, assistence, help.

ala *f* wing; (*sport*) winger.

alabastro *m* alabaster.

alba *f* dawn, daybreak, sunrise.

alberello *m* sapling.

albergo *m* hotel.

albero *m* tree; mast; (*mar*) spar; shaft:—**albero a gomiti** *m* crankshaft:—**albero a camme** *m* camshaft.

albicocca *f* apricot.

album *m* album.

alchimia *f* alchemy.

alcolico *m* alcoholic.

alcolico *m* alcoholic:—**bevande alcoliche** *fpl* liquor.

alcolismo *m* alcoholism.

alcool *m* alcohol, (*fam*) booze:—**alcool denaturato** *m* methylated spirits.

alcuno *adj* some:—*pron* **alcuni** some.

alfabetico *adj* alphabetical:—**in ordine alfabetico** in alphabetical order.

alfabeto *m* alphabet:—**alfabeto Morse** *m* Morse code.

algebra *f* algebra.

alghe *fpl* algae; seaweed.

alias *adv* alias.

alibi *m* alibi.

alimentare *vt* to feed.

alimentari *m* grocery:—**negoziante di alimentari** *m* grocer.

aliscafo *m* hydrofoil.

alito *m* breath.

alitosi *f* halitosis.

allacciare *vt* to tie; to lace; to buckle:—*vr* ~**rsi** to buckle, fasten.

allarme *m* alarm, alert:—**falso allarme** *m* false alarm.

alleanza *f* alliance.

alleato *adj* allied:—*m* ally.

allegato *m* enclosure.

allegria *f* gaiety; merriment.

allegro *m* cheerful, jolly, merry; perky.

allenamento *m* training.

allergia *f* allergy.

alleviare *vt* to alleviate; to ease; to relieve.

alligatore *m* alligator.

allodola *f* lark, skylark.

alloggiamento *m* housing.

alloggiare *vt* to accommodate; to house:—*vi* to lodge; to stay.

alloggio *m* accommodation.

allora *adv* then:—**da allora** since.

alloro *m* bay, laurel.

alludere *vt* to hint.

alluminio *m* aluminium.

allungare *vt* to elongate; to lengthen.

almeno *adv* at least.

alpinismo *m* climbing; mountaineering.

alpinista *m/f* climber; mountaineer.

alpino *adj* alpine.

alquanto *adv* somewhat.

altare *m* altar.

alterco *m* wrangle.

alternativa *f* alternative:—**come alternativa** alternatively.

alternativo *adj* alternative.

alternato *adj* alternate.

altezza *f* height; headroom; highness:—**essere all'altezza** to live up to.

altitudine *f* altitude.

alto *adj* high; tall:—**in alto** aloft:—**il più alto** topmost:—**verso l'alto** upwards:—*adv* **in alto** overhead:—*m* high.

altoparlante *m* *invar* loudspeaker; speaker.

altrettanto *adv* just as; likewise.

altrimenti *adv* else; otherwise.

altro *pron*: **un altro** another; other:—**l'un l'altro** one another:—*adj* other; more:—*adv* else.

alzare *vt* to heighten; to raise; to turn up:—*vr* ~**rsi** to rise; to stand up.

amaca *f* hammock.

amante *m/f* lover; *f* mistress.

amare *vt* to love.

amaro *adj* bitter.

ambasciata *f* embassy.

ambasciatore *m* ambassador.

ambedue *adj* both.

ambidestro *adj* ambidextrous.

ambientale *adj* environmental.

ambientalista *m/f* conservationist.

ambientarsi *vr* to find one's feet.

ambiente *m* environment; setting:—**ambiente sociale** *m* milieu.

ambiguo *adj* ambiguous; dubious.

ambito *m* scope.

ambizione *f* ambition.

ambulanza *f* ambulance.

ambulatorio *m* surgery.

ametista *f* amethyst.

amica *f* girlfriend.

amichevole *adj* amicable; friendly.

amicizia *f* friendship.

amico *m* friend; pal:—**amico del cuore** bosom friend.

ammazzare *vt* to kill.

ammettere *vt* to accept, admit:—**bisogna ammettere che** admittedly.

ammiccare *vi* to wink.

amministrare *vt* to administer.

amministrativo *adj* administrative.

amministratore *m* administrator; trustee:—**amministratore delegato** managing director.

amministrazione *f* administration:—**amministrazione della casa** *f* housekeeping:—**cattiva amministrazione** *f* mismanagement.

ammirare *vt* to admire.

ammiratore *m* admirer; well-wisher.

ammirazione *f* admiration.

ammissibile *adj* admissible, allowable.

ammissione *f* acknowledgement, admission: entrance.

ammettere *vt* to concede, countenance; to own up.

ammissibile *adj* permissible.

ammobiliato *adj* furnished.

ammonitorio *adj* cautionary.

ammutinamento *m* mutiny.

amnesia *f* amnesia.

amnistia *f* amnesty.

amorale *adj* amoral.

amore *m* love.

amorfo *adj* amorphous.

ampio *adj* ample.

ampliare *vt* amplify; to enlarge; to widen.

ampolla *f* cruet.

amputare *vt* amputate.

anacardio *m* cashew.

anacronismo *m* anachronism.

analcolico *m* soft drink:—*adj* non-alcoholic.

analfabeta *m/f*, *adj* illiterate.

analisi *f inv* analysis.

analista *m/f* analyst:—**analista sistemi** systems analyst.

analitico *adj* analytic(al).

analizzare *vt* to analyse.

ananas *m inv* pineapple.

anarchia *f* anarchy.

anatomia *f* anatomy.

anca *f* hip.

ancestrale *adj* ancestral.

anche *adv* also; too; as well.

ancora *adv* again; another; even; still; already:—*adj* more.

ancora *f* anchor.

andare *vi* to go.

andata *f*: **biglietto di andata** *m* single ticket.

anello *m* ring.

anemia *f* anaemia.

anemico *adj* anaemic.

anemone *m* (*bot*) anemone.

anestetico *m* anaesthetic.

anfiteatro *m* amphitheatre.

angelo *m* angel.

anglicismo *m* anglicism.

anglicizzare *vt* anglicise.

angolo *m* angle; corner.

angoscia *f* anguish; distress:—*vr* ~**rsi** to agonise over.

anguilla *f* eel.

anguria *f* watermelon.

angusto *adj* cramped; poky.

anice *m* aniseed.

anima *f* soul.

animale *adj* animal:—*m* animal:—**animale domestico** *m* pet:—**animali nocivi** *mpl* vermin.

animare *vt* to animate; to pep up.

animosità *f inv* animosity.

annegare *vt*, *vi* to drown.

anniversario *m* anniversary.

anno *m* year; session:—**anno nuovo** *m* New Year:—**anno luce** *m* light year:—**all'anno** per annum.

annoiare *vt* to bore.

annotare *vt* to annotate; to record.

annuale *adj* yearly.

annunciare *vt* to announce.

annunciatore *m* newscaster.

annuncio *m* advertisement; announcement.

anonimato *m* anonymity; obscurity.

anonimo *adj* anonymous; unnamed.

anoressia *f* anorexia.

anormale *adj* abnormal; freak.

anormalità *f* abnormality.

ansia *f* anxiety.

ansioso *adj* nervous; solicitous.

antagonismo *m* antagonism.

antartico *adj* antarctic.

antecedente *adj* antecedent.

antenna *f* aerial, antenna; feeler.

anteriore *adj* anterior; fore.

antibiotico *m* antibiotic.

antichità *f* antiquity.

anticipo *m* advance; down payment.

antico *adj* ancient, antique.

anticoncezionale *adj*, *m* contraceptive.

antidolorifico *m* painkiller.

antidoto *m* antidote.

antifurto *m inv* burglar alarm.

antilope *f* antelope.

antincendio *adj*: **allarme antincendio** *f* fire alarm.

antipasto *m* hors d'oeuvres, starter.

antipatico *adj* objectionable; unlovable.

antipodi *mpl* antipodes.

antiquato *adj* antiquated; dated; old-fashioned; stuffy.

antirrino *m* antirrhinum.

antisemitico *adj* antisemitic.

anziano *adj* aged; elderly; old:—*m* elder.

aorta *f* aorta.

apartheid *f* apartheid.

ape *f* bee.

aperitivo *m* aperitif.

aperto *adj* open; broad-minded; open-minded; gaping:—**all'aperto** outdoor.

apertura *f* aperture; opening; spread.

apiario *m* apiary.

apostrofo *m* apostrophe.

appagare *vt* to quench.

apparecchio *m* set; appliance:—**apparecchio acustico** *m* hearing aid: —**apparecchio ortodontico** *m* brace.

apparenza *f* semblance.

apparire *vi* to appear:—**apparire indistintamente** to loom.

appartamento *m* apartment; flat; suite.

appartenere *vi* to belong.

appassionante *adj* gripping.

appassionato *adj* devotee; enthusiastic; passionate:—*m* enthusiast.

appellante *m*/*f* appellant.

appena *adv* barely; just; hardly; fresh, freshly; scarcely; just.

appendere *vt* to hang.

appetito *m* appetite.

applaudire *vt* to applaud; to clap.

applauso *m* applause, acclaim; clapping.

applicare *vt* to enforce:—*vr* **~rsi** to apply.

appoggiare *vt* to back; to lean; to support.

apporre *vt* affix, append.

apprezzare *vt* to appreciate.

appropriato *adj* apt; proper; suitable.

approvare *vt* to approve; to assent.

appuntamento *m* appointment; date; rendezvous.

apribottiglie *m inv* bottle-opener.

aprile *m* April.

aprire *vt* to open; to unlock.

apriscatole *m inv* tin-opener.

aquila *f* eagle.

arabo *adj, m* Arab.

arachide *f* peanut.

arancia *f* orange.

aranciata *f* orangeade.

archeologia *f* archeology.

archeologico *adj* archaeological.

archeologo *m* archaelogist.

architettare *vt* to engineer.

architetto *m* architect.

architettura *f* architecture.

arco *m* arch; bow:—**tiro con l'arco** archery:—*adj* **ad arco** arched.

arcobaleno *m* rainbow.

area *f* area.

argento *m* silver.

argomento *m* argument; subject; topic.

Ariete *m* Aries.

aristocrazia *f* aristocracy.

aritmetica *f* arithmetic.

aritmetico *adj* arithmetical.

arma *f* weapon:—**arma da fuoco** firearm.

armadio *m* cupboard.

armare *vt* to arm.

armato *adj* armed.

armonia *f* concord; harmony.

armonica *f* harmonica; mouth organ.

aroma *m* aroma.

arrabbiare *vt* **far arrabbiare** to make someone angry; to enrage.

arrabbiato *adj* angry.

arredare *vt* to furnish.

arrivare *vi* to arrive; to turn up.

arrivederci *excl* goodbye.

arrosto *m* roast.

arte *f* art; craft:—**le belle arti** *fpl* the fine arts.

articolo *m* article; item; story.

artigiano *m* craftsman; artisan.

artigliere *m* gunner.

asciugacapelli *m inv* hairdryer.

asciugamano *m* towel.

asciugare *vt* to dry; to blot (ink).

ascoltare *vi* to listen.

asma *f* asthma.

asmatico *adj* asthmatic.

aspettare *vt* to await; to expect:—*vi* to wait.

aspirina *f* aspirin.

assaggiare *vt* to taste; to sample.

assassinare *vt* to assassinate; to murder.

assassinio *m* assassination; murder; foul play.

asse *f* board; axis:—**asse da stiro** ironing board:—**asse di pavimento** floorboard.

assegnare *vt* to assign; to award; to set.

assemblea *f* assembly.

assicurare *vt* to assure; to insure; to secure.

assistenza *f* help; aid:—**assistenza post-operatoria** aftercare:—**servizio assistenza clienti** after-sales service:—**assistenza sociale** social work.

assomigliare *vi* to look like; to take after.

assorbente *m* sanitary towel:—*adj* absorbent.

assurdità *f* absurdity.

assurdo *adj* absurd; preposterous:—*m* (an) absurdity.

astratto *adj* abstract.

astringente *adj, m* astringent.

astrologia *f* astrology.

astronauta *m/f* astronaut; spaceman/woman.

astronomia *f* astronomy.

astronomico *adj* astronomical.

atavico *adj* ancestral.

ateismo *m* atheism.

ateo *m* atheist.

atipico *adj* atypical.

atlante *m* atlas.

atleta *m/f* athlete.

atletico *adj* athletic.

atmosfera *f* atmosphere.

atomico *adj* atomic.

atomo *m* atom.

atrocità *f inv* atrocity; enormity; outrage.

atrofia *f* atrophy.

attaccare *vt* to affix; to charge (*mil*); to attach, attack; to hitch up.

attacco *m* attack; strike; onslaught; fit; bout (illness); seizure.

attento *adj* careful; observant; watchful:—**stare attento** to beware.

attenuante *adj* extenuating.

attenzione *f* attention; care; heed; caution.

atterraggio *m* landing; touchdown:—**atterraggio forzato** forced landing.

atterrare *vi* to land.

attesa *f* wait; waiting:—**lista d'attesa** waiting list:—**sala d'attesa** waiting room.

attestare *vt* to certify; to attest.

attestazione *f* certification.

attirare *vt* to attract; to draw.

attività *f* activity; business; pursuit.

atto *m* act:—**atto di proprietà** title deed.

attore *m* actor; plaintiff.

attrattiva *f* attraction.

attraversare *vt* to cross; to span.

attraverso *prep* across; through.

attrazione *f* attraction; pull.

attrezzo *m* tool:—**cassetta degli attrezzi** *f* toolbox.

attribuire *vt* attribute; ascribe; apportion; to give.

attrice *f* actress.

attuale *adj* current; present; prevailing; up-to-date.

attualità *fpl* news

audacia *f* audacity; boldness; daring; temerity.

auditorio *m* auditorium.

augurare *vt* to wish.

augurio *m* wish.

augusto *adj* august.

aula *f* classroom.

aumentare *vt* to augment; to increase; to grow; to gain; to heighten:—*vi* increase; to heighten; to rise; to accrue.

aumento *m* raise; gain; increase; rise:—**aumento di valore** *m* appreciation.

ausiliario *adj, m* ancillary.

autenticità *f* authenticity.

autentico *adj* authentic.

autista *m* chauffeur; *m/f* driver.

autoaffondare *vt* to scuttle.

autoarticolato *m* articulated lorry.

autobiografia *f* autobiography.

autoblinda *f* armoured car.

autobus *m* bus.

autocarro *m* lorry:—**autocarro della nettezza urbana** *m* dustcart.

autodifesa *f* self-defence.

autodisciplina *f* self-discipline.

autografo *m* autograph.

automobile *f* car:—**automobile sportiva** sports car.

autopsia *f* autopsy; post-mortem.

autore *m* author; writer.

autorimessa *f* garage.

autorità *f* authority.

autoritratto *m* self-portrait.

autorizzare *vt* to authorise.

autorizzazione *f* authorisation; clearance; permit; licence; leave.

autostop *m* hitchhiking: —**fare l'autostop** to hitch (a lift), hitchhike.

autostrada *f* motorway.

autrice *f* authoress.

autunnale *adj* autumnal.

autunno *m* autumn.

avanguardia *f* avant-garde; forefront: —**d'avanguardia** *adj* avant-garde.

avanti *adv* ahead; forwards: —**in avanti** onwards: —**in avanti** *adj* forward: —**più avanti** further, farther.

avaro *adj* avaricious; mean: —*m* miser.

avere *vt* to have.

aviazione *f* aviation.

avido *adj* avid, greedy, grasping.

avorio *m*, *adj* ivory.

avvalersi *vr*: **avvalersi di** to avail oneself of.

avvallamento *m* subsidence.

avvelenare *vt* to poison.

avvenimento *m* event; happening; incident.

avventura *f* adventure; affair.

avverbio *m* adverb.

avversario *m* adversary; opponent: —*adj* opposing.

avvertimento *m* warning.

avvisare *vt* advise.

avviso *m* notice; advice.

avvocato *m* advocate; lawyer; solicitor; attorney, barrister, counsel.

avvolgere *vt* to wind; to envelop; to coil; to swathe; to shroud.

avvoltoio *m* vulture.

azalea *f* azalea.

azienda *f* company.

azione *f* action; deed; share: —**azioni** *fpl* holdings.

azionista *m/f* shareholder.

azzurro *adj* azure; blue.

B

babbo *m* pa(pa), dad(dy).

bacca *f* berry.

baciare *vt* to kiss.

bacio *m* kiss.

badia *f* abbey.

badminton *m* badminton

baffo *m*: **baffi** *mpl* moustache; whiskers.

bagaglio *m* baggage: —**bagagli** *mpl* luggage.

bagnante *m/f* bather.

bagnare *vt* to wet, to bathe.

bagnato *adj* wet, soggy.

bagnino *m* lifeguard.

bagno *m* bath.

baia *f* bay; cove.

balcone *m* balcony.

baldacchino *m* canopy: —**letto a baldacchino** four-poster (bed).

balena *f* whale.

ballare *vt vi* to dance.

ballo *m* dance; ball:—**sala da ballo** dance hall.

balsamo *m* (hair) conditioner; balm.

bambino *m* infant; baby; child (*pl* children).

bambola *f* doll.

banana *f* banana.

banca *f* bank.

banchetto *m* banquet; feast; spread.

banco *m* counter; pew; form; shoal, school (of fish).

bandiera *f* flag; colours.

bar *m* bar; café.

bara *f* coffin.

barattolo *m* jar; canister:—**barattolo del tè** tea caddy.

barba *f* beard:—**senza barba** *adj* clean-shaven:—**barba corta** *f* stubble.

barbiere *m* barber.

barbuto *adj* bearded.

barca *f* boat.

barella *f* stretcher.

barista *m/f* barman, barmaid, bartender.

base *f* base; basis; staple; grass roots.

basilico *m* basil.

basso *adj* low; short; bass:—*m* (*mus*) bass.

basta *interj* that's enough.

bastardo *m* bastard; (*sl*) sod; mongrel.

bastare *vi* to be enough; to suffice:—**far bastare** *vt* to eke out, stretch.

bastoncino *m* stick; chopstick.

bastone *m* rod; club; cane.

battaglia *f* battle:—**campo** *m* **di battaglia** battlefield.

battello *m* boat:—**battello a ruote** *m* paddle steamer.

battere *vt* to hit; to beat.

batteria *f* battery; drums; set.

battezzare *vt* to christen; to baptise.

battistrada *m inv* tread.

baule *m* chest, trunk.

beatificare *vt* to beatify.

becco *m* bill, beak; spout.

begonia *f* begonia.

beige *m adj* beige.

bellezza *f* beauty.

bello *adj* beautiful; handsome; good-looking, lovely.

benché *conj* notwithstanding; though; although.

bene *m* good; welfare:—*excl* fine:—*adv* right; all right; well:—*adj* well:—**voler bene a** *vt* to love.

benedizione *f* benediction; blessing.

beni *mpl* assets.

benvenuto *adj, m* welcome.

bere *m* drinking:—*vt* to drink; to imbibe:—*vi* to drink.

bestemmia *f* curse; blasphemy.

bestia *f* beast:—**bestia da soma** beast of burden.

bestiale *adj* bestial.

bettola *f* dive.

betulla *f* birch.

bevanda *f* drink:—**bevanda gasata** *f* fizzy drink.

biancheria *f* laundry:—**biancheria intima** *f* lingerie, underwear.

bianco *adj* blank; white:—*m* white.

biancospino *m* hawthorn.

bibita *f* drink.

biblioteca *f* library.

bicchiere *m* glass; beaker; tumbler.

bici *f inv* bike.

bicicletta *f* bicycle, cycle:—**andare in bicicletta** *vi* to cycle.

biforcazione *f* fork; bifurcation.

biforcuto *adj* forked.
biglietteria *f* ticket office.
biglietto *m* card; note; ticket.
bikini *m inv* bikini.
bilancia *f* scales.
Bilancia *f* Libra.
bilione *m* billion.
bimbo *m* baby.
binario *m* platform; track.
biologia *f* biology.
biondo *m, adj* blond.
birra *f* beer; ale:—**birra bionda** *f* lager.
bisbigliare *vt vi* to whisper.
bisbiglio *m* whisper, whispering.
biscia *f* grass snake.
biscotto *m* biscuit.
bisestile *adj*: **anno bisestile** *m* leap year.
bisogno *m* need; want:—**aver bisogno di** *vt* to need.
bistecca *f* steak:—**bistecca di manzo** *f* steak:—**bistecca di maiale** *f* pork chop.
bisturi *m inv* lancet; scalpel.
bizzarria *f* quirk; oddity.
bizzarro *adj* droll; kinky; bizarre; weird.
bleso *adj*: **essere bleso** *vi* to lisp:—**pronuncia blesa** *f* lisp.
blocco *m* bloc; block; blockade; freeze.
blusa *f* smock.
bocca *m* mouth:—**guardare a bocca aperta** *vt* to gape.
bocchetta *f* nozzle.
body *m inv* leotard.
bollire *vi* to boil; to seethe.
bollitore *m* kettle.
bomba *f* bomb, bombshell:—**bomba incendiaria** *f* incendiary (bomb):—**bomba a orologieria** *f* time bomb.

bombo *m* bumblebee.
bontà *f* goodness.
bordeaux *adj* maroon.
bordo *m* edge, edging; surround.
borsa *f* handbag; pouch; bag:—**borsa di studio** bursary, grant, scholarship.
bosco *m* wood.
boscoso *adj* wooded:—**zona boscosa** *f* woodland.
botteghino *m* box office.
bottiglia *f* bottle.
bottino *m* loot; plunder; booty; spoil.
bottone *m* button:—**bottone automatico** *m* popper.
bovino *adj* bovine.
braccialetto *m* bracelet, bangle.
braccio *m* arm; jib; fathom.
bracconaggio *m* poaching.
bracconiere *m* poacher.
branco *m* drove; gaggle (of geese); pride; pack.
brancolare *vi* to fumble.
brandy *m inv* brandy.
bravo *adj* good.
breccia *f* opening; breach.
breve *adj* brief; short.
brevettare *vt* to patent.
brevettato *adj* patented.
brevetto *m* patent.
brevità *f* brevity.
brezza *f* breeze:—**brezza marina** *f* sea breeze.
bric-a-brac *m* bric-a-brac.
briciola *f* breadcrumb; crumb.
bricolage *m* do-it-yourself.
bridge *m* bridge.
brigata *f* brigade.
briglia *f* bridle; *fpl* harness.
brillante *adj* brilliant.
brillare *vi* to shine.

brina *f* frost; hoarfrost.

brindare *vt* to toast.

brindisi *m inv* toast:—**qui ci vuole un brindisi!** this calls for a drink!

brio *m* liveliness.

brocca *f* jug; pitcher.

broccato *m* brocade.

broccoli *mpl* broccoli.

brochure *f* brochure.

brodo *m* broth; stock:—**brodo ristretto** *m* consommé.

bronchiale *adj* bronchial.

bronchite *f* bronchitis.

broncio *m* pout:—**tenere il broncio** *vi* to sulk:—**fare il broncio** *vi* to pout.

brontolare *vi* to grumble; to grouse; to rumble.

bronzo *m* bronze.

brucare *vt* to crop.

bruciacchiare *vt* to singe; to scorch.

bruciacchiatura *f* scorch.

bruciapelo *adj*: **a bruciapelo** point-blank.

bruciare *vt* to burn:—*vi* to smart; to sting; to rankle.

bruciato *m* burning.

bruciatore *m* burner.

bruciatura *f* burn.

bruco *m* caterpillar.

brughiera *f* moor, heath.

brulicare *vi* to teem.

brumoso *adj* misty.

bruna *f* brunette.

bruscamente *adv* sharply; abruptly.

brusco *adj* abrupt, brusque, bluff, blunt, off-hand, curt; sharp; unceremonious; rude.

brutale *adj* brutal.

brutalità *f* brutality.

brutalmente *adv* roughly.

bruto *m*, brute:—*adj* brute; bad; ugly.

bruttezza *f* ugliness.

brutto *adj* bad; ugly.

bubble-gum *m inv* bubble gum.

buca *f* hole; pothole; pit:—**buca di sabbia** *f* sandpit.

bucaneve *m inv* snowdrop.

bucare *vt* to hole; to prick.

bucato *m* washing.

buccia *f* peel; skin; rind; zest.

buco *m* hole.

bucolico *adj* bucolic.

buddismo *m* Buddhism.

budello *m* gut:—**budella** *fpl* guts.

budino *m* pudding.

bue *m* ox.

bufalo *m* buffalo.

bufera *f* gale:—**bufera di neve** blizzard.

buffet *m inv* buffet.

buffo *adj* funny, comic.

buffone *m* buffoon; fool; jester.

buffoneria *f* antics.

bugia *f* lie:—**bugia pietosa** *f* white lie.

bugiardo *adj* lying:—*m m* liar, fibber.

buio *adj* dark; gloom; *m* dark, darkness.

bulbo *m* bulb:—**bulbo oculare** *m* eyeball.

bulldog *m inv* bulldog.

bulldozer *m inv* bulldozer.

bulletta *f* tack.

bullo *m* bully.

bullone *m* bolt.

bungalow *m inv* bungalow.

bunker *m inv* bunker.

buoi *mpl* oxen.

buo-ngustaio *m* epicure; gourmet.

buono *m* coupon; token:—**buono premio** *m* gift voucher:—*adj* good.

burattino *m* puppet.

burbero *adj* gruff; surly.

burla *f* prank.
burlone *m* joker; tease.
burocrate *m/f* bureaucrat.
burocrazia *f* bureaucracy; (*fig*) red tape.
burrasca *f* squall.
burrascoso *adj* rough; stormy; tempestuous.
burro *m* butter.
burrone *m* gully; ravine.
bussare *vi* to knock; to tap:—*vt* to rap.

bussata *f* rap.
bussola *f* compass.
busta *f* envelope.
bustarella *f* backhander; bribe.
bustina *f* sachet.
busto *m* bust; girdle, corset.
buttafuori *m inv* bouncer.
buttar *vt*: **buttar fuori** to turf out:—**buttar via** to throw away.
byte *m* byte.

C

cabina *f* booth; (lorry) cab; (plane) cabin; cubicle:—**cabina di pilotaggio** cockpit, flight deck:—**cabina telefonica** *f* telephone booth, callbox.
cacao *m* cocoa.
cacciare *vi* to hunt.
cactus *m inv* cactus.
cadere *vi* to fall; to topple over; to slump:—*vt* **lasciar cadere** to drop.
caffè *m* café; coffee:—**pausa per il caffè** *f* coffee break.
caffettiera *f* coffee pot:—**caffettiera a filtro** *f* percolator.
cagnolino *m* puppy.
calamaro *m* squid.
calare *vi* to drop; to wane:—*vt* to lower; to drop.
calcagno *m* heel.
calcare *m* limestone.
calce *f* lime:—**bianco di calce** *m* whitewash.
calcestruzzo *m* concrete:—**rivestire di calcestruzzo** *vt* to concrete.

calciatore *m* footballer.
calcificare *vt* to calcify.
calcio *m* kick; calcium; football; soccer.
calcolare *vt* to calculate; to compute; to reckon.
calcolatore *m* calculator.
caldo *adj* hot, warm.
caleidoscopio *m* kaleidoscope.
calendario *m* calendar.
calendola *f* marigold.
callo *m* corn.
calma *f* calm; cool; composure.
calmante *adj* soothing; sedative:—*m* sedative.
calmare *vt* to calm; to lull; to pacify; to steady; to soothe.
caloroso *adj* warm, appreciative.
calmo *adj* calm; cool.
calo *m* fall; drop.
calore *m* heat; warmth.
calvo *adj* bald.
calza *f* stocking:—**calze** *fpl* hosiery.
calzettone *m* sock.

calzoncini *mpl* shorts.

cambiamento *m* change; shift: — **cambiamento continuo** *m* flux.

cambiare *vt* to change.

cambio *m* change; exchange.

camelia *f* camellia.

camera *f* room; chamber; (*pol*) house: — **camera da letto** *f* bedroom.

cameraman *m inv* cameraman.

cameriere *m* waiter.

camicetta *f* blouse.

camicia *f* shirt: — **camicia di forza** *f* straitjacket.

camino *m* chimney.

camion *m inv* lorry, truck.

cammeo *m* cameo.

camminare *vi* walk.

campagna *f* country, countryside; campaign.

campagnolo *m* countryman.

campana *f* bell.

campanello *m* bell; doorbell.

campanile *m* belfry; steeple.

campeggiare *vi* to camp.

campione *m* champion.

campo *m* ground, field; pitch.

cancellare *vt* to cancel.

Cancer *m* Cancer.

cancro *m* cancer.

candela *f* candle; sparking plug.

candida *f* thrush.

candidato *m* candidate.

candidatura *f* candidacy.

cane *m* dog: — **cane per ciechi** *m* guide dog.

canna *f* cane.

canoa *f* canoe.

canottiera *f* vest.

cantante *m/f* singer.

cantare *vi* to sing; to crow: — *vt* to sing; to chant.

canto *m* song; singing; crow; chant: — **canto funebre** *m* dirge.

canzone *f* song: — **canzone folk** *f* folksong.

capacità *f* capability.

capelli *mpl* hair.

capire *vt* to understand; to comprehend.

capitale *f* capital (city).

capitano *m* captain, skipper.

capo *m* boss, chief; commander; leader.

Capodanno *m* New Year's Day.

cappa *f* cape; cloak.

cappella *f* chapel.

cappellaio *m* hatter.

cappellano *m* chaplain.

cappello *m* hat.

capra *f* goat.

capretto *m* kid.

Capricorno *m* Capricorn.

carattere *m* character; type.

caratteristica *f* feature; trait.

carbone *m* coal; charcoal.

carciofo *m* artichoke.

cardiaco *adj* cardiac.

carenza *f* shortage.

caricare *vt* to load.

carino *adj* sweet.

carità *f* charity.

carne *f* meat; flesh.

caro *adj* dear; darling; expensive.

carota *f* carrot.

carta *f* paper; charter; map.

cartellino *m* docket.

cartello *m* placard; cartel: — **cartello stradale** *m* roadsign.

cartolina *f* postcard.

cartone *m* cardboard.

casa *f* house; home.

casalinga *f* housewife.

casco *m* helmet, crash helmet.

caserma *f* barracks:—**caserma dei pompieri** *f* fire station.

caso *m* (*med*, *gr*) case; chance:—**per caso** *adv* by accident, by chance.

cassetto *m* drawer.

cassettone *m* chest of drawers.

castagna *f* chestnut.

castello *m* castle.

castigare *vt* to castigate; to chasten; to discipline.

catacombe *fpl* catacombs.

catalizzatore *m* catalyst.

catalogo *m* catalogue.

categoria *f* category.

cattedrale *f* cathedral.

cattivo *adj* bad; ill; evil; nasty.

cattolicesimo *m* Catholicism.

cattolico *adj*, *m* Catholic, Roman Catholic.

caucciù *m* rubber.

causa *f* cause; law suit.

causare *vt* to cause.

cavalletta *f* grasshopper.

cavallo *m* horse; horsepower.

caverna *f* cave, cavern.

caviglia *f* ankle.

cavolfiore *m* cauliflower.

cavolino *m*:—**cavolini** *mpl* **di Bruxelles** Brussels sprouts.

cavolo *m* cabbage.

cazzo *m* prick.

celebrazione *f* celebration.

cena *f* dinner, supper.

cenere *f* ash.

cenotafio *m* cenotaph.

centesimo *m* cent; hundredth:—*adj* hundredth.

centigrado *adj* centigrade.

centilitro *m* centilitre.

centimetro *m* centimetre.

cento *adj*, *m* hundred.

centrale *adj* central; middle.

centro *m* centre; middle.

ceramica *f* ceramic; pottery.

cercare *vt* to try; to look for.

cerchio *m* circle.

certamente *adv* definitely.

certo *adj* certain; some; sure:—*pron* **certi** some.

certosino *m* Carthusian.

cervello *m* brain; mastermind.

cervo *m* deer.

cesareo *adj* Caesarian.

cespuglio *m* bush, shrub.

cessare *vt* to cease:—*vi* to cease, stop.

cestino *m* basket.

cetriolo *m* cucumber.

champagne *m inv* champagne.

che *rel pron* that; which; who, whom:—*conj* that; then:—*adj* what.

chewing-gum *m inv* chewing gum.

chi *pron* who, whom:—*poss pron* **di chi** whose.

chiacchierare *vi* to chat, chatter; to gossip; to jabber.

chiamare *vt* to call; to name; to term.

chiamata *f* call:—**chiamata alle armi** *f* (*mil*) call-up.

chiarimento *m* explanation:—**fornire un chiarimento a** *vt* to enlighten.

chiave *f* key.

chiaro *adj* clear; articulate; fair; light; straightforward.

chic *adj* chic, classy; smart.

chiedere *vt* to ask.

chiesa *f* church.

chilo *m* kilo.

chilogrammo *m* kilogram(me).

chilometraggio *m* mileage.

chilometro *m* kilometre.

chimica *f* chemistry.

chimico *adj* chemical:—*m* chemist:—**prodotto chimico** chemical.

chiocciola *f* snail.

chiostro *m* cloister.

chip *m inv* silicon chip; microchip.

chirurgo *m* surgeon.

chitarra *f* guitar.

chiudere *vt* to close; to shut:—*vr* ~**rsi** to shut.

chiunque *pron* anybody; who.

chiuso *adj* closed.

ci *pers pron* us.

ciao *interj* hullo, goodbye.

ciascuno *adv* apiece:—*adj, pron, adv* each.

cibo *m* food; (*fam*) grub.

cicatrice *f* scar.

ciclo *m* cycle.

ciclomotore *m* moped.

cicogna *f* stork.

cieco *adj, m* blind.

cielo *m* heaven; sky.

ciglio *m* eyelash, lash; side.

ciliegia *f* cherry.

cima *f* crown (of hill); peak; summit; top.

cimitero *m* cemetery; churchyard; graveyard.

cinema *m inv* cinema.

cinghiale *m* boar.

cinquanta *m, adj* fifty.

cinque *m, adj* five.

cintura *f* belt:—**cintura di sicurezza** *f* seatbelt, safety belt.

cioccolato *m* chocolate.

cioè *adv* i.e.; namely.

cipolla *f* onion; (*med*) bunion.

cipresso *m* cypress.

circa *adv* around; some; somewhere.

circolo *m* club; clubhouse.

circostanza *f* circumstance.

citofono *m* entryphone.

citrico *adj* citric.

città *f inv* city, town.

cittadino *m* citizen; national:—**semplice cittadino** *m* commoner.

civilizzare *vt* to civilise.

classe *f* class, form; style.

classico *adj* classic(al); standard.

clemente *adj* clement.

clero *m* clergy.

cliente *m/f* client, customer.

clima *m* climate.

climatizzato *adj* air-conditioned.

clinica *f* clinic; nursing home.

cloro *m* chlorine.

club *m* club.

coagulare *vt* to coagulate:—*vr* ~**rsi** to clot, coagulate.

coalizione *f* coalition.

cobalto *m* cobalt.

coccolare *vt* to cuddle.

cocomero *m* watermelon.

coda *f* queue; tail; tailback.

cogliere *vt* to pluck; to pick; to seize.

cognac *m inv* cognac.

cognata *f* sister-in-law.

cognato *m* brother-in-law.

cognome *m* surname.

coincidere *vi* to coincide; to concur.

colazione *f*: **prima colazione** breakfast:—**seconda colazione** lunch.

colibrì *m inv* humming-bird.

collaboratore *m* (journal) contributor; collaborator.

collaborazione *f* collaboration.

collasso *m* collapse.

collaudare *vt* to test.

collaudo *m* test.

collina *f* hill; foothill.

collirio *m* eyedrops.

collo *m* collar; neck; instep.

collocare *vt* to locate; to site.

colombo *m* dove.

colon *m inv* (*med*) colon.

colonia *f* colony.

colorante *m* dye; stain.

colorare *vt* to colour.

colpevole *m* culprit:—*adj* guilty; culpable:—*vt* **riconoscere colpevole** to convict.

colpire *vt* to hit; to knock; to smite; to strike; to clout; to impress.

coltellata *f* stab.

coltello *m* knife:—**coltello a serramanico** jack-knife.

coltivare *vt* to cultivate; to grow, farm, till.

coltivazione *f* crop; cultivation.

colto *adj* cultured, learned, educated.

coma *m inv* coma.

comandamento *m* commandment.

comandare *vt* to command.

comando *m* control; command; order.

comatoso *adj* comatose.

combattente *m/f* combatant; fighter.

combattere *vi* to battle:—*vt* to combat; to fight.

combattimento *m* combat, fight, fighting.

combinare *vt* to combine.

combinazione *f* combination.

combustibile *adj* combustible:—*m* fuel.

combustione *f* combustion.

come *conj* as:—*adv* how:—*prep* like:—*adj* such as.

cometa *f* comet.

comico *adj* comic:—*m* comedian.

comignolo *m* chimney stack.

cominciare *vt* to begin, commence; to start; to take up:—*vi* to begin; to get; to start.

comitato *m* committee:—**comitato elettorale** *m* caucus.

comizio *m* rally:—**comizi elettorali** *mpl* hustings.

commando *m* commando.

commedia *f* comedy; play.

commediànte *m/f* player; comedian.

commemorare *vt* to commemorate.

commemorativo *adj* commemorative.

commemorazione *f* commemoration.

commentare *vt* to commentate.

commento *m* comment; commentary.

commerciale *adj* commercial; trading.

commercialista *m* chartered accountant.

commerciante *m/f* dealer, merchant, trader.

commerciare *vi* to trade.

commercio *m* commerce, trade, trading.

commessa *f* saleswoman.

commesso *m* salesman.

commestibile *adj* edible, eatable.

commettere *vt* to commit.

commiserazione *f* commiseration.

commissariato *m* commissariat.

commissario *m*:—**commissario di bordo** *m* purser.

commissionare *vt* to commission.

commissione *f* commision; board; errand.

commosso *adj* affected, touched.

commovente *adj* appealing, moving, touching, emotive.

commozione *f* emotion:—**commozione cerebrale** *f* concussion.

commuovere *vt* to move, touch.

commutare *vt* to commute.

comodità *f* convenience.

comodo *adj* comfortable; convenient; handy.

compagnia *f* company, society.

compagno *m* companion; comrade; mate:—**compagno di classe** *m* classmate:—**compagno di studi** *m* fellow student:—**compagno di viaggio** *m* fellow traveller.

comparativo *adj* comparative.

comparire *vi* to appear.

comparsa *f* appearance.

compassione *f* compassion, pity.

compassionevole *adj* compassionate.

compasso *m* compass:—**compasso a punte fisse** *m* dividers.

compatibile *adj* compatible.

compatire *vt* to pity:—*vi* to sympathise.

compatriota *m/f* compatriot, fellow countryman.

compatto *adj* compact.

compendiare *vt* abridge.

compensare *vt* to compensate.

compensato *m* plywood.

compenso *m* compensation.

competente *adj* competent, proficient.

competenza *f* competence, proficiency.

competere *vi* to compete.

compiacente *adj* compliant.

compiacimento *m* complacency.

compiaciuto *adj* complacent; smug, self-righteous.

compiere *vt* to do; to accomplish; to fulfil.

compilare *vt* to compile.

compilazione *f* compilation.

compimento *m* fulfilment.

compito *m* homework; job; task.

compleanno *m* birthday.

complementare *adj* complementary; subsidiary.

complemento *m* complement.

complessità *f inv* complexity; intricacy; sophistication; involvement.

complessivo *adj* aggregate.

complesso *m* complex; ensemble, entirety; group; hang-up:—**nel complesso** by and large.

completamente *adv* completely, fully; totally; wholly.

completamento *m* completion; accomplishment.

completare *vt* to complete; to fill in (form, etc).

completo *adj* complete.

complicare *vt* to complicate.

complicato *adj* complicated, elaborate; involved.

complicazione *f* complication.

complice *m/f* accomplice, accessory:— **essere complice di** *vt* to aid and abet.

complicità *f* complicity.

complimentarsi *vr* to compliment.

complimento *m* compliment.

complottare *vi, vt* to plot.

complotto *m* plot.

componente *adj* component:—*m* component; constituent.

comporre *vt* to compose.

comportamento *m* behaviour.

comportare *vt* to entail:—*vr* ~**rsi** to act; to behave:—**comportare male** to misbehave.

composito *adj* composite.

compositore *m* composer; compositor.

composizione *f* composition; make-up.

composto *m* compound:—*adj* self-possessed; composed; compound: — (*gr*) **parola composta** *f* compound.

comprare *vt* to buy.

compratore *m* buyer.

comprendere *vt* to comprise; to comprehend; to encompass.

comprensibile *adj* comprehensible, understandable.

comprensione *f* comprehension, appreciation, understanding; sympathy.

comprensivo *adj* understanding, sympathetic.

compressa *f* compress; tablet.

comprimere *vt* to compress.

compromesso *m* compromise.

comprovare *vt* to substantiate.

computer *m* computer: — **personal computer** *m* personal computer.

comune *adj* common; routine; ordinary: — *m* borough; municipality: — **in comune** *adj* communal: — **in comune** *adv* jointly.

comunemente *adj* commonly.

comunicare *vt* to communicate; to impart; to commune.

comunicazione *f* communication; (road, etc): — **di grande comunicazione** arterial.

comunione *f* communion.

comunismo *m* communism.

comunista *m/f* communist.

comunità *f inv* community.

comunque *adv* anyhow: — *conj* however.

con *prep* with.

conato *m*: — **avere dei conati di vomito** to retch.

concavo *adj* concave.

concedere *vt* allow.

concentramento *m* concentration: — **campo di concentramento** *m* concentration camp.

concentrare *vt* to concentrate.

concentrato *m* concentrate; strong: — **concentrato di frutta** *m* fruit squash.

concentrazione *f* concentration.

concentrico *adj* concentric.

concepibile *adj* conceivable.

concepimento *m* conception.

concepire *vt* to conceive.

concerto *m* concert, concerto, recital.

concessione *f* concession, franchise.

concetto *m* concept.

conchiglia *f* shell.

conciare *vt* to cure.

conciliabile *adj* reconcilable.

conciliare *vt* to accommodate (differences).

conciliante *adj* accommodating, amenable.

concordare *vt* to agree, conciliate: — *vi* to agree.

conciliatorio *adj* conciliatory.

conciliazione *f* conciliation.

concimare *vt* to manure.

concime *m* compost, manure.

conciso *adj* concise; crisp; terse.

concittadino *m* fellow citizen.

concludere *vt* to conclude; to clinch: — *vi* to conclude; to tie up.

conclusione *f* conclusion: — **conclusioni** *fpl* findings.

conclusivo *adj* conclusive; closing.

concomitante *adj* concomitant.

concordanza *f* concordance.

concordare *vi* to settle.

concorrente *m/f* competitor; contestant, entrant.

concorrenza *f* competition.

concorrenziale *adj* competitive.

concorso *m* competition, contest.

concreto *adj* concrete.

concubina *f* concubine.

concupire *vt* to covet.

condanna *f* conviction, sentence.

condannare *vt* to condemn; to sentence; to decry.

condensare *vt* to condense.

condensato *adj* potted.
condensazione *f* condensation.
condiglianze *fpl* condolences.
condimento *m* condiment, seasoning; dressing, relish:—**condimento per l'insalata** *m* salad dressing.
condire *vt* to dress, season.
condiscendente *adj* condescending; acquiescent.
condiscendenza *f* compliance:— **trattare con condiscendenza** *vt* to patronise.
condividere *vt* to share.
condizionale *adj* conditional.
condizionare *vt* to condition.
condizionato *adj* qualified.
condizione *f* condition; state:— **condizione indispensabile** *f* precondition:—**condizioni** *fpl* terms.
condotta *f* conduct:—**cattiva condotta** *f* misbehaviour, misconduct.
conducente *m* driver.
condurre *vt* to conduct; to lead; (ship) to sail.
conduttività *f* conductivity.
conduttore *m* (*phys*) conductor.
conduttura *f* conduit; pipeline:— **conduttura principale** *f* main:— **conduttura dell'acqua** *f* water main.
conduzione *f* conduction.
confederarsi *vr* to confederate.
confederato *adj* confederate.
confederazione *f* confederacy.
conferenza *f* talk; lecture:— **conferenza stampa** *f* press conference:—**tenere una conferenza** *vt* to lecture.
conferire *vt* to bestow, confer.
conferma *f* confirmation.
confermare *vt* to confirm.

confessare *vt* to confess.
confessionale *m* confessional.
confessione *f* confession; denomination.
confessore *m* confessor.
confezionare *vt* to package; to tailor.
conficcare *vt* to stick; to plunge; to jab.
confidare *vt* to confide.
confidente *m* confidant.
confidenziale *adj* private.
configurazione *f* configuration.
confinante *adj* neighbouring.
confine *m* border, boundary, frontier.
confisca *f* confiscation; seizure.
confiscare *vt* to confiscate.
conflagrazione *f* conflagration.
conflitto *m* conflict; clash; strife.
confluenza *f* confluence.
confluire *vi* to merge:—*vt* to join.
confondere *vt* to confuse; to baffle.
conformarsi *vr* to conform.
conformità *f* conformity; compliance.
confortare *vt* to comfort.
conforto *m* comfort.
confusione *f* confusion, muddle; turmoil.
confuso *adj* confused.
confutare *vt* to disprove; to refute; to rebut.
congedare *vt* to dismiss.
congedo *m* dismissal; furlough.
congegno *m* device; contrivance.
congelamento *m* freezing, frostbite: —**punto di congelamento** *m* freezing point
congelare *vt* to freeze:—*vr* ~**rsi** to freeze.
congelato *adj* frozen, frostbitten.
congelatore *m* freezer, deep-freeze.
congenito *adj* congenital, inbred.
congestionato *adj* congested.

congestione f congestion.

congettura f conjecture, surmise, guesswork.

congetturare vt to conjecture, surmise.

congiuntivo adj, m subjunctive.

congiuntura f conjuncture; juncture.

congiunzione f conjunction.

congiura f conspiracy.

congiurare vi to conspire.

conglomerato m conglomerate.

congratularsi vr to congratulate.

congratulazioni fpl congratulations.

congregazione f congregation.

congresso m congress.

congruità f congruity.

congruo adj congruous.

coniare vt to mint.

conico adj conic(al).

conifera f conifer.

conifero adj coniferous.

conigliera f rabbit hutch.

coniglio m rabbit.

coniugale adj conjugal, matrimonial, marital.

coniugare vt to conjugate.

coniugato adj married.

coniugazione f conjugation.

connivente adj; **essere ~ in** to connive.

connivenza f connivance.

cono m cone.

conoscente m/f acquaintance.

conoscenza f acquaintance; knowledge; consciousness: — **privo di conoscenza** adj insensible.

conoscere vt become acquainted with; to know.

conosciuto adj familiar.

conquista f conquest.

conquistare vt to conquer; to win.

conquistatore m conqueror.

consacrare vt to consecrate, hallow.

consacrazione f consecration.

consapevole adj aware; mindful.

consapevolezza f awareness.

consapevolmente adv wittingly.

consciamente adv knowingly.

consecutivo adj consecutive; successive.

consegna f delivery.

consegnare vt to consign; to hand over; to deliver; to turn in.

conseguente adj consequent.

conseguenza f consequence; after-effect: — **conseguenze** fpl aftermath: — **di conseguenza** adv consequently.

consenso m consensus; acquiescence; agreement.

conserva f preserve.

conservante m preservative.

conservare vt to conserve, preserve; to retain.

conservatore m conservative; curator (of museum): — adj conservative.

conservatorio m conservatory.

conservazione f conservation, preservation.

considerare vt to consider; to regard; to deliberate; to treat.

considerazione f consideration.

considerevole adj considerable, handsome, sizeable.

consigliabile adj advisable.

consigliare vt advise; to recommend.

consigliere m adviser; councillor, counsellor.

consigli mpl guidance.

consiglio m advice; council, counsel: —(pol) **Consiglio dei Ministri** the Cabinet.

consistenza f consistency; texture.

consistere *vi* to consist.

consociato *adj* associate.

consolare *adj* consular:—*vt* to console.

consolato *m* consulate.

consolazione *f* consolation, comfort, solace.

console *m* consul.

consolidare *vt* to consolidate:—*vr* ~rsi to strengthen.

consolidazione *f* consolidation.

consonante *f* consonant.

consorte *m/f* consort.

consorzio *m* consortium.

consueto *adj* customary.

consuetudine *f* custom.

consulente *m/f* adviser, consultant.

consulenza *f* consultancy.

consultare *vt* to consult:—*vi* to refer:—*vr* ~rsi to confer.

consultazione *f* consultation.

consultivo *adj* advisory.

consumare *vt* to consummate; to consume; to wear:—*vi* to fray:—*vr* ~rsi to wear away.

consumato *adj* threadbare, worn.

consumatore *m* consumer.

consumazione *f* consummation.

consumista *adj*: **società consumista** consumer society.

consumo *m* consumption:—**beni di consumo** *mpl* consumer goods.

consunto *adj* worn-out.

consunzione *f* (*med*) tuberculosis, consumption.

contabile *m/f* accountant, bookkeeper.

contabilità *f* accountancy, bookkeeping.

contachilometri *m inv* mileometer.

contadino *m* peasant, rustic.

contagioso *adj* catching, contagious.

contagocce *m inv* dropper.

contaminare *vt* to contaminate.

contaminato *adj* tainted.

contaminazione *f* contamination.

contanti *mpl*: **in contanti** in cash.

contare *vt* to count:—**contare su** to depend on, rely on; to number:—*vi* to count.

contatore *m* meter:—**contatore del gas** *m* gas meter.

contatto *m* contact:—**lenti a contatto** *fpl* contact lenses.

contattare *vt* to contact.

contatto *m* touch.

conte *m* count, earl.

contea *f* county, shire.

conteggio *m* count.

contegno *m* demeanour.

contegnoso *adj* demure.

contemplare *vt* to contemplate.

contemplativo *adj* contemplative.

contemplazione *f* contemplation.

contemporaneo *adj* contemporary, contemporaneous.

contendente *m/f* contender.

contendere *vi* to contend:—*vr* ~rsi to vie.

contenere *vt* to contain.

contenitore *m* container, holder.

contentare *vt* to suit.

contentezza *f* content, contentment.

contentissimo *adj* delighted.

contento *adj* content; contented; glad; happy; pleased.

contenuto *m* contents.

contenzioso *adj* contentious.

contessa *f* countess.

contestare *vt* to contest; to dispute; to query.

contestatore *m* protestor.

contesto *m* context.

contiguo *adj* contiguous; adjoining:—
  essere contiguo a *vt* to adjoin.

continentale *adj* continental.

continente *m* continent; mainland.

contingente *m* contingent.

contingenza *f* contingency.

continuare *vt* to carry on, continue: —
  vi to continue; to go on.

continuazione *f* continuance, continuation.

continuità *f* continuity.

continuo *adj* continual; continuous;
  constant; non-stop.

conto *m* account; bill:—**dover
  rendere conto a qualcuno** to be answerable to someone:—**non tenere
  conto di** to override:—**per conto di**
  on behalf of:—**conto in banca** *m*
  bank account:—**conto scoperto**
  overdraft:—**estratto conto** statement:—**conto spese** *m* expense account:—**rendersi conto di** *vr* to realise.

contorcere *vt* to contort:—*vr* **~rsi** to
  squirm; to writhe.

contorno *m* contour, outline.

contorsione *f* contortion.

contrabbandare *vt* to smuggle.

contrabbandiere *m* smuggler.

contrabbando *m* contraband; smuggling.

contraccambiare *vt* to reciprocate; to
  requite.

contraccezione *f* contraception, birth
  control.

contraddire *vt* to contradict.

contraddittorio *adj* contradictory, conflicting; inconsistent.

contraddizione *f* contradiction.

contraereo *adj*:—**fuoco contraereo**
  m flak.

contrafatto *adj* counterfeit.

contraffare *vt* to counterfeit, forge.

contraffattore *m* forger.

contraffazione *f* forgery.

contrafforte *m* buttress.

contrappeso *m* counterbalance.

contrariare *vt* to put out.

contrariato *adj* disgruntled.

contrario *m* contrary, opposite:—*adj*
  contrary:—**al contrario** conversely.

contrarre *vt* to contract; to incur.

contrarsi *vr* to twitch.

contrastante *adj* contrasting.

contrastare *vi* to contrast.

contrasto *m* contrast.

contrattare *vi* to bargain, haggle.

contrattempo *m* contretemps, upset.

contratto *m* contract:—**contratto d'
  affitto** *m* lease.

contrattuale *adj* contractual.

contravvenire *vt* to contravene; to
  flout.

contravvenzione *f* contravention.

contrazione *f* contraction.

contribuente *m/f* taxpayer.

contribuire *vi*, *vt* to contribute:—**che
  contribuisce** *adj* contributory.

contribuzione *f* contribution.

contro *prep* against, versus.

controbilianciare *vt* to counterbalance.

controcultura *f* underground.

controfigura *f* stand-in.

controfiletto *m* sirloin.

controfirmare *vt* to countersign.

controllare *vt* to check; to inspect; to
  control; to test.

controllo *m* control; inspection:—
  controllo delle nascite *m* birth control:—**visita di controllo** *f* (*med*)
  check-up.

controllore *m* inspector.

controproducente *adj* counterproductive.

controversia *f* controversy, dispute.

controverso *adj* controversial.

contumacia *f* default.

contusione *f* contusion.

conurbazione *f* conurbation.

convalescente *adj, m/f* convalescent.

convalescenza *f* convalescence; recuperation: — **fare la convalescenza** to convalesce.

convalescenziario *m* sanatorium.

convalidare *vt* to authenticate; to validate.

convegno *m* conference: — **convegno galante** *m* assignation.

convenire *vit* to convene, to agree.

convento *m* convent.

convenuto *adj* agreed: — *m* respondent.

convenzionale *adj* conventional.

convenzione *f* convention.

convergente *adj* convergent.

convergenza *f* convergence.

convergere *vi* to converge.

conversare *vi* to converse.

conversazione *f* talk; conversation.

conversione *f* conversion.

convertibile *adj* convertible.

convertire *vt* to convert.

convertito *m* convert.

convertitore *m* converter.

convesso *adj* convex.

convettore *m* convector.

convezione *f* convection.

convincente *adj* convincing; cogent; forcible.

convincere *vt* to convince; to coax: — **convincere con le buone** to cajole.

convinzione *f* conviction; belief.

convocare *vt* to summon; to convoke; to convene.

convoglio *m* convoy.

convulsione *f* convulsion.

convulso *adj* convulsive.

cooperare *vi* to cooperate.

cooperativa *f* cooperative.

cooperativo *adj* cooperative.

cooperazione *f* cooperation.

cooptare *vt* to coopt.

coordinamento *m* coordinate: — *vt* to coordinate.

coordinata *f* coordinate.

coordinatore *m* coordinator.

coordinazione *f* coordination.

coperchio *m* cover, lid.

coperta *f* blanket; deck: — **coperte** *fpl* bedclothes: — **coperta termica** *f* electric blanket.

coperto *adj* covered; cloudy, overcast.

copertura *f* cover, covering.

copia *f* copy.

copiare *vt* to copy; to crib.

copiatrice *f* copier.

copione *m* scenario, script.

copioso *adj* profuse.

coppia *f* couple, pair, twosome.

copricapo *m* headdress.

coprifuoco *m* curfew.

copriletto *m* bedspread, counterpane.

coprimozzo *m* hubcap.

coprire *vt* to cover; to defray.

coraggio *m* courage, bravery; pluck; spirit; valour.

coraggioso *adj* brave, courageous, plucky, valiant.

corale *adj* choral.

corallino *m* coral reef.

corallo *m* coral.

corda *f* cord; string; rope; chord: — **corda del bucato** *f* clothes line: — **corda da acrobata** *f* tightrope.

cordame *m* rigging.

cordiale *m* cordial:—*adj* cordial, genial.

cordialità *f* friendliness.

cordicella *f* twine.

cordone *m* cord:—**cordone ombelicale** *m* umbilical cord.

coreografia *f* choreography.

coreografo *m* choreographer.

coriaceo *adj* thick-skinned.

coriandoli *mpl* confetti.

coriandolo *m* coriander.

corista *m/f* chorister.

cornacchia *f* crow.

cornamusa *f* bagpipes:—**suonatore di cornamusa** *m* piper.

cornea *f* cornea.

cornetta *f* cornet.

cornetto *m* croissant; cornet.

cornice *f* frame.

cornicione *m* cornice.

corno *m* horn.

coro *m* choir; chorus.

corollario *m* corollary.

corona *f* crown.

coronario *adj* coronary.

coroncina *f* coronet.

coroner *m inv* coroner.

corpino *m* bodice.

corpo *m* body; corps.

corporale *adj* corporal, corporeal.

corporatura *f* build; frame.

corporazione *f* guild.

corpulento *adj* corpulent, portly.

corpulenza *f* corpulence.

corredino *m* layette.

correggere *vt* to correct; to emend; to right; to mark.

correlare *vt* to correlate.

correlativo *adj* correlative.

correlato *adj* interrelated.

correlazione *f* correlation.

corrente *adj* current; fluent; running:—*f* current; flow.

correo *m* co-respondent.

correre *vi* to race; to run:—*vt* to run.

correttezza *f* fair play.

correttivo *adj* corrective; remedial.

corretto *adj* correct; right.

correzione *f* correction; emendation.

corrida *f* bull fight.

corridoio *m* corridor.

corridore *m* runner; racer.

corriera *f* coach.

corriere *m* carrier; courier.

corrimano *m* handrail, rail.

corrispondente *m/f* correspondent; pen friend:—*adj* corrisponding.

corrispondenza *f* correspondence:—**vendita per corrispondenza** *f* mail order.

corrispondere *vi* to correspond; to match; to tally:—*vt* to correspond.

corroborare *vt* to corroborate.

corroborazione *f* corroboration.

corrodere *vt* to corrode:—*vr* **~rsi** to corrode.

corrompere *vt* to corrupt; to bribe; to debauch.

corrosione *f* corrosion.

corrosivo *adj* corrosive.

corrotto *adj* corrupt.

corruttibile *adj* corruptible.

corruzione *f* corruption; bribery.

corsa *f* dash; race; run; racing.

corsia *f* ward.

corsivo *adj* italic.

corso *m* course:—**corso serale** *m* evening class:—**moneta a corso legale** *f* legal tender:—**in corso** *adj* ongoing.

corte *f* court:—**corte marziale** *f* court-martial.

corteccia f bark.

corteggiare vt to court, woo.

corteggiatore m suitor.

corto adj short.

cosa pron what: — f thing.

coscia f thigh; haunch; leg: — **coscia di pollo** f drumstick.

cosciente adj conscious.

così adv so: — **così così** so-so; such; thus; that.

cosmetico adj, m cosmetic.

costa f coast.

costare vt to cost.

costituzione f constitution.

costo m cost.

costola f rib.

costoletta f chop.

costoso adj costly, expensive.

costrizione f compulsion; constraint; constriction.

costruire vt to construct, build.

costruttore m builder.

cotoletta f cutlet.

cotone m cotton: — **cotone idrofilo** m cotton wool.

cottage m cottage.

cotto adj cooked: — **poco cotto** underdone.

cranio m skull.

cravatta f tie.

creazione f creation; brainchild.

credenziali fpl credentials.

credere vt to believe; to feel; to reckon; to understand: — **non credere** to disbelieve: — vi to believe; to think.

credibile adj credible; believable.

credibilità f credibility.

credito m credit: — **lettera di credito** f letter of credit.

creditore m creditor.

credo m creed.

credulità f credulity; gullibility.

credulo adj credulous.

credulone adj gullible.

crema f cream.

crepuscolo m dusk, nightfall, twilight.

crescente adj growing; increasing; rising.

crescere vi to grow.

cresima f confirmation.

cresimare vt to confirm.

cricket m cricket.

criminale m/f, adj criminal, felon.

criminalità f crime.

criniera f mane.

cristallizzare vt to crystalise: — vr ~**rsi** to crystallise.

cristianesimo m Christianity.

cristianità f Christianity, Christendom.

cristiano m, adj Christian.

Cristo m Christ.

criticare vt to criticise; to fault; to slate.

critico m critic, critique: — adj critical.

croccante adj crisp, crunchy.

croce f cross.

crociata f crusade.

crociato m crusader.

crociera f cruise.

crocifisso m crucifix.

croco m crocus.

cronico adj chronic.

cronista m reporter.

crostata f tart.

cruciverba m inv crossword.

crudeltà f cruelty.

crudo adj raw; uncooked.

crumiro m blackleg; scab.

crup m croup.

cucchiaino m teaspoon.

cucchiaio m spoon: — **cucchiaio da portata** serving spoon.

cucciolo m pup, cub.

cucina *f* cooker, cookery; kitchen.

cucitrice *f* stapler.

cucitura *f* seam.

cuculo *m* cuckoo.

cugino *m* cousin.

cui *rel pron* **il ~** whose.

culla *f* crib, cradle, cot: — **culla trasportabile** carrycot.

culo *m* (*sl*) bum, arse.

culto *m* cult.

cultura *f* culture, learning, edification.

cuocere *vt* to cook: — **cuocere al forno** to bake: — **cuocere in bianco** to poach.

cuoco *m* cook.

cuoio *m* hide, leather: — **cuoio capelluto** *m* scalp.

cuore *m* heart: — **prendersi a cuore** to befriend: — **di cuore** *adv* heartily: — **dal cuore tenero** *adj* soft-hearted.

cupola *f* dome.

cura *f* cure: — **aver cura di** *vt* to groom.

curare *vt* to care for; to tend; to treat.

curiosità *f inv* curio; curiosity.

curioso *adj* curious; inquisitive, nos(e)y.

curriculum vitae *m inv* curriculum vitae.

curry *m* curry.

curva *f* curve, bend, turn, turning.

cuscinetto *m* pad.

cuscino *m* cushion.

custode *m/f* custodian, attendant.

custodia *f* case; custody.

D

da *prep* to; out; off; since; from, by, for.

dalia *f* dahlia.

daltonico *adj* colour-blind.

damigella *f* damsel: — **damigella d'onore** bridesmaid.

dandy *m* dandy.

dannazione *f* damnation.

danneggiare *vt* to damage, hurt; to impair.

danno *m* damage.

danzare *vi* to dance.

danza *f* dance.

dappertutto *adv* everywhere; throughout.

dapprima *adv* at first.

dare *vt* to give: — **dare su** to overlook: — *vi* to give.

data *f* date.

dati *mpl* data.

dattilografo *m* typist.

davanti *adv* ahead: — *prep* by: — *m* front, fore: — *adj* front.

davvero *adv* really.

debole *adj* weak, frail, feeble: — *m* penchant; foible

debutto *m* debut.

decaffeinato *adj* decaffeinated.

decennio *m* decade.

decente *adj* decent, proper.

decentramento *m* decentralisation, devolution.

decidere *vi* to decide; to elect; to resolve: — **decidere su** adjudicate.

decimo *adj*, *m* tenth.

decisione *f* decision.

decollare *vi* to take off.

decorativo *adj* decorative.

decrepito *adj* decrepit.

dedizione *f* dedication.

defezionare *vi* to defect.

deficit *m inv* deficit.

definire *vt* to define; to class; to settle; to finalise.

definitivo *adj* definitive, definite; firm.

deflazione *f* deflation.

deformità *f* deformity.

delfino *m* dolphin.

delinquente *m* delinquent.

delirio *m* delirium.

delitto *m* crime.

delizia *f* delight.

deludente *adj* disappointing.

deludere *vt* to disappoint.

demolire *vt* to demolish, pull down, knock down; to scrap.

demonio *m* demon, fiend.

dente *m* tooth; cog.

dentiera *f* dentures.

dentifricio *m* toothpaste.

dentista *m/f* dentist.

dentro *prep* into; within; inside:—*adv* inside.

deputazione *f* deputation.

derivare *vt* to derive.

dermatite *f* dermatitis.

dermatologia *f* dermatology.

descrivere *vt* to describe.

deserto *m* desert; wilderness.

desiderare *vt, vi* to desire; to wish; to want; to long for; to lust after.

desiderio *m* desire; wish.

desolato *adj* bleak, desolate, dreary.

dessert *m inv* dessert, pudding.

destinatario *m* recipient.

destino *m* destiny, fate, lot; doom.

destra *f* right.

detective *m* detective.

detenzione *f* detention; custody.

deterioramento *m* deterioration.

detersivo *m* detergent; soap powder.

detestare *vt* to detest, loathe.

detonare *vi* to detonate.

dettagliare *vt* to detail.

dettaglio *m* detail:—**al dettaglio** *adj* (*com*) retail:—**vendere al dettaglio** *vt* to retail.

detto *m* saying.

devolvere *vt* to devolve.

devoto *adj* devoted, devout.

di *prep* of; any.

diabetico *adj, m* diabetic.

diabolico *adj* devilish, diabolical, fiendish.

diagnosi *f inv* diagnosis.

diagnosticare *vt* to diagnose.

diagonale *adj* diagonal.

diagramma *m* diagram.

dialetto *m* dialect.

dialogo *m* dialogue.

diamante *m* diamond.

diapositiva *f* slide, transparency.

diario *m* diary.

diarrea *f* diarrhoea.

diavolo *m* devil.

dibattere *vt* to debate:—*vr* **~rsi** to flounder.

dicembre *m* December.

dichiarazione *f* declaration.

diciannove *adj, m* nineteenth

diciassette *adj, m* seventeen.

diciassettesimo *adj, m* seventeenth.

diciottesimo *adj, m* eighteenth.

diciotto *adj, m* eighteen.

dieci *adj, m inv* ten.

dieta *f* diet:—**seguire una dieta** *vi* to diet.

dietro *prep* behind:—*m* back.

difendere *vt* to defend; to champion; to plead.

differenza *f* difference.

difficile *adj* difficult, hard, tricky, stiff.

difficoltà *f inv* difficulty.

digeribile *adj* digestible.

digerire *vt* to digest.

digestione *f* digestion.

digitale *adj* digital:—*f* foxglove.

dignità *f* dignity.

dilemma *m* dilemma.

diligente *adj* diligent, industrious.

diluire *vt* to dilute.

diluvio *m* deluge.

dimagrante *adj* slimming.

dimensione *f* dimension:—**dimensioni** *fpl* size.

dimenticare *vi* to forget.

diminuire *vt* to diminish; to decrease; to lessen.

diminuzione *f* decrease.

dimissioni *fpl* resignation.

dimostrare *vt* to demonstrate; to prove.

dinamite *f* dynamite.

dinastia *f* dynasty.

dinosauro *m* dinosaur.

dio *m* god:—**per amor di Dio!** *excl* for God's sake!

dipendente *m/f* employee.

dipendere *vi* to depend:—**dipendere da** to be contingent on.

dipingere *vt* to paint.

diploma *m* diploma, degree.

diplomatico *m*, *adj* diplomat.

dire *vt* to speak; to tell; to say:—*vi* to say:—**va detto che** *adv* admittedly.

direttamente *adv* directly; squarely; straight.

diretto *adj* direct; first hand; non-stop.

direttore *m* director; editor; (*mus*) conductor.

direttrice *f* manageress.

direzione *f* direction, way; leadership; administration.

dirigere *vt* to direct; to administer; (*mus*) to conduct; to run.

diritto *m* right; law.

diritti *mpl* dues:—**diritti d'autore** *mpl* royalties.

disapprovare *vi* to disapprove.

disarmo *m* disarmament.

disattenzione *f* carelessness.

discesa *f* descent:—**in discesa** *adv* downhill.

dischetto *m* floppy disk.

disciplina *f* discipline.

disco *m* disc, discus; record:—**disco volante** *m* flying saucer.

discorsivo *m* discursive.

discorso *m* discourse, speech, address.

discoteca *f* disco.

disegnare *vt* to draw.

disgraziato *adj* unlucky; wretched.

disgustare *vt* to disgust.

disinfettante *m* disinfectant.

disoccupato *adj* unemployed, jobless.

disorganizzato *adj* disorganised, unorganised.

dispari *adj inv* odd.

dispensario *m* dispensary.

disperare *vi* to despair.

disponibile *adj* available; disposable.

disprezzare *vt* to despise; to scorn.

disputa *f* dispute, contention.

disputarsi *vr* to dispute.

dissenteria *f* dysentery.

dissentire *vt* to dissent.

dissertazione *f* dissertation.

dissolvere *vt* to dissolve.

distante *adj* distant:—*adv* off:—*adj* far.

distanza *f* distance:—**a distanza** *adv* apart.

distanziare *vt* to distance, space.

disteso *adj* recumbent; outstretched.

distinto *adj* distinct.

distinzione *f* distinction:—**senza distinzioni** *adv* regardless.

distorcere *vt* to distort.

distorsione *f* distortion.

distribuzione *f* distribution.

distruggere *vt* to destroy; to wreck.

disturbare *vt* to disturb; to trouble.

disturbo *m* disturbance; static:—**fare azione di disturbo** *vt* to heckle.

disubbidiente *adj* disobedient, naughty.

disubbidienza *f* disobedience.

disubbidire *vt* to disobey.

disuguale *adj* unequal.

disuso *m* disuse:—**essere in disuso** *vi* to be in abeyance:—**cadere in disuso** *vi* to fall into disuse.

ditale *m* thimble.

dito *m* finger:—**dito del piede** *m* toe.

ditta *f* firm.

dittatore *m* dictator.

dittatoriale *adj* dictatorial.

dittatura *f* dictatorship.

dittongo *m* diphthong.

diuretico *adj* diuretic.

divagare *vi* to digress, ramble.

divampare *vi* to blaze, flame.

divano *m* couch, settee.

divenire *vi* to become.

diventare *vi* to become:—**diventare grande** to grow up.

divergente *adj* divergent.

divergenza *f* divergence.

divergere *vi* to diverge.

diversamente *adv* differently, other than.

diversificare *vi* to diversify.

diversità *f* diversity.

diverso *adj* different; diversi *adj* sundry.

divertente *adj* amusing, entertaining.

divertimento *m* amusement, enjoyment, fun.

divertire *vt* amuse:—*vr* ~**rsi** to enjoy oneself, have a good time.

dividendo *m* dividend.

dividere *vt* to divide, split, share.

divieto *m* ban.

divinità *f* divinity, godhead, deity.

divino *adj* divine, heavenly, godlike.

divisa *f* uniform, strip.

divisibile *adj* divisible.

divisione *f* division.

diviso *adj* divided.

divisore *m* divisor.

divo *m* star:—**divo del cinema** *m* film star.

divorare *vt* to devour, wolf.

divorziare *vt*, *vi* to divorce.

divorziato *adj* divorced:—*m* divorcee.

divorzio *m* divorce.

divulgare *vt* to divulge; to leak.

dizionario *m* dictionary:—**dizionario dei sinonimi** *m* thesaurus.

dizione *f* diction, elocution.

doccia *f* shower:—**fare la doccia** *vi* to shower.

docente *adj* teaching:—*m* **docente universitario** lecturer, don.

docile *adj* docile.

documentare *vt* to document.

documentario *adj*, *m* documentary.

documento *m* document:—**documenti** *mpl* papers.

dodicesimo *adj*, *m* twelfth.

dodici *adj*, *m inv* twelve.

dogana *f* customs:—**esente da dogana** *adj* duty free.

doganiere *m* customs officer.

doglie *fpl* labour: — **avere le doglie** *vi* to be in labour.

dogma *m* dogma.

dogmatico *adj* dogmatic, opinionated.

dolce *adj* sweet; gentle; soft: — **dalla voce dolce** *adv* soft-spoken: — *m* sweet, pudding;

dolcemente *adv* gently.

dolcezza *f* sweetness.

dolcificante *m* sweetener.

dolciumi *mpl* confectionery.

dollaro *m* dollar.

dolore *m* ache, pain; grief, sorrow, woe.

doloroso *adj* painful, sore.

domanda *f* question; inquiry; query; application: — **fare una domanda** *vi* to ask a question.

domandarsi *vt* to wonder.

domani *adv, m inv* tomorrow.

domare *vt* to tame.

domenica *f* Sunday, Sabbath.

domestico *adj* domestic: — *m* servant.

domicilio *m* domicile, abode.

dominante *adj* dominant, uppermost.

dominare *vt* to dominate; to control; to subdue; to master.

dominazione *f* domination.

dominio *m* dominion, domain, domino.

donare *vt* to donate.

donatore *m* contributor; donor: — **donatore di sangue** blood donor.

donazione *f* endowment, donation.

donchisciottesco *adj* quixotic.

dondolare *vt* to swing; to dangle: — *vi* to swing; to rock.

dondolo *adj*: — **sedia a dondolo** *f* rocking chair.

dongiovanni *m inv* ladykiller.

donna *f* woman: — **donna d'affari** *f* businesswoman.

donnaiolo *m* philanderer.

donnola *f* weasel.

dono *m* gift: — **dono del cielo** *m* godsend.

dopo *prep* after: — *adv* after; next: — **dopotutto** after all; afterwards.

dopobarba *m inv* aftershave.

doppiamente *adv* doubly.

doppiare *vt* to dub.

doppio *adj* dual, double; twofold: — **camera doppia** *f* double room.

dorare *vt* to gild.

doratura *f* gilding, gilt.

dormire *vi* to sleep, slumber.

dormitorio *m* dormitory.

dorso *m* backstroke.

dosare *vt* to dose.

dose *f* dose.

dossier *m inv* dossier; (*law*) brief.

dotare *vt* to endow.

dotato *adj* gifted.

dote *f* dowry; accomplishment: — **doti** *fpl* abilities.

dotto *adj* scholarly.

dottore *m* doctor.

dottrina *f* doctrine.

dottrinale *m* doctrinal.

double-face *adj* reversible.

dove *adv* where, whereabouts: — *conj* where.

dovere *mod.vb* to have to; to owe.

dovunque *conj* wherever.

dovuto *adj* due.

dozzina *f* dozen.

draga *f* dredge.

dragamine *m inv* minesweeper.

dragare *vt* to drag, dredge.

drago *m* dragon.

dragoncello *m* tarragon.

drammatico *adj* dramatic.

dramma *m* drama.

drammatizzare *vt* to dramatise.
drammaturgo *m* playwright, dramatist.
drappeggiare *vt* to drape.
drappo *m* cloth:—**drappo funebre** *m* pall.
drastico *adj* drastic.
drenaggio *m* drain, drainage.
drenare *vt* to drain.
dribbling *m* dribble.
dritto *adj* erect:—*adv* straight.
droga *f* drug, dope; spice.
drogare *vt* to drug; to spice.
drogato *m* drug addict, junkie.
dubbio *adj* dubious:—*m* doubt.
dubitare *vt* to doubt.
duca *m* duke.
duchessa *f* duchess.
due *m* two:—*adj* two:—**tutti e due** both:—**a due porte** two-door:—*adv* **due volte** twice.

duello *m* duel.
duetto *m* duet.
dumping *m* dumping.
duna *f* dune.
duodenale *adj* duodenal.
duodeno *m* duodenum.
duplicare *vt* to duplicate.
duplicato *m* duplicate.
duplice *adj* dual.
duplicità *f* duplicity.
durante *prep* during.
durare *vi* to last, wear.
durata *f* length, duration.
duraturo *adj* enduring, lasting.
durevole *adj* durable.
durevolezza *f* durability.
durezza *f* hardness.
duro *adj* hard, stiff; trying:—**duro d'orecchio** hard of hearing:—**duro di cuore** hard-hearted.

E

e *conj* and.
ebano *m* ebony.
ebbrezza *f* intoxication.
ebraico *adj m* Hebrew.
ebrea *f* Jewess.
ebreo *m* Jew, Hebrew:—*adj* Jewish, Hebrew.
eccedenza *f* excess.
eccedere *vt* to exceed.
eccellente *adj* excellent.
eccentricità *f* eccentricity.
eccentrico *m* eccentric; crank; freak:—*adj* eccentric.
eccesso *m* excess.
eccetto *prep* except.

eccezionale *adj* exceptional.
eccezione *f* exception.
eccitare *vt* to excite.
ecclesiastico *adj* ecclesiastical.
eco *m/f* echo.
ecologia *f* ecology.
economia *f* economy, economics.
economico *adj* economical, inexpensive.
eczema *m* eczema.
edera *f* ivy.
edificio *m* building, edifice.
editore *m* publisher.
editoria *f* publishing.
editoriale *m* editorial.

edizione f edition.
edonismo m hedonism.
educare vt to educate.
educato adj polite.
educazione f education; politeness; upbringing: — **(buona) educazione** f breeding, good manners: — **educazione fisica** f physical education.
effeminato adj effeminate.
effetto m effect; spin (of ball).
effettuare vt to effect.
effigie f effigy.
effimero adj ephemeral.
egli pron he.
ego m ego.
egocentrico adj self-centred.
egoista m/f egoist: — adj selfish.
egualitario adj egalitarian.
eiaculare vt to ejaculate.
elaborare vt to elaborate; to evolve; to hatch (a plot).
elastico adj elastic; resilient: — m elastic; rubber band.
elefante m elephant.
elegante adj elegant; dressy; smart.
eleganza f elegance, smartness.
eleggere vt to elect.
eleggibile adj elegible.
elementare adj elementary.
elemento m element.
elencare vt to list.
elenco m list; directory: — **elenco telefonico** m telephone directory.
elettorato m electorate.
elettricità f electricity.
elevare vt to elevate.
elezione f election.
elicottero m helicopter.
eliminare vt to eliminate; to remove.
elio m helium.

élite f inv élite.
ella pron she.
eloquente adj eloquent.
emancipare vt to emancipate.
emblema m emblem.
emblematico adj emblematic.
emendare vt amend.
emergenza f emergency.
emergere vi to emerge.
emigrante m/f emigrant.
emigrare vi to emigrate.
emigrazione f emigration.
emisfero m hemisphere.
emittente f transmitter.
emofilia f haemophilia.
emorroidi fpl haemorrhoids, piles.
emotivo adj emotional (person), emotive (film, etc).
emozione f emotion.
enciclopedia f encyclopaedia.
endovenoso adj intravenous.
energia f energy.
energico adj energetic, spirited; strenuous.
enfasi f emphasis, stress.
enigma m enigma.
enigmatico adj enigmatic, cryptic.
enorme adj enormous, huge, tremendous, terrific.
ente m corporation.
entità f inv entity.
entrare vi to enter, go in, come in: — **lasciare entrare** to admit: — vt to enter, go in: — **questo non c'entra** this doesn't enter into it.
entrata f entrance, entry, hall.
entroterra m (Australia) outback: — **nell'entroterra** adv inland.
epatite f hepatitis.
epidemia f epidemic.
Epifania f Epiphany.

epilessia *f* epilepsy.

epilettico *adj, m* epileptic

episodio *m* episode, incident.

epoca *f* epoch, day, age.

equatore *m* equator.

equatoriale *adj* equatorial.

equazione *f* equation.

equipaggiamento *m* equipment.

equipaggiare *vt* to fit out.

equipaggio *m* crew.

equità *f* equity.

equitazione *f* riding; horsemanship: — **scuola di equitazione** *f* riding school.

equivalente *m/f* counterpart: — *adj* equivalent.

equivoco *m* misapprehension: — *adj* equivocal.

era *f* era, age, time.

erba *f* grass.

ereditare *vt* to inherit.

erezione *f* erection.

ermellino *m* ermine, stoat.

erodere *vt* to erode.

eroe *m* hero.

eroico *adj* heroic.

eroina *f* heroin; heroine.

erotico *adj* erotic.

errore *m* error; mistake; fallacy.

eruzione *f* eruption: — **essere in eruzione** *vi* to erupt.

esagerare *vt* to exaggerate; to overstate.

esagonale *adj* hexagonal.

esagono *m* hexagon.

esame *m* examination; test.

esaminare *vt* to examine; to vet; to survey.

esattamente *adv* exactly.

esattezza *f* accuracy, exactness, exactitude.

esatto *adj* exact, accurate, spot-on.

esattore *m* (tax) collector: — **esattore delle imposte** *m* tax collector.

esauriente *adj* exhaustive, comprehensive.

esaurientemente *adv* at length.

esaurimento *m* exhaustion: — **esaurimento nervoso** *m* nervous break-down.

esaurire *vt* to deplete; to exhaust.

esaurito *adj* exhausted; spent; out of print.

esca *f* bait.

eschimese *adj* Eskimo: — **cane eschimese** *m* husky (dog).

esclamare *vt* to exclaim.

esclamazione *f* exclamation.

escludere *vt* to exclude, debar, except.

esclusione *f* exclusion.

esclusivo *adj* exclusive, select; sole.

escursionista *m/f* rambler.

esecutivo *adj* executive.

esecutore *m* executor.

esempio *m* example, instance.

esemplare *adj* exemplary.

esentare *vt* to exempt.

esenzione *f* exemption.

esercitare *vt* to exercise; to drill; to exert; to ply: — *vr* **~rsi** to practise.

esercitazione *f* drill.

esercito *m* military, army.

esercizio *m* exercise, practice.

esibirsi *vr* to appear; to perform.

esibizionista *m/f* show-off.

esigente *adj* exacting, demanding.

esigenza *f* requirement.

esigere *vt* to expect; to demand; to exact.

esilio *m* exile.

esistenza *f* existence.

esistere *vi* to exist.

esitante *adj* hesitant; tentative.
esitare *vi* to hesitate; to dither.
esitazione *f* hesitation.
esodo *m* exodus.
esofago *m* oesophagus.
esonerare *vt* to excuse.
esorbitante *adj* exorbitant; extortionate.
esorcismo *m* exorcism.
esorcizzare *vt* to exorcise.
esortare *vt* to exhort.
esoterico *adj* esoteric.
esotico *adj* exotic.
espandere *vt* to expand.
espansione *f* expansion.
espansivo *adj* expansive, effusive, gushing, demonstrative.
espatriato *adj, m* expatriate.
espediente *m* expedient.
espellere *vt* to expel; to eject.
esperienza *f* experience.
esperimentare *vt* to experience.
esperimento *m* experiment.
esperto *adj* accomplished; experienced; expert: — *m* expert; adept; troubleshooter; pundit.
espirare *vt* to exhale.
esplicativo *adj* explanatory.
esplicito *adj* explicit.
esplodere *vi* to explode: — *vt* to blow up.
esplorare *vt* to explore; to prospect.
esploratore *m* explorer.
esplorazione *f* exploration.
esplosione *f* explosion; blast.
esplosivo *adj, m* explosive.
esponente *m/f* exponent.
esportare *vt* to export.
esportazione *f* export.
espositore *m* exhibitor.
esposizione *f* display, exposition; show; exposure.

esposto *adj* exposed.
espressione *f* expression.
espressivo *adj* expressive.
espresso *adj* express.
esprimere *vt* to express; to air; to phrase; to voice: — *vr* ~rsi to express oneself.
espropriare *vt* to expropriate.
esproprio *m* expropriation.
espulsione *f* expulsion, ejection.
essenza *f* essence.
essenziale *adj* essential.
essenzialmente *adv* essentially.
essere *vi* to be: — *m* being.
essi *pers pron* they.
essiccare *vt* to dry.
essiccato *adj* dried; desiccated.
essistenza *f* being.
esso *m* it.
est *m* east: — *adv* **verso est** eastwards.
estasi *f inv* ecstasy; rapture: — **mandare in estasi** *vt* to entrance.
estasiare *vt* to enrapture; to ravish.
estasiato *adj* rapturous.
estate *f* summer: — **piena estate** *f* midsummer.
estatico *adj* ecstatic.
estendersi *vr* to reach; to range.
estensione *f* extent.
estenuante *adj* gruelling; wearisome.
esterno *adj* external, exterior; outside; outward; outer.
estero *adj* foreign; overseas: — **all'estero** *adv* overseas: — **andare all'estero** *vi* to go abroad.
esteso *adj* extensive.
estetico *adj* aesthetic.
estinguere *vt* to extinguish; to write off.
estinto *adj* extinct.
estintore *m* (fire) extinguisher.
estinzione *f* extinction.

estirpare *vt* to extirpate.

estorcere *vt* to extort.

estorsione *f* extortion.

estradare *vt* to extradite.

estradizione *f* extradition.

estramurale *adj* extramural.

estraneo *adj* foreign; alien; extraneous: — *m* outsider.

estrarre *vi* to abstract: — *vt* to mine; to draw; to extract.

estratto *m* excerpt.

estrazione *f* extraction; draw: — **estrazione mineraria** *f* mining.

estremamente *adv* extremely.

estremista *m/f* extremist.

estremità *f* end, extremity.

estremo *adj* far; extreme; utmost: — *m* extreme.

estrinseco *adj* extrinsic.

estrogeno *m* oestrogen.

estroverso *adj, m* extrovert.

estuario *m* estuary.

esuberante *adj* exuberant.

esuberanza *f* exuberance.

esule *m/f* exile.

esultante *adj* elated, jubilant.

esultanza *f* elation, jubilation.

esultare *vi* to exult.

esumare *vt* to exhume.

età *f inv* age.

etere *m* ether.

eternamente *adv* forever.

eternità *f* eternity.

eterno *adj* eternal; everlasting; timeless.

eterodosso *adj* heterodox.

eterogeneo *adj* heterogeneous.

eterosessuale *adj*, heterosexual; (*fam*) straight.

etica *f* ethics.

etichetta *f* label; tag; etiquette.

etico *adj* ethical.

etimologia *f* etymology.

etimologico *adj* etymological.

etnico *adj* ethnic.

eucalipto *m* gum tree; eucalyptus.

Eucaristia *f* Eucharist.

eufemismo *m* euphemism.

euforia *f* euphoria.

eunuco *m* eunuch.

eutanasia *f* euthanasia.

evacuare *vt* to evacuate.

evacuazione *f* evacuation.

evadere *vi* to escape; to break out; to abscond: — *vt* to evade.

evangelico *adj* evangelic(al).

evangelista *m* evangelist.

evaporare *vi* to evaporate.

evaporazione *f* evaporation.

evasione *f* evasion; escape; breakout; escapism.

evasivo *adj* evasive; non-committal.

evento *m* occurrence.

eventuale *adj* eventual.

eventualità *f* eventuality.

evidente *adj* evident; plain; overt.

evitabile *adj* avoidable.

evitare *vt* to avoid; to shun; to miss; to eschew.

evocare *vt* to evoke.

evocativo *adj* evocative.

evoluzione *f* evolution.

evolversi *vr* to evolve.

extra *adj* extra.

extra-coniugale *adj* extramarital.

extrasensoriale *adj* extrasensory.

extraterrestre *m* alien.

F

fa *adv* ago:—**quanto tempo fa?** how long ago?

fabbrica *f* factory; mill; works:— **fabbrica di birra** brewery.

fabbricante *m* manufacturer:—**fabbricante di birra** brewer.

fabbricare *vt* to manufacture; to make; to fabricate.

faccia *f* face; side.

facciata *f* facade.

facile *adj* easy; effortless.

facilità *f* facility; easiness.

facilitare *vt* to facilitate; to ease.

facilmente *adv* easily.

facoltà *f inv* faculty; school.

facoltativo *adj* optional.

facsimile *m* facsimile; fax.

faggio *m* beech.

fagiano *m* pheasant.

fagiolo *m* bean:—**fagiolo bianco** *m* haricot.

faglia *f* (*geol*) fault.

fai da te *m* do-it-yourself.

falce *f* scythe, sickle.

falco *m* hawk, falcon:—**falco pescatore** *m* osprey.

falconiera *f* falconry.

fallire *vi* to fail, abort, backfire.

fallo *m* foul.

falò *m* bonfire.

falsificare *vt* to falsify, fake.

falso *adj* false, fake.

fama *f* fame.

fame *f* hunger.

famiglia *f* family, household.

famoso *adj* famous, famed, noted.

fan *m* fan.

fanciulla *f* girl.

fanciullesco *adj* boyish.

fanciullo *m* boy.

fango *m* mud.

fantasia *f* fantasy.

fantasma *m* ghost, apparition, phantom.

faraone *m* Pharoah.

farcire *vt* to stuff.

fare *vt* to do; to make:—**fare lo stupido** to act the fool:—*vt, vi* **fare male** to hurt.

farfalla *f* bow tie; butterfly.

farina *f* flour; meal.

farmaceutico *adj* pharmaceutical.

farmacia *f* dispensary, pharmacy.

farmacista *m/f* chemist, pharmacist.

faro *m* lighthouse; beacon.

fascino *m* glamour, fascination, allure, charm, mystique.

fascio *m* sheaf.

fascismo *m* fascism.

fascista *m/f* fascist.

fase *f* phase.

fastidio *m* annoyance.

fastidioso *adj* troublesome.

fasto *m* pomp.

fasullo *adj* bogus, fake, phoney.

fata *f* fairy.

fatale *adj* fatal; vital.

fatalismo *m* fatalism.

fatica *f* fatigue; toil.

faticare *vi* to labour, toil, slog.

faticata *f* slog.

faticoso *adj* strenuous, uphill, tough, tiring, laborious.

fatidico *adj* fateful.

fatiscente *adj* derelict.

fattibile *adj* workable.

fattibilità *f* feasibility.

fatto *pp* done:—*m* fact:—*adj* **ben fatto** shapely.

fattore *m* bailiff; factor.

fattoria *f* farm.

fattorino *m* errand boy.

fattura *f* bill, invoice; workmanship.

fatturare *vt* to invoice.

fatuo *adj* fatuous.

fauna *f* fauna.

fautore *m* campaigner.

fava *f* broad bean.

favo *m* honeycomb.

favola *f* fable.

favoloso *adj* fabulous.

favore *m* favour:—**a favore di** *prep* for.

favorevole *adj* favourable; auspicious.

favorire *vt* to favour, further, farther; to advance; to be conducive to.

favoritismo *m* favouritism.

favorito *adj* favoured, favourite.

fax *m* fax.

fazione *f* faction.

fazzolettino *m*:—**fazzolettino di carta** tissue.

fazzoletto *m* handkerchief.

fazzolettone *m* bandanna.

febbraio *m* February.

febbre *f* fever.

febbrile *adj* feverish.

feccia *f* dregs, scum.

feci *fpl* faeces.

fecondare *vt* to fertilise.

fecondo *adj* fertile:—**in età feconda** of childbearing age.

fede *f* faith, belief; wedding ring.

fedele *adj* faithful; true; regular; accurate:—*m/f* churchgoer, worshipper.

fedeltà *f* faithfulness, fidelity; accuracy.

felice *adj* happy.

femmina *adj*, *f* female.

fenice *f* phoenix.

fenicottero *m* flamingo.

feriale *adj*:—**giorno feriale** *m* weekday.

ferire *vt* to hurt, injure, wound.

ferita *f* wound; injury.

fermaglio *m* clip, paperclip.

fermare *vt* to halt; to stop; to stay.

fermata *f* stop; halt:—**fermata d'autobus** bus stop.

fermo *adj* firm; still.

feroce *adj* ferocious, fierce.

ferocia *f* ferocity, fierceness; savagery.

ferro *m* iron.

ferrovia *f* railway.

fertile *adj* fertile.

festa *f* party, feast, festival, festivity, fête, gala:—**di festa** *adj* festive.

festeggiamenti *mpl* rejoicings.

fetido *adj* fetid.

feto *m* foetus.

fetta *f* slice.

fettuccia *f* tape.

feudale *adj* feudal.

fiamma *f* flame; pennant.

fiammifero *m* match.

fianco *m* side; flank.

fiasco *m* flask, fiasco; flop.

fibbia *f* buckle.

fico *m* fig.

fidanzamento *m* engagement; betrothal.

fidanzare *vt* to betroth.

fiera *f* fair; show.

figlia *f* daughter.
figlio *m* son.
figura *f* figure.
filamento *m* filament.
filantropia *f* philanthropy.
filantropo *m* philanthropist.
filatelia *f* philately.
filetto *m* fillet.
filigrana *f* filigree; watermark.
film *m inv* film, motion picture, movie.
filmare *vt* to film.
filo *m* thread; string; wire; flex.
filologia *f* philology.
filosofia *f* philosophy.
filosofo *m* philosopher.
filtrare *vt* to percolate; to filter.
filtro *m* filter: — **con filtro** *adj* filter-tipped.
finale *adj* final; eventual; finale.
finalista *m/f* finalist.
finalmente *adv* at last.
finanza *f* finance.
finanziare *vt* to finance; to fund.
finanziario *adj* financial.
finché *conj* until.
fine *adj* fine; acute: — *f* end; close; ending; finish: — **senza fine** endless
finemente *adv* finely.
finestra *f* window: — **finestra a saliscendi** *f* sash window.
finezza *f* finesse.
fingere *vi* to fake, pretend; to sham: — *vt* to pretend; to sham.
finire *vt* to finish: — *vi* to finish, end.
finito *adj* over; through; finite.
fino *adj* fine: — *prep* **fino a** until.
finto *adj* dummy, mock.
finzione *f* fiction, make-believe.
fionda *f* catapult, sling.
fiore *m* flower; bloom.
firma *f* signature.

firmare *vt* to sign, autograph: — *vi* to sign.
fisarmonica *f* accordion.
fiscale *adj* fiscal.
fisica *f* physics.
fisiologico *adj* physiological.
fisioterapia *f* physiotherapy.
fisso *adj* fixed; set; steady.
fittizio *adj* fictitious.
fiume *m* river, stream.
flaccido *adj* flabby, flaccid.
flanella *f* flannel.
flash *m inv* flash, flash cube; newsflash.
flautista *m/f* flautist.
flauto *m* flute, recorder.
flemma *f* phlegm.
flessibile *adj* flexible; supple, limber.
flipper *m* pinball machine.
flirt *m inv* flirtation.
flora *f* flora.
floscio *adj* floppy.
fluido *adj*, *m* fluid.
fluire *vi* to flow.
fluorescente *adj* fluorescent.
fluoruro *m* fluoride.
fluttuare *vi* to fluctuate.
fobia *f* phobia.
foca *f* seal.
focale *adj* focal.
focena *f* porpoise.
focoso *adj* fiery, hot.
foglia *f* leaf.
foglio *m* folio, leaf (of paper), sheet.
fohn *m* hairdrier.
fondamentale *adj* fundamental, basic; seminal.
fondare *vt* to establish, found.
fondo *m* fund; bottom; sediment.
fondi *mpl* grounds.
fontana *f* fountain.

fonte *m* spring, source.
forbici *fpl* scissors:—**forbici per potare** *fpl* secateurs.
forchetta *f* fork.
foresta *f* forest.
forestale *adj* forest:—**guardia forestale** *f* forester.
forfora *f* dandruff.
forma *f* shape; fitness; form:—**in forma** *adj* fit.
formattare *vt* to format.
formazione *f* formation; education; background.
formica *f* ant.
formidabile *adj* formidable.
formoso *adj* curvaceous.
fornello *m* gas ring.
fornire *vt* to furnish, provide, supply.
fornitore *m* supplier, stockist, tradesman, purveyor.
fornitura *f* supply, provision.
forno *m* oven.
foro *m* forum; hole, bore.
forse *adj* perhaps:—*adv* maybe.
forsennato *adj* frenzied; berserk.
forte *m* (*mus*) forte; hard; loud; strong.
fortezza *f* fortress, fort, stronghold; strength.
fortificare *vt* to fortify.
fortificato *adj* walled.
fortificazione *f* fortification.
fortuna *f* luck; fortune.
forza *f* force; might; power; strength.
fossa *f* ditch.
fossile *adj*, *m* fossil
foto *f inv* photo.
fotocopia *f* photocopy.
fotografare *vt* to photograph, snap.
fotografia *f* photograph, photography.
fottere *vt* to fuck.
fra *prep* between.

fracasso *m* fracas, crash, smash, noise, racket.
fragile *adj* fragile, breakable, brittle.
fragola *f* strawberry.
fragranza *f* fragrance.
fraintendere *vt* to be at cross-purposes.
frana *f* landslide.
franco *m* franc, frank:—*adj* candid; straightforward.
francobollo *m* stamp, postage stamp.
frasario *m* phrase book.
frase *f* sentence; phrase.
frassino *m* (*bot*) ash.
fratello *m* brother.
frattempo *adv*:—**nel frattempo** in the meantime, in the meanwhile.
frattura *f* fracture.
fraudolento *adj* fraudulent.
frazione *f* fraction.
freccia *f* arrow; indicator:—**mettere la freccia** *vi* to indicate
frecciata *f* gibe:—**lanciare frecciate a** *vi* to gibe.
freddo *adj* cold, chill; stand-offish:—*m* cold, chill.
fregare *vt* to pinch, nick.
frenare *vt* to curb; to control:—*vi* to brake.
freno *m* brake; curb.
frequente *adj* frequent.
fresco *adj* fresh; crisp; cool; chilly:—**mettere in fresco** *vt* to chill.
fretta *f* hurry, haste, rush.
frigo *m* fridge.
frigorifero *m* refrigerator.
frittata *f* omelette.
frivolezza *f* frivolity; triviality; levity.
frizzare *vi* to fizz.
frodo *m*:—**cacciare di frodo** *vt*, *vi* to poach.
fronte *m* front; *f* forehead.

frontiera *f* frontier.
frusta *f* whip.
frustrare *vt* to frustrate; to foil.
frutta *f* fruit.
fruttare *vt* to yield.
frutteto *m* orchard.
fruttifero *adj* fruitful.
fruttivendolo *m* fruiterer, greengrocer.
frutto *m* fruit: — **frutti di mare** *mpl* seafood.
fruttuoso *adj* fruitful.
fucilare *vt* to shoot.
fucilazione *f* shooting.
fucile *m* gun, rifle: — **fucile ad aria compressa** air gun: — **fucile da caccia** *m* shotgun.
fucina *f* smithy.
fuco *m* drone.
fucsia *f* fuchsia.
fuga *f* flight; escape; fugue: — **fuga romantica** *f* elopement: — **fuga precipitosa** *f* stampede.
fuggifuggi *m* debacle.
fuggire *vi* to abscond; to elope; to flee: — *vt* to flee.
fuggitivo *adj*, *m* fugitive, runaway.
fulcro *m* hub, fulcrum.
fuliggine *f* soot: — **granellino di fuliggine** *m* smut.
fulminare *vt* to electrocute: — *vt* fulminare con lo sguardo to glare at.
fulmine *m* lightning, bolt of lightning, thunderbolt.
fulvo *m*, *adj* fawn.
fumante *adj* smoking.
fumare *vt* to smoke: — *vi* to smoke; to steam: — **vietato fumare** no smoking.
fumatore *m* smoker.
fumo *m* smoke, smoking: — **senza fumo** *adj* smokeless: — **emettere fumo** *vt* to fume.

fumoso *adj* smoky.
fune *f* rope.
funebre *adj*: — **carro funebre** *m* hearse.
funerale *m* funeral.
funereo *adj* funereal.
fungo *m* mushroom: — **fungo velenoso** *m* toadstool: — **fungo del legno** *m* dry rot.
funivia *f* cable-car.
funzionale *adj* functional.
funzionamento *m* function: — **cattivo funzionamento** *m* malfunction.
funzionare *vi* to operate; to work; to run: — *vt* **far funzionare** to operate.
funzionario *m* official: — **funzionario del fisco** assessor.
funzione *f* function; service.
fuoco *m* fire; focus: — **fuoco incrociato** crossfire: — **cessate il fuoco** ceasefire: — **resistente al fuoco** *adj* fireproof: — **fuochi d'artificio** *mpl* fireworks.
fuori *adv* outside; out: — *prep* out: — **fuori di** outside.
fuoribordo *adj* outboard.
fuorigioco *adj*: — **in fuorigioco** offside.
fuorilegge *m* outlaw.
furberia *f* craftiness.
furbizia *f* cunning.
furbo *adj* crafty, cunning, artful.
furetto *m* ferret.
furfante *m* knave.
furgone *m* van.
furia *f* fury, rage.
furibondo *adj* wild, livid.
furiere *m* quartermaster.
furioso *adj* furious; raging: — **rendere furioso** *vt* to infuriate.
furtivamente *adv* by stealth: — **procedere furtivamente** *vi* to sidle.
furtivo *adj* furtive, stealthy, surreptitious.

furto *m* theft; snatch; larceny:—**furto con scasso** burglary.

fusa *fpl* purr:—**far le fusa** *vi* to purr.

fusciacca *f* sash.

fusibile *m* fuse:—**scatola dei fusibili** *f* fusebox.

fusione *f* fusion; merger:—**punto di fusione** *m* melting point.

fuso *m* spindle:—*adj* molten.

fusoliera *f* fuselage.

fustigazione *f* flogging.

fusto *m* he-man.

futile *adj* futile, self-defeating.

futilità *f* futility.

futuro *adj* future; prospective; coming; succeeding; elect:—*m* future.

G

gabbia *f* cage; hutch:—**mettere in gabbia** *vt* to cage.

gabbiano *m* (sea)gull.

gabinetto *m* lavatory.

gag *f inv* gag.

galassia *f* galaxy.

galleria *f* gallery, arcade; tunnel:—**galleria d'arte** art gallery.

gallina *f* hen.

gallo *m* cock, rooster.

gamba *f* leg.

gancio *m* hook; catch; clasp.

garage *m inv* garage.

garantire *vt* to guarantee; to ensure; to secure:—*vi* to vouch.

gargolla *f* gargoyle.

garofano *m* carnation.

gas *m inv* gas; throttle.

gasolio *m* diesel.

gassato *adj* carbonated:—**non gassato** *adj* still.

gattino *m* kitten.

gatto *m* cat, tomcat.

gazzetta *f* gazette.

gel *m inv* gel.

gelare *vt*, *vi* to freeze.

gelato *m* ice, ice cream.

gelo *m* frost.

gelosia *f* jealousy.

Gemelli *mpl* Gemini.

gemello *adj*, *m* twin.

gemma *f* gem.

gene *m* gene.

generalità *f inv* generality.

generalizzare *vi* to generalise.

genere *m* gender; kind, sort, genus.

generosità *f* generosity.

gengiva *f* gum.

geniale *adj* brainy.

genio *m* genius.

genitali *mpl* genitals.

genitore *m* parent.

gennaio *m* January.

gente *f* people, folk.

gentile *adj* kind, nice, good.

gentiluomo *m* gentleman.

genuino *adj* genuine, sterling.

geografia *f* geography.

geranio *m* geranium.

gerarchia *f* hierarchy.

gesso *m* chalk; plaster; (*med*) cast.

gestazione *f* gestation.

gesticolare *vi* to gesticulate; to wave.

gesto *m* gesture, sign.

gestore *m* manager.

Gesù *m* Jesus.

gettare *vt* to throw; to chuck; to sprout; to cast.

geyser *m inv* geyser.

ghiaccio *m* ice:—**ghiaccio invisibile** *m* black ice.

ghiacciolo *m* icicle.

ghiaia *f* gravel.

ghianda *f* acorn.

ghiandola *f* gland.

ghigliottina *f* guillotine.

ghirlanda *f* garland, wreath.

già *adv* already; yet.

giacca *f* jacket:—**giacca a vento** *f* anorak, windcheater.

giacinto *m* hyacinth.

giada *f* jade.

giaietto *m* jet.

giallo *adj*:—*m* yellow; (traffic lights) amber.

giardinaggio *m* gardening.

giardino *m* garden.

giarrettiera *f* garter.

gigante *m* giant.

gigantesco *adj* gigantic, monster.

giglio *m* lily.

gin *m inv* gin.

ginecologo *m* gynaecologist.

ginepro *m* juniper.

ginocchio *m* knee.

giocare *vt, vi* to play.

giocatore *m* player:—**giocatore d'azzardo** gambler.

giocattolo *m* toy.

gioco *m* game; play.

gioia *f* joy, glee.

gioielliere *m* jeweller.

gioiello *m* jewel:—**gioielli** *mpl* jewellery.

giornale *m* (news)paper:—**giornale radio** *m* news.

giornaliero *adj* daily.

giornalismo *m* journalism.

giornalista *m/ f* journalist, columnist.

giornata *f* day.

giorno *m* day, daytime:—**giorno per giorno** day by day:—**di giorno** by day:—**buon giorno** *excl* good morning:—**un giorno** *adv* sometime.

giostra *f* merry-go-round, roundabout, carousel.

giovane *adj* young.

giovedì *m inv* Thursday.

gioventù *f* youth.

giraffa *f* giraffe.

girare *vt* to revolve; to spin; to turn.

girasole *m* sunflower.

girino *m* tadpole.

giro *m* tour; round; circuit; turn; walk; ride; run.

gita *f* jaunt; excursion; trip.

giù *adv* down:—**in giù** downwards.

giubileo *m* jubilee.

giubilo *m* exultation.

giudicare *vt* to judge; to deem; to adjudicate.

giudice *m* judge.

giugno *m* June.

giungla *f* jungle, wilderness.

giunta *f* junta.

giuntare *vt* to splice.

giuntura *f* join.

giuramento *m* oath.

giurare *vt* to swear, vow:—*vi* to swear.

giurato *m* juror.

giustamente *adv* right.

giustificare *vt* to justify.

giustizia *f* justice.

giustiziare *vt* to execute.

giusto *adj* right; just; fair; proper.

globale *adj* global; comprehensive; blanket.

globo *m* globe.

gnocco *m* dumpling.

gnomo *m* gnome.

gnu *m inv* gnu.

goccia *f* drop, drip.

godere *vt* to enjoy.

godimento *m* enjoyment.

gol *m inv* goal.

gola *f* throat, gullet; gorge.

golf *m* golf.

goloso *adj* greedy.

gomito *m* elbow.

gomma *f* rubber.

gonfiabile *adj* inflatable.

gonfiare *vt* to inflate; to swell.

gonfio *adj* swollen; puffy, bloated: — **essere gonfio di** *vi* to bulge.

gonna *f* skirt.

gonorrea *f* gonorrhoea.

gonzo *m* dupe.

gorgogliare *vi* to gurgle.

gorilla *m inv* gorilla.

gotico *adj* gothic.

gotta *f* gout.

gradevole *adj* pleasant: — **gradevole al palato** palatable.

gradiente *m* gradient.

gradino *m* step.

gradito *adj* welcome; acceptable: — **non gradito** unwelcome.

grado *m* degree; grade; rank.

graduale *adj* gradual.

gradualmente *adv* little by little.

graduare *vt* to grade.

graffio *m* scratch.

graffiti *mpl* graffiti.

grafica *f* graphics.

grafico *adj* graphic(al): — *m* graph.

grammatica *f* grammar.

grammo *m* gram.

grammofono *m* gramophone.

grana *f* grain.

granchio *m* crab.

grande *adj* big, large, great.

grandiosità *f* grandeur.

granito *m* granite.

grano *m* corn, wheat: — **campo di grano** *m* cornfield.

grasso *m* grease.

grasso *m* fat: — **grasso dell'arrosto** *m* dripping: — **grasso di balena** blubber: — *adj* fat, fatty: — **piante grasse** *fpl* succulent plants.

gratis *adv* gratis.

gratitudine *f* gratitude, thankfulness.

grato *adj* grateful; appreciative; thankful.

grattacapo *m* (*fig*) headache.

grattacielo *m* skyscraper.

gratuito *adj* free; gratuitous.

grave *adj* grave; serious; acute.

gravità *f* gravity.

gravitare *vi* to gravitate.

gravitazione *f* gravitation.

grazia *f* grace: — **grazie** *fpl* thanks.

greco *adj m* Greek.

greggio *adj* unrefined, raw.

grembo *m* lap, womb.

grida *fpl* shouting.

gridare *vi*, *vt* to cry, shout.

grido *m* cry; shout: — **grido di incoraggiamento** *m* cheer.

griffone *m* griffin.

grigio *m* grey: — *adj* grey, drab.

griglia *f* grill: — **cuocere alla griglia** *vt* to grill.

grilletto *m* trigger.

grillo *m* cricket.

grinta *f* drive.

grondare *vt* to stream.

groppa *f* rump.

grossa *f* gross.

grossista *m/f* wholesaler.

grosso *adj* big; thick.

grossolanamente *adv* roughly.

grossolano *adj* gross; crude; earthy.

grotta *f* grotto; cave.

grottesco *adj* grotesque.

groviglio *m* entanglement, tangle.

gru *f inv* crane.

gruccia *f* (coat)hanger.

grugnire *vi* to grunt.

grugnito *m* grunt.

grumo *m* clot, lump.

gruppo *m* group; cluster; batch:—**gruppo sanguigno** blood group.

gruzzolo *m* hoard; nest egg.

guadagnare *vt* to earn; to gain.

guadagno *m* gain; return:—**guadagni** *mpl* earnings.

guadare *vt* to ford.

guado *m* ford.

guai *mpl* trouble.

guaina *f* sheath.

guaio *m* scrape, fix.

guaire *vi* to whine.

guaito *m* whine.

guancia *f* cheek.

guanciale *m* pillow.

guanto *m* glove; gauntlet.

guantoni *mpl* boxing gloves.

guardacaccia *m inv* gamekeeper.

guardacoste *m inv* coastguard.

guardalinee *m inv* linesman.

guardare *vi* to look; to watch:—**guardare i bambini** to babysit.

guardaroba *m inv* wardrobe; cloak-room.

guardia *f* guard; watch:—**guardia del corpo** bodyguard:—**corpo di guar-**dia *m* guardroom:—**guardia forestale** *f* ranger:—**cane da guardia** *m* watchdog:—**fare la guardia a** *vt* to guard.

guardiano *m* watchman; keeper.

guaribile *adj* curable.

guarigione *f* cure.

guarire *vt* to cure; to heal.

guarnigione *f* garrison.

guarnire *vt* to garnish.

guarnizione *f* gasket.

guastafeste *m/ f inv* spoilsport, kill-joy.

guastare *vt* to vitiate:—*vr* ~**rsi** *vr* to go off, spoil.

guasto *m* breakdown.

guerra *f* war:—**guerra civile** *f* civil war.

guerriero *m* warrior.

guerriglia *f* guerrilla warfare.

guerrigliero *m* guerrilla.

gufo *m* owl.

guglia *f* spire.

guida *f* leader; guide; guidebook; driving; guidance; runner.

guidare *vt* to drive; to guide; to steer; to lead.

guidatore *m* driver.

guinzaglio *m* leash, lead.

gulasch *m inv* goulash.

guru *m inv* guru.

guscio *m* shell; husk:—**guscio d'uovo** *m* eggshell:—**guscio di noce** *m* nutshell.

gustare *vt* to relish.

gusto *m* flavour; taste; relish:—**di gusto** *adv* heartily:—**di gusto** *adj* tasteful:—**di cattivo gusto** *adj* tasteless.

gutturale *adj* guttural.

H

habitat *m inv* habitat; home.
hamburger *m inv* hamburger.
handicap *m* handicap.
handicappato *adj* handicapped.
harem *m inv* harem.
hascisc *m* hash(ish).
herpes *m inv* cold sore:—**herpes zoster** *m* (*med*) shingles.

hi-fi *m inv* hi-fi.
hobby *m inv* hobby.
hockey *m* hockey.
hostess *f inv* stewardess.
hot dog *m inv* hot dog.
hotel *m inv* hotel.
house boat *f inv* houseboat.

I

ibrido *adj, m* hybrid.
iceberg *m inv* iceberg.
icona *f* icon.
idea *f* idea; notion.
ideale *adj, m* ideal.
identico *adj* identical.
identificare *vt* to identify; to equate.
ideologia *f* ideology.
idillico *adj* idyllic.
idiota *m/f* idiot; moron.
idoneità *f* fitness.
idrante *m* hydrant.
idrogeno *m* hydrogen.
iena *f* hyena.
ieri *adv* yesterday.
igiene *f* hygiene.
ignizione *f* ignition.
ignorante *adj* ignorant.
il *def art* the.
illegale *adj* illegal.
illeggibile *adj* illegible.

illustrazione *f* illustration.
imballaggio *m* packing.
imbarazzante *adj* embarrassing, awkward.
imbarcare *vt* to embark; to ship:—*vr* ~**rsi** to board.
imbecille *m* imbecile.
imbiancare *vt* to whitewash.
imbottigliare *vt* to bottle.
imitare *vt* to imitate, impersonate, copy, mimic.
immaginazione *f* imagination.
immagine *f* image.
immangiabile *adj* inedible, unpalatable.
immaturo *adj* immature; callow.
immediato *adj* immediate, instant.
immenso *adj* immense.
immerso *adj* engrossed.
immigrato *m* immigrant.
immigrazione *f* immigration.

immorale *adj* immoral.
immoralità *f* immorality.
immune *adj* immune.
imparare *vt* to learn.
imparziale *adj* impartial, fair, unbiased, detached.
impaziente *adj* impatient.
impazienza *f* impatience.
impazzire *vi* to go mad: — far impazzire to *vt* madden.
impedire *vt* to stop, hinder.
impegnare *vt* to pledge, pawn: — *vr* ~rsi to covenant.
impegno *m* commitment; bond; engagement.
imperativo *adj* imperative.
imperatore *m* emperor.
imperatrice *f* empress.
imperdonabile *adj* unforgivable, inexcusable.
imperfetto *adj* imperfect.
imperiale *adj* imperial.
impermeabile *adj* impermeable; waterproof: — *m* mackintosh, raincoat.
impero *m* empire.
impersonale *adj* impersonal.
impervio *adj* impervious.
impestare *vt* to foul.
impianto *m* plant: — impianto elettrico *m* wiring; *mpl* fixtures.
impiegare *vt* to employ.
impiegato *m* clerk, office worker.
impiego *m* job, position; use.
implicare *vt* to implicate, imply.
implicazione *f* implication.
implicito *adj* implicit.
implorare *vt* to implore.
imponente *adj* imposing, impressive, awe-inspiring.
imponibile *adj* taxable.
importante *adj* important; momentous;

weighty: — il più importante foremost.
importanza *f* importance: — avere più importanza di *vt* to outweigh.
importare *vt* to import: — *vi* to matter: — non mi importa I don't care.
importatore *m* importer.
importazione *f* import, importation.
importo *m* amount.
impossibile *adj* impossible; hopeless.
impossibilità *f* impossibility.
imposta *f* tax; levy.
impostazione *f* layout.
impotente *adj* impotent, powerless.
impotenza *f* impotence.
impraticabile *adj* impracticable.
impreciso *adj* imprecise.
impregnare *vt* to impregnate, steep.
imprenditore *m* entrepreneur.
impresa *f* concern; undertaking.
impressionabile *adj* impressionable.
impressione *f* impression, feeling, hunch: — fare impressione a *vt* to impress.
imprevedibile *adj* unforeseeable, unpredictable.
imprigionare *vt* to imprison, incarcerate.
imprimere *vt* to imprint.
improbabile *adj* improbable, unlikely.
improbabilità *f* improbability, unlikelihood.
improduttivo *adj* unproductive.
improvvisamente *adv* all at once.
improvvisare *vi* to improvise.
improvvisato *adj* impromptu.
improvviso *adj* sudden, snap.
impulsivo *adj* impulsive.
impulso *m* impulse, urge.
impunemente *adv* with impunity.
impunito *adj* unpunished.

impurità *f inv* impurity.
impuro *adj* impure.
imputare *vt* to indict.
imputato *m* defendant, accused.
imputazione *f* charge, indictment.
in *prep* in; into; **in treno** by train: — **in vettura** *adv* aboard.
inabilità *f* inability.
inabitabile *adj* uninhabitable.
inaccessibile *adj* inaccessible.
inadatto *adj* inappropriate, unfit, unsuitable
inadeguato *adj* inadequate.
inafferrabile *adj* elusive.
inalare *vt* to inhale.
inalterabile *adj* unalterable.
inammissibile *adj* inadmissible.
inanimato *adj* inanimate.
inatteso *adj* unexpected.
inattività *f* inactivity.
inattuabile *adj* unworkable.
inaugurale *adj* inaugural, maiden.
inaugurare *vt* to inaugurate.
inazione *f* inaction.
incandescente *adj* incandescent, white-hot.
incantare *vt* to enchant.
incantevole *adj* enchanting, ravishing.
incanto *m* charm.
incapace *adj* incapable, unable.
incarnazione *f* incarnation, embodiment.
incartare *vt* to wrap.
incassare *vt* to cash.
incendio *m* fire, blaze.
incenso *m* incense.
incertezza *f* uncertainty, suspense.
incerto *adj* unsure, uncertain, touch-and-go.
inchiesta *f* inquest, inquiry.

inchinarsi *vr* to bow.
inchiostro *m* ink.
incidente *m* accident.
incidenza *f* incidence.
incidere *vt* to incise; to engrave; to cut.
incidere su *vt* affect.
incinta *adj* pregnant, expecting.
incivile *adj* uncivil.
inclinare *vt* to tilt, slant.
includere *vt* to include.
incollare *vt* to glue, stick.
incolpare *vt* to blame.
incolto *adj* uncultivated, fallow; uneducated.
incomodare *vt* to inconvenience.
incomparabile *adj* incomparable.
incompatibile *adj* incompatible.
incompetente *adj* incompetent.
incompetenza *f* incompetence.
inconfondibile *adj* unmistakable.
inconscio *adj, m* unconscious.
incontestato *adj* unchallenged.
incontrare *vt* to meet, encounter.
incontro *m* encounter; meeting; match; (boxing) bout.
inconveniente *m* drawback.
incoraggiare *vt* to encourage.
incorniciare *vt* to frame.
incoronare *vt* to crown.
incorporare *vt* to incorporate.
incorruttibile *adj* incorruptible.
incredibile *adj* incredible, unbelievable.
incriminare *vt* to incriminate.
incrociare *vt* to cross.
incrocio *m* crossing, crossroads, junction; crossbreed.
incubo *m* nightmare.
incurabile *adj* incurable, terminal.
indagare *vt* to investigate, inquire (into).

indagine *f* investigation; survey.
indebolire *vt* to weaken, enfeeble: — *vr* ~**rsi** to weaken.
indecente *adj* indecent, rude.
indeciso *adj* undecided; indecisive; doubtful.
indecoroso *adj* unseemly.
indelebile *adj* indelible.
indennità *f* allowance; compensation.
indennizzare *vt* to indemnify.
indicazione *f* indication.
indice *m* index; forefinger, index finger.
indietro *adv* behind; back, backwards.
indifeso *adj* defenceless, unprotected.
indifferente *adj* indifferent, cold, uninterested, unmoved.
indigeno *adj* indigenous, native.
indigestione *f* indigestion.
indignato *adj* indignant.
indignazione *f* indignation.
indipendente *adj* independent; self-contained.
indiretto *adj* indirect.
indirizzare *vt* to address.
indirizzo *m* address.
indiscreto *adj* indiscreet.
indiscrezione *f* indiscretion.
indispensabile *adj* indispensable.
indistinto *adj* indistinct.
indistruttibile *adj* indestructible.
individuale *adj* individual, one-man.
indolenza *f* indolence, lethargy.
indossare *vt* to wear; to model.
indovinare *vt, vi* to guess.
indubbiamente *adv* doubtless.
indubbio *adj* undoubted.
indulgenza *f* indulgence.
industria *f* industry, trade.
inebriare *vt* to intoxicate.
inefficace *adj* ineffective, ineffectual.

inefficiente *adj* inefficient.
ineguaglianza *f* inequality.
ineguale *adj* uneven.
inesperto *adj* inexperienced; unskilful.
inespressivo *adj* expressionless.
inesprimibile *adj* inexpressable.
inetto *adj* inept.
infamia *f* infamy.
infangare *vt* to soil; to taint.
infantile *adj* infantile, babyish, childish.
infanzia *f* infancy, childhood: — **prima infanzia** *f* babyhood.
infastidire *vt* to annoy, bother.
infaticabile *adj* indefatigable, untiring.
infatti *adv* indeed.
infatuazione *f* infatuation.
infedele *adj* unfaithful, infidel: — *m* infidel.
infedeltà *f inv* unfaithfulness, infidelity.
infelice *adj* unhappy, miserable.
infelicità *f* unhappiness.
inferiore *adj* inferior, lower.
infermiere *m* nurse.
infermo *adj* infirm.
inferno *m* hell.
infestare *vt* to infest.
infettare *vt* to infect.
infettivo *adj* infectious.
infezione *f* infection.
infilare *vt* to thread; to string.
infiltrarsi *vr* to infiltrate.
infilzare *vt* to spike.
infine *adv* lastly.
infinità *f* infinity.
infinitivo *adj* infinitive.
inflazione *f* inflation.
inflessibile *adj* inflexible; adamant.
influenza *f* influence, influenza.

inforcatura f crotch.

informale adj informal, casual.

informare vt to inform.

informatica f computer science.

informato adj knowledgeable.

informazione f information.

inframmezzare vt to intersperse.

ingresso m entrance; admission, admittance.

inimicarsi vr to antagonise.

infrangere vt to infringe.

infrarosso adj infra-red.

infrastruttura f infrastructure.

infrazione f offence, infraction.

infrequente adj infrequent.

infruttuoso adj unfruitful, barren.

infusione f infusion:—**lasciare in infusione** vt to infuse.

infuso m brew.

ingaggiare vt to engage.

ingannare vt to deceive, fool, hoax, trick.

inganno m trick, deceit, deception:—**trarre in inganno** vt to mislead.

ingegnere m engineer:—**ingegnere civile** m civil engineer.

ingegneria f engineering.

ingegnoso adj ingenious.

ingenuo adj naïve, ingenuous, artless, simple.

ingiustizia f injustice.

ingiusto adj wrong, wrongful, unfair, unjust.

ingovernabile adj ungovernable.

ingozzare vt to guzzle.

ingrandimento m enlargement.

ingrandire vt to enlarge, magnify.

ingrassare vt to fatten.

ingratitudine f ingratitude.

ingraziarsi vr to ingratiate.

ingrediente m ingredient.

ingresso m entrance, entry.

ingrosso adj:—**all'ingrosso** adv wholesale.

inguine m groin.

inibire vt to inhibit.

inibizione f inhibition.

iniettare vt to inject.

iniezione f injection, shot.

inimicizia f enmity.

inimmaginabile adj unimaginable, inconceivable.

inintelligibile adj unintelligible.

ininterrotto adj unbroken, uninterrupted.

iniquità f iniquity.

iniziale f, adj initial.

iniziare vt to begin, start; to initiate: — vi to begin.

iniziativa f initiative, enterprise.

inizio m beginning.

innaffiare vt to water.

innamorare vt to enamour:—vr ~**rsi** to fall in love.

innato adj innate, in-born.

innervosire vt to fluster.

inno m hymn, anthem.

innocente adj innocent.

innocenza f innocence.

innocuo adj innocuous, harmless.

innovazione f innovation.

innumerevole adj innumerable, countless.

inoculare vt to inoculate.

inoculazione f inoculation.

inodore adj odourless, scentless.

inoffensivo adj unoffending, inoffensive.

inoltre adv furthermore, besides, moreover.

inondare vt to inundate, flood, swamp.

inondazione f inundation, flood.

inopportuno *adj* inopportune, unsuitable; ill-timed.

inorganico *adj* inorganic.

inorridire *vt* to horrify.

inorridito *adj* aghast.

inospitale *adj* inhospitable.

inquietante *adj* disquieting.

inquieto *adj* uneasy.

inquilino *m* tenant, occupant, occupier.

inquinamento *m* pollution.

inquinare *vt* to pollute.

insalata *f* salad.

insalatiera *f* salad bowl.

insalubre *adj* unhygienic.

insegnamento *m* teaching.

insegnante *m/f* teacher; *m* master, schoolmaster.

insegnare *vt, vi* to teach.

inseguire *vt* to chase, pursue.

inseminazione *f* insemination.

insensibile *adj* insensitive, unfeeling, callous.

inseparabile *adj* inseparable.

inserire *vt* to insert.

inserviente *m* orderly.

insetto *m* insect.

insicurezza *f* insecurity.

insidioso *adj* insidious.

insieme *adv, adj* together.

insignificante *adj* insignificant.

insincerità *f* insincerity.

insincero *adj* insincere.

insinuare *vt* to insinuate:—*vr* ~**rsi** to worm.

insipido *adj* insipid, flavourless, tasteless.

insistente *adj* insistent.

insoddisfacente *adj* unsatisfying.

insoddisfatto *adj* dissatisfied.

insolazione *f* sunstroke.

insolito *adj* uncommon, unusual.

insolubile *adj* insoluble.

insonnia *f* insomnia.

insopportabile *adj* insufferable, unendurable.

insormontabile *adj* insurmountable.

insostenibile *adj* untenable.

inspiegato *adj* unexplained.

instillare *vt* to instil.

insufficiente *adj* insufficient, unsatisfactory.

insufficienza *f* insufficiency, deficiency.

insulare *adj* insular.

insulina *f* insulin.

insultare *vt* to insult, abuse; to revile.

insulto *m* insult.

insuperato *adj* unequalled.

insurrezione *f* insurrection, uprising.

intaglio *m* carving.

intarsiare *vt* to inlay.

integrale *adj* complete, integral, (bread) wholemeal.

integrante *adj* integral.

intelletto *m* intellect.

intellettuale *m/f, adj* intellectual.

intelligente *adj* intelligent, clever.

intelligenza *f* intelligence, cleverness, wit.

intendere *vt* to intend, mean.

intenditore *m* connoisseur.

intensivo *adj* intensive.

intenzionale *adj* intentional.

intercettare *vt* to intercept; to tap.

interessante *adj* interesting.

interessare *vt* to interest:—*vr* ~**rsi di** to care about.

interferire *vt* to interfere.

interiezione *f* interjection.

interiore *adj* inner, inward.

interlocutore *m* speaker.

intermediario *m* intermediary, go-between.

intermedio *adj* intermediate, in-between.

intero *adj* entire, whole.

interporre *vt* to interpose.

interpretare *vt* to interpret; to render; to act.

interpretazione *f* interpretation, performance.

interprete *m/f* interpreter.

interrogare *vt* to interrogate, cross-examine; to quiz, question.

interrompere *vt* to interrupt.

interurbano *adj* long-distance.

intervallo *m* interval, interlude, break, recess.

intervenire *vt* to intervene.

intervista *f* interview.

intesa *f* understanding.

intestino *m* intestine; bowels; gut.

intimidire *vt* to intimidate.

intimità *f* intimacy.

intimo *adj* intimate.

intonacare *vt* to plaster.

intonaco *m* plaster.

intorno *adv* around: —*prep* **intorno a** about, around; round.

intorpidimento *m* numbness.

intossicazione *f* poisoning: —**intossicazione alimentare** *f* food poisoning.

intraducibile *adj* untranslatable.

intralcio *m* hindrance.

intransigenza *f* intransigence.

intransitabile *adj* impassable.

intransitivo *adj* intransitive.

intrepido *adj* intrepid, fearless.

intricato *adj* intricate.

intrigo *m* intrigue.

intrinseco *adj* intrinsic, inherent.

introdurre *vt* to introduce.

introduzione *f* introduction.

introiti *mpl* takings.

intromettersi *vr* to intrude, interfere.

introverso *m* introvert.

intrusione *f* intrusion.

intruso *m* intruder, interloper, gatecrasher.

intuire *vt* to sense, divine.

intuito *m* intuition.

inumanità *f* inhumanity.

inumano *adj* inhuman.

inumidire *vt* to damp, dampen, moisten.

inutile *adj* useless, unnecessary.

inutilità *f* uselessness.

inutilizzato *adj* unused.

invalido *adj* disabled; invalid: —*m* invalid.

invano *adv* to no avail.

invariabile *adj* invariable.

invariato *adj* unchanged.

invasare *vt* to pot.

invasione *f* invasion.

invasore *m* invader.

invece *adv* instead: —**invece di** in lieu of.

invecchiare *vi* to age.

inveire *vi* to rail (against).

invendibile *adj* unsaleable.

invenduto *adj* unsold.

inventare *vt* to invent; to make up; to concoct (a story).

inventario *m* inventory, stocktaking.

inventivo *adj* inventive.

inventore *m* inventor.

invenzione *f* invention.

invernale *adj* winter, wintry.

inverno *m* winter: —**pieno inverno** *m* midwinter.

inverosimile *adj* unlikely.

inversione *f* inversion, reversal.
inverso *m* converse:—*adj* inverse, reverse.
invertebrato *m* invertebrate.
invertire *vt* to reverse; to switch.
investigatore *m* investigator, detective.
investimento *m* investment.
investire *vt* to invest.
inveterato *adj* inveterate, confirmed.
invettiva *f* invective.
inviare *vt* to send, dispatch.
inviato *m* envoy.
invidia *f* envy.
invidiabile *adj* enviable:—**poco invidiabile** unenviable.
invidiare *vt* to grudge, begrudge.
invidioso *adj* envious.
invincibile *adj* invincible, unconquerable.
invio *m* dispatch.
inviolabile *adj* inviolable.
invisibile *adj* invisible.
invitante *adj* inviting.
invitare *vt* to invite; to ask out; to take out.
invitato *m* guest.
invito *m* invitation.
invocare *vt* to invoke.
involontario *adj* involuntary.
involontario *adj* inadvertent, accidental, unwitting, unintentional.
involtino di fegato *m* faggot.
invulnerabile *adj* invulnerable.
inzuppare *vt* to drench, soak, dunk.
inzuppato *adj* waterlogged.
io *pron* I.
iodio *m* iodine.
iperbole *f* hyperbole.
ipermercato *m* hypermarket.
ipersensibile *adj* highly strung.
ipertensione *f* hypertension.
ipnosi *f* hypnosis.

ipnotico *adj* hypnotic.
ipnotismo *m* hypnotism.
ipnotizzare *vt* to hynotise, mesmerise.
ipocondria *f* hypochondria.
ipocondriaco *m* hypochondriac.
ipocrisia *f* hypocrisy.
ipocrita *m/f* hypocrite;
ipodermico *adj* hypodermic.
ipoteca *f* mortgage.
ipotecare *vt* to mortgage.
ipotesi *f inv* hypothesis.
ipotetico *adj* hypothetical.
ippocastano *m* horse chestnut.
ippoglosso *m* halibut.
ippopotamo *m* hippopotamus.
ira *f* wrath.
irato *adj* irate.
iride *f* iris.
iris *f inv* iris.
ironia *f* irony.
ironico *adj* ironic.
irradiare *vt* to irradiate.
irraggiare *vt* to radiate.
irraggiungibile *adj* unattainable.
irragionevole *adj* irrational.
irrazionale *adj* unreasonable.
irreale *adj* unreal.
irreconciliabile *adj* irreconcilable.
irrecuperabile *adj* irretrievable.
irregolare *adj* irregular.
irreligioso *adj* irreligious.
irremovibile *adj* unshakable.
irreparabile *adj* irrepairable.
irreprensibile *adj* blameless
irreprensibile *adj* irreproachable, unimpeachable.
irrequieto *adj* restive, restless, fidgety:
—**persona irrequieta** *f* fidget.
irresistibile *adj* irresistible.
irresponsabile *adj* irresponsible, feckless.

irriconoscibile *adj* unrecognisable.
irrigare *vt* to irrigate.
irrigazione *f* irrigation.
irrilevante *adj* immaterial.
irripetibile *adj* unrepeatable.
irrisorio *adj* paltry.
irritabile *adj* irritable.
irritante *adj* irritating.
irritare *vt* to irritate.
irritato *adj* irritated, vexed.
irritazione *f* irritation.
irriverente *adj* irreverent, disrespectful, flippant.
irriverenza *f* irreverence.
iscrivere *vt* to enrol:—*vr* ~**rsi** to register.
iscrizione *f* inscription; enrolment; membership.
Islam *m inv* Islam.
isola *f* island, isle.
isolamento *m* insulation; isolation, seclusion.

isolare *vt* to insulate; to isolate.
ispessire *vt* to thicken.
ispettore *m* inspector.
ispezione *f* inspection,
ispirare *vt* to inspire.
ispirazione *f* inspiration.
issare *vt* to hoist.
istante *m* instant.
isterismo *m* hysteria.
istigare *vt* to instigate.
istigazione *f* instigation.
istinto *m* instinct.
istituire *vt* to institute, establish.
istituzione *f* institution, establishment.
istruire *vt* to instruct, educate.
istruttivo *adj* instructive.
istruttore *m* instructor.
istruzione *f* instruction, education.
itinerante *adj* travelling.
itinerario *m* itinerary, route.
iuta *f* jute.
IVA *f* VAT.

J

jazz *m* jazz.
jeans *mpl* jeans; **tessuto jeans** *m* denim.
jeep *f inv* jeep.

jet *m inv* jet.
jolly *m* joker.
judo *m* judo.
juke-box *m inv* juke-box.

K

K.O. *m inv* knock-out.
karate *m* karate.
ketchup *m* ketchup.

kilt *m inv* kilt.
kolossal *m* spectacular.

L

la *def art* the:—*pron* her.
là *adv* there.
labbro *m* lip.
labirinto *m* labyrinth, maze.
laboratorio *m* laboratory.
lacca *f* lacquer, hairspray.
laccio *m* (shoe)lace.
lacerare *vt* to lacerate.
lacrima *f* tear.
ladro *m* thief.
lago *m* lake, (*Scot*) loch.
laguna *f* lagoon.
laim *m* lime.
lama *f* blade.
lamentare *vt* to lament.
lampada *f* lamp.
lampadina *f* (light) bulb.
lampeggiare *vi* to flash.
lampo *m* flash; lightning.
lampone *m* raspberry, raspberry bush.
lana *f* wool.
lancia *f* lance, spear.
lanciare *vt* to throw.
lanterna *f* lantern.
lapide *f* gravestone; tablet.
lapis *m* pencil.
larghezza *f* width, breadth.
largo *adj* broad, wide.
laringe *f* larynx.
larva *f* larva.
lasciapassare *m inv* pass.
lasciare *vt* to leave.
laser *m inv* laser.
lassativo *m* laxative.
laterale *adj* lateral, side.
lato *m* side.

latta *f* can.
latte *m* milk.
latteo *adj* milky:—**Via Lattea** *f* Milky Way.
lattina *f* can, tin.
lattuga *f* lettuce.
laureato *m* graduate.
lavabo *m* washbasin.
lavagna *f* blackboard.
lavandino *m* basin.
lavare *vt* to wash.
lavastoviglie *f inv* dishwasher.
lavatrice *f* washing machine.
lavorare *vi* to work.
lavoratore *m* worker.
lavoro *m* work.
leader *m* leader.
lecca lecca *m inv* lollipop.
leccapiedi *m/f* sycophant.
leccare *vt* to lick, lap.
lega *f* league.
legale *adj* legal, lawful.
legalità *f* legality.
legalizzare *vt* to legalise.
legare *vt* to tie.
legge *f* law.
leggere *vt, vi* to read.
leggero *adj* light, flimsy.
leggibile *adj* legible; readable.
legione *f* legion.
legislativo *adj* legislative:—**corpo legislativo** *m* legislature.
legislazione *f* legislation.
legittimare *vt* to legitimise.
legittimità *f* legitimacy.
legna *f* wood.

legname *m* timber.

legno *m* wood.

lei *pron* her, she:—**di lei** hers:—*pers pron* you.

lente *f* lens.

lentiggine *f* freckle.

lento *adj* slow.

lenzuolo *m* sheet.

leone *m* lion.

leonessa *f* lioness.

leopardo *m* leopard.

lepre *f* hare.

lesbica *f* lesbian; (*sl*) dyke.

lesione *f* lesion; hurt.

lessico *m* lexicon.

letale *adj* lethal.

letame *m* muck.

letargico *adj* lethargic.

lettera *f* letter.

letterale *adj* literal.

letterario *adj* literary.

letteratura *f* literature.

lettino *m* cot.

letto *m* bed.

lettore *m* reader.

leucemia *f* leukaemia.

leva *f* lever.

levriero *m* greyhound.

lezione *f* lesson.

li *pers pron* them.

lì *adv* there.

libbra *f* pound.

libellula *f* dragonfly.

liberale *adj* liberal.

liberare *vt* to liberate.

libero *adj* free, unattached, unoccupied.

libertà *f* liberty.

libidine *f* lust.

libido *f inv* libido.

libraio *m* bookseller.

libreria *f* bookshop; bookcase.

libretto *m* libretto; booklet.

libro *m* book.

licenza *f* licence; leave.

licenzioso *adj* licentious.

lichene *m* lichen.

lieto *adj* pleased, glad, joyful, joyous.

lievitare *vi* to rise.

lievito *m* yeast.

ligustro *m* privet.

lilla *m inv* lilac.

lima *f* file.

limare *vt* to file.

limitare *vt* to limit.

limitazione *f* limitation, check.

limite *m* limit:—**limite di velocità** *m* speed limit.

limiti *mpl* bounds.

limonata *f* lemonade.

limone *m* lemon.

limousine *f inv* limousine.

limpido *adj* limpid.

lince *f* lynx.

linea *f* line; figure.

linfa *f* sap, lymph.

lingua *f* language; tongue.

linguaggio *m* language, speech.

linguetta *f* flap, tab.

linguista *m/f* linguist.

linguistica *f* linguistics.

linguistico *adj* linguistic.

linimento *m* liniment.

linoleum *m* linoleum.

liquidare *vt* to liquidate.

liquidazione *f* liquidation.

liquido *adj*, *m* liquid.

liquore *m* liqueur.

liquori *mpl* spirits.

lirico *adj* lyrical; operatic.

lisca *f* fishbone.

lisciare *vt* to smooth.

liscio *adj* smooth.
litania *f* litany.
lite *f* row.
litigare *vi* to argue.
litigio *m* quarrel.
litigioso *adj* litigious, quarrelsome.
litografia *f* lithograph, lithography.
litorale *m* coast.
litro *m* litre.
liturgia *f* liturgy.
liuto *m* lute.
livellare *vt* to level; to equalise.
livello *m* level.
livido *m* bruise:—*adj* livid:—**farsi un livido a** *vt* to bruise.
livrea *f* livery.
lo *pron* him.
lobo *m* lobe.
locale *adj* local.
locali *mpl* premises.
località *f inv* locality.
localizzare *vt* to localise:—**localizzare con esatezza** to pinpoint.
locanda *f* inn.
locandiere *m* innkeeper.
locomotiva *f* locomotive, engine.
locusta *f* locust.
lodevole *adj* laudable.
logica *f* logic.
logo *m inv* logo.
logoramento *m* wear.
logorarsi *vr* to wear out.
logoro *adj* effete.
lombata *f* loin.
lombrico *m* earthworm.
longevità *f* longevity.
longitudine *f* longitude.
lontananza *f* distance.
lontano *adj* distant, far, faraway:—**più lontano** farthest.
lontra *f* otter.

loquace *adj* loquacious, talkative.
loquacità *f* loquacity.
loro *pers* you; them:—*poss adj* your(s), their; *pron*:—your(s).
lordo *adj* gross.
losanga *f* lozenge.
losco *adj* shifty.
lotta *f* fight.
lottare *vt* to fight, struggle.
lottatore *m* wrestler.
lottèria *f* lottery, draw.
lotto *m* lot.
lozione *f* lotion.
lubrificante *m* lubricant.
lubrificare *vt* to lubricate, grease.
lucchetto *m* padlock.
luccicare *vi* to glisten.
luccichio *m* gleam.
luccio *m* pike.
lucciola *f* firefly.
luce *f* light.
lucente *adj* shining.
lucentezza *f* gloss, shine, sheen.
lucernario *m* skylight.
lucertola *f* lizard.
lucidare *vt* to polish, buff.
lucidato *adj* polished.
lucidata *f* polish.
lucido *adj* shiny, glossy; lucid:—*m* polish:—**lucido da scarpe** boot polish.
lucrativo *adj* lucrative.
luglio *m* July.
lugubre *adj* lugubrious, mournful.
lui *pron* him, he.
lumaca *f* slug.
luminosità *f* brightness.
luminoso *adj* luminous, bright.
luna *f* moon.
lunare *adj* lunar.
lunatico *adj* moody.

lunedì *m inv* Monday.
lunghezza *f* length.
lungo *adj* long.
lungomare *m* esplanade, seafront.
luogo *m* place.
lupo *m* wolf.
luppolo *m* hop.
lusingare *vt* to flatter.

lusso *m* luxury.
lussuoso *adj* luxurious.
lussureggiante *adj* lush, luxuriant.
lustrare *vt* to shine, polish.
lustrino *m* sequin, spangle.
lustro *m* lustre.
lutto *m* mourning; bereavement:—**in lutto** *adj* bereaved.

M

ma *conj* but; yet.
macabro *adj* macabre; grim; sick.
macadam *m*:—**macadam al catrame** *m* tarmac.
maccheroni *mpl* macaroni.
macchia *f* spot, smudge, stain.
macchiare *vt* to mark, stain.
macchiato *adj* spotted.
macchina *f* machine; car:—**macchina fotografica** *f* camera.
macchinari *mpl* machinery.
macchinazione *f* machination.
macchinista *m* engine driver.
macedonia *f* fruit salad.
macellaio *m* butcher.
macellare *vt* to butcher, slaughter.
macelleria *f* butcher's shop.
macello *m* shambles.
macigno *m* boulder.
madre *f* mother.
madrelingua *f* native language.
madreperla *f* mother-of-pearl.
madrina *f* godmother.
maestà *f* majesty.
maestra *f* teacher, schoolmistress.
maestria *f* craftsmanship.

maestro *m* maestro; teacher, schoolmaster.
maga *f* sorceress.
magazzino *m* warehouse.
maggio *m* May.
maggioranza *f* majority.
maggiordomo *m* butler.
maggiore *adj* elder, eldest; senior.
magia *f* magic.
magico *adj* magic.
magistrale *adj* masterly.
magistrato *m* magistrate.
maglia *f* jersey.
maglieria *f* knitwear.
maglietta *f* T-shirt.
maglione *m* jumper, sweater.
magnanimità *f* magnanimity.
magnanimo *adj* magnanimous.
magnate *m* magnate, tycoon.
magnesio *m* magnesium.
magnetico *adj* magnetic.
magnificenza *f* magnificence.
magnifico *adj* magnificent, grand.
mago *m* magician, wizard.
magro *adj* thin, lean.
mai *adv* never, ever.

maiale *m* pig, pork.
maionese *f* mayonnaise.
maiuscolo *adj* capital.
malaria *f* malaria.
malato *adj* ill, sick, diseased.
malattia *f* illness, sickness, disease, malady
malavita *f* underworld.
malcontento *adj, m* malcontent.
male *m* harm, wrong, evil.
maledetto *adj* damned, accursed, bloody.
maledire *vt* to curse.
maledizione *f* curse.
maleducato *adj* bad-mannered, ill-bred.
maleducazione *f* rudeness.
malevolenza *f* ill-will.
malevolo *adj* malevolent, acrimonious.
malfamato *adj* low, seamy.
malgrado *prep* despite: — *conj* in spite of.
malinconia *f* melancholy.
malizia *f* malice.
malleabile *adj* malleable, pliable.
malsano *adj* unhealthy.
malsicuro *adj* insecure.
malto *m* malt.
maltrattare *vt* to maltreat, mistreat.
malva *f* mallow: — *adj* mauve.
malvone *m* hollyhock.
mamma *f* (*inf*) mummy.
mammella *f* breast; udder.
mammifero *m* mammal.
mammut *m inv* mammoth.
manager *m inv* manager.
mancante *adj* missing, deficient.
mancanza *f* lack; deficiency.
mancare *vt* to miss: — *vi* to lack.
mancia *f* tip; gratuity.
manciata *f* handful.

mancino *adj* left-handed.
mandare *vt* to send.
mandarino *m* mandarin.
mandolino *m* mandolin.
mandorla *f* almond.
mandria *f* herd.
maneggevole *adj* manageable.
maneggio *m* stables.
manetta *f* manacle.
manette *fpl* handcuffs.
manganese *m* manganese.
mangiabile *adj* edible.
mangiare *vt* to eat: — **dare da mangiare a** *vt* to feed.
mangiata *f* feed.
mangiatoia *f* manger, crib, trough.
mango *m* mango.
mania *f* mania, craze.
maniaco *adj* manic: — *m* maniac.
manica *f* sleeve: — **la Manica** the English Channel.
manichino *m* dummy.
manico *m* handle.
manicure *f inv* manicure.
maniera *f* manner.
manifestare *vt* to demonstrate, manifest, evince.
manifestazione *f* demonstration, manifestation, show.
manifesto *m* manifesto, poster.
manipolare *vt* to manipulate.
mano *f* hand.
manoscritto *m* manuscript.
manovra *f* manoeuvre.
manovrare *vi, vt* to manoeuvre.
mansarda *f* attic.
mantella *f* cloak.
mantello *m* cape.
mantenere *vt* to maintain; to support.
mantenimento *m* maintenance.
manuale *m* handbook.

manutenzione *f* maintenance.
manzo *m* beef.
mappa *f* map.
mappamondo *m* globe.
maratona *f* marathon.
marca *f* make, brand.
marcato *adj* pronounced; rugged.
marcatore *m* marker.
marchiare *vt* to brand.
marchio *m* hallmark, trademark.
marciapiede *m* pavement.
marciare *vi* to march.
marco *m* mark (*curr*).
mare *m* sea.
marea *f* tide.
margarina *f* margarine.
marginale *adj* marginal.
margine *m* border, margin.
marijuana *f* marijuana.
marina *f* navy.
marinaio *m* sailor.
marinare *vt* to marinate.
marino *adj* marine.
marito *m* husband.
marketing *m* marketing.
marmellata *f* jam: — **marmellata di arance** *f* marmalade.
marmo *m* marble.
marrone *adj* brown.
marsupiale *m, adj* marsupial.
marsupio *m* pouch.
martedì *m inv* Tuesday: — **martedì grasso** *m* Shrove Tuesday.
martello *m* hammer.
martin *m inv*: — **martin pescatore** *m* kingfisher.
martire *m* martyr.
martirio *m* martyrdom.
marzapane *m* marzipan.
marziale *adj* martial.
marzo *m* March.

mascara *m inv* mascara.
mascella *f* jaw.
maschera *f* mask.
mascherare *vt* to mask; to disguise.
mascherata *f* masquerade.
maschiaccio *m* tomboy.
maschile *adj* male, masculine: — *m* masculine.
maschilismo *m* male chauvinism.
maschilista *m* male chauvinist.
maschio *adj, m* male; (*zool*) buck.
masochista *m/f* masochist.
mass media *m pl* mass media.
massa *f* mass, body, bulk.
massacro *m* massacre, slaughter.
massaggiare *vt* to massage.
massaggiatore *m* masseur.
massaggiatrice *f* masseuse.
massiccio *adj* massive.
massimo *adj* utmost, maximum.
masticare *vt* to masticate, chew.
mastro *m* master: — **libro mastro** *m* ledger.
masturbarsi *vr* to masturbate.
masturbatore *m* masturbator, (*sl*) wanker.
matassa *f* skein.
matematica *f* mathematics, maths.
matematico *adj* mathematical: — *m* mathematician.
materasso *m* mattress.
materia *f* matter; subject.
materiale *adj* material.
materialismo *m* materialism.
maternità *f* motherhood, maternity.
matinée *f inv* matinée.
matita *f* pencil.
matrice *f* stencil.
matrigna *f* stepmother.
matrimoniale *adj* matrimonial: — **letto matrimoniale** *m* double bed.

matrimonio *m* marriage.
mattatoio *m* slaughterhouse.
matterello *m* rolling pin.
mattina *f* morning, forenoon.
matto *adj* crazy.
mattone *m* brick.
mattonella *f* tile.
mattutino *m* matins.
maturare *vi* to ripen.
maturità *f* maturity.
mausoleo *m* mausoleum.
mazzo *m* bunch.
mazzolino *m* posy, spray.
mazzuolo *m* mallet.
me *pron* me.
meccanica *f* mechanics.
meccanico *m* mechanic.
meccanismo *m* mechanism.
meccanizzare *vt* to mechanise.
mecenate *m/f* patron.
medaglia *f* medal.
medaglione *m* medallion; locket.
media *mpl* media:—*f* average:— **sopra la media** *adj* above par.
mediatore *m* mediator; broker.
medicare *vt* to medicate.
medicato *adj* medicated.
medicina *f* medicine; drug.
medicinale *adj* medicinal:—*m* drug.
medico *m* doctor.
medievale *adj* medieval.
medio *adj* average.
mediocre *adj* mediocre.
mediocrità *f* mediocrity.
meditare *vi* to meditate, cogitate.
meditativo *adj* meditative.
meditazione *f* meditation.
mediterraneo *adj* Mediterranean.
medusa *f* jellyfish.
megalomane *m/f* megalomaniac.
meglio *adv* better, best.

mela *f* apple.
melagrana *f* pomegranate.
melanzana *f* aubergine.
melassa *f* treacle, molasses.
melma *f* slime.
melmoso *adj* slimy.
melodia *f* melody, tune.
melodioso *adj* melodious, tuneful.
melodramma *m* melodrama.
melone *m* melon.
membrana *f* membrane.
membro *m* member, fellow.
memorabile *adj* memorable.
memorandum *m inv* memorandum.
memoria *f* memory.
mendicante *m/f* beggar.
mendicare *vt* to beg.
meno *prep* less; minus.
menopausa *f* menopause.
mensa *f* canteen.
mensile *adj* monthly.
mensola *f* bracket; cantilever.
menta *f* mint.
mentale *adj* mental.
mentalità *f inv* mentality.
mentalmente *adv* mentally.
mente *f* mind:— **di mente aperta** *adj* open-minded.
mentire *vi* to lie.
mento *m* chin.
mentore *m* mentor.
mentre *conj* as, whereas, while.
menù *m inv* menu.
menzione *f* mention.
meraviglia *f* marvel.
meraviglioso *adj* marvellous, great, smashing.
mercato *m* market.
merce *f* merchandise.
mercenario *adj, m* mercenary.
merceria *f* haberdashery.

merciaio *m* haberdasher.
merci *fpl* goods.
mercoledì *m inv* Wednesday.
mercurio *m* mercury, quicksilver.
merda *f* shit.
meridiana *f* sundial:—*adj*, *m* meridian.
meridionale *adj* south.
meringa *f* meringue.
meritare *vt* to merit, deserve.
merito *m* merit.
merlango *m* whiting.
merlo *m* blackbird.
merluzzo *m* cod.
mescolanza *f* mix.
mescolare *vt* to mix.
mescolata *f* shuffle.
mese *m* month.
messa *f* mass.
messaggero *m* messenger.
messaggio *m* message.
mestolo *m* ladle, scoop.
mestruazione *f* menstruation.
metà *f inv* half.
metabolismo *m* metabolism.
metafisica *f* metaphysics.
metafora *f* metaphor.
metaforico *adj* metaphoric(al).
metallo *m* metal.
metallurgia *f* metallurgy.
metamorfosi *f inv* metamorphosis.
metano *m* methane.
meteora *f* meteor.
meteorite *m* meteorite.
meteorologia *f* meteorology.
meticcio *m* half-caste.
metodico *adj* methodical.
metodo *m* method.
metrico *adj* metric.
metro *m* metre.
metrò *m inv* underground railway.
metropolitana *f* underground railway.

mettere *vt* to put.
mezz'ora *f* half-hour.
mezzaluna *f* half-moon, crescent.
mezzanino *m* mezzanine.
mezzanotte *f* midnight.
mezzo *m* middle, medium.
mezzogiorno *m* noon, midday.
mi *pron* me.
mia *poss adj* my.
microbo *m* germ, microbe.
microfono *m* microphone.
microonda *f* microwave.
microscopio *m* microscope.
midollo *m* marrow.
miele *m* honey.
miglio *m* mile; millet.
migliorare *vt* to improve; to better: —
  vi to improve.
migliore *adj* better, best, topmost:—*m*
  best.
migrare *vi* to migrate.
migrazione *f* migration.
milionario *m* millionaire.
milione *m* million.
milionesimo *m* millionth.
militante *m/f* militant.
militare *adj* military:—*vi* to militate.
mille *adj*, *m* thousand.
millennio *m* millennium.
millepiedi *m inv* centipede, millipede.
millesimo *adj*, *m* thousandth.
milligrammo *m* milligramme.
millilitro *m* millilitre.
millimetro *m* millimetre.
milza *f* spleen.
mimare *vt*, *vi* to mime.
mimo *m* mime.
mina *f* mine.
minaccia *f* threat, menace.
minacciare *vt* to threaten, menace.
minare *vt* to mine; to undermine.

minato *m*: — **campo minato** minefield.
minatore *m* miner, coalminer.
minerale *m* mineral.
minestra *f* soup.
mingherlino *m* weakling: — *adj* thin, skinny.
miniatura *f* miniature.
miniera *f* mine.
minima *f* minimum.
minimo *adj* least; minimal.
ministeriale *adj* ministerial.
ministero *m* ministry.
ministro *m* minister; clergyman: — **Primo Ministro** *m* Prime Minister.
minoranza *f* minority.
minore *adj* minor, lesser, younger.
minuscolo *adj* tiny, minute.
minuto *adj* minute, tiny.
minuzioso *adj* thorough.
mio *poss adj* my; *poss pron* mine.
miope *adj* short-sighted, near-sighted, myopic.
miopia *f* short-sightedness.
miracolo *m* miracle, wonder.
miraggio *m* mirage.
mirino *m* viewfinder, sight.
mirra *f* myrrh.
mirtillo *m* bilberry.
mirto *m* myrtle.
misantropo *m* misanthropist.
miscela *f* mixture, blend.
miscellanea *f* miscellany.
mischiare *vt* to blend.
miseria *f* poverty, want, misery.
misericordia *f* mercy.
misero *adj* poor.
misogino *m* misogynist.
missile *m* missile.
missionario *m* missionary.
missione *f* mission.
misterioso *adj* mysterious.

mistero *m* mystery.
misto *adj* mixed.
mistura *f* mixture.
misura *f* size; measure.
misurare *vt* to measure; to gauge.
mito *m* myth.
mitologia *f* mythology.
mitra *f* mitre.
mittente *m/f* sender.
mobile *adj* mobile, moving.
mobili *mpl* furniture, furnishings.
mobilità *f* mobility.
moccio *m* snot.
moda *f* fashion.
modellare *vt* to model, fashion.
modello *m* pattern; model; mock-up.
moderato *adj* moderate; sparing.
moderazione *f* moderation.
modernizzare *vt* to modernise.
moderno *adj* modern.
modestia *f* modesty.
modesto *adj* modest, unassuming.
modifica *f* modification.
modificare *vt* to modify.
modo *m* way; mode.
moffetta *f* skunk.
mogano *m* mahogany.
moglie *f* wife.
mohair *m* mohair.
molare *m* molar.
molecola *f* molecule.
molestare *vt* to molest.
molla *f* spring: — **a molla** *adj* clockwork.
molle *adj* limp.
mollusco *m* mollusc.
molo *m* jetty, quay.
moltiplicare *vt* to multiply.
moltitudine *f* host, throng, multitude.
molto *adj* much.
molti *pron* many.
momento *m* moment.

monaco *m* monk.

monarca *m* monarch.

monarchia *f* monarchy.

monastero *m* monastery.

monastico *adj* monastic.

mondiale *adj* world, worldwide.

mondo *m* world.

moneta *f* coin; currency.

mongolfiera *f* hot air balloon.

monolocale *adj*: — **appartamento monolocale** *m* studio apartment.

monopolio *m* monopoly.

monotonia *f* monotony; sameness; flatness.

montagna *f* mountain: — **montagne russe** big dipper.

montagnoso *adj* mountainous.

montare *vt* to assemble; to mount.

monte *m* mount: — **monte di pietà** *m* pawnshop.

montone *m* ram; sheepskin; *m* mutton.

monumentale *adj* monumental.

monumento *m* monument, memorial.

moquette *f* (fitted) carpet.

mora *f* bramble; blackberry.

moraie *f* moral.

moraleggiante *adj* sanctimonious.

moraleggiare *vi* to moralise.

morbido *adj* soft.

morbillo *m* measles.

morboso *adj* morbid.

mordere *vt* to bite.

morfina *f* morphine.

morire *vi* to die.

mortale *adj* mortal; deadly.

mortalità *f* mortality.

morte *f* death; dying.

morto *adj* dead.

mosaico *m* mosaic.

mosca *f* fly.

moschea *f* mosque.

moscone *m* bluebottle.

mostra *f* display; exhibition.

mostrare *vt* to show

mostro *m* monster.

motel *m inv* motel.

motivo *m* reason, motive.

moto *f invar* (*fam*) motorbike.

motocicletta *f* motorcycle.

motolancia *f* launch.

motore *m* motor, engine.

motoscafo *m* motorboat: — **motoscafo da corsa** *m* speedboat.

motto *m* motto.

mousse *f inv* mousse.

movibile *adj* movable.

movimentato *adj* eventful, hectic.

movimento *m* movement, motion.

mucca *f* cow.

mucchio *m* heap, pile, mound, stack.

muco *m* mucus.

muffa *f* fungus, mildew, mould.

mughetto *m* lily of the valley.

mugnaio *m* miller.

mulino *m* mill: — **mulino a vento** *m* windmill.

mulo *m* mule.

multa *f* fine: — **multa per sosta vietata** *f* parking ticket.

multare *vt* to fine.

multiplo *adj*, *m* multiple.

moltiplicazione *f* multiplication.

mummia *f* mummy.

municipale *adj* municipal.

municipio *m* town hall.

muovere *vt* to move.

murale *adj* mural.

muratore *m* bricklayer, builder, mason.

muro *m* wall.

musa *f* muse.

muschio *m* moss; musk: — **bacca del muschio** *f* cranberry.

muscolare *adj* muscular.
muscolo *m* muscle.
muscoso *adj* mossy.
museo *m* museum, gallery.
musicale *adj* musical.
musicista *m/f* musician.
mutabile *adj* fickle.

mutande *fpl* pants, knickers.
mutandine *fpl* panties, briefs.
mutante *adj*, *m* mutant.
mutare *vi* to change.
mutazione *f* mutation:—**subire una mutazione** *vi* to mutate.
muto *adj* mute, dumb.

N

nailon *m* nylon.
nano *m* midget, dwarf.
nappa *f* tassel.
narciso *m* narcissus.
narcotico *adj*, *m* narcotic.
narice *f* nostril.
narrativa *f* fiction.
nasale *adj* nasal.
nascita *f* birth.
nascondere *vt* to hide.
naso *m* nose.
nastro *m* ribbon; tape.
nasturzio *m* nasturtium.
Natale *m* Christmas, Xmas.
natica *f* buttock.
nativo *m* native.
natura *f* nature.
naturale *adj* natural; unaffected.
naturalista *m/f* naturalist.
naufragio *m* (ship)wreck.
nausea *f* nausea.
nauseato *adj* squeamish, queasy.
nautico *adj* nautical.
navale *adj* naval.
navata *f* nave, aisle.
nave *f* ship, boat.
navetta *f* shuttle.
navigare *vt* to navigate.

navigazione *f* navigation.
nazionale *adj* national.
nazionalità *f inv* nationality.
nazione *f* nation.
né *conj* neither, nor.
nebbia *f* fog.
necessario *adj* necessary.
necrologio *m* obituary.
negare *vt* to deny.
negativa *f* (*gr*; *foto*) negative.
negativo *adj* negative.
negligente *adj* negligent.
negoziante *m/f* shopkeeper.
negozio *m* shop.
negra *f* Negress.
negro *adj*, *m* Negro.
nemmeno *conj* neither.
neon *m* neon:—**insegna al neon** *f* neon light.
neonato *adj* newborn, baby.
nepotismo *m* nepotism.
neppure *conj* neither.
nero *adj*, *m* black.
nervo *m* nerve.
nervoso *adj* nervous, jumpy.
nessuno *pron* none, nobody.
netturbino *m* dustman.
neutrale *adj* neutral.

neve *f* snow.
nevicare *vi* to snow.
nicotina *f* nicotine.
nido *m* nest.
niente *pron* none.
ninfea *f* waterlily.
nipote *m* nephew, *f* niece; *m/f* grand-child.
nipotina *f* granddaughter.
nipotino *m* grandson.
nitido *adj* clear, sharp.
no *adv* no.
nobile *adj*, *m* noble.
nobiltà *f* nobility.
nocciola *f* hazelnut: — *adj* hazel.
nocciolina *f* peanut.
noce *f* walnut; *m* walnut tree.
nocivo *adj* noxious, harmful.
nodo *m* knot, crux.
nodulo *m* lump.
noi *pers pron* us,we
noia *f* bore; boredom.
noioso *m* bore: — *adj* dull, boring, tedious: — **diventare noioso** *vi* to pall.
nome *m* name, first name.
non *adv* not.
nondimeno *adv* nonetheless.
nonna *f* grandmother, granny.
nonno *m* grandfather, granddad.
nono *adj*, *m* ninth.
nonostante *conj* in spite of.
nord *adj* north.
nordest *m* northeast.
nordovest *m* northwest.

norma *f* norm.
nostro *adj* our: — *pron* ours.
notaio *m* notary; conveyancer.
notifica *f* notification.
noto *adj* well-known; distinguished.
notorietà *f* notoriety.
notte *f* night.
notturno *adj* nocturnal.
novantesimo *adj*, *m* ninetieth.
nove *adj*, *m inv* nine.
novembre *m* November.
novità *f* novelty.
novizio *m* novice.
nozze *fpl* wedding.
nube *f* cloud.
nucleare *adj* nuclear.
nudista *adj*, *m/f* nudist.
nudità *f* nudity.
nudo *adj* nude, naked, bare.
numerale *m* numeral.
numerare *vt* to number.
numerico *adj* numerical.
numero *m* number.
nuocere *vt* to harm.
nuora *f* daughter-in-law.
nuotare *vt*, *vi* to swim.
nuotata *f* swim.
nuovo *adj* new.
nutriente *adj* nourishing, nutritious.
nutrimento *m* nourishment.
nutrire *vt* to nourish.
nuvola *f* cloud.
nuvoloso *adj* cloudy.
nuziale *adj* nuptial, bridal.

O

o *conj* or, either.

oasi *f inv* oasis.

obbligatorio *adj* mandatory.

obbligo *m* obligation.

obeso *adj* obese, gross.

oblungo *adj* oblong.

oboe *m* oboe.

obsoleto *adj* obsolete.

oca *f* goose.

occasionale *adj* occasional.

occasione *f* occasion.

occhiali *mpl* glasses, spectacles.

occhiata *f* look, glance.

occhio *m* eye.

occidentale *adj* west, western.

occorrente *adj*, *m* requisite.

occupare *vt* to take up, occupy.

occuparsi *vr* to deal with, look after.

occupato *adj* busy.

oceano *m* ocean.

ocra *f* ochre.

oculista *m/ f* oculist.

odiare *vt* to hate.

odioso *adj* hateful, horrid, odious.

odissea *f* odyssey.

odontoiatria *f* dentistry.

odore *m* odour, smell.

offendere *vt* to offend.

offensivo *adj* offensive.

offerta *f* bid, offer.

offesa *f* offence.

officina *f* garage, workshop.

offrire *vt* to offer.

offuscare *vt* to blur.

oggetto *m* object.

oggi *adv m inv* today.

oggigiorno *adv* nowadays.

ogni *adj* every, each.

ognuno *pron* each, everybody.

oleandro *m* oleander.

oleoso *adj* oily.

olfatto *m* smell.

oliare *vt* to oil.

oliatore *m* oilcan.

olio *m* oil.

oliva *f* olive.

olmo *m* elm.

olocausto *m* holocaust.

oltre *prep* besides, aside from.

oltremarino *adj*, *m* ultramarine.

omaggio *m* homage:—**in omaggio** complimentary.

ombelico *m* navel.

ombra *f* shade, shadow.

ombrello *m* umbrella.

ombretto *m* eyeshadow.

omeopatia *f* homoeopathy.

omettere *vt* to omit.

omicida *adj* homicidal.

omicidio *m* murder, homicide.

omissione *f* omission.

omogeneità *f* homogeneity.

omogeneo *adj* smooth, homogeneous.

omonimo *m* homonym, namesake.

omosessuale *adj*, *m/f* homosexual, (*fam*) gay.

onda *f* wave.

ondulato *adj* corrugated.

onere *m* burden, onus.

onestà *f* honesty.

onesto *adj* honest.

onnivoro *adj* omnivorous.

onorare *vt* to grace, honour.
onorario *adj* honorary, fee, retainer.
onore *m* honour.
onorevole *adj* honourable.
opaco *adj* opaque, matt.
opale *m/ f* opal.
opera *f* work, opera.
operaio *adj* blue-collar, worker.
operazione *f* operation, transaction.
operoso *adj* industrious.
opinione *f* opinion, belief.
oppio *m* opium.
opporsi *vr* to oppose.
opportunista *m/f* opportunist.
opportuno *adj* fitting, timely.
opposizione *f* opposition.
opprimente *adj* oppressive, heavy.
opprimere *vt* to oppress, burden.
optare *vi* to opt (for).
opulento *adj* opulent.
opzione *f* option.
ora *adv, conj* now: —*f* hour, time.
oracolo *m* oracle.
orale *adj, m* oral.
oralmente *adv* orally.
orario *m* timetable.
orbitare *vi* to orbit.
orchestra *f* orchestra.
orchidea *f* orchid.
ordinare *vt* to order; to ordain.
ordine *m* order, command.
orecchino *m* earring.
orecchio *m* ear.
orfano *adj, m* orphan.
organigramma *m* flow chart.
organismo *m* organism.
organista *m/ f* organist.
organizzare *vt* to organise.
organo *m* organ.
orgasmo *m* orgasm, climax.
orgia *f* orgy.

orgoglio *m* pride.
orientale *adj* oriental, easterly, eastern.
orientare *vt* to orientate.
oriente *m* east.
orifizio *m* orifice.
origano *m* oregano.
originale *adj, m* original.
originalità *f* originality.
origine *f* origin.
orina *f* urine.
orinare *vi* to urinate.
orizzontale *adj* horizontal.
orizzonte *m* horizon.
ormone *m* hormone.
ornamentale *adj* ornamental.
ornato *adj* ornate.
ornitologo *m* bird watcher.
oro *m* gold.
orologio *m* clock.
oroscopo *m* horoscope.
orribile *adj* horrible, hideous.
orrore *m* horror.
orsacchiotto *m* teddy bear.
orso *m* bear.
ortensia *f* hydrangea.
orticaria *f* rash.
orticoltura *f* horticulture.
orto *m* vegetable garden, kitchen garden.
ortodossia *f* orthodoxy.
ortografia *f* spelling.
orzo *m* barley.
oscenità *f* obscenity.
oscillazione *f* swing.
oscurità *f* dark, darkness, blackness.
oscuro *adj* obscure.
ospedale *m* hospital.
ospitare *vt* to put up.
ospite *m/f* host, guest, visitor.
osservanza *f* observance.
osservare *vt* to remark, observe.

osservatore *m* observer.
osservazione *f* remark, observation, comment.
ossidare *vt* to tarnish, oxidise.
ossigeno *m* oxygen.
osso *m* bone.
ostacolo *m* hurdle, obstacle.
ostaggio *m* hostage.
ostello *m* hostel.
osteopatia *f* osteopathy.
ostetrica *f* midwife.
ostile *adj* hostile, unfriendly.
ostilità *f* hostility.
ostinato *adj* obstinate, wilful.
ostinazione *f* wilfulness.
ostracizzare *vt* to ostracise.

ostrica *f* oyster.
ostruire *vt* to obstruct.
ottanta *adj*, *m* eighty.
ottantesimo *adj* eightieth.
ottavo *adj* eighth.
ottenere *vt* to gain, get, obtain.
otto *adj*, *m* eight.
ottobre *m* October.
ottone *m* brass.
ovaia *f* ovary.
ovale *adj*, *m* oval.
overdose *f inv* overdose.
ovest *adj*, *m* west, westward.
ovvio *adj* obvious.
oziare *vi* to laze.
ozono *m* ozone.

P

pace *f* peace, calm.
padella *f* frying pan; bedpan.
padre *m* father.
padrino *m* godfather.
padrona *f* mistress.
padrone *m* boss, master.
paesaggio *m* scenery, landscape.
paese *m* land, country, village.
paesino *m* hamlet.
pagamento *m* payment.
pagano *m* heathen.
pagare *vi*, *vt* to pay.
pagina *f* page.
paglia *f* straw.
pagliaccio *m* clown.
paio *m* pair.
pala *f* shovel.
palazzo *m* palace, mansion:—**palazzo per uffici** *m* office block.

palco *m* stage.
palestra *f* gym.
palla *f* ball.
pallacanestro *f* basketball.
pallavolo *f* volleyball.
pallido *adj* pale, wan.
pallone *m* ball.
palo *m* stake, goalpost.
pancetta *f* bacon.
pancia *f* belly, tummy.
panciotto *m* waistcoat.
pane *m* bread, loaf.
panificio *m* bakery.
panino *m* roll, sandwich.
panna *f* cream:—**panna montata** *f* whipped cream.
pantaloni *mpl* trousers.
pantofola *f* slipper.
papà *m* (*inf*) dad(dy).

pappa *f* mush, feed.
parabrezza *m inv* windscreen.
paragonare *vt* to liken, compare.
parare *vt* to save.
parasole *m* sunshade.
parassita *m/f* parasite, hanger-on.
parco *m* park: — **parco comunale** *m* common.
parecchio *adj* several.
pareggiare *vi* to equalise, draw, tie.
parente *m/f* relation, relative.
parentesi *f inv* bracket.
parere *vi* to seem.
pari *adj*, equal, even.
paria *m inv* untouchable.
parlamentare *m/f* member of parliament.
parlare *vi* to talk, tell, speak.
parodia *f* parody, ravesty.
parola *f* word.
parolaccia *f* swearword.
parrucca *f* wig.
parrucchiere *m* hairdresser.
parsimonioso *adj* thrifty.
parte *f* part, share, side.
partecipare *vi* to participate.
partenza *f* departure.
particolare *adj* particular, special, especial, detail.
partire *vi* to leave, depart, start.
partita *f* lot, consignment; match, game.
parvenu *m inv* upstart.
Pasqua *f* Easter.
passare *vi*, *vt* to pass, go by.
passatempo *m* hobby.
passeggiare *vi* to walk.
passeggiata *f* walk.
passerella *f* gangway, footbridge.
passero *m* sparrow.
passionale *adj* passionate, sultry.

passo *m* step, pace.
pastello *m* crayon.
pasticceria *f* cake shop.
pasticciere *m* confectioner.
pasticcino *m* cake.
pasticcio *m* pie.
pastiglia *f* lozenge.
pastore *m* shepherd; clergyman, vicar.
patata *f* potato.
patatina *f* crisp.
patente *f* licence: — **patente di guida** *f* driving licence.
patria *f* home, homeland.
patrigno *m* stepfather.
patrimonio *m* heritage, estate, wealth.
pattinare *vi* to skate.
paura *f* fear: — **avere paura di** *vt* to fear.
pauroso *adj* fearful.
pausa *f* pause, stop, rest.
pavimento *m* floor.
pazzo *adj* demented, mad, insane, lunatic.
peccare *vi* to sin.
peccato *m* shame, sin.
peccatore *m* sinner.
pecora *f* ewe, sheep.
peculiarità *f inv* idiosyncracy.
peggio *adj*, *adv*, *m/f* worse, worst.
peggiorare *vt* to worsen, compound.
peggiore *adj*, *m/f* worse, worst.
pelle *f* skin, leather.
pellicola *f* skin, film.
pelo *m* hair, fur.
pena *f* punishment.
pendere *vi* to slant, hang, lean.
penna *f* pen; feather.
pennello *m* brush.
pennino *m* nib.
pensare *vi* to think, expect.
pensiero *m* thought.

pensione *f* pension, retirement.
Pentecoste *f* Whit Sunday.
pentola *f* saucepan.
penzolare *vi* to swing.
pepe *m* pepper.
per *prep* for, from, to, through.
percepibile *adj* discernible, noticeable.
perchè *conj* why, because, what for.
perciò *adv* thus.
perdere *vt* to lose; to miss.
perdersi *vt* to get lost, go astray.
perdonare *vt* to forgive, condone.
perfetto *adj* perfect, flawless.
pericolo *m* danger.
pericoloso *adj* dangerous, unsafe.
periferia *f* suburbia, outskirts.
periferico *adj* outlying.
periodico *m* journal.
periodo *m* period, spell, time.
perizia *f* expertise, survey.
perlina *f* bead.
permanente *adj* permanent.
permesso *m* leave.
permettere *vt* to allow.
permissività *f* laxity.
permissivo *adj* lax.
perplesso *adj* puzzled, bemused.
persiana *f* shutter.
persistente *adj* lingering, niggling.
personaggio *m* character.
personale *m* staff.
persuadere *vt* to persuade, induce.
pesante *adj* heavy, hefty.
pesare *vt, vi* to weigh.
pesca *f* fishing.
pescare *vi, vt* to fish.
pesce *m* fish:—**pesce rosso** *m* goldfish.
pescecane *m* shark.
pescivendolo *m* fishmonger.
peso *m* weight, encumbrance.
pessimo *adj* wretched, lousy.

peste *f* terror, scamp.
petroliera *f* oil tanker.
petrolio *m* petroleum, oil.
pettinare *vt* to comb.
pettine *m* comb.
pettirosso *m* robin.
petto *m* breast, chest.
pezzo *m* piece, bit.
piacere *vt* to please:—**non piacere** *vt* to dislike.
piacevole *adj* nice, agreeable.
piangere *vt, vi* to cry, weep.
piano *m* floor, storey.
pianta *f* map; plant.
pianto *m* cry.
piastrella *f* tile.
piastrellare *vt* to tile.
piattino *m* saucer.
piatto *m* plate, dish; turntable.
piazza *f* square.
piazzale *m* forecourt.
piccante *adj* spicy, hot.
picchio *m* woodpecker.
piccione *m* pigeon:—**piccione viaggiatore** *m* carrier pigeon.
piccolino *adj* smallish.
piccolo *adj* small, little.
piede *m* foot.
piega *f* crease, fold, twist.
piegare *vt* to bend, fold:—*vr* ~**rsi** to bend, fold.
pieno *adj* full.
pietanza *f* dish.
pietoso *adj* sorry.
pietra *f* stone.
pietrisco *m* grit.
pignolo *adj* fastidious, fussy.
pigro *adj* lazy, idle.
pila *f* battery, torch.
pilota *m* pilot.
pioggia *f* rain.

piombo *m* lead.
piovere *vi* to rain.
piovra *f* octopus.
pipa *f* pipe.
pipistrello *m* bat.
piscina *f* swimming pool, baths.
pisolino *m* doze, nap.
pista *f* scent; track; runway.
pistola *f* pistol, gun.
pittoresco *adj* scenic.
più *adv*, *adj* more, most.
piuma *f* feather: — **piume** *fpl* down.
piumone *m* duvet.
piuttosto *adv* sooner, somewhat, rather.
pizzicare *vt* to nip, sting.
placenta *f* afterbirth.
plastica *f* plastic.
poco *m* a little: — **pochi** *mpl* few.
podio *m* rostrum.
poesia *f* verse.
poggiare *vi* to rest.
poi *adv* then.
poiché *conj* inasmuch as, for.
polemico *adj* argumentative.
polena *f* (*naut*) figurehead.
polizia *f* police.
poliziotto *m* policemen.
polizza *f* policy: — **polizza d'assicurazione** *f* insurance policy.
pollame *m* fowl.
pollice *m* inch; thumb.
pollo *m* chicken.
polmone *m* lung.
polo *m* pole: — **polo nord** *m* North Pole.
polso *m* wrist.
poltrona *f* armchair.
polvere *f* dust, powder.
polveroso *adj* dusty.
pomeriggio *m* afternoon.
pomodoro *m* tomato.

pompa *f* pump; pomp.
pompelmo *m* grapefruit.
pompiere *m* fireman.
ponente *m* west: — **di ponente** *adj* westerly.
ponte *m* bridge.
popolo *m* people.
poppa *f* stern.
porcellana *f* china.
porcellino *m* piglet.
porco *m* pig, hog.
porta *f* door, gateway.
portacenere *m inv* ashtray.
portachiavi *m* key ring.
portafoglio *m* wallet.
portafortuna *m inv* mascot.
posta *f* post: — **posta aerea** airmail.
portare *vt* to wear; to carry; to take; to bring.
portauovo *m* eggcup.
portavoce *m inv* spokesman.
portiere *m* porter, doorman.
porto *m* port, harbour.
porzione *f* helping.
posizione *f* position.
possessore *m* holder.
possibile *adj* possible
posta *f* post, mail.
posteggio *m* parking.
posteriore *adj* hind, hindquarters.
posto *m* seat.
potabile *adj* drinkable.
potere *vt* to be able to: — *m* power.
povero *adj* poor.
pozzo *m* well.
pranzare *vi* to dine.
pranzo *m* lunch, feast.
prato *m* meadow, lawn.
preavvertire *vt* to forewarn.
preavviso *m* notice.
precedente *adj* former.

preciso *adj* accurate.
prego *excl* not at all.
preferire *vt* to prefer.
prefisso *m* dialling code.
prematuro *adj* untimely, early.
premere *vt* to squeeze.
premiare *vt* to reward.
premio *m* prize, award.
premura *f* rush.
prendere *vt* to take.
prenotare *vt* to reserve, book.
prenotazione *f* reservation.
preoccupare *vt* to worry, trouble.
presentatore *m* announcer, TV host, compère.
presentare *vt* to introduce.
presente *adj, m* present.
presentimento *m* foreboding.
preservativo *m* condom, sheath.
presidente *m* president, chairman.
pressione *f* pressure.
prestare *vt* to lend.
prestito *m* loan:—**prendere in prestito** *vt* to borrow.
presto *adv* early, soon.
pretendere *vt* to expect, claim.
prevalere *vi* to prevail.
prevedere *vt* to foresee, forecast.
prezioso *adj* valuable.
prezzo *m* price.
prigione *f* prison.
prima *adv* before.
primavera *f* spring, springtime.
primo *adj* first, early, former.
principale *adj* main, chief.
principe *m* prince.
principiante *m/f* beginner, learner.
principio *m* beginning, inception; principle, tenet.
privare *vt* to deprive.
probabile *adj* probable, likely.

problema *m* problem.
procedere *vi* to proceed.
processo *m* trial, process.
prodotto *m* product, commodity.
produzione *f* production, output, generation.
professionale *adj* professional, vocational.
professore *m* professor, teacher.
profondo *adj* deep.
profumare *vt* to scent.
profumo *m* scent, smell.
progenitori *mpl* forefathers.
progettare *vt* to design.
progetto *m* design.
programma *m* programme, syllabus, schedule.
progresso *m* progress.
proiettile *m* bullet.
prolungare *vt* to lengthen, extend.
promotore *m* sponsor.
pronto *adj* ready:—**pronto!** *excl* (*tel*) hello.
propenso *adj* inclined.
proporzionato *adj* commensurate.
proposito *m* intention.
proprietà *f* ownership.
proprietario *m* owner, landlord.
proprio *adj* own.
prosciutto *m* ham.
prossimo *adj* next.
proteggere *vt* to shield.
protestare *vi* to protest.
protezione *f* guard.
prova *f* test.
provare *vt* to rehearse; to feel; to try.
provenire *vi* to emanate.
provvisorio *adj* temporary, interim.
prudente *adj* careful, cautious.
prurito *m* itch.
pubblicare *vt* to publish, issue.

pubblicazione *f* publication.
pubblicità *f* commercial, advertisement.
pubblico *m* audience.
pugnale *m* dagger.
pugno *m* fist.
pulce *f* flea.
pulire *vt* to clean.
pulito *adj* clean.
pulsare *vi* to throb.
punire *vt* to chastise, discipline.
punta *f* tip.

punteggio *m* score.
punto *m* dot, point, stop, stitch.
pupazzo *m* puppet.
puro *adj* pure, sheer.
purtroppo *adv* unluckily.
putrefarsi *vr* to decay.
puttana *f* prostitute, whore.
puzzare *vi* to smell, stink, reek.
puzzle *m* (jigsaw) puzzle.
puzzo *m* stench, reek, stink, smell.
puzzolente *adj* smelly, rank.

Q

qua *adv* here.
quacchero *adj*, *m* Quaker.
quaderno *m* exercise book.
quadrangolo *m* quadrangle.
quadrante *m* dial, face (of watch, etc), quadrant.
quadrato *adj*, *m* square.
quadrilatero *adj*, *m* quadrilateral.
quadro *m* square; painting, picture.
quadruplo *adj* quadruple, fourfold.
quaglia *f* quail.
qualche *adj* some.
qualcosa *pron* something.
qualcuno *pron* anybody, somebody.
quale *adj* what, which.
qualificare *vt* to qualify.
qualità *f* quality.
qualsiasi *adj* any:—**qualsiasi cosa** *pron* whatever.
quantità *f inv* quantity.
quantitativo *adj* quantitative.
quanto *adj* how much:—**quanti** *adj* how many.
quaranta *m inv* forty.

quarantena *f* quarantine.
quarantesimo *adj*, *m* fortieth.
quartetto *m* quartet.
quartiere *m* quarter.
quarto *m* quarter, fourth.
quarzo *m* quartz.
quasi *adv* almost, nearly.
quattordicesimo *adj*, *m* fourteenth.
quattordici *adj*, *m* fourteen.
quattro *adj*, *m* four.
quel *adj* that:—**quelli** *pron* those.
quercia *f* oak.
questo *dem adj*, *dem pron* this:—
questi *dem adj*, *dem pron* these.
questione *f* question.
qui *adv* here.
quietare *vt* to hush.
quindi *adv* therefore, consequently.
quindicesimo *adj* fifteenth.
quindici *m*, *adj* fifteen:—**quindici giorni** *m* fortnight.
quintetto *m* quintet.
quinto *adj*, *m* fifth.
quiz *m inv* quiz.

quorum *m inv* quorum.
quota *f* quota, dues.
quotare *vt* to quote.

quotazione *f* quotation.
quotidiano *adj* daily:—*m* daily (news-paper).

R

rabbia *f* anger; rabies:—**con rabbia** *adv* angrily.
rabbino *m* rabbi.
racchetta *f* racket.
raccogliere *vt* to collect.
raccolta *f* collection, set.
raccomandabile *adj* advisable.
raccomandare *vt* to recommend.
raccomandazione *f* recommendation.
raccontare *vt* to relate, tell.
raddobbare *vt* to refit.
raddrizzare *vt* to straighten, right.
radersi *vr* to shave.
radiante *adj* radiant.
radiatore *m* radiator.
radicale *adj* radical.
radicare *vi* to root.
radicato *adj* entrenched.
radice *f* root.
radio *f* radio.
radiografia *f* X-ray, radiography.
rafano *m* horseradish.
raffica *f* gust.
raffinare *vt* to refine.
raffinato *adj* polished, cultured.
raffreddare *vt* to cool.
raffreddore *m* cold.
ragazza *f* girl.
ragazzo *m* boy, lad; boyfriend.
raggio *m* spoke; radius; ray.
raggiungere *vt* to hit, reach.
raggruppare *vt* to group.

ragionare *vi* to reason.
ragione *f* reason, sense.
ragioniere *m/f* accountant.
ragnatela *f* web, spider-web.
ragno *m* spider.
ramato *adj* auburn.
rame *m* copper.
ramo *m* branch, bough.
ramoscello *m* sprig, twig.
rampa *f* ramp.
rampante *adj* rampant.
rampicante *f* creeper.
rana *f* frog.
ranch *m inv* ranch.
rancido *adj* rancid, rank.
rancore *m* grudge, ill feeling, rancour.
rango *m* standing.
rantolo *m* rattle.
ranuncolo *m* buttercup.
rapa *f* turnip.
rapporto *m* report, relation, rapport.
rappresentare *vt* to represent.
rappresentativo *adj* representative.
rapsodia *f* rhapsody.
raramente *adv* seldom.
rarità *f* rarity.
raro *adj* rare.
raschiare *vt* to scrape.
raso *m* satin.
rasoio *m* razor:—**rasoio elettrico** *m* shaver.
rassegnato *adj* resigned.

rassicurare *vt* to reassure.
rata *f* instalment.
ratifica *f* ratification.
ratificare *vt* to ratify.
ratto *m* rat.
rattristare *vt* to sadden.
ravanello *m* radish.
ravvivare *vt* to liven up.
razionalità *f* rationality.
razionare *vt* to ration.
razione *f* ration.
razza *f* race, strain, breed.
razzismo *m* racism.
razzista *m/f* racialist.
razzo *m* rocket.
re *m inv* king.
reagire *vi* to react.
reale *adj* real, actual, royal.
reali *mpl* royalty.
realistico *adj* realistic, lifelike.
realizzabile *adj* feasible.
realizzare *vt* to realise, accomplish.
realtà *f* reality:—**in realtà** in fact.
reazionario *m* reactionary.
reazione *f* reaction.
rebus *m* puzzle.
recensire *vt* to review.
recensore *m* reviewer.
recente *adj* recent.
reception *f inv* reception.
recessione *f* recession.
recintare *vt* to enclose, fence.
recinto *m* fence.
recipiente *m* vessel, receptacle.
reciproco *adj* mutual, reciprocal.
reciso *adj* cut.
recitare *vt, vi* to recite.
reclamizzare *vt* to publicise.
reclusione *f* imprisonment, confinement.
recluso *adj* recluse.

record *m inv* record.
recriminare *vt* to recriminate.
redazionale *adj* editorial.
redditività *f* profitability.
reddito *m* income, revenue.
Redentore *m* Redeemer.
redenzione *f* redemption.
redigere *vt* to edit.
redine *f* rein.
referendum *m inv* referendum.
referenza *f* reference.
refettorio *m* refectory.
refrigerante *m* coolant.
refrigerare *vt* to refrigerate.
regalare *vt* to give.
regale *adj* regal.
regalo *m* gift.
regata *f* regatta.
reggimento *m* regiment.
reggiseno *m* bra; brassiere.
regime *m* régime.
regina *f* queen.
regionale *adj* regional.
regione *f* region.
registrare *vt* to register, record.
registratore *m* tape recorder, recorder.
regnare *vi* to rule, reign.
regno *m* kingdom.
regola *f* rule.
regolare *vt* to regulate.
regressivo *adj* regressive.
reincarnazione *f* reincarnation.
reintegrare *vt* to reinstate.
reinvestire *vt* to plough back.
reiterare *vt* to reiterate.
relativo *adj* relative.
relax *m* relaxation.
relazione *f* paper; relation, relationship.
relè *m* relay.
religione *f* religion.

religioso *adj* religious, holy.
reliquia *f* relic.
relitto *m* wreck.
remare *vi* to row, scull.
reminiscenza *f* reminiscence.
remissione *f* remission.
remo *m* oar.
remoto *adj* remote.
renale *adj* renal.
rendere *vt* to render.
rene *m* kidney.
renna *f* reindeer.
reparto *m* unit, department.
reperto *m* exhibit.
repertorio *m* repertory, repertoire.
replica *f* repeat, replica.
reportage *m inv* report.
repressione *f* suppression, repression.
reprimere *vt* to suppress.
repubblica *f* republic.
reputazione *f* reputation.
requisire *vt* to comandeer, requisition.
rescindere *vt* to rescind.
residente *adj*, *m* resident.
residuo *m* residue:—*adj* residual.
resina *f* resin.
resinoso *adj* resinous.
resistente *adj* tough, hard-wearing.
resistere *vt* to resist, withstand.
respingente *m* buffer.
respingere *vt* to repulse, repel, spurn, quash.
respirare *vt* to breathe.
respiro *m* breath.
responsabile *adj* responsible, liable.
responsabilità *f* responsibility, liability.
restare *vt* to stay, remain.
restaurare *vt* to restore.
resti *mpl* remains.
restio *adj* reluctant.

restituire *vt* to give back.
resto *m* rest, change.
restringere *vt* to narrow:—*vr* ~**rsi** to shrink.
restrittivo *adj* restrictive.
retata *f* roundup, catch, haul.
rete *f* net, network, grid.
retina *f* retina.
retorica *f* rhetoric.
retorico *adj* rhetorical.
retribuzione *f* retribution.
retro *m* back.
retrodatare *vt* to backdate.
retrogrado *adj* retrograde.
retromarcia *f* reverse.
retrospettiva *f* retrospective.
retrovisore *m* rear-view mirror.
rettangolo *m* rectangle, oblong.
rettificare *vt* to rectify.
rettile *m* reptile.
rettilineo *adj* rectilinear.
rettitudine *f* righteousness, rectitude.
rettore *m* vice-chancellor, rector.
reumatico *adj* rheumatic.
revisione *f* review, service.
rianimare *vt* to revive.
riaprire *vt* to reopen.
riarso *adj* parched.
riassunto *m* summary, résumé.
ribaltabile *adj* reclining.
ribattino *m* rivet.
ribellarsi *vr* to revolt, rebel.
ribelle *adj* rebel.
ribellione *f* rebellion.
ribes *m inv* currant.
ricadere *vi* to relapse.
ricamare *vt* to embroider.
ricambiare *vt* to repay, exchange.
ricaricare *vt* to recharge.
ricattare *vt* to blackmail.
ricchezza *f* wealth, richness.

riccio *m* hedgehog:—*adj* curly.
ricciolo *m* curl.
ricco *adj* wealthy, rich.
ricerca *f* research.
ricetta *f* prescription, recipe.
ricettario *m* cookery book.
ricevere *vt* to receive, get.
ricevimento *m* reception.
ricevuta *f* receipt.
richiedere *vt* to request, require.
riconoscere *vt* to recognise, know.
riconsiderare *vt* to reconsider.
ricoprire *vt* to recover, coat.
ricordare *vt* to recall, remember, remind.
ricordo *m* souvenir.
ricorrente *adj* recurrent.
ricorrere *vi* to return.
ricorso *m* recourse, resort:—**far ricorso a** *vt* to resort to.
ricreazione *f* recreation.
ricuperare *vt* to salvage, recover.
ridere *vi* to laugh, scoff.
ridicolo *m* ridicule.
ridondante *adj* redundant.
ridotto *adj* diminished.
ridurre *vt* to reduce.
riduzione *f* cut, cutback, reduction.
riempire *vt* to fill, refill to stuff.
rievocare *vt* to conjure up.
riferimento *m* reference.
riferirsi *vr* to refer.
rifiutare *vt* to refuse, turn down.
rifiuto *m* refusal.
riflessione *f* reflection.
riflessivo *adj* reflexive.
riflesso *m* reflection, reflex.
riflettere *vt* to mirror, think over, reflect.
riflettore *m* searchlight, floodlight, spotlight.

rifluire *vi* to ebb.
riflusso *m* ebb.
riforma *f* reform.
riformare *vt* to reform.
riformatorio *m* borstal.
rifornire *vt* to stock.
rifugiato *m* refugee.
rifugio *m* shelter.
riga *f* stripe, line, (hair) parting.
rigare *vt* to streak, rule.
rigato *adj* lined.
rigetto *m* rejection.
righello *m* ruler.
rigidezza *f* rigidity.
rigidità *f* stiffness.
rigido *adj* rigid, stiff.
rigonfiamento *m* bulge.
rigore *m* rigour.
rigoroso *adj* stringent, rigorous.
riguadagnare *vt* to regain.
riguardare *vt* to regard, concern.
rilasciare *vt* to release, issue.
rilassare *vt* to relax:—*vr* **~rsi** to relax.
rilevamento *m* survey.
rilievo *m* relief.
riluttanza *f* reluctance, disinclination.
rima *f* rhyme.
rimanere *vi* to stay, remain.
rimbalzare *vi* to bounce, rebound.
rimborsare *vt* to refund.
rimediare *vt* to remedy.
rimedio *m* remedy.
rimettere *vt* to remit.
rimorso *m* remorse.
rimpiangere *vt* to regret.
rimunerazione *f* remuneration.
Rinascimento *m* Renaissance.
rinforzo *m* brace.
rinfrescare *vi*, *vt* to freshen, refresh.
ringhiera *f* banisters.
ringraziare *vt* to thank.

rinnovare *vt* to refurbish, renovate.
rinoceronte *m* rhinoceros.
rinunciare *vt* to renounce, surrender.
rinvigorire *vt* to exhilarate.
riorganizzare *vt* to reorganise.
riparare *vt* to repair.
ripassare *vt* to revise.
ripasso *m* revision.
ripensare *vi* to think over.
ripetere *vt* to repeat.
ripiano *m* shelf.
ripido *adj* steep.
ripiegare *vt* to refold.
riposante *adj* restful.
riposare *vi* to rest, stand.
riprendersi *vi* to recover.
riprodurre *vt* to reproduce.
ripudiare *vt* to repudiate.
ripugnante *adj* repulsive.
ripulsione *f* repulsion.
risata *f* laugh, laughter.
riscaldamento *m* heating.
rischiare *vt* to risk, venture.
rischio *m* risk, hazard, chance.
risciacquare *vt* to rinse, swill.
risciò *m inv* rickshaw.
riservare *vt* to reserve, book.
riso *m* rice.
risoluto *adj* resolute.
risparmiare *vt* to spare, save.
rispecchiare *vt* to reflect.
rispettare *vt* to respect.
rispondere *vi* to answer, respond.
risposarsi *vr* to remarry.
risposta *f* reply, response, retort.
ristagno *m* stagnation.
ristampa *f* reprint, reissue.
ristorante *m* restaurant.
ristrutturare *vt* to convert.
risultare *vi* to result, emerge.
risultato *m* result.

risuscitare *vt* to resuscitate.
risvolto *m* lapel.
ritagliare *vt* to clip.
ritardare *vt* to hold up, delay.
ritardo *m* delay:—**in ritardo** *adj* late.
ritirare *vt* to withdraw, retract.
ritiro *m* withdrawal.
ritmo *m* rhythm, beat, swing.
rito *m* rite, ceremonial.
ritornare *vi* to revert, go back.
ritornello *m* chorus, refrain.
ritorno *m* return.
ritratto *m* portrait.
rituale *adj, m* ritual.
riunione *f* meeting, reunion.
riunire *vt* to rally, reunite.
riuscire *vi* to succeed.
riva *f* bank (river):—**riva del mare** *f* seashore.
rivale *adj, m* rival.
rivedere *vt* to revise.
rivelare *vt* to give away, disclose, reveal.
rivestimento *m* facing, casing.
rivestire *vt* to cover.
rivista *f* magazine, review.
rivolta *f* revolt.
rivoltante *adj* revolting.
rivoltare *vt* to revolt.
rivoluzionario *adj, m* revolutionary.
rivoluzione *f* revolution.
rizzarsi *vi* to bristle.
roano *m* roan.
roba *f* stuff, things.
robot *m inv* robot.
robustezza *f* sturdiness.
roccia *f* rock.
roditore *m* rodent.
rododendro *m* rhododendron.
rognone *m* kidney.
romantico *adj* romantic.
romanziere *m* novelist.

romanzo *m* novel.
rompere *vt* to snap, break.
rondella *f* washer.
rondine *f* swallow.
rondone *m* swift.
rosa *f* rose.
rosario *m* rosary.
rosbif *m* roast beef.
rosicchiare *vt* to gnaw, nibble.
rosmarino *m* rosemary.
rospo *m* toad.
rossetto *m* lipstick.
rosso *adj*, *m* red.
rosticceria *f* takeaway.
rotare *vi* to rotate.
rotatoria *f* roundabout.
roteare *vi* to gyrate.
rotella *f* caster, roller.
rotolare *vi*, *vt* to roll: — *vr* ~**rsi** to wallow.
rotondo *adj* round.
rotula *f* kneecap.
roulotte *f inv* caravan.
round *m inv* round.
routine *f* routine.
rovente *adj* red-hot.
rovescia *f* lapel: — **alla rovescia** *adj* inside out.

rovina *f* ruin, undoing, downfall.
rovinare *vt* to spoil, ruin.
rovo *m* bramble bush.
rubare *vt* to steal.
rubinetto *m* tap, (water)cock.
rublo *m* rouble.
rubrica *f* rubric.
rudere *m* ruin.
rudimentale *adj* rough and ready.
rudimento *m* rudiment.
ruga *f* wrinkle, line.
rugby *m* rugby.
ruggire *vi* to roar.
rugiada *f* dew.
rullino *m* film, roll.
rum *m inv* rum.
rumore *m* noise, sound.
ruolo *m* role.
ruota *f* wheel.
rurale *adj* rural.
russare *vi* to snore.
rustico *adj* rustic.
rusticone *m* bumpkin.
ruttare *vi* to belch, burp.
rutto *m* burp, belch.
ruvidità *f* roughness.
ruvido *adj* rough, coarse.
ruzzolare *vi* to tumble.

S

sabato *m* Saturday, Sabbath.
sabbia *f* sand.
sabbioso *adj* sandy.
sabotaggio *m* sabotage.
sabotare *vt* to sabotage.
saccarina *f* saccharin.
saccheggiare *vt* to sack, raid, pillage.

sacchetto *m* carrier bag, bag.
sacco *m* sack: — **sacco a pelo** *m* sleeping bag.
sacerdote *m* clergyman.
sacramento *m* sacrament.
sacrificare *vt* to sacrifice.
sacrificio *m* sacrifice.

sacrilegio *m* sacrilege.
sacro *adj* sacred.
sadico *m* sadist.
sadico *adj* sadistic.
sadismo *m* sadism.
safari *m inv* safari.
saga *f* saga.
saggio *adj* wise:—*m* essay; sage.
Sagittario *m.*Sagittarius.
sagoma *f* silhouette, template.
sagrestano *m* sacristan.
sagrestia *f* vestry.
sagù *m* sago.
sala *f* room, hall.
salame *m* salami, sausage.
salare *vt* to salt, cure.
salariato *m* wage earner.
salato *adj* savoury, salty.
saldare *vt* to weld, solder; to settle.
saldarsi *vr* to set.
saldo *adj* steady, firm.
sale *m* salt.
salice *m* willow.
salicone *m* pussy willow.
saliente *adj* salient.
saliera *f* salt cellar.
salino *adj* saline.
salire *vt, vi* to ascend, mount, climb.
salita *f* rise, climb, slope.
saliva *f* saliva.
salivare *vi* to salivate.
salma *f* corpse.
salmo *m* psalm.
salmone *m* salmon.
salnitro *m* saltpeter.
salone *m* salon, saloon, lounge, hall.
saloon *m inv* saloon.
salopette *f inv* dungarees.
salotto *m* parlour, sitting room.
salsa *f* sauce:—**salsa indiana** *f* chutney.

salsiccia *f* sausage.
saltare *vi, vt* to jump.
saltatore *m* jumper.
saltuario *adj* casual (labour).
salubre *adj* wholesome, salubrious.
salumeria *f* delicatessen.
salutare *adj* salutary:—*vt* to salute, greet.
salute *f* health.
saluto *m* greeting, salute.
salva *f* salvo.
salvadanaio *m* piggy bank.
salvaguardare *vt* to safeguard.
salvare *vt* to save, rescue.
salvatore *m* saviour.
salvia *f* sage.
sambuco *m* elder.
San Silvestro *m:*—**la notte di San Silvestro** *f* New Year's Eve.
sandalo *m* sandal.
sandwich *m* sandwich.
sangue *m* blood.
sanguinaccio *m* black pudding.
sanguinare *vi* to bleed.
sanguisuga *f* leech, bloodsucker.
sanità *f* soundness.
sano *adj* healthy, sound.
santificare *vt* to sanctify.
santo *m* saint.
santuario *m* sanctuary, shrine.
sanzione *f* sanction.
sapere *vi* to know, smell (of).
sapone *m* soap.
sapore *m* taste, flavour, savour:—**sapore forte** *m* tang.
saporito *adj* tasty.
saracinesca *f* shutter.
sarcasmo *m* sarcasm.
sarcofago *m* sarcophagus.
sardina *f* sardine, pilchard.
sassofono *m* saxophone.

Satana *m* Satan.

satanico *adj* satanic.

satellite *m* satellite.

satira *f* satire, lampoon.

satiro *m* satyr.

saturare *vt* to saturate.

saziare *vt* to satiate.

sbaciucchiarsi *vr* to smooch.

sbadigliare *vi* to yawn.

sbadiglio *m* yawn.

sbagliare *vt* to make a mistake.

sbagliato *adj* wrong.

sbaglio *m* mistake, slip.

sbalordire *vt* to stagger, astound.

sbaragliare *vt* to rout.

sbarcare *vi* to disembark, land.

sbarra *f* rail, bar.

sbarramento *m* barrage.

sbiadirsi *vr* to fade.

sbiancare *vt* to whiten.

sbigottire *vt* to dumbfound.

sbirciare *vi* to peek, peep.

sbloccare *vt* to unblock.

sborsare *vt* to disburse, fork out.

sbottonare *vt* to unbutton.

sbrigare *vt* to deal with, polish off.

sbrinare *vt* to defrost.

sbrodolare *vt* to dribble.

sbrogliare *vt* to untangle, disentangle.

sbronzo *adj* drunk, tight.

sbucciapatate *m* potato peeler.

sbucciare *vt* to peel, skin.

scacchi *mpl* chess.

scacchiera *f* chessboard.

scacco *m* check (chess):—**scacco matto** *m* checkmate.

scadente *adj* shoddy, third-rate, ropy.

scadenza *f* expiry, deadline.

scadere *vi* to fall due, lapse, expire.

scaduto *adj* out-of-date, overdue.

scaffalature *fpl* shelving.

scaglia *f* scale, flake.

scala *f* scale, ladder, staircase.

scalare *vt* to scale, climb.

scaldabagno *m* water-heater, geyser.

scaldare *vt* to warm, heat.

scalino *m* stair.

scalogno *m* shallot.

scalpello *m* chisel.

scambiare *vt* to swap, exchange.

scambio *m* exchange, swap.

scampare *vt* to escape.

scampolo *m* remnant.

scanalatura *f* slot.

scandagliare *vt* to plumb.

scandalizzare *vt* to scandalise, shock.

scandalo *m* scandal.

scansare *vt* to shirk.

scappare *vi* to escape, abscond.

scappatoia *f* loophole.

scarabeo *m* beetle.

scarabocchio *m* scribble, doodle.

scarafaggio *m* cockroach.

scaramuccia *f* skirmish.

scardinare *vt* to unhinge.

scarica *f* discharge.

scaricare *vt* to dump, unload.

scarico *m* drain, plughole, outlet.

scarlattina *f* scarlet fever.

scarlatto *adj, m* scarlet.

scarpa *f* shoes

scarpetta *f* bootee.

scarpone *m* boot, brogue.

scarsità *f* dearth, scarcity, scarceness.

scarto *m* reject.

scassato *adj* dilapidated.

scatenare *vt* to trigger (off).

scatola *f* tin, box.

scattare *vi* to click.

scatto *m* click.

scavare *vt* to excavate, dig.

scavezzacollo *m* daredevil.

scavo *m* excavation.

scegliere *vt* to single out, select, choose.

sceicco *m* sheik.

scemo *m* nit, twit.

scendere *vt, vi* to come down, descend.

sceneggiatura *f* screenplay.

sceriffo *m* sheriff.

scetticismo *m* scepticism.

scheda *f* index card.

scheletro *m* skeleton.

schematico *adj* schematic.

scherma *f* fencing.

schermo *m* screen.

scherno *m* mockery.

scherzare *vi* to joke.

scherzo *m* joke, lark, trick.

schiaccianoci *m inv* nutcrackers.

schiaffeggiare *vt* to smack.

schiaffo *m* slap, smack.

schiavitù *f* slavery.

schiavo *m* slave.

schiena *f* back.

schietto *adj* frank, outright, forthright.

schiffo *m* cuff.

schifoso *adj* lousy, rotten.

schiuma *f* froth, foam, lather.

schiumoso *adj* frothy.

schizofrenia *f* schizophrenia.

schizzare *vt* to splash, squirt; to sketch.

schooner *m inv* schooner.

sci *m inv* ski, skiing.

sciacallo *m* jackal.

sciacquare *vt* to rinse.

sciarada *f* charade.

sciarpa *f* scarf.

sciatica *f* sciatica.

scientifico *adj* scientific.

scienza *f* science.

scimmia *f* monkey, ape.

scimpanzé *m inv* chimpanzee.

scintilla *f* spark.

scintillare *vi* to twinkle, sparkle, glint.

scioccare *vt* to shock.

sciocco *m* fool.

sciogliere *vt* to melt, dissolve.

scioltezza *f* fluency.

scioperare *vi* to strike.

sciopero *m* strike, stoppage.

sciovinismo *m* chauvinism.

sciovinista *m/f* chauvinist.

scisma *m* schism.

scissione *f* split.

sciupare *vt* to mar.

scivolare *vi* to slide, slip.

scivolo *m* slide, chute.

scivolone *m* slide.

sclerosi *f* sclerosis.

scoiato *adj* skinned.

scoiattolo *m* squirrel.

scollato *adj* low-cut.

scollatura *f* cleavage.

scommessa *f* wager, bet.

scommettere *vi, vt* to bet, wager.

scomodità *f* inconvenience.

scomodo *adj* uncomfortable, inconvenient.

scompartimento *m* compartment.

scomunicare *vt* to excommunicate.

scongelare *vt* to thaw.

sconosciuto *adj* strange, unknown.

sconsiderato *adj* thoughtless.

sconsolato *adj* disconsolate, forlorn.

sconto *m* discount.

scontrarsi *vr* to crash, collide, clash.

scontro *m* clash, smash.

sconvolgere *vt* to convulse.

scooter *m inv* scooter.

scopa *f* broom.

scopare *vt, vi* to sweep, brush.

scoperta *f* discovery, detection, find.

scoperto *adj* exposed.

scoppiare *vi* to burst, break out.
scoppiettare *vi* to sputter, crackle.
scoprire *vt* to uncover, find out.
scoraggiamento *m* discouragement.
scorbutico *adj* grumpy.
scorbuto *m* scurvy.
scoreggia *f* fart.
scoreggiare *vi* to fart.
Scorpione *m* Scorpio.
scorpione *m* scorpion.
scorrettezza *f* impropriety.
scorretto *adj* incorrect, improper.
scorrevole *adj* sliding, fluent.
scorso *adj* last.
scortare *vt* to escort.
scortese *adj* discourteous, unkind, impolite.
scotch *m inv* whisky, adhesive tape, sellotape.
scotennare *vt* to scalp.
scottare *vt* to scald, blanch.
scottato *adj* sunburnt.
scovolino *m* pipe cleaner.
scozzese *adj* Scottish:—**tessuto scozzese** *m* plaid.
screditare *vt* to discredit:—*vr* ~**rsi** to cheapen oneself.
scremato *adj* skimmed.
scriba *m* scribe.
scribacchiare *vt* to scrawl.
scricciolo *m* wren.
scrigno *m* casket.
scrittore *m* writer.
scrittura *f* writing, handwriting.
scrivania *f* desk, writing desk.
scrivere *vt*, *vi* to write.
scroccare *vi* to sponge, scrounge.
scroccone *m/f* scrounger, sponger.
scrollata *f* shaking.
scroto *m* scrotum.
scrupolo *m* scruple, qualm.

scrutare *vt* to scan, peer, eye, scrutinise.
scuderia *f* stable.
scudo *m* shield.
scultore *m* sculptor.
scultura *f* sculpture.
scuola *f* school.
scuro *adj* dark.
scusa *f* excuse.
scusare *vt* to excuse:—*vr* ~**rsi** to apologise.
sdegnare *vt* to disdain.
sdentato *adj* toothless.
sdraiarsi *vr* to lie down.
sdrucciolevole *adj* slippery.
se *conj* if, whether.
se stessi *pers pron* themselves.
secca *f* shallow:—**in secca** *adv* aground.
seccare *vt* to dry.
secernare *vt* to secrete.
secondario *adj* secondary, incidental.
secondino *m* screw.
secondo *prep* according to, under.
secretaire *m* bureau.
secrezione *f* secretion, discharge.
sedano *m* celery.
sedativo *m*, *adj* sedative.
sede *f* seat, head office.
sedentario *adj* sedentary.
sedere *vi* to sit.
sedia *f* chair, seat.
sedicesimo *adj*, *m* sixteenth.
sedici *adj*, *m* sixteen.
sedile *m* seat.
sedimento *m* sediment, lees.
seducente *adj* glamorous, seductive.
sedurre *vt* to seduce.
sega *f* saw.
segale *f* rye.
segare *vt* to saw.

seggiolone *m* high chair.
seghetto *m* hacksaw.
segmento *m* segment.
segnalare *vt*, *vi* to signal.
segnale *m* signal, sign.
segnalibro *m* bookmark.
segnare *vt* to show, write down, mark.
segnatura *f* signature.
segnavento *m inv* weather vane.
segno *m* indicator, token, tick, sign, mark.
segregazione *f* segregation.
segretario *m* secretary.
segreteria telefonica *f* answering machine.
segreto *adj* secret, sneaking:—*m* secret.
seguire *vt* to follow:—*vi* to ensue.
sei *adj*, *m* six.
selezionare *vt* to select.
self-service *adj inv* self-service.
sella *f* saddle.
selvaggio *adj* uncivilised, wild, savage.
selvatico *adj* wild.
semaforo *m* traffic lights.
semantica *f* semantics.
sembianza *f* guise.
sembrare *vi* to seem, appear.
seme *m* seed, pip.
semestrale *adj* half-yearly.
semicerchio *m* semicircle.
semifinale *f* semifinal.
semiprezioso *adj* semiprecious.
semolino *m* semolina.
semplice *adj* simple, plain.
sempre *adv* always, ever.
sempreverde *m/f* evergreen.
senato *m* senate.
senile *adj* senile.
seno *m* bosom, breast; sinus.

sensibile *adj* tender, sensitive.
senso *m* sense, feeling.
sensuale *adj* sensual.
sentenza *f* sentence.
sentiero *m* track, trail, path.
sentimentale *adj* sentimental.
sentire *vt* to feel, hear.
senza *prep* without, apart from.
separabile *adj* separable.
separare *vt* to separate, part.
sepolcro *m* sepulchre.
seppellire *vt* to bury, inter.
seppia *f* cuttlefish.
sera *f* evening.
serata *f* evening.
serenata *f* serenade.
serenità *f* serenity, equanimity.
serie *f inv* succession, series, run.
serigrafia *f* silk-screen printing.
serio *adj* serious, earnest.
sermone *m* sermon.
serpente *m* snake, serpent.
serra *f* hot-house.
serratura *f* lock.
servile *adj* servile; menial.
servire *vi* to wait, serve, dish.
servizio *m* service.
sessanta *adj*, *m* sixty.
sessantesimo *adj*, *m* sixtieth.
sessismo *m* sexism.
sesso *m* sex.
sessuale *adj* sexual.
sessualità *f* sexuality.
sestante *m* sextant.
sesto *adj*, *m* sixth.
set *m inv* set.
seta *f* silk.
sete *f* thirst.
setola *f* bristle.
setta *f* sect.
settanta *adj m* seventy.

settantesimo *adj, m* seventieth.
settario *adj* sectarian.
sette *adj, m* seven.
settembre *m* September.
settentrionale *adj* northern.
settentrione *m* north.
setter *m inv* setter.
setticemia *f* septicaemia.
settico *adj* septic.
settimana *f* week: — **fine settimana** *m inv* weekend.
settimanale *adj, m* weekly.
settimo *adj, m* seventh.
settore *m* sector.
severità *f* strictness, harshness, severity.
severo *adj* severe, harsh, strict.
sexy *adj inv* sexy.
sezionamento *m* dissection.
sezionare *vt* to dissect.
sezione *f* section, department.
sfacelo *m* dilapidation.
sfarzo *m* pageantry.
sfavorevole *adj* unfavourable, adverse.
sfortuna *f* adversity.
simile *adj* alike.
sfera *f* sphere.
sfidante *m/f* challenger.
sfidare *vt* to defy.
sfigurare *vt* to disfigure.
sfilare *vt* to unthread: — *vi* to parade.
sfilata *f* parade, marchpast.
sfinge *f* sphinx.
sfocato *adj* fuzzy, hazy.
sfoderato *adj* unlined.
sfogare *vt* to vent.
sformato *adj* baggy.
sfortunatamente *adv* unfortunately, unhappily.
sforzarsi *vr* to strive, exert oneself.

sforzo *m* stress, exertion, effort.
sfregare *vt* to rub, chafe.
sfrontato *adj* unashamed, brash.
sfruttamento *m* exploitation.
sfruttare *vt* to tap, exploit.
sfumatura *f* tint, nuance.
sgabello *m* stool.
sgangherato *adj* ramshackle.
sgargiante *adj* garish.
sgocciolare *vi* to drip.
sgonfiare *vt* to deflate.
sgorgare *vi* to well up, gush.
sgradevole *adj* undesirable, distasteful, nasty.
sgranare *vt* to shell.
sgualdrina *f* tart, slut.
sguardo *m* look, gaze.
shampoo *m inv* shampoo.
shock *m inv* shock.
show-room *m inv* showroom.
si *pers pron* itself, themselves.
sì *adv, m* yes, yeah.
sibilo *m* hiss.
siccità *f* drought.
siccome *conj* since.
sicomoro *m* sycamore.
sicurezza *f* safety, security.
sidro *m* cider.
siepe *f* hedge.
siero *m* serum.
sifilide *f* syphilis.
sifone *m* siphon.
sigaretta *f* cigarette, (*fam*) fag.
sigaro *m* cigar.
sigillare *vt* to seal.
sigillo *m* seal.
sigla *f* abbreviation: — **sigla editoriale** *f* imprint.
significare *vt* to signify, mean.
significativo *adj* meaningful, significant.

significato *m* meaning, significance.
signora *f* lady, madam, Mrs.
signore *m* sir, gentleman, lord, Mr.
signorina *f* Miss.
silenzio *m* silence, quiet, hush.
silice *f* flint.
sillaba *f* syllable.
silo *m* silo.
simbolo *m* symbol.
simile *adj* similar, comparable.
similitudine *f* simile.
simmetria *f* symmetry.
simpatia *f* liking, fellow feeling.
simpatico *adj* likeable, nice, congenial.
simposio *m* symposium.
simulare *vt* to simulate, feign.
simulato *adj* sham.
simulazione *f* simulation.
simultaneo *adj* simultaneous, concurrent.
sinagoga *m* synagogue.
sincerità *f* sincerity.
sincronizzare *vt* to synchronise.
sindacato *m* syndicate, trade union, union.
sindrome *f* syndrome.
sinfonia *f* symphony.
singolare *adj* singular, quaint.
singolo *adj* single:—*m* singles (tennis).
sinistra *f* left hand:—**a sinistra** *adv* on the left.
sinistro *adj* left; eerie, sinister, spooky.
sinodo *m* synod.
sinonimo *m* synonym, byword:—*adj* synonymous.
sinossi *f inv* synopsis.
sintassi *f* syntax.
sintesi *f inv* synthesis.
sintomo *m* symptom.
sirena *f* siren, hooter, mermaid.

siringa *f* syringe.
sistema *m* system.
sistemare *vt* to settle, position.
sistematico *adj* systematic.
situare *vt* to place.
situato *adj* situated.
situazione *f* situation.
skate-board *m inv* skate-board.
slang *m* slang.
slitta *f* sled, sledge, sleigh.
slittare *vi* to skid.
slogan *m inv* slogan.
slogare *vt* to wrench, strain.
smaltare *vt* to enamel.
smalto *m* enamel, glaze.
smarrire *vt* to mislay.
smeraldo *m* emerald.
smettere *vt* to quit, stop.
smistare *vt* to sort, shunt.
smog *m inv* smog.
smontare *vt* to take down, dismantle.
smorfia *f* grimace.
smorto *adj* pasty.
smottamento *m* landslip.
snazionalizzare *vt* to denationalise.
snello *adj* trim, slender.
sniffare *vt* to sniff.
snob *m/f inv* snob.
snobbare *vt* to snub, slight.
sobborgo *m* suburb.
sobrietà *f* sobriety.
sobrio *adj* sober.
socchiuso *adj* ajar.
soccombere *vi* to succumb.
soccorrere *vt* to help, aid.
soccorso *m* help:—**pronto soccorso** *m* first aid.
socialismo *m* socialism.
socialista *m/f* socialist.
società *f inv* society, company, corporation.

socio *m* partner, member.
sociologia *f* sociology.
sociologo *m* sociologist.
soda *f* soda.
soddisfacente *adj* satisfactory.
soddisfare *vt* to satisfy, content.
sodo *adj* hard-boiled.
sofà *m inv* sofa.
soffiare *vi* to puff, blow.
soffice *adj* soft.
soffitta *f* attic.
soffitto *m* ceiling.
soffocante *adj* sweltering, overpowering.
soffocare *vt* to suffocate, stifle, choke.
soffrire *vt*, *vi* to suffer.
sofisticare *vt* to adulterate.
sofisticato *adj* sophisticated.
soggetto *m* subject.
soggiorno *m* living room; stay.
sognare *vt*, *vi* to dream.
sogno *m* dream, fantasy.
soia *f* soya.
solamente *adv* only.
solare *adj* solar.
solarium *m inv* solarium.
solco *m* rut, groove, furrow.
soldato *m* soldier.
soldo *m* penny, cent: — **soldi** *mpl* money.
solenne *adj* solemn.
solfato *m* sulphate.
solido *adj* solid, sturdy.
solista *m/f* soloist.
solitario *adj* solitary, lonely.
solitudine *f* solitude, loneliness.
sollecitare *vt* to solicit, invite.
sollevare *vt* to raise, lift, uplift.
solo *adj* alone, single.
solstizio *m* solstice.
soltanto *adv* only, just.

solubile *adj* soluble, (coffee) instant.
soluzione *f* solution.
solvente *adj*, *m* solvent.
solvenza *f* solvency.
somiglianza *f* similarity, resemblance.
somigliare *vt* to resemble.
somma *f* sum, amount.
sommare *vt* to add.
somministrare *vt* to dose, administer.
somministrazione *f* administration.
sonata *f* sonata.
sondare *vt* to sound, probe.
sonetto *m* sonnet.
sonnambulismo *m* sleepwalking.
sonnambulo *m* sleepwalker.
sonnifero *m* sleeping pill.
sonno *m* slumber, sleep.
sontuoso *adj* palatial, sumptuous.
sopportabile *adj* bearable, endurable.
sopportare *vt* to bear, stand, endure.
sopprimere *vt* to suppress, put down.
sopra *prep* over, above, on.
sopracciglio *m* eyebrow.
sopraggiungere *vi* to intervene.
soprammenzionato *adj* above-mentioned.
soprannaturale *adj*, *m* supernatural.
sopratutto *adv* above all.
sopravvivenza *f* subsistence.
sorbetto *m* sorbet, sherbet.
sordido *adj* sordid.
sordità *f* deafness.
sordo *adj* deaf.
sordomuto *adj* deaf-and-dumb.
sorella *f* sister.
sorgere *vi* to rise, spring.
sorprendente *adj* surprising, startling, astonishing.
sorprendere *vt* to surprise, catch.
sorpresa *f* surprise.
sorpresina *f* treat.

sorridere *vi* to smile.
sorriso *m* smile.
sorsata *f* draught.
sorseggiare *vt* to sip.
sorso *m* sip.
sorte *f* fate, lot.
sorteggio *m* draw.
sorveglianza *f* supervision, watch.
sorvegliare *vt* to supervise, invigilate, oversee.
S.O.S. *m* S.O.S.
sosia *m inv* double.
sospendere *vt* to suspend.
sospensione *f* suspension.
sospettare *vt* to suspect.
sospettoso *adj* suspicious.
sospirare *vi* to sigh.
sospiro *m* sigh.
sosta *f* stop, stopover, halt.
sostantivo *adj* substantive.
sostanza *f* substance.
sostanziale *adj* substantial.
sostegno *m* support, prop, mainstay.
sostenere *vt* to support.
sostentamento *m* livelihood.
sostituire *vt* to substitute.
sostituzione *f* substitution.
sottaceti *mpl* pickles.
sotterfugio *m* subterfuge.
sotterraneo *adj* subterranean, underground.
sottile *adj* subtle, thin, fine.
sottilmente *adv* subtly.
sotto *adv*, *prep* under.
sottobicchiere *m* coaster.
sottobosco *m* undergrowth.
sottolineare *vt* to underline, emphasise.
sottomettere *vt* to subdue.
sottopassaggio *m* subway, underpass.
sottoporre *vt* to subject.

sottoprodotto *m* by-product.
sottoscrivere *vt* to sign, underwrite.
sottosegretario *m* undersecretary.
sottosopra *adj*, *adv* topsy-turvy, upside down.
sottosviluppato *adj* underdeveloped.
sottotitolo *m* subtitle, caption.
sottovento *adj* lee, leeward.
sottoveste *f* slip, petticoat.
sottrarre *vt* to subtract.
sottrazione *f* subtraction.
soufflé *m inv* soufflé.
souvenir *m inv* souvenir.
soviet *m inv* soviet.
sovrabbondanza *f* surfeit, glut.
sovraffollato *adj* overcrowded.
sovranità *f* sovereignty.
sovrano *m* ruler, sovereign.
sovrapporsi *vr* to overlap.
sovrastruttura *f* superstructure.
sovrumano *adj* superhuman.
sovvenzionare *vt* to subsidise.
sovvenzione *f* grant, subsidy.
sovvertire *vt* to subvert.
spaccare *vt* to split, chop.
spacco *m* slit, vent, split.
spaccone *m* braggart.
spada *f* sword: — **pesce spada** *m* swordfish.
spaghetti *mpl* spaghetti.
spago *m* string.
spalare *vt* to shovel.
spalla *f* shoulder.
spallina *f* strap.
spaniel *m inv* spaniel.
spanna *f* span.
sparare *vt* to fire, shoot.
spareggio *m* disparity.
sparlare *vi* to backbite.
sparo *m* shot, gunshot.
spartano *adj* spartan.

spartizione *f* share-out.
sparviero *m* sparrowhawk.
spasmo *m* spasm.
spassionato *adj* dispassionate.
spassosissimo *adj* hilarious.
spastico *m*, *adj* spastic.
spatola *f* spatula.
spavalderia *f* bravado.
spaventapasseri *m inv* scarecrow.
spaventare *vt* to frighten, startle, scare.
spaventoso *adj* frightening, abysmal, horrific.
spaziale *adj* spatial.
spazio *m* room, space, gap.
spazzacamino *m* chimney sweep.
spazzare *vt*, *vi* to sweep.
spazzatura *f* trash, rubbish.
spazzola *f* brush: — **spazzola per capelli** *f* hairbrush.
spazzolare *vt* to brush.
spazzolino *m* small brush: — **spazzolino da denti** *m* toothbrush.
specchio *m* mirror.
speciale *adj* special.
specialista *m/f* (*med*) consultant, specialist.
specialità *f inv* speciality.
specializzato *adj* specialist, skilled.
specie *f inv* sort, species.
specificare *vt* to specify.
specificazione *f* specification.
specifico *adj* specific.
specioso *adj* specious.
speculare *vi* to speculate, profiteer.
speculativo *adj* speculative.
speculatore *m* profiteer.
spedire *vt* to ship, send, dispatch.
spedizione *f* trek, expedition, dispatch.
spegnere *vt* to switch off, extinguish.
spellare *vt* to skin.
spendere *vt* to spend, expend.

spennare *vt* to pluck.
spensierato *adj* happy-go-lucky.
spento *adj* dull, off.
speranza *f* hope.
sperare *vt* to hope.
sperduto *adj* godforsaken.
spericolato *adj* reckless.
sperimentare *vt* to test.
sperma *m* sperm, semen.
sperone *m* spur.
sperperare *vt* to squander.
spesa *f* expense, shopping, groceries.
spesso *adj* thick: — *adv* often.
spettacolo *m* spectacle, show.
spettare *vi* to be due, appertain.
spettatore *m* spectator, onlooker.
spettinato *adj* uncombed.
spettrale *adj* spectral.
spettro *m* spectre.
spezie *fpl* spice.
spezzato *adj* broken.
spia *f* spy.
spiacevole *adj* unpleasant, disagreeable.
spiaggia *f* seaside, beach.
spianare *vt* to smooth, level.
spiare *vi* to peep, spy.
spiccioli *m pl* small change.
spiedino *m* kebab.
spiedo *m* spit, skewer.
spiegabile *adj* explicable.
spiegare *vt* to unfold, spread; to explain.
spiegazione *f* explanation, elucidation.
spietato *adj* pitiless, ruthless, remorseless.
spiffero *m* draught.
spilla *f* brooch: — **spilla di balia** *f* safety pin.
spillo *m* pin.
spilungone *adj* lanky.

spina f plug, thorn, prickle.
spinaci mpl spinach.
spinale adj spinal.
spinello m joint.
spingere vt to push.
spinta f push, impetus, boost.
spinto adj suggestive.
spionaggio m spying, espionage.
spioncino m peephole.
spione m telltale, sneak.
spirale adj spiral.
spirare vi to expire.
spiritista m/f spiritualist.
spirito m spirit.
spiritoso adj humorous.
spirituale adj spiritual.
splendido adj splendid, stunning, gorgeous.
splendore m radiance, splendour.
spogliare vt to undress, despoil.
spogliarellista m/f stripper.
spogliarello m striptease.
spoglio adj bare.
spola f shuttle.
spolverare vt, vi to dust.
sponda f shore.
sponsorizzare vt to sponsor.
sponsorizzazione f sponsorship.
spontaneità f spontaneity.
spontaneo adj unstudied, spontaneous.
spopolare vt to depopulate.
sporadico adj sporadic.
sporcare vt to soil, foul.
sporcizia f dirtiness.
sporco adj dirty, smutty:— m dirt.
sporgere vi to protrude.
sport m inv sport.
sportello m door.
sposa f bride, wife.
sposare vt to wed, marry.

sposato adj married.
sposo m spouse, bridegroom.
spostare vt to budge, shift.
spot m inv spotlight, (TV) commercial.
spratto m sprat.
spray m inv spray.
sprecare vt to fritter (away), waste.
sprecato adj misspent.
spreco m wastage, waste.
spregevole adj contemptible, despicable.
spregiativo adj derogatory.
spremere vt to squeeze.
sprint m inv sprint.
spronare vt to spur, urge on.
sprone m yoke, boost, spur.
sproporzionato adj disproportionate.
sprovvisto adj lacking.
spruzzare vt to spray, squirt.
spruzzatina f sprinkling.
spruzzo m splash, spray.
spudorato adj shameless.
spugna f towelling, sponge.
spugnoso adj spongy.
spumoso adj foamy.
spuntare vt to tick, trim.
spuntino m snack.
sputacchiare vi to splutter.
sputare vt, vi to spit.
sputo m spit, spittle.
squadra f team, side.
squadrare vt to square.
squadrone m troop, squadron.
squalificare vt to disqualify.
squallido adj seedy, sleazy, squalid, dingy.
squallore m squalor.
squalo m shark.
squash m squash.
squaw f inv squaw.
squilibrato adj unbalanced.

squilibrio *m* imbalance.

squillo *m* ring.

squisito *adj* exquisite.

squittio *m* squeak.

squittire *vi* to peep, squeak.

sradicare *vt* to eradicate, uproot.

stabile *adj* stable.

stabilimento *m* establishment, plant.

stabilire *vt* to establish.

stabilità *f* stability.

stabilito *adj* set.

stabilizzare *vt* to stabilise.

staccabile *adj* detachable.

staccare *vt* to unplug, disconnect.

staccato *adj* unattached, detached.

stadio *m* stage, stadium.

staffa *f* stirrup.

stagionare *vt* to season.

stagionato *adj* ripe.

stagione *f* season.

stagnare *vi* to stagnate.

stagno *adj* watertight: — *m* tin.

stalagmite *f* stalagmite.

stalattite *f* stalactite.

stalla *f* stable, stall, barn, cowshed.

stallo *m* stalemate.

stallone *m* stud, stallion.

stame *m* stamen.

stampa *f* press, print, printing.

stampante *m* printer.

stampare *vt* to print.

stampato *m* print.

stampella *f* crutch.

stampo *m* cast, mould.

stancare *vt* to tire.

stanchezza *f* tiredness, weariness, fatigue.

stanco *adj* weary, tired: — **stanco morto** *adj* dead tired.

stantio *adj* stale, musty.

stanza *f* room.

stanziamento *m* allocation

stanziare *vt* to station.

stappare *vt* to uncork.

stare *vi* to stay, stand, to be.

starnutire *vi* to sneeze.

starnuto *m* sneeze.

starter *m inv* starter.

stasera *adv* tonight.

statico *adj* static.

statista *m* statesman.

statistica *f* statistics.

stato *m* status, state.

statua *f* statue.

statuario *adj* statuesque, statuary.

statura *f* stature.

status *m* status.

statuto *m* statute, charter.

stazionario *adj* stationary,

stazione *f* station.

steeplechase *m inv* steeplechase.

stella *f* star.

stelo *m* stem.

stendardo *m* banner.

stendibiancheria *m inv* clothes horse.

stenografia *f* stenography, shorthand.

stentato *adj* laboured.

sterco *m* dung.

stereo *m inv* stereo, hi-fi.

stereofonia *f* stereo.

stereotipo *m* stereotype.

sterile *adj* barren, sterile.

sterilità *f* sterility.

sterilizzare *vt* to sterilise.

sterlina *f* pound (sterling).

sterminare *vt* to exterminate.

sterno *m* sternum, breastbone.

sterzo *m* lock.

stesso *adj* self, same, self-same, very.

stetoscopio *m* stethoscope.

steward *m inv* steward.

stigma *m* stigma.

stigmatizzare vt to stigmatise.
stile m style, panache.
stiletto m stiletto.
stima f esteem, valuation, estimation.
stimabile adj reputable.
stimare vt to treasure, esteem.
stimolante m stimulant.
stimolare vt to stimulate, whet, arouse.
stimolo m stimulus.
stinco m shank, shin.
stipato adj crammed.
stipendio m wages, salary.
stipulazione f stipulation.
stirare vt to press, iron.
stirpe f stock.
stitichezza f constipation.
stitico adj constipated.
stivale m boot.
stivare vt to stow.
stock m stock.
stoffa f fabric, cloth.
stola f stole.
stomaco m stomach.
stonato adj flat, off-key.
stop m stop sign.
stoppia f stubble.
stoppino m wick.
stordito adj light headed, in a daze, dazed.
storia f story, history.
storico adj historic(al).
storione m sturgeon.
storno adj starling.
storpiare vt to maim.
storta f retort.
storto adj crooked, awry.
strabico adj cross-eyed.
strabismo m squint, cast.
stracciare vt to shred.
stracciato adj ragged.
straccio m duster, rag.

strada f street, road, way.
stradina f lane.
strage f slaughter.
strambo adj odd, strange.
strangolare vt to strangle.
straniero m alien, foreigner.
strano adj strange, peculiar, odd.
straordinario adj extraordinary.
strapazzare vt to overwork.
strappare vt to tear, rip.
straripare vi to flood.
strascicare vt to shuffle, drawl.
stratagemma m stratagem, ploy.
strategia f strategy.
strato m stratum.
strattone m tug, wrench.
stravagante adj extravagant.
stravaganze f extravagance.
stravedere vi to dote.
stravolto adj distraught.
straziante adj harrowing.
strega f witch.
stregare vt to bewitch.
stregone m sorcerer.
stregoneria f witchcraft, sorcery.
stremare vt to exhaust.
stress m stress.
stressante adj stressful.
stretta f squeeze.
stretto adj tight, strict, narrow.
striare vt to streak.
stricnina f strychnine.
stridere vi to screech.
strillare vi to yell.
strillo m scream, shriek.
stringa f shoelace.
stringente adj stringent.
stringere vt to tighten, grip.
striscia f streak, strip, band.
strisciare vi to creep, trail.
striscione m banner.

strizzare *vt* to squeeze, wring.
strizzata *f* squeeze.
strizzatina *f*:—**una strizzatina d'occhio** *f* wink.
strofinaccio *m* dishcloth.
strofinare *vt* to scrub, rub.
stroncare *vt* to scotch, quash.
stronza *f* bitch.
stronzo *m* turd, pig.
stropicciare *vt* to wrinkle.
strozzare *vt* to throttle, strangle.
struggente *adj* poignant.
strumentale *adj* instrumental.
strumento *m* instrument, tool.
struzzo *m* ostrich.
stucchevole *adj* sickly.
stucco *m* stucco, putty.
studente *m* student.
studiare *vt, vi* to study, read.
studio *m* studio, study.
studioso *adj* studious.
stufa *f* fire, heater, stove.
stufare *vt* to stew.
stufato *m* stew.
stufo *adj* fed-up.
stunt-man *m inv* stuntman.
stupendo *adj* stupendous.
stupidità *f* stupidity.
stupido *adj* stupid.
stupire *vt* to stupefy, amaze.
stupore *m* wonder, astonishment, amazement.
stuprare *vt* to rape.
stupratore *m* rapist.
stupro *m* rape.
stuzzicadenti *m inv* toothpick.
su *adv* up, above:—*prep* over, on.
subacqueo *adj* underwater.
subaffittare *vt, vi* to sublet.
subalterno *adj, m* subordinate.
subappaltare *vt* to subcontract.

subconscio *m* subconscious.
subcosciente *adj* subconscious.
subdolo *adj* devious.
subire *vt* to undergo, sustain.
subito *adv* at once, straight away.
sublimare *vt* to sublimate.
sublime *adj* sublime.
subnormale *adj* subnormal.
subordinare *vt* to subordinate.
suburbano *adj* suburban.
succedere *vi* to happen, transpire.
successione *f* succession, sequence.
successivo *adj* subsequent.
successo *m* success, hit.
successone *m* smash.
successore *m* successor.
succhiare *vt, vi* to suck.
succo *m* juice, gist.
succoso *adj* juicy.
succulento *adj* succulent.
sud *adj, m* south.
sudare *vt, vi* to sweat.
sudario *m* shroud.
suddetto *adj* aforementioned.
suddito *m* subject.
suddividere *vt* to subdivide.
sudicio *m* filth.
sudiciume *m* grime, filth.
sudore *m* sweat.
sufficiente *adj* sufficient.
suffragetta *f* suffragette.
suffragio *m* suffrage.
suffumicare *vt* to fumigate.
suggerimento *m* tip, suggestion.
suggerire *vt* to suggest, prompt.
suggeritore *m* prompter.
sughero *m* cork.
sugo *m* sauce.
suicidio *m* suicide.
suite *f inv* suite.
sultanina *f* sultana.

sultano *m* sultan.

suo *poss adj*, *pron* your(s), her(s), his, its.

suocera *f* mother-in-law.

suocero *m* father-in-law.

suola *f* sole.

suonare *vt*, *vi* to sound, play, ring.

suono *m* sound.

suora *f* nun, sister.

superare *vt* to pass, top, excel, surpass.

superbo *adj* superb, haughty.

superficiale *adj* superficial.

superficie *f* top, surface.

superfluo *adj* superfluous.

superiore *adj* upper, senior.

superiorità *f* superiority.

superlativo *adj*, *m* superlative.

supermercato *m* supermarket.

superpetroliera *f* supertanker.

superpotenza *f* superpower.

supersonico *adj* supersonic.

superstite *m/f* survivor.

superstizione *f* superstition.

superuomo *m* superman.

supino *adj* supine.

supplemento *m* supplement.

supplica *f* supplication.

supplicare *vt* to beg, appeal.

supportabile *adj* tolerable, bearable.

supportare *vt* to bear.

supporto *m* strut.

supposizione *f* assumption, supposition, guess.

supposta *f* suppository.

suppurare *vi* to fester.

supremazia *f* supremacy.

supremo *adj* ultimate, crowning.

surf *m* surfboard.

surgelare *vt* to freeze.

surplus *m inv* surplus.

surrealismo *m* surrealism.

surrogato *adj*, *m* surrogate.

suscettibilità *f* susceptibility, sensibility.

susina *f* plum, damson.

suspense *m* suspense.

sussidiario *m* subsidiary.

sussidio *m* help.

sutura *f* suture.

svago *m* leisure.

svalutazione *f* devaluation.

svanire *vi* to vanish.

svantaggio *m* disadvantage.

svantaggioso *adj* disadvantageous.

svariato *adj* diverse, multifarious.

svasato *adj* flared.

svastica *f* swastika.

sveglia *f* alarm.

svegliare *vt* to awake, rouse.

svelare *vt* to unveil.

svelto *adj* agile, smart.

svendita *f* sale.

svenire *vi* to swoon, faint.

sventolare *vt* to wave.

sventrare *vt* to gut.

sventurato *adj* luckless.

sverniciare *vt* to strip.

svilire *vt* to debase.

sviluppare *vt* to develop.

sviluppo *m* development, twist.

svista *f* oversight, lapse.

svitare *vt* to unscrew.

svogliato *adj* half-hearted.

svolazzare *vi* to flit, flutter.

svolazzo *m* flourish.

svolgere *vt* to perform.

svuotare *vt* to drain.

swing *m* swing.

T

tabaccaio *m* tobacconist.
tabacco *m* tobacco.
tabella *f* chart.
tabellone *m* billboard, scoreboard.
tabù *m inv* taboo.
tacca *f* notch.
taccagno *adj* miserly.
taccheggiare *vi* to shoplift.
taccheggiatore *m* shoplifter.
tacchino *m* turkey.
tacco *m* heel.
taccuino *m* notebook.
tachimetro *m* speedometer.
tacito *adj* tacit, unwritten.
tafano *m* horsefly.
taffettà *m* taffeta.
taglia *f* size: — **taglia forte** *f* outsize.
tagliaboschi *m inv* woodcutter.
tagliaerba *m inv* lawnmower.
taglialegna *m inv* lumberjack.
tagliare *vt* to cut.
tagliatelle *fpl* noodles.
tagliaunghie *m* clippers.
tagliere *m* chopping board, breadboard.
taglio *m* cut, cutback, slash.
talco *m* talc, talcum powder.
tale *adj* such.
talento *m* talent.
talpa *f* mole.
tamburino *m* tambourine.
tamburo *m* drum.
tampone *m* tampon, wad.
tanga *m inv* G-string.
tangente *f* tangent.
tangibile *adj* tangible.

tanto *adj, pron* so much, so many.
tappa *f* stage.
tappare *vt* to bung, cap, cork, plug.
tappetino *m* mat.
tappeto *m* carpet, rug.
tappezzare *vt* to paper.
tappezzeria *f* upholstery.
tappo *m* top, bung, stopper.
tarantola *f* tarantula.
tardi *adj* late.
tariffa *f* rate, tariff.
tarlo *m* woodworm.
tarma *f* moth.
tartan *m inv* tartan.
tartaro *m* tartar.
tartaruga *f* tortoise.
tartufo *m* truffle.
tasca *f* pocket.
tascabile *m* paperback.
tassa *f* duty, tax.
tassare *vt* to tax.
tassativo *adj* imperative.
tassazione *f* taxation.
tassista *m/f* taxi-driver.
tasso *m* rate; badger; yew.
tastare *vt* to feel.
tastiera *f* keyboard.
tasto *m* key.
tattica *f* tactic, tactics.
tattico *adj* tactical.
tatto *m* touch, tact, feel.
tatuaggio *m* tattoo.
tatuare *vt* to tattoo.
tautologia *f* tautology.
tautologico *adj* tautological.

taverna f tavern.
tavola f table, plank.
tavolino m coffee table.
tavolo m table.
taxi m inv taxi, cab.
tazza f cup.
tazzone m mug.
tè m inv tea.
teatrale adj theatrical.
teatro m theatre.
tecnica f skill, technique.
tecnicità f technicality.
tecnico m technician.
tecnologia f technology.
tedio m tedium.
tee m inv tee.
teenager m/f inv teenager.
tela f web, canvas.
telaio m frame, loom.
telecomando m remote control.
telecomunicazioni fpl telecommunications.
telecronaca f commentary.
telecronista m/f commentator.
telefonare vi to phone, ring, call.
telefonata f telephone call.
telefonista m/f telephonist.
telefono m telephone.
telegiornale m TV news.
telegrafo m telegraph.
telegramma m telegram.
telenovella f soap opera.
telepatia f telepathy.
telescopio m telescope.
telespettatore m viewer.
televisione f television.
televisore m television set.
telex m inv telex.
telone m tarpaulin.
tema m theme.
temerario adj foolhardy.

temere vt vi to fear, dread.
tempera f distemper.
temperamatite m inv sharpener.
temperamento m temperament, temper.
temperare vt to sharpen.
temperato adj temperate.
temperatura f temperature.
temperino m penknife.
tempesta f tempest, storm.
tempia f temple.
tempio m temple.
tempo m time; weather; tense.
temporale m storm.
temporaneamente adv temporarily.
tenace adj tenacious, dogged.
tenacia f tenacity.
tenda f tent, curtain.
tendenza f tendency.
tender m inv tender.
tendere vt to tend, stretch.
tendine m tendon, sinew.
tendone m awning.
tenente m lieutenant.
tenere vt to keep.
tenerezza f tenderness, gentleness.
tenero adj tender, endearing.
tenia f tapeworm.
tennis m tennis.
tennista m/f tennis player.
tenore m tenor.
tensione f tension, stress.
tentacolo m tentacle.
tentare vt to tempt, attempt.
tentazione f temptation.
teologia f theology.
teorema m theorem.
teoretico adj theoretical.
teoria f theory.
teorico m theorist.
teorizzare vi to theorise.

terapeutico *adj* therapeutic.

terapia *f* therapy.

tergicristallo *m* windscreen wiper.

tergo *m* back: — **a tergo** *adv* overleaf.

termale *adj* thermal: — **stazione termale** *f* spa.

terminale *adj*, *m* terminal.

terminare *vi*, *vt* to end, terminate.

termine *m* term, limit, end.

termite *f* termite.

termometro *m* thermometer.

termosifone *m* radiator.

termostato *m* thermostat.

terra *f* land, ground, earth.

terrazza *f* patio, terrace.

terremoto *m* earthquake.

terreno *m* ground, land, terrain.

terrestre *adj* terrestrial.

terribile *adj* terrible.

terrier *m inv* terrier.

terrificare *vt* to terrify.

territoriale *adj* territorial.

terrore *m* terror, dread.

terrorismo *m* terrorism.

terrorista *m/f* terrorist.

terzo *adj*, *m* third.

teschio *m* skull.

tesi *f inv* thesis, contention.

tesoro *m* treasure; exchequer; darling, sweetheart.

tessera *f* card.

tessere *vt*, *vi* to weave.

tessile *adj* textile.

tessitura *f* weaving.

tessuti *mpl* textiles.

tessuto *f* fabric, cloth, tissue, material.

test *m* test.

testa *f* head.

testamento *m* testament, will.

testicolo *m* testicle.

testimone *m* witness.

testimoniare *vi* to testify, witness.

testo *m* text.

tetano *m* tetanus.

tetro *adj* bleak.

tetta *(fam)* *f* tit, boob.

tettarella *f* teat.

tetto *m* roof.

thermos *m inv* vacuum flask.

thriller *m inv* thriller.

tibia *f* shinbone.

tic *m inv* tic, twitch.

tiepido *adj* tepid, lukewarm.

tifo *m* typhus.

tifone *m* typhoon.

tifoso *m* fan, supporter.

tigre *f* tiger, tigress.

timbrare *vt* to stamp.

timbro *m* stamp.

timidezza *f* timidity.

timido *adj* shy, diffident.

timo *m* thyme.

timore *m* fear.

timpano *m* eardrum.

tingere *vt* to stain.

tinta *f* paint, hue.

tintoria *f* dyeworks.

tintura *f* dye.

tipico *adj* typical.

tipo *m* type.

tirannia *f* tyranny.

tirare *vi* to pull.

tiroide *f* thyroid.

titillare *vt* to titillate.

titolare *m* bearer, occupant, occupier.

titolo *m* title.

toccare *vt* to touch.

toga *f* gown.

togliere *vi* to take away, remove.

toilette *f inv* toilet, dressing table.

tollerare *vt* to tolerate, suffer.

tomba *f* tomb, grave.

tombola f bingo.
tomo m tome.
tonalità f shade.
tonare vi to thunder.
tonica f tonic.
tonificante adj invigorating, bracing.
tonnellaggio m tonnage.
tonnellata f ton.
tonno m tuna.
tono m tone.
tonsilla f tonsil.
tonsillite f tonsillitis.
tonsura f tonsure.
tonto adj stupid.
topazio m topaz.
topo m mouse.
topografia f topography.
toporagno m shrew.
torace m thorax.
torbido adj murky.
torcia f torch.
tordo m thrush.
torero m bullfighter.
tormentare vt to torment.
tormento m torment.
tornado m inv tornado.
tornare vi to return.
torneo m tournament.
tornire vt to turn.
toro m bull.
Toro m Taurus.
torre f tower.
torrefare vt to roast (coffee).
torrente m torrent.
torrenziale adj torrential.
torretta f turret.
torrido adj torrid.
torrone m nougat.
torso m torso.
torsolo m stalk, core.
torta f pie, cake.

tortora f turtledove.
tortuoso adj circuitous, tortuous.
tortura f torture.
torturare vt to torture.
tosse f cough.
tossico adj toxic.
tossicodipendente m/f drug addict.
tossicodipendenza f addiction.
tossicomane m/f addict.
tossina f toxin.
tossire vi to cough.
tostare vt to toast.
totale adj total.
totalità f totality.
totalitario adj totalitarian.
tovaglia f tablecloth.
tovagliolo m napkin, serviette.
tra prep between.
traccia f smear, trace.
tracciare vt to chart.
trachea f trachea, windpipe.
tracolla f strap.
tradimento m betrayal, treason.
tradire vt to betray, shop.
traditore m traitor.
tradizionale adj traditional.
tradizione f tradition.
tradurre vt, vi to translate.
traduttore m translator.
traduzione f translation.
trafficante m/f trafficker.
trafficare vi to traffic.
traffico m traffic.
tragedia f tragedy.
traghetto m ferry.
tragico adj tragic.
tragicommedia f tragicomedy.
tragitto m haul, run.
tram m inv tram.
trama f story, plot, weave.
trambusto m commotion.

tramontare *vi* to set.

tramonto *m* sundown, sunset.

tramortire *vt* to stun.

trampolino *m* springboard, diving board.

trance *f inv* trance.

tranquillamente *adv* happily.

tranquillante *m* tranquilliser.

tranquillità *f* ease.

tranquillo *adj* leisurely.

transatlantico *m* liner.

transatlantico *adj* transatlantic.

transistor *m inv* transistor.

transito *m* transit.

transitorio *adj* transient.

transizione *f* transition.

trapano *m* drill.

trapezio *m* trapeze.

trapiantare *vt* to transplant.

trappola *f* trap, snare.

trascorrere *vi* to elapse, spend.

trascrizione *f* transcription.

trascurabile *adj* unimportant.

trascurare *vt* to neglect.

trasferire *vt* to shift, transfer.

trasformare *vt* adapt.

trasfusione *f* transfusion.

trasgredire *vt* to transgress.

trasgressione *f* misdemeanour.

trasgressore *m* offender.

traslocare *vt, vi* to move.

trasloco *m* removal, move.

trasmettere *vt* to transmit.

trasparente *adj* transparent.

traspirare *vi* to perspire.

trasportare *vt* to convey, transport.

trasporto *m* transport.

tratta *f* (bank) draft.

trattamento *m* treatment.

trattare *vt* to treat.

trattato *m* treaty, treatise.

trattino *m* dash, hyphen.

trattore *m* tractor.

trauma *m* trauma.

trave *f* beam, girder.

traveller's cheque *m inv* traveller's cheque.

traversata *f* crossing.

traverso *adj* cross.

travestire *vt* to disguise.

travestito *m* transvestite.

tre *adj, m* three.

treccia *f* plait, braid.

treccina *f* pigtail.

tredicesimo *adj, m* thirteenth.

tredici *adj, m inv* thirteen.

tredimensionale *adj* three-dimensional.

tregua *f* respite.

tremare *vi* to quiver.

tremendo *adj* dreadful.

trementina *f* turpentine.

tremolare *vi* to flicker.

trench *m inv* trench coat.

treno *m* train.

trenta *adj, m* thirty.

trentesimo *adj, m* thirtieth.

trepidazione *f* trepidation.

treppiede *m* tripod.

tresca *f* intrigue.

triangolare *adj* triangular.

triangolo *m* triangle.

tribale *adj* tribal.

tribolazione *f* tribulation.

tribù *f* tribe.

tribunale *m* law court, tribunal.

tributo *m* tribute.

tricheco *m* walrus.

triciclo *m* tricycle.

tricofizia *f* ringworm.

trigonometria *f* trigonometry.

trillare *vi* to trill.

trillo *m* trill.
trilogia *f* trilogy.
trimestrale *adj* quarterly.
trimestre *m* term.
trincea *f* trench.
Trinità *f* Trinity.
trio *m* trio.
trionfo *m* triumph.
trip *m inv* trip.
triplicare *vt* to treble.
triplo *adj* triple, treble.
trippa *f* tripe.
triste *adj* sad, woeful.
tristezza *f* misery, sadness.
tritacarne *m inv* mincer.
tritare *vt* to mince.
tritone *m* newt.
trofeo *m* trophy.
tromba *f* trumpet.
trombone *m* trombone; daffodil.
trombosi *f* thrombosis.
tronco *m* log, trunk.
trono *m* throne.
tropicale *adj* tropical.
troppo *adv* too.
trota *f* trout.
trottare *vi* to trot.
trotto *m* trot.
trottola *f* top.

trovare *vt* to find.
trovata *f* gimmick.
trucco *m* trick.
truffare *vt* to swindle.
tu *pers pron* you.
tuba *f* tuba.
tubature *fpl* piping.
tubercolosi *f* tuberculosis.
tubo *m* tube, pipe.
tuffarsi *vr* to plunge, dive.
tulipano *m* tulip.
tumore *m* tumour.
tumultuare *vi* riot.
tumultuoso *adj* tumultuous.
tunica *f* robe, tunic.
tunnel *m inv* tunnel.
tuo *poss adj, pron* your(s).
tuono *m* thunder.
tuorlo *m* yolk.
turbina *f* turbine.
turbolenza *f* turbulence.
turchese *adj*, *m* turquoise.
turismo *m* sightseeing, tourism.
turista *m/f* tourist.
turno *m* shift, turn.
tutela *f* guardianship.
tutore *m* guardian.
tuttavia *conj* however, yet, all the same.
twist *m* twist.

U

ubbidire *vi*, *vt* to obey.
ubicazione *f* site.
ubriachezza *f* drunkenness.
ubriaco *adj* drunk, inebriated.
uccelliera *f* aviary.
uccellino *m* fledgling.

uccello *m* bird.
uccidere *vt* to kill.
udibile *adj* audible.
udito *m* hearing.
ufficiale *adj* official.
ufficiare *vi* to officiate.

ufficio *m* office, bureau.
uguaglianza *f* equality.
uguagliare *vt* to touch, match, equal.
uguale *m/f* match:—*adj* equal.
ulcera *f* ulcer.
ulivo *m* olive tree.
ulteriore *adj* ulterior.
ultimamente *adv* lately.
ultimatum *m inv* ultimatum.
ultimo *adj* last.
ululare *vi* to howl.
umanamente *adv* humanly.
umanista *m/f* humanist.
umanità *f* humanity, mankind.
umanitario *adj* humanitarian, humane.
umano *adj* human.
umidità *f* humidity.
umido *adj* damp, humid.
umile *adj* lowly, humble.
umiliare *vt* to demean, humiliate.
umiltà *f* humility.
umore *m* mood, frame of mind, humour.
unanime *adj* unamity.
unanimità *f* unanimity.
undicesimo *adj, m* eleventh.
undici *adj, m* eleven.
ungere *vt* to anoint.
unghia *f* fingernail, nail, claw.
unguento *m* ointment, salve.
unico *adj* sole.
unicorno *m* unicorn.
unificante *adj* cohesive.
unificare *vt* to unify, unite.
uniforme *adj* uniform.
uniformemente *adv* evenly.
uniformità *f* uniformity.
unilaterale *adj* one-sided, unilateral.
unione *f* union, unity.

unire *vt* to join, unify.
unisono *m* unison.
unità *f inv* unit, unity.
unito *adj* united.
universale *adj* universal.
università *f* university.
universo *m* universe.
uno *adj, m* one.
unto *m* grease.
unzione *f* unction.
uomo *m* (*pl* **uomini**). man.
uovo *m* (*pl* (*f*) **uova**) egg.
uragano *m* hurricane.
uranio *m* uranium.
urbano *adj* urban; urbane.
urgente *adj* urgent.
urgenza *f* urgency.
urlare *vi, vt* to howl.
urlo *m* scream, yell.
urna *f* urn.
urogallo *m* grouse.
usabile *adj* expendabile.
usanza *f* usage.
usare *vt* to use.
uscente *adj* outgoing.
usciere *m* usher.
uscire *vi* to go out.
uscita *f* exit, release.
usignolo *m* nightingale.
uso *m* usage, use.
usurpare *vt* to usurp, encroach.
utensile *m* utensil.
utero *m* uterus, womb.
utile *adj* useful, helpful.
utilità *f* usefulness, utility.
utilizzare *vt* to utilise.
uva *f* grapes.
uvetta *f* raisin.

V

vacanza *f* vacation, holiday.
vacca *f* cow.
vaccinare *vt* to vaccinate.
vaccinazione *f* vaccination.
vaccino *m* vaccine.
vacillare *vi* to totter, falter.
vacuo *adj* blank, vacant.
vagabondo *m* tramp, vagabond.
vagare *vi* to rove, drift.
vagina *f* vagina.
vaglia *m* draft.
vagliare *vt* to screen.
vago *adj* faint, woolly.
vagone *m* carriage.
vaiolo *m* smallpox.
valere *vi* to be worth.
validità *f* validity, soundness.
valido *adj* valid.
valutare *f* to appraise.
valigia *f* suitcase.
valle *f* valley.
vallone *m* glen.
valore *m* value, worth.
valorizzare *vt* to enhance.
valoroso *adj* valiant, manful.
valuta *f* currency.
valutare *vt* to value, assess, evaluate.
valutazione *f* valuation, appraisal.
valvola *f* valve.
valzer *m inv* waltz.
vampiro *m* vampire.
vandalizzare *vt* to vandalise.
vanga *f* spade.
vangare *vt* to dig.
vangelo *m* gospel.
vaniglia *f* vanilla.

vanità *f inv* vanity, conceit.
vanitoso *adj* vain, conceited.
vantaggio *m* advantage.
vantare *vt* to boast.
vapore *m* vapour, steam.
variare *vt, vi* to vary, range.
varicella *f* chickenpox.
varietà *f inv* variety.
variopinto *adj* mottled, motley.
vasaio *m* potter.
vasca *f* basin.
vaschetta *f* tub.
vasectomia *f* vasectomy.
vaselina *f* vaseline.
vasellame *m* crockery.
vasetto *m* pot.
vasino *m* potty.
vaso *m* vase.
vassoio *m* tray, salver.
vastità *f* magnitude.
vasto *adj* vast.
vecchiaia *f* old age.
vecchio *adj* old.
veci *f* duties.
vedere *vi, vt* to see.
vedova *f* widow.
vedovo *m* widower.
veduta *f* outlook, view.
vegetare *vi* to vegetate.
vegetariano *adj, m* vegetarian.
vegetazione *f* vegetation.
veglia *f* wake, vigil.
veicolo *m* vehicle.
vela *f* sail.
velare *vt* to veil.
veleno *m* poison, venom.

vello *m* fleece.
vellutato *adj* silky.
velluto *m* velvet.
velo *m* veil, ply.
veloce *adj* quick.
velocità *f* speed.
vena *f* vein, seam, streak.
venale *adj* venal.
vendere *vt* to sell.
vendetta *f* vendetta.
vendicare *vt* to avenge.
vendita *f* sale.
venditore *m* seller, vendor.
venerabile *adj* venerable.
venerare *vt* to venerate.
venerazione *f* veneration.
venerdì *m* Friday: — **Venerdì Santo** *m* Good Friday.
venereo *adj* venereal.
venial *adj* veniale.
venire *vi* to come.
ventaglio *m* fan.
ventesimo *adj*, *m* twentieth.
venti *adj*, *m* twenty.
venticello *m* breeze.
ventilare *vt* to ventilate.
ventilatore *m* fan, ventilator.
ventilazione *f* ventilation.
vento *m* wind.
ventre *m* stomach.
veramente *adv* truly, really.
veranda *f* veranda(h), porch.
verbo *m* verb.
verde *adj*, *m* green.
verdetto *m* verdict.
verdura *f* greens.
vergine *adj*, *f* virgin.
Vergine *f* Virgo.
verginità *f* virginity.
vergogna *f* shame.
vergognare *vt* to shame.

verificare *vt* to verify, try, check.
verità *f inv* truth.
verme *m* worm.
vermut *m inv* vermouth.
vernice *f* paint, paintwork.
verniciare *vt* to paint.
vero *adj* true, real, veritable.
versare *vt* to spill.
versatile *adj* versatile.
versione *f* version.
verso *prep* toward(s): — *m* verse.
vertebra *f* vertebra.
verticale *adj*, *f* vertical.
vertigine *f* dizziness.
verve *f* verve.
vescica *f* blister, bladder.
vescovo *m* bishop.
vespa *f* wasp.
vespasiano *m* urinal.
vestaglia *f* dressing gown.
vestire *m* dressing: — *vt* to clothe, dress.
vestito *m* dress.
veterano *m* veteran.
veterinario *adj* veterinary.
veto *m* veto.
vetraio *m* glazier.
vetrina *f* showcase, window.
vetro *m* glass, windowpane.
vetta *f* summit.
via *f* road.
via *prep* via, by.
viadotto *m* viaduct.
viaggiare *vi* to travel.
viaggio *m* journey.
viale *m* avenue.
vibrante *adj* vibrant.
vibrare *vi* to vibrate.
vibrazione *f* vibration.
vicepresidente *m* vice-president.
viceversa *adv* vice versa.
vicinanza *f* proximity.

vicinato *m* neighbourhood.
vicino *m* neighbour.
vicolo *m* alley.
video *m inv* video.
vietare *vt* to prohibit.
vigilanza *f* vigilance.
vigilia *f* eve:—**la vigilia di Natale** *f* Christmas Eve.
vigliacco *m*, *adj* coward.
vigna *f* vineyard.
vigneto *m* vineyard.
vignetta *f* cartoon.
vigore *m* vigour.
vigoroso *adj* vigorous.
vile *adj* base.
villa *f* villa.
villano *adj* rude.
vimine *m* wicker.
vincere *vt*, *vi* to win.
vinile *m* vinyl.
vino *m* wine:—**vino bianco** white wine:—**vino rosso** red wine.
viola *m*, *adj* purple.
violare *vt* to violate.
violazione *f* breach.
violentare *vt* to rape.
violentatore *m* rapist.
violenza *f* violence.
violetto *adj*, *m* violet.
violinista *m/f* violinist.
violino *m* violin, fiddle.
violoncello *m* violoncello, cello.
vipera *f* viper, adder.
virare *vi* to turn.
virgola *f* comma, point.
virgoletta *f* inverted comma:—**virgolette** *fpl* quotation marks.
virile *adj* manly, virile.
virilità *f* virility.
virtù *f inv* virtue.
virtuoso *adj* virtuous, righteous.

virus *m inv* virus.
vischio *m* mistletoe.
viscido *adj* slimy.
viscoso *adj* viscous.
visibile *adj* visible.
visione *f* vision.
visita *f* visit.
visitare *vt* to visit, examine.
viso *m* face.
visone *m* mink.
vispo *adj* frisky, bright.
vista *f* sight, vista.
vistoso *adj* showy.
vita *f* life.
vitamina *f* vitamin.
vite *f* vine, grapevine.
vitello *m* calf, veal.
vittima *f* victim.
vitto *m* board.
vittoria *f* victory.
vivace *adj* sprightly.
vivacità *f* liveliness.
vivere *vi* to live, subsist.
vivisezione *f* vivisection.
viziare *vt* to indulge, pamper.
viziato *adj* spoilt.
vizio *m* vice, fault.
vocabolario *m* vocabulary, dictionary.
vocale *f* vowel.
vocazione *f* vocation, calling.
voce *f* voice.
vodka *f inv* vodka.
voglia *f* fancy, inclination.
voi *pers pron* you.
volano *m* shuttlecock.
volantino *m* leaflet.
volare *vi* to fly.
volere *vt* to want, wish.
volgare *adj* coarse, vulgar.
volo *m* flight.
volontà *f* will.

volontario *m* volunteer.
volpe *f* fox.
volta *f* time; vault.
voltaggio *m* voltage.
voltare *vt* to turn, turn over.
volume *m* volume.
voluminoso *adj* bulky.
voluttuoso *adj* sensuous, voluptuous.
vomitare *vi* to vomit, be sick.
vomito *m* vomit.
vongola *f* clam.

vorace *adj* voracious.
vortice *m* whirl, whirlpool.
vostro *poss adj, pron* your(s).
votare *vt, vi* to vote.
votazione *f* poll, vote.
voto *m* mark, grade, vow.
vulcanico *adj* volcanic.
vulcano *m* volcano.
vulnerabile *adj* vulnerable.
vuotare *vt* to empty, bale out.
vuoto *m* vacuum, vacancy, void.

W X Y Z

wagon-lit *m inv* sleeping car.
walzer *m inv* waltz.
WC *m inv* WC, toilet.
weekend *m inv* weekend.
würstel *m inv* frankfurter.
xilofono *m* xylophone.
yacht *m inv* yacht.
yankee *m/f inv* yankee.
yard *f inv* yard.
yen *m inv* yen.
yoga *m* yoga.
yogurt *m inv* yoghurt.
yuppy *m/f* yuppie.
zafferano *m* saffron.
zaffiro *m* sapphire.
zampa *f* paw.
zampata *f* kick.
zangola *f* churn.
zanna *f* fang, tusk.
zanzara *f* mosquito, gnat.
zanzarone *m* daddy-long-legs.
zappa *f* hoe.
zar *m inv* czar, tsar.
zarina *f* czarina.

zattera *f* raft.
zebra *f* zebra.
zecca *f* mint; tick, louse.
zelante *adj* zealous.
zelo *m* zeal.
zenit *m inv* zenith.
zenzero *m* ginger.
zerbino *m* doormat.
zero *m* nought, zero, nil.
zia *f* aunt.
zigomo *m* cheekbone.
zigzag *m inv* zigzag.
zinco *m* zinc.
zingaro *m* gypsy.
zio *m* uncle.
zip *m inv* zip.
zitella *f* spinster.
zoccolo *m* hoof, clog.
zodiaco *m* zodiac.
zolfo *m* sulphur.
zolla *f* clod, sod.
zolletta *f* lump.
zona *f* zone.
zoo *m inv* zoo.

zoologico *adj* zoological.
zoologia *f* zoology.
zoom *m inv* zoom.
zoppicare *vi* to hobble, limp.
zoppo *m* cripple:—*adj* lame.
zoster *m*:—**herpes zoster** *m* shingles.
zotico *m* lout.
zoticone *m* oaf, boor.
zucca *f* pumpkin, marrow, gourd.

zuccherare *vt* to sugar, sweeten.
zucchero *m* sugar.
zucchetto *m* skullcap.
zucchina *f* courgette.
zuccone *m* blockhead.
zuffa *f* fray, dust-up, set-to.
zuppa *f* soup:—**zuppa inglese** *f* (*culin*) trifle.
zuppiera *f* tureen.

English–Italian
Dictionary

A

a *art* un, uno, una, un':—*prep* a, per.

a.m. *adv* del mattino.

abandon *vt* abbandonare:—*n* disinvoltura *f*; brio *m*.

abbey *n* badia *f*.

abbot *n* abate *m*.

abbreviate *vt* abbreviare.

abbreviation *n* abbreviazione *f*.

abdicate *vt* abdicare a, rinunciare a.

abdication *n* abdicazione *f*.

abdomen *n* addome *m*.

ability *n* capacità *f*, abilità *f*:—**abilities** *npl* doti *fpl*.

ablaze *adj* in fiamme.

able *adj* capace, abile, intelligente: —**to be able to do** poter fare.

able-bodied *adj* robusto, valido.

abnormal *adj* anormale.

abnormality *n* anormalità *f*, anomalia *f*.

aboard *adv* a bordo, in vettura.

abolish *vt* abolire.

abolition *n* abolizione *f*.

aboriginal *adj* aborigeno.

abortion *n* aborto *m*.

about *prep* intorno a.

above *prep* sopra:—*adv* al di sopra: —**above all** soprattutto:—**above-mentioned** sopra menzionato.

abroad *adv* all'estero:—**to go abroad** andare all'estero.

abrupt *adj* brusco.

abscess *n* ascesso *m*.

absence *n* assenza *f*, mancanza *f*.

absent *adj* mancante, assente:—**absent-minded** distratto.

absolute *adj* assoluto; totale; categorico:—**absolutely** *adv* assolutamente, completamente:

absorb *vt* assorbire, ammortizzare, assimilare.

absorbent *adj* assorbente.

abstain *vi* astenersi.

abstract *adj* astratto:—*n* riassunto *m*.

absurd *adj* assurdo, ridicolo.

absurdity *n* assurdità *f*, assurdo *m*.

abundance *n* abbondanza *f*, gran quantità *f*.

abundant *adj* abbondante:—**abundant in** ricco di.

abuse *vt* insultare; abusare di.

abusive *adj* offensivo, ingiurioso.

academic *adj* accademico *m*.

academy *n* accademia *f*.

accelerate *vt* vi accelerare.

acceleration *n* accelerazione *f*.

accelerator *n* acceleratore *m*.

accent *n* accento *m*.

accentuate *vt* accentuare; mettere in risalto.

accept *vt* accettare, ammettere.

acceptable *adj* accettabile; gradito.

acceptance *n* accettazione *f*; accoglienza *f*.

access *vt* accedere a:—*n* accesso *m*.

accessible *adj* accessibile; facilmente reperibile.

accident *n* incidente *m*, disgrazia *f*; caso *m*.

accidental *adj* fortuito; involontario:—**accidentally** *adv* per caso; senza volere.

acclimatise *vt* acclimatare:—*vi* acclimatarsi, adattarsi.

accommodate *vt* ospitare, alloggiare.

accommodation *n* sistemazione *f*, alloggio *m*.

accompaniment *n* accompagnamento *m*.

accompany *vt* accompagnare.

accomplish *vt* compiere, portare a termine, realizzare.

accomplished *adj* esperto.

accord *n* accordo *m*:—**with one accord** all'unanimità: **of one's own accord** spontaneamente.

accordance *n*:—**in accordance with** secondo *m*, in conformità di/a.

according to *prep* secondo, stando a; conforme a:—**accordingly** *adv* di conseguenza.

account *n* conto *m*; relazione *f*, resoconto *m*; considerazione *f*:— **on no account** per nessun motivo; in nessun caso:—**on account** in acconto:—**on account of** a causa di:—*vt* **account for** rendere conto di; spiegare.

account number *n* numero *m* di conto.

accountancy *n* ragioneria *f*, contabilità *f*.

accountant *n* ragioniere *m*, ragioneria *f*, contabile *m/f*.

accumulate *vt* accumulare; *vi* accumularsi.

accuracy *n* esattezza *f*; accuratezza *f*; precisione *f*; fedeltà *f*.

accurate *adj* accurato, esatto, preciso; corretto; fedele.

accusation *n* accusa *f*.

accuse *vt* accusare.

accused *n* accusato *m*, imputato *m*.

accuser *n* accusatore *m*, accusatrice *f*.

accustom *vt* abituare.

ace *n* asso *m*.

ache *n* dolore *m*:—*vi* far male.

achieve *vt* raggiungere; realizzare.

achievement *n* realizzazione *f*; raggiungimento *m*.

acid *adj* acido, caustico:—*n* acido *m*.

acknowledge *vt* riconoscere, ammettere; ricambiare.

acknowledgement *n* riconoscimento *m*, ammissione *f*, (*of letter, etc*) riscontro *m*.

acne *n* acne *f*.

acoustics *n* acustica *f*.

acquaintance *n* conoscenza *f*; conoscente *m/f*.

acquit *vt* assolvere.

acre *n* acro *m*.

across *adv* dall'altra parte:—*prep* attraverso.

act *vt* interpretare:—*vi* recitare; agire; *vr* comportarsi:—*n* (*deed*) atto *m*; (*law*) legge *f*; (*theatre*) atto *m*.

action *n* azione *f*.

activity *n* attività *f*.

actor *n* attore *m*.

actress *n* attrice *f*.

actual *adj* reale, effettivo:—**actually** *adv* veramente, addirittura.

acute *adj* acuto; fine; intenso; grave; perspicace.

ad-lib *vt* improvvisare:—*adj* improvvisato.

adamant *adj* inflessibile.

adapt *vt* modificare; trasformare; adattare.

adaptation *n* adattamento *m*.

adaptor *n* presa multipla *f*, riduttore *m*.

add *vt* aggiungere, sommare, addizionare.

addict *n* tossicomane *m/f*, drogato *m*.

addictive *adj* che induce al vizio.

addition *n* aggiunta *f*, addizione *f*:— there has been an addition to the family la famiglia si è accresciuta.

additive *n* additivo *m*.

address *vt* indirizzare; rivolgere:—*n* indirizzo *m*.

adequate *adj* sufficiente; adeguato.

adhesive *n* adesivo *m*.

adhesive tape *n* nastro adesivo *m*.

adjacent *adj* adiacente.

adjective *n* aggettivo *m*.

adjudicate *vt* giudicare; decidere su.

adjust *vt* regolare; modificare; aggiustare.

adjustable *adj* regolabile.

adjustment *n* regolazione *f*, modifica *f*, adattamento *m*.

administer *vt* dirigere, gestire, amministrare; somministrare.

administration *n* direzione *f*, gestione *f*, amministrazione *f*; somministrazione *f*.

administrative *adj* amministrativo.

administrator *n* amministratore *m*, amministratrice *f*.

admirable *adj* ammirevole.

admiral *n* ammiraglio *m*.

admiration *n* ammirazione *f*.

admire *vt* ammirare.

admirer *n* ammiratore *m*, ammiratrice *f*.

admission *adj* ammissione, ingresso.

admit *vt* lasciar entrare; ammettere.

adolescence *n* adolescenza *f*.

adolescent *n* adolescente *m/f*.

adopt *vt* adottare.

adopted *adj* adottato.

adoption *n* adozione *f*.

adorable *adj* adorabile.

adore *vt* adorare.

adult *adj* adulto:—*n* adulto *m*, adulta *f*.

adulterer *n* adultero *m*.

adulteress *n* adultera *f*.

adulterous *adj* adultero.

adultery *n* adulterio *m*.

advance *vt* anticipare; favorire:—*vi* avanzare; progredire.

advanced *adj* avanzato, superiore.

advantage *n* vantaggio *m*:—to take advantage of approfittare di.

adventure *n* avventura *f*.

adventurous *adj* avventuroso.

adverb *n* avverbio *m*.

advertise *vt* fare pubblicità, reclamizzare.

advertisement *n* pubblicità *f*, inserzione *f*, annuncio *m*.

advertising *n* pubblicità *f*.

advice *n* consiglio *m*; avviso *m*.

advisable *adj* consigliabile; raccomandabile.

advise *vt* consigliare; avvisare.

adviser *n* consigliere *m*, consulente *m/f*.

advisory *adj* consultivo.

aerial *n* antenna *f*:—*adj* aereo.

aerobics *npl* aerobica *f*.

aerosol *n* aerosol *m*.

affair *n* faccenda *f*, affare *m*; relazione *f*, avventura *f*.

affect *vt* influire su, incidere su.

affected *adj* affettato; commosso.

affection *n* affetto *m*.

affectionate *adj* affezionato.

affirm *vt* affermare, asserire.

affirmative *adj* affermativo.

affix *vt* apporre, attaccare.

affluence *n* ricchezza *f*, abbondanza *f*.

affluent *adj* ricco.

afford *vt* permettersi.

afraid *adj*:—**to be afraid** aver paura; temere.

after *prep* dopo:—*adv* **after all** dopotutto; malgrado tutto.

after-effects *npl* ripercussione *f*, conseguenza *f*; reazione *f*.

afterlife *n* vita *f* dell'aldilà.

aftermath *n* conseguenze *fpl*.

afternoon *n* pomeriggio *m*.

aftershave *n* dopobarba *m*.

afterwards *adv* dopo, più tardi, in seguito.

again *adv* ancora, di nuovo, un'altra volta:—**again and again** ripetutamente:—**then again** d'altra parte.

against *prep* contro.

age *n* età *f*, epoca *f*, era *f*:—*adj* **underage** minorenne:—*vi* invecchiare.

agency *n* agenzia *f*.

agent *n* agente *m/f*.

aggression *n* aggressione *f*.

aggressive *adj* aggressivo.

aggressor *n* aggressore *m*.

ago *adv* fa:—**how long ago?** quanto tempo fa?

agony *n* dolore *m* atroce.

agree *vt* essere d'accordo con; (*gram*) concordare.

agreeable *adj* piacevole.

agreed *adj* convenuto.

agreement *n* accordo *m*, consenso *m*.

agricultural *adj* agricolo.

agriculture *n* agricoltura *f*.

ahead *adv* avanti; davanti; in anticipo.

aid *vt* aiuto *m*; assistenza *f*.

AIDS *n* AIDS *m*.

aim *vt* puntare, mirare:—*n* mira *f*; scopo *m*.

air force *n* aeronautica *f* militare.

air freshener *n* deodorante *m* per l'ambiente.

air *n* aria *f*:—*vt* arieggiare; esprimere.

air terminal *n* terminal *m*.

air-conditioned *adj* ad/con aria condizionata, climatizzato.

air-conditioning *n* aria *f* condizionata.

aircraft *n* aeromobile *m*.

airlift *n* ponte *m* aereo.

airline *n* linea *f* aerea.

airport *n* aeroporto *m*.

aisle *n* navata *f*.

alarm *n* allarme *m*, sveglia *f*:—*vt* allarmare.

album *n* album *m*.

alcohol *n* alcool *m*.

alcoholic *adj* alcolico:—*n* alcolizzato *m*.

alcoholism *n* alcolismo *m*.

ale *n* birra *f*.

alert *adj* sveglio; vigile:—*n* allarme *m*: —*vt* avvertire.

alibi *n* alibi *m*.

alike *adj* simile.

alive *adj* vivo.

all *adj* tutto.

all-night *adj* aperto/che dura tutta la notte.

all right *adv* bene.

all-time *adj* senza precedente.

allegation *n* accusa *f*.

allergy *n* allergia *f*.
alley *n* vicolo *m*.
alliance *n* alleanza *f*.
allied *adj* alleato.
alligator *n* alligatore *m*.
allow *vt* permettere; concedere.
allowable *adj* ammissibile.
ally *n* alleato *m*:—*vt* allearsi.
almond *n* mandorla *f*.
almost *adv* quasi.
alone *adj* solo:—*adv* da solo:—**to leave alone** lasciare in pace.
along *prep* lungo.
alphabet *n* alfabeto *m*.
alphabetical *adj* alfabetico:—**alphabetically** *adv* in ordine alfabetico.
alpine *n* alpino *m*.
already *adv* già.
also *adv* anche, pure.
altar *n* altare *m*.
alter *vt* modificare.
alteration *n* modifica *f*.
alternative *n* alternativa *f*.
although *conj* benché.
altogether *adv* tutto sommato.
always *adv* sempre.
amateur *n* dilettante *m/f*.
amaze *vt* stupire.
amazing *adj* sorprendente.
ambassador *n* ambasciatore *m*.
ambiguous *adj* ambiguo.
ambition *n* ambizione *f*.
ambitious *adj* ambizioso.
ambulance *n* ambulanza *f*.
amenities *npl* attrezzatura *f*.
America *n* America *f*.
American *adj* americano.
amnesia *n* amnesia *f*.
among(st) *prep* tra, in mezzo a.
amount *n* somma *f*, importo *m*, quantità *f*:—*vi* ammontare a.

amphitheatre *n* anfiteatro *m*.
amputate *vt* amputare.
amuse *vt* divertire.
amusing *adj* divertente.
an *art* un, uno, una.
anaemia *n* anemia *f*.
anaemic *adj* anemico.
anaesthetic *n* anestetico *m*.
analysis *n* analisi *f*.
anchor *n* ancora *f*.
anchovy *n* acciuga *f*.
ancient *adj* antico.
and *conj* e:—**faster and faster** sempre più veloce.
angel *n* angelo *m*.
anger *n* rabbia *f*:—*vt* far arrabbiare.
angle *n* angolo *m*:—*vt* pescare con la lenza.
anglicism *n* anglicismo *m*.
angrily *adv* con rabbia.
angry *adj* arrabbiato.
animal *adj*, *n* animale *m*.
ankle *n* caviglia *f*:—**ankle socks** calzini *mpl*.
anniversary *n* anniversario *m*.
announce *vt* annunciare.
announcement *n* annuncio *m*.
annoy *vt* infastidire.
annoying *adj* irritante.
annual *adj* annuo.
anorak *n* giacca *f* a vento.
anorexia *n* anoressia *f*.
another *adj* un altro, ancora:—**one another** l'un l'altro.
answer *vt* rispondere:—*n* risposta *f*.
answering machine *n* segreteria *f* telefonica.
ant *n* formica *f*.
antarctic *adj* antartico.
antenna *n* antenna *f*.
anthem *n* inno *m*.

antibiotic n antibiotico m.
anticipate vt prevedere.
anticipation n attesa f.
anticlockwise adj antiorario: —adv in senso antiorario.
antidote n antidoto m.
antihistamine n antistaminico m.
antique adj antico: —n pezzo m di antiquariato.
antiquity n antichità f.
antiseptic adj, n antisettico m.
anxiety n ansia f.
anxious adj preoccupato.
any adj del, dello, della, dei, degli, delle, qualche, un po'.
apart adv a distanza; separatamente; a pezzi; a parte.
apartheid n apartheid f.
apartment n appartamento m.
aperitif n aperitivo m.
apologetic adj (pieno) di scuse.
apologise vt scusarsi.
apology n scuse fpl.
apostrophe n apostrofo m.
apparatus n attrezzatura f.
apparent adj evidente: —**apparently** adv a quanto pare.
appeal vi supplicare; (law) appellarsi: —n (law) appello m.
appealing adj attraente; commovente.
appear vi apparire; comparire; sembrare; esibirsi.
appearance n aspetto m; comparsa f.
appease vt placare.
appetising adj appetitoso.
appetite n appetito m.
applaud vi applaudire.
applause n applauso m.
apple n mela f.
appliance n apparecchio m.

applicable adj applicabile.
apply vt applicare; applicarsi; rivolgersi.
appointment n appuntamento m; nomina f.
appreciate vt apprezzare: —vi aumentare di valore.
appreciation n apprezzamento m.
apprehensive adj apprensivo, timoroso.
approach vt vi avvicinar(si) a: —n approccio m.
appropriate vt appropriarsi di: —adj adatto.
approval n approvazione f.
approve (of) vt approvare.
approximate adj approssimativo.
apricot n albicocca f: —**apricot tree** albicocco m.
April n aprile m.
aptitude n abilità f.
Aquarius n Acquario m.
Arab n, adj arabo m.
arcade n arcata f; galleria f.
arch n arco m: —adj principale; malizioso.
archaeology n archeologia m.
arched adj ad arco.
architect n architetto m.
architecture n architettura f.
archway n passaggio m a volta.
area n area f.
arena n arena f.
argue vi litigare.
argument n discussione f.
Aries n Ariete m.
aristocracy n aristocrazia f.
arithmetic n aritmetica f.
arm n braccio m: —vt armare.
armchair n poltrona f.
armpit n ascella f.
army n esercito m.
around prep intorno: —adv circa.

arrange *vt* sistemare; organizzare.

arrest *n* arresto *m*:—*vt* arrestare.

arrival *n* arrivo *m*.

arrive *vt* arrivare.

arse *n* culo *m*.

art gallery *n* galleria *n* d'arte.

art *n* arte *f*:—**arts** *npl* lettere *fpl*, studi *mpl* umanistici.

artery *n* arteria *f*.

arthritis *n* artrite *f*.

arctic *adj* artico.

artichoke *n* carciofo *m*.

article *n* articolo *m*.

artificial *adj* artificiale.

artisan *n* artigiano *m*.

artist *m* artista *m/f*.

as *conj* mentre; come:—**as to, as for** quanto a.

ascent *n* ascensione *f*.

ash *n* (*bot*) frassino *m*; cenere *f*.

ashtray *n* portacenere *m*.

ask *vt* chiedere:—**ask a question** fare una domanda.

asleep *adj* addormentato.

asparagus *n* asparago *m*.

asphyxia *n* asfissia *f*.

aspire *vt* aspirare.

aspirin *n* aspirina *f*.

assassin *n* assassino *m*.

assault *n* assalto *m*:—*vt* assaltare.

assembly *n* assemblea *f*; montaggio *m*.

assignment *n* incarico *m*.

assist *vt* aiutare.

assistant *n* aiutante *m/f*.

associate *vt* associare:—*adj* consociato:—*n* collega *m/f*.

assurance *n* assicurazione *f*.

assure *vt* assicurare.

asthma *n* asma *f*.

asthmatic *adj* asmatico.

astrology *n* astrologia *f*.

astronomy *n* astronomia *f*.

asylum *n* asilo *m*; manicomio *m*.

at *prep* a:—**at once** subito:—**at all** affatto:—**at first** dapprima:—**at last** finalmente.

athlete *n* atleta *m/f*.

athletic *adj* atletico.

atlas *n* atlante *m*.

atmosphere *n* atmosfera *f*.

atmospheric *adj* atmosferico.

atom *n* atomo *m*.

attach *vt* attaccare.

attack *vt* attaccare:—*n* attacco *m*.

attempt *vt* tentare:—*n* tentativo *m*.

attend *vt* frequentare:—**attend to** occuparsi di.

attendant *n* custode *m/f*.

attention *n* attenzione *f*.

attic *n* soffitta *f*, mansarda *f*.

attract *vt* attirare.

attractive *adj* attraente.

attribute *vt* attribuire:—*n* attributo *m*.

aubergine *n* melanzana *f*.

auction *n* asta *f*.

audience *n* pubblico *m*; udienza *f*.

auditorium *n* auditorio *m*.

August *n* agosto *m*.

aunt *n* zia *f*.

austere *adj* austero.

authentic *adj* autentico.

author *n* autore *m*.

authority *n* autorità *f*.

automatic *adj* automatico.

autumn *n* autunno *m*.

available *adj* disponibile.

avenue *n* viale *m*.

average *n* media *f*:—*adj* medio.

avocado *n* avocado *m*.

avoid *vt* evitare.

awake *vt* svegliare:—*adj* sveglio.

award *vt* assegnare:—*n* premio *m*.
aware *adj* consapevole.
away *adv* lontano:—**far and away** di gran lunga.

away game *n* partita *f* in trasferta.
awful *adj* terribile.
awkward *adj* imbarazzante; goffo.
axe *n* ascia:—*vt* ridurre drasticamente.

B

baby *n* bambino *m*, bimbo *m*, neonato *m*.
baby-sit *vi* guardare i bambini.
baby-sitter *n* baby sitter *m/f*.
bachelor *n* scapolo *m*; (*univ*) dottore *m*, dottoressa *f*.
back *n* schiena *f*; dietro *m*; retro *m*:—*adj* posteriore.
backbone *n* spina *f* dorsale.
backside *n* sedere *m*.
backward *adj* all'indietro.
backwards *adv* indietro.
bacon *n* pancetta *f*.
bacteria *n* batteri *mpl*.
bad *adj* cattivo; brutto.
badge *n* distintivo *m*.
badminton *n* badminton *m*.
bag *n* borsa *f*, sacchetto *m*.
baggage *n* bagaglio *m*.
bail *n* cauzione *f*.
bake *vt* cuocere (al forno).
baker *n* fornaio *m*.
bakery *n* panificio *m*.
balaclava *n* passamontagna *m*.
balance *n* equilibrio *m*; bilancio *m*.
balcony *n* balcone *m*.
bald *adj* calvo.
ball *n* palla *f*; ballo *m*.
ballad *n* ballata *f*.
ballerina *n* ballerina *f*.

ballet *n* danza *f* classica.
balloon *n* palloncino *m*:—**hot air balloon** mongolfiera *f*.
ballpoint (pen) *n* penna *f* a sfera.
ballroom *n* sala *f* da ballo.
balm *n* balsamo *m*.
bamboo *n* bambù *m*.
ban *n* divieto *m*:—*vt* proibire.
banana *n* banana *f*:—**banana tree** banano *m*.
band *n* banda *f*; striscia *f*.
bandage *n* fascia *f*.
bandit *n* bandito *m*.
bandstand *n* palco *m* dell'orchestra.
bang *n* colpo *m*:—*vt vi* sbattere.
banger *n* salsiccia *f*; petardo *m*.
bangle *n* braccialetto *m*.
banjo *n* banjo *m*.
bank *n* riva *f*; banca *f*.
bank account *n* conto *m* in banca.
banker *n* banchiere *m*.
banknote *n* banconota *f*.
bankrupt *adj* fallito:—*n* fallito *m*.
bank statement *n* estratto *m* conto.
banner *n* stendardo *m*; striscione *m*.
banquet *n* banchetto *m*.
baptise *vt* battezzare.
bar *n* bar *m*; sbarra *f*:—*vt* sbarrare:—*prep* tranne.
barbecue *n* barbecue *m*.

barber n barbiere m.

bare adj nudo; spoglio; semplice.

barely adv appena.

bargain n affare m: — vi contrattare.

bark n corteccia f; abbaiare m: — vi abbaiare.

barley n orzo m.

barmaid n barista f.

barman n barista m.

barn n stalla f.

barometer n barometro m.

baroque adj barocco.

barrel n barile m; canna f.

barrier n barriera f.

barrister n avvocato m.

bartender n barista m.

base n base f: — vt basare: — adj ignobile, vile.

baseball n baseball m.

basement n seminterrato m.

bash n botta: — vt picchiare.

basic adj fondamentale.

basil n basilico m.

basin n lavandino m.

basis n base f.

basket n cestino m.

basketball n pallacanestro f.

bass adj basso.

bassoon n fagotto m.

bastard adj bastardo.

bat n (zool) pipistrello m; (sport) mazza f.

bath n bagno m: — vt fare il bagno.

bathing cap n cuffia f.

bathing costume n costume m.

bathroom n (stanza da) bagno m.

baths npl piscina f.

batter vt colpire violentemente: — n pastella f.

battery n pila f, batteria f.

battle n battaglia f, lotta f: — vi lottare, combattere.

battleship n nave f da guerra.

bay n baia f; alloro m: — vt latrare.

bayonet n baionetta f.

bazaar n bazar m.

be vi essere.

beach n spiaggia f.

bead n perlina f.

beak n becco m.

bean n fagiolo m; chicco m.

bear n orso m: — vt portare; sopportare; partorire.

bearable adj sopportabile.

beard n barba f.

beast n bestia f: — **beast of burden** bestia da soma.

beastly adj insopportabile.

beat vt battere: — vi palpitare: — n battito m; ritmo m.

beautiful adj bello; splendido.

beautify vt abbellire.

beauty n bellezza f: — **beauty spot** neo m.

because conj perché.

become vi diventare; divenire.

becoming adj adatto.

bed n letto m.

bedclothes npl coperte fpl.

bedroom n camera f da letto.

bee n ape f.

beef n manzo m.

beefsteak n bistecca (di manzo) f.

beer n birra f.

beetle n scarabeo m.

before adv prima di.

beg vt mendicare; supplicare.

beggar n mendicante m/f.

begin vt vi cominciare, incominciare, iniziare.

beginning n inizio m, principio m.

behave vi comportarsi.

behaviour n comportamento m.

behind prep dietro.

being n essere m, esistenza f.

belief n fede f; convinzione f; opinione f.

believable adj credibile.

believe vt vi credere.

bell n campanello m.

belly n pancia f.

belong vi appartenere.

belongings npl effetti mpl personali.

below prep, adv sotto.

belt n cintura f: — vi filare.

bench n panchina f.

bend vt piegare: — vi piegarsi: — n curva f.

beneath adv, prep sotto.

beneficial adj benefico.

beneficiary n beneficiario m.

benefit n vantaggio m: — vt giovare: — vi trarre vantaggio.

benign adj benevolo; benigno.

bent n inclinazione f.

bereaved adj in lutto.

bereavement n lutto.

beret n berretto m.

berry n bacca f.

beside prep accanto a.

besides prep oltre a: — adv inoltre.

best adj migliore: — adv meglio: — n il migliore.

bestseller n bestseller m.

bet vt vi scommettere: — n scommessa f.

betray vt tradire.

betrayal n tradimento m.

betroth vt fidanzare.

betrothal n fidanzamento m.

better adj migliore: — adv meglio: — vt migliorare.

between prep tra, fra.

beware vi stare attento.

beyond prep oltre; al di là.

Bible n bibbia f.

bicycle n bicicletta f.

bid vt offrire: — vi dichiarare: — n offerto m; tentativo m.

big adj grande; grosso.

bikini n bikini m.

bile n bile f.

bilingual adj bilingue.

bill n becco m; fattura f; conto m.

billiards npl biliardo m.

billion n miliardo m.

bin n bidone m.

bind vt legare; rilegare.

bingo n tombola f.

binoculars n binocolo m.

biographer n biografo m.

biography n biografia f.

biological adj biologico.

biology n biologia f.

bird n uccello m.

birth n nascita f; parto m.

birthday n compleanno m.

biscuit n biscotto m.

bishop n vescovo m; (chess) alfiere m.

bison n bisonte m.

bit n punta f; pezzo m; morso m.

bitch n cagna f; (fam) stronza f.

bite vt mordere; pungere: — **bite the dust** lasciarci la pelle: — n morso m; puntura f.

bitter adj amaro; aspro.

bizarre adj bizzarro.

black adj nero: — n nero: — vt boicottare.

blackberry n mora f.

blackbird n merlo m.

blackboard n lavagna f.

blackhead n punto m nero.

blacklist n lista f nera.

blackmail n ricatto m: — vt ricattare.

black sheep n pecora f nera.

blacksmith *n* fabbro *m*.
bladder *n* vescica *f*.
blade *n* lama *f*.
blame *vt* incolpare; rimproverare:—*n* colpa *f*.
blameless *adj* irreprensibile.
bland *adj* blando.
blank *adj* bianco; vacuo:—*n* vuoto *m*.
blank cheque *n* assegno *m* in bianco.
blanket *n* coperta *f*:—*adj* globale.
blaspheme *vi* bestemmiare.
blasphemous *adj* blasfemo.
blasphemy *n* bestemmia *f*.
blast *n* esplosione *f*; raffica *f*:—*vt* far saltare:—*excl* **blast!** mannaggia!
blaze *n* incendio *m*:—*vi* ardere; divampare.
blazer *n* blazer *m*.
bleach *vt* candeggiare:—*n* candeggina *f*.
bleak *adj* tetro; desolato.
bleed *vi* sanguinare:—*vt* spurgare.
bleeding *n* emorragia *f*:—*adj* sanguinante.
bless *vt* benedire.
blessed *adj* benedetto.
blessing *n* benedizione *f*.
blind *adj n* cieco *m*:—*vt* accecare:— **Venetian blind** tenda *f* avvolgibile.
blindness *n* cecità *f*.
blink *vt* sbattere le palpebre:—*n* battito *m* di ciglia.
blister *n* vescica *f*.
blizzard *n* bufera *f* di neve.
blond(e) *adj n* biondo *m*.
blood *n* sangue *m*.
blossom *n* fiori *mpl*.
blouse *n* camicetta *f*.
blow *vi* soffiare:—*vt* suonare; esplodere:—*n* colpo *m*.
blue *adj* azzurro, celeste.

bluebottle *n* moscone *m*.
blunder *n* gaffe *f*.
blunt *adj* non tagliente; brusco.
blush *n* rossore *m*:—*vi* arrossire.
board *n* asse *f*; (*chess*) scacchiera *f*; vitto *m*; commissione *f*:—*vt* imbarcarsi su; salire su:—*vi* essere a pensione da.
boast *vt* vantare:—*n* vanteria *f*.
boat *n* barca *f*; nave *f*.
body *n* corpo *m*; cadavere *m*; massa *f*.
bogus *adj* fasullo.
boil *vi* bollire:—*vt* (far) lessare:—*n* foruncolo *m*.
boisterous *adj* animato.
bold *adj* audace.
bollard *n* colonnina *f*.
bolt *n* chiavistello *m*.
bomb *n* bomba *f*; *vt* bombardare.
bond *n* impegno *m*; legame *m*; titolo *m*.
bone *n* osso *m*; (*fish*) lisca *f*.
bonfire *n* falló *m*.
bonus *n* gratifica *f*; premio *m*.
bony *adj* osseo.
boo *vt* fischiare.
boob *n* gaffe *f*; tetta *f*.
book *n* libro *m*; quaderno *m*:—*vt* prenotare, riservare.
bookkeeper *n* contabile *m/f*.
bookkeeping *n* contabilità *f*.
booklet *n* opuscolo *m*.
bookshop *n* libreria *f*.
boom *n* boma *f*.
boot *n* stivale *m*.
booth *n* cabina *f*.
booze *vi* alzare il gomito:—*n* alcol *m*.
boozer *n* osteria *f*.
bore *vt* trivellare; annoiare:—*n* foro *m*; calibro *m*; noia *f*; noioso *m*.
boredom *n* noia *f*.

boring *adj* noioso.

born *adj* nato.

borough *n* comune *m*.

borrow *vt* prendere in prestito.

bosom *n* petto *m*, seno *m*.

boss *n* capo *m*, padrone *m*.

botany *n* botanica *f*.

both *adj* entrambi; ambedue; tutti e due.

bother *vt* infastidire:—**a bother** *n* una seccatura.

bottle *n* bottiglia *f*:—*vt* imbottigliare.

bottom *n* fondo *m*; sedere *m*.

bough *n* ramo *m*.

boulder *n* macigno *m*.

bound(s) *n* limiti *mpl*.

boundary *n* confine *m*.

bountiful *adj* abbondante; munifico.

bouquet *n* bouquet *m*.

bow *vt* chinare:—*vi* inchinarsi:—*n* inchino *m*; prua *f*.

bowl *n* scodella *f*:—*vt* lanciare.

box *n* scatola *f*; palco *m*:—*vi* fare il pugile.

boxing *n* pugilato *m*.

boxer *n* pugile *m*.

box office *n* botteghino *m*.

boy *n* ragazzo *m*; fanciullo *m*.

bra *n* reggiseno *m*.

bracelet *n* braccialetto *m*.

bracket *n* mensola *f*; parentesi *f*.

brain *n* cervello *m*.

brake *n* freno *vi* frenare.

bran *n* crusca *f*.

branch *n* ramo *m*:—*vi* diramarsi.

brand *n* marca *f*:—*vt* marchiare.

brandy *n* brandy *m*.

brass *n* ottone *m*.

brave *adj* coraggioso.

bread *n* pane *m*.

breadcrumbs *n* pangrattato *m*.

breadth *n* larghezza *f*.

break *vt* rompere:—*vi* rompersi.

breakable *adj* fragile.

breakdown *n* guasto *m*; esaurimento *m* nervoso.

breakfast *n* prima colazione *f*.

breast *n* petto *m*; seno *m*; mammella *f*.

breastbone *n* sterno *m*.

breath *n* fiato *n*; alito *m*.

breathe *vt* respirare.

breathing *n* respiro *m*, respirazione *f*.

breathless *adj* senza fiato.

breed *n* razza *f*:—*vt* allevare:—*vi* riprodursi.

breeze *n* brezza *f*, venticello *m*.

brewery *n* fabbrica *f* di birra.

bribe *n* bustarella *f*:—*vt* corrompere.

bribery *n* corruzione *f*.

brick *n* mattone *m*.

bride *n* sposa *f*.

bridegroom *n* sposo *m*.

bridesmaid *n* damigella *f* d'onere.

bridge *n* ponte *m*; bridge *m*.

brief *adj* breve:—*n* dossier:—*vt* dare istruzioni a.

briefcase *n* cartella *f*.

briefs *n* slip; mutandine *fpl*.

bright *adj* luminoso; vispo.

brightness *n* luminosità *f*.

brilliance *n* intensità *f*; intelligenza *f* scintillante.

brilliant *adj* brillante.

bring *vt* portare.

brisk *adj* sbrigativo; attivo.

brittle *adj* fragile.

broad *adj* largo.

broadcast *n* trasmissione *f*:—*vt* trasmettere.

brochure *n* depliant *m*; brochure *f*.

broken *adj* rotto, spezzato.

brolly *n* ombrello *m*.

bronchitis n bronchite f.

bronze n bronzo m.

brooch n spilla f.

brood vi covare, rimuginare: — n covata f; prole f.

broom n scopa f; (bot) ginestra f.

broth n brodo m.

brothel n bordello m.

brother n fratello m.

brother-in-law n cognato m.

brotherly adj fraterno.

brown adj marrone.

bruise vt farsi un livido a: — n livido m.

brush n spazzola f: — vt spazzolare; scopare; sfiorare.

brutal adj brutale.

bubble n bolla f.

bucket n secchio m.

buckle n fibbia f: — vt allacciare: — vi allacciarsi.

bud n bocciolo m.

Buddhism m buddismo m.

budgerigar n pappagallino m.

budget n bilancio m.

buffalo n bufalo m.

buffet n schiaffo; buffet m: — vt sballottare.

bug n insetto m.

build n corporatura f: — vt costruire.

builder n costruttore m; muratore m.

building n costruzione f; edificio m.

bulb n bulbo m; lampadina f.

bulk n volume m; massa f.

bull n toro m.

bulldozer n bulldozer m.

bullet n proiettile m.

bulletin n bollettino m.

bulletproof adj a prova di proiettile.

bullion n oro m in lingotti.

bully n bullo m: — vt fare il prepotente.

bumblebee n bombo m.

bump n botta f; bernoccolo m: — vt sbattere.

bun n panino m dolce; chignon m.

bunch n mazzo m; grappolo m.

bungalow n bungalow m.

bunion n (med) cipolla f.

bunk n cuccetta f.

bunker n bunker m.

buoy n (mar) boa f.

buoyant adj galleggiante.

burden n carico m; onere m: — vt opprimere; oberare.

bureau n ufficio m; secrétaire m.

bureaucracy n burocrazia f.

bureaucrat n burocrate m/f.

burglar n ladro m.

burgle vt svaligiare.

burial n sepoltura f.

burn vt bruciare: — n bruciatura f, ustione f.

burp n rutto m: — vi ruttare.

burrow n tana f: — vt scavare.

bursary n borsa f di studio.

burst vi scoppiare.

bury vt seppellire.

bus n autobus m.

bush n cespuglio m.

busily adv alacremente.

business n affari mpl; attività f.

businessman n uomo m d'affari.

bus stop n fermata f d'autobus.

bust n busto m; petto m.

busy adj occupato.

but conj ma: — adv solo: — prep tranne.

butcher n macellaio m: — vt macellare.

butcher's shop n macelleria f.

butler n maggiordomo m.

butt n botte f; mozzicone m: — vt dare una testata.

butter *n* burro *m*.
buttercup *n* ranuncolo *m*.
butterfly *n* farfalla *f*.
buttock *n* natica *f*.
button *n* bottone *m*.
buy *vt* comprare.

by *adv* vicino:—*prep* vicino; via; davanti.
bygone *adj* passato.
bypass *n* circonvallazione *f*.
by-product *n* sottoprodotto *m*.
byte *n* (*comput*) byte *m*.

C

cab *n* taxi *m*; cabina *f*.
cabbage *n* cavolo *m*.
cabin *n* capanna *f*; cabina *f*.
cabinet *n* armadietto *m*; Consiglio *m* dei Ministri.
cable *n* cavo *m*.
cable car *n* funivia *f*.
cactus *n* cactus *m*.
café *n* caffè *m*; bar *m*.
caffeine *n* caffeina *f*.
cage *n* gabbia *f*:—*vt* mettere in gabbia.
cake *n* torta *f*; pasticcino *m*.
cake shop *n* pasticceria *f*.
calculate *vt* calcolare.
calculator *n* calcolatore *m*.
calendar *n* calendario *m*.
calf *n* vitello *m*.
call *vt* chiamare; telefonare a.
calm *n* calma *f*; pace *f*.
calorie *n* caloria *f*.
camel *n* camello *m*.
camera *n* macchina *f* fotografica.
camomile *n* camomilla *f*.
camouflage *n* mimetizzazione *f*.
camp *n* accampamento *m*:—*vi* campeggiare.
campaign *n* campagna *f*:—*vi* fare una campagna.

camping *n* campeggio *m*.
campsite *n* campeggio *m*.
can *v aux* potere:—*n* latta *f*; lattina *f*.
canal *n* canale *m*.
cancel *vt* cancellare.
cancellation *n* cancellazione *f*.
cancer *n* cancro *m*.
Cancer *n* Cancro *m*.
candelabra *n* candelabro *m*.
candidate *n* candidato *m*.
candle *n* candela *f*.
candlestick *n* candeliere *m*.
cane *n* canna *f*; bastone *m*.
canine *adj* canino.
canister *n* barattolo *m*.
cannabis *n* canapa *f* indiana.
cannon *n* cannone *m*.
canoe *n* canoa *f*.
canteen *n* mensa *f*.
canvas *n* tela *f*.
canyon *n* canyon *m*.
cap *n* berretto *m*.
capability *n* capacità *f*.
capable *adj* capace.
capacity *n* capacità *f*.
cape *n* capo *m*; cappa *f*; mantello *m*.
capital *n* lettera maiuscola *f*; (city) capitale *f*; (*econ*) capitale *m*.

capitalism n capitalismo m.
capitalist n capitalista m/f.
Capricorn n Capricorno m.
captain n capitano m.
caption n sottotitolo m.
captivity n prigionia f; cattività f.
capture n cattura f.
car n macchina f, automobile f.
caramel n caramello m.
carat n carato m.
caravan n roulotte f.
carbonated adj gassato.
card n biglietto m; tessera f; carta f.
cardboard n cartone m.
card game n gioco m di carte.
cardiac adj cardiaco.
cardinal adj cardinale:—n cardinale m.
care n preoccupazione f; attenzione f: —vi interessarsi.
career n carriera f.
careful adj attento; accurato; prudente.
careless adj distratto; negligente.
caress n carezza f:—vt carezzare.
caretaker n portinaio m.
carnival n carnevale m.
carpet n tappeto m; moquette f.
carriage n carrozza f; vagone m; portamento m.
carriageway n carreggiata f.
carrier n corriere m; (med) portatore; portaerei f; sacchetto m.
carrot n carota f.
carry vt portare; tenere; riportare; approvare.
cart n carretto m.
carton n cartone m.
cartoon n vignetta f; cartone m animato.
carve vt tagliere; incidere; scolpire.
case n valigia f; custodia f; astuccio m;

cassa f; (gr, med) caso m:—**in case** caso mai.
cash n soldi mpl:—vt incassare.
cashier n cassiere m.
cassette n cassetta f.
cassette recorder n registratore m a cassette.
cast vt gettare; lanciare; affidare:—n gesso m; cast m; stampo m; strabismo m.
castle n castello m.
casual adj casuale; informale; saltuario; indifferente.
casualty n vittima f.
cat n gatto m.
catalogue n catalogo m.
catarrh n catarro m.
catastrophe n catastrofe f.
catch vt afferrare; prendere; sorprendere; sentire.
category n categoria f.
cater vi provvedere a.
caterpillar n bruco m.
cathedral n cattedrale f; duomo m.
catholic adj cattolico; ampio.
Catholicism n cattolicesimo m.
cattle n bestiame m.
cauliflower n cavolfiore m.
cause n causa f; motivo m:—vt causare.
caution n attenzione; prudenza f.
cautious adj cauto; prudente.
cave n brocca f; caverna f.
caviar n caviale m.
cease vt, vi cessare.
ceasefire n cessate il fuoco m.
ceiling n soffitto m.
celebrate vt festeggiare.
celebrity n celebrità f.
celibacy n astinenza sassuale f.
cell n cella f.

cellar n cantina f.

cello n violoncello m.

cellular adj cellulare.

cement n cemento m.

cemetery n cimitero m.

censorship n censura f.

centenary n centenario m.

centigrade n centigrado m.

centilitre n centilitro m.

centimetre n centimetro m.

centipede n millepiedi m.

central adj centrale.

century n secolo m.

ceramic adj di ceramica.

cereal n cereale m.

ceremony n cerimonia f.

certain adj certo; sicuro.

certainty n certezza f.

certificate n certificato m.

certify vt certificare; attestare.

cessation n cessazione f.

cesspit n pozzo m nero.

chain n catena f:—vt incatenare.

chair n sedia f, poltrona f:—vt presiedere.

chairman n presidente m.

chalk n gesso m.

challenge n sfida f:—vt sfidare.

chamber n camera f.

chameleon n camaleonte m.

champagne n champagne m.

champion n campione m:—vt difendere.

chance n caso m; occasione f; probabilità f; rischio m:—vt rischiare.

chancellor n cancelliere m.

chandelier n lampadario m.

change vt cambiare; trasformare:—vi mutare:—n cambiamento m; resto m; spiccioli mpl.

channel n canale m:—vt scavare.

chaos n caos m.

chapel n cappella f.

chapter n capitolo m.

character n carattere m; personaggio m.

charcoal n carbone m, carboncino m.

charge vt accusare; (mil) attaccare; far pagare:—n imputazione f; (mil) carica f; tariffa f.

charity n carità f; beneficenza f.

chase vt inseguire:—n inseguimento m; caccia f.

chat vi chiacchierare:—n chiacchierata f.

chauvinism n maschilismo m; sciovinismo m.

chauvinist n maschilista m; sciovinista m/f.

cheap adj a buon prezzo.

cheat vt imbrogliare:—n imbroglione m.

check vt verificare; controllare:—n limitazione f; controllo m; (chess) scacco m.

checkout n cassa f.

cheek n guancia f; (fam) faccia f tosta.

cheerful adj allegro.

cheese n formaggio m.

chef n chef m.

chemical adj chimico:—n prodotto m chimico.

chemist n chimico m; farmacista m/f.

cheque n assegno m.

cherry n ciliegia f.

cherub n cherubino m.

chess n scacchi mpl.

chessboard n scacchiera f.

chessman n pezzo m degli scacchi.

chest n petto m; baule m.

chew vt masticare.

chewing gum n chewing-gum m.

chicken n pollo m.

chickenpox n varicella f.

chief *adj* principale:—*n* capo *m*.

child *n* bambino *m*.

chill *adj* freddo *m*:—*n* freddo:—*vt* mettere in fresco.

chilly *adj* fresco.

chimney *n* camino *m*.

chin *n* mento *m*.

chip *vt* scheggiare:—*n* frammento *m*; patatina *f* fritta; scheggiatura *f*.

chisel *n* scalpello *m*.

chlorine *n* cloro *m*.

chocolate *n* cioccolato *m*.

choice *n* scelta *f*:—*adj* di prima scelta.

choir *n* coro *m*.

choke *vt* soffocare:—*n* aria *f*.

cholera *n* colera *m*.

choose *vt* scegliere.

chop *vt* tagliare; spaccare:—*n* colpo *m* secco; costoletta *f*.

choral *adj* corale.

chord *n* corda *f*.

choreography *n* coreografia *f*.

chorus *n* coro *m*; ritornello *m*.

Christ *n* Cristo *m*.

christen *vt* battezzare.

Christian *adj n* cristiano *m*.

Christianity *n* cristianesimo *m*.

Christmas *n* Natale *m*.

Christmas Eve *n* vigilia *f* di Natale.

chrome *n* metallo *m* cromato.

chronological *adj* cronologico.

chronology *n* cronologia *f*.

chum *n* amicone *m*.

chunk *n* bel pezzo *m*.

church *n* chiesa *f*.

churn *n* zangola *f*:—*vt* agitare.

chutney *n* salsa *f* indiana.

cider *n* sidro *m*.

cigar *n* sigaro *m*.

cigarette *n* sigaretta *f*.

cinema *n* cinema *m*.

circle *n* cerchio *m*:—*vt* accerchiare.

circuit *n* giro *m*; circuito *m*.

circular *adj* circolare:—*n* circolare *f*.

circulation *n* circolazione *f*.

circumference *n* circonferenza *f*.

circus *n* circo *m*.

citizen *n* cittadino *m*.

citrus *n* agrume *m*.

city *n* città *f*.

civic *adj* civico.

civil *adj* civile.

civilian *n* civile *m*, borghese *m*.

civilisation *n* civiltà *f*.

civilise *vt* civilizzare.

claim *vt* rivendicare; pretendere:—*n* pretesa *f*; affermazione *f*.

clam *n* vongola *f*.

clamp *n* morsetto *m*:—*vt* stringere.

clap *vt* applaudire:—*n* battimano *m*.

claret *n* chiaretto *m*.

clarify *vt* chiarire.

clarinet *n* clarinetto *m*.

clarity *n* chiarezza *f*.

clasp *n* gancio *m*:—*vt* afferrare.

class *n* classe *f*, tipo *m*; categoria *f*:— *vt* definire.

classic(al) *adj* classico.

classification *n* classificazione *f*.

classify *vt* classificare.

classroom *n* aula *f*.

claustrophobia *n* claustrofobia *f*.

claw *n* unghia *f*; artiglio *m*:—*vt* graffiare.

clay *n* argilla *f*.

clean *adj* pulito; corretto *m*:—*vt* pulire.

clear *adj* chiaro; trasparente; nitido; sgombero:—*vt* liberare; sgomberare; superare.

clearly *adv* chiaramente.

clergy *n* clero *m*.

clergyman *n* sacerdote *m*; pastore *m*; ministro *m*.

clerk *n* impiegato *m*.

clever *adj* intelligente.

client *n* cliente *m/f*.

cliff *n* scogliera *f*.

climate *n* clima *m*.

climatic *adj* climatico.

climax *n* culmine *m*; orgasmo *m*.

climb *vt*, *vi* salire; arrampicarsi.

clinic *n* clinica *f*.

clip *n* (*cin*) sequenza *f*; fermaglio *m*; moletta *f*: — *vt* tosare; ritagliare.

cloak *n* cappa *f*; mantella *f*.

cloakroom *n* guardaroba *m*.

clock *n* orologio *m*.

clockwise *adv* in senso orario.

clockwork *adj* a molla.

close *vt* chiudere: — *adj adv* vicino: — *n* fine *f*; chiusura *f*.

closed *adj* chiuso.

closely *adv* strettamente.

cloth *n* tessuto *m*, stoffa *f*.

clothe *vt* vestire.

clothes *npl* vestiti *mpl*.

cloud *n* nuvola *f*; nube *f*: — *vt* intorbidare.

clown *n* pagliaccio *m*.

club *n* randello *m*; mazza *f*; bastone *m*; circolo *m*; club *m*; (*cards*) fiori *mpl*.

clue *n* indicazione *f*; indizio *m*.

coach *n* corriera *f*; pullman *m*; carrozza *f*; allenatore *m*: — *vt* allenare.

coal *n* carbone *m*.

coalition *n* coalizione *f*.

coarse *adj* ruvido; volgare.

coast *n* costa *f*; litorale *m*: — *vt* andare in folle.

coastal *adj* costiero.

coaster *n* sottobicchiere *m*.

coastline *n* litorale *m*.

coat *n* capotto *m*; mano *f*: — *vt* ricoprire.

coat hanger *n* gruccia *f*.

coax *vt* convincere.

cocaine *n* cocaina *f*.

cock *n* gallo *m*; rubinetto *m*.

cockerel *n* galletto *m*.

cockroach *n* scarafaggio *m*.

cocktail *n* cocktail *m*.

cocoa *n* cacao *m*.

coconut *n* noce *f* di cocco.

cod *n* merluzzo *m*.

code *n* codice *m*: — *vt* cifrare.

coffee *n* caffè *m*.

coffin *n* barra *f*.

cognac *n* cognac *m*.

coil *n* rotolo *m*; bobina *f*; spirale *f*: — *vt* avvolgere: — *vi* attorcigliarsi.

coin *n* moneta *f*.

coincide *vi* coincidere.

coincidence *n* coincidenza *f*.

cold *adj* freddo; indifferente: — *n* freddo *m*; raffreddore *m*.

cold sore *n* herpes *m*.

coleslaw *n* insalata *f* di cavolo bianco.

colic *n* colica *f*.

collaborate *vt* collaborare.

collaboration *n* collaborazione *f*.

collaborator *n* collaboratore *m*.

collapse *n* crollo *m*; collasso *m*: — *vi* crollare.

collar *n* collo *m*.

colleague *n* collega *m/f*.

collect *vt* raccogliere: — *vi* radunarsi.

collection *n* raccolta *f*.

collector *n* esattore *m*; collezionista *m/f*.

college *n* college *m*; collegio *m*; istituto *m* superiore.

collision *n* scontro *m*.

colloquial *adj* familiare.

colon *n* (*med*) colon *m*; (*gram*) due punti *mpl*.

colonel n colonnello m.

colossal adj colossale.

colour n colore m; ~s bandiera f: — vt colorare; tingere.

column n colonna f.

coma n coma m.

comb n pettine m: — vt pettinare.

combat n lotta f; combattimento m: — vt combattere.

combination n combinazione f.

combine vt combinare.

come vi venire.

comedian n comico m.

comedy n commedia f.

comet n cometa f.

comfort n consolazione f; conforto m: — vt confortare.

comfortable adj confortevole, comodo.

comic(al) adj comico; buffo.

coming adj prossimo; futuro: — n avvento m.

comma n virgola f.

command vt comandare; disporre di: — n ordine m; commando m.

commemorate vt commemorare.

comment n commento m; osservazione f.

commentary n commento m; telecronaca f.

commerce n commercio m.

commercial adj commerciale: — n pubblicità f.

commission n commissione f: — vt commissionare; incaricare.

commit vt commettere.

commitment n impegno m.

committee n comitato m.

common adj comune: — n parco comunale.

communication n comunicazione f.

communion n comunione f.

communism n comunismo m.

communist n comunista m/f.

community n comunità f.

commute vt commutare: — vi fare il pendolare.

compact adj compatto: — n portacipria m.

companion n compagno m.

companionship n cameratismo m.

company n compagnia f; società f.

comparable adj simile.

compare vt paragonare.

comparison n paragone m.

compartment n scompartimento m.

compass n bussola f; compasso m.

compassion n compassione f.

compete vt competere.

competent adj competente.

competition n concorrenza f; concorso m; gara f.

competitive adj competitvo, agonistico; concorrenziale.

complain vi lamentarsi.

complaint n lamentela f.

complement n complemento m.

complete adj completo: — vt completare.

complex adj complesso.

complexion n carnagione f.

compliance n conformità f.

complicate vt complicare.

complication n complicazione f.

compliment n complimento m: — vi complimentarsi.

comply vi attenersi a.

component adj n componente m.

compose vt comporre.

composer n compositore m.

composition n composizione f.

compound n composto m.

comprehend vt capire, comprendere.

comprehensive *adj* esauriente; globale.

compress *vt* comprimere:—*n* compressa *f*.

comprise *vt* comprendere.

compromise *n* compromesso *m*.

compulsory *adj* obbligatorio.

compute *vt* calcolare.

computer *n* elaboratore *m*; computer *m*.

comrade *n* compagno *m*.

concave *adj* concavo.

conceal *vt* nascondere.

conceive *vt* concepire.

concentrate *vt* concentrare.

concentration *n* concentrazione *f*.

concept *n* concetto *m*.

conception *n* concepimento *m*.

concern *vt* riguardare:—*n* preoccupazione *f*; impresa *f*.

concert *n* concerto *m*.

concession *n* concessione *f*.

concise *adj* conciso.

conclude *vt, vi* concludere.

conclusion *n* conclusione *f*.

conclusive *adj* conclusivo.

concrete *n* calcestruzzo *m*:—*adj* concreto; di calcestruzzo *m*.

concussion *n* commozione *f* cerebrale.

condemn *vt* condannare.

condensation *n* condensazione *f*.

condense *vt* condensare.

condiment *n* condimento *m*.

condition *vt* condizionare:—*n* condizione *f*.

conditional *adj* condizionale.

conditioner *n* balsamo *m*.

condom *n* preservativo *m*.

conduct *vt* condurre; (*mus*) dirigere:—*n* condotta *f*.

conductor *n* (*mus*) direttore; (*elect*) conduttore *m*.

cone *n* cono *m*; pigna *f*.

confectioner *n* pasticciere *m*.

confectionery *n* dolciumi *mpl*.

confer *vt* conferire:—*vi* consultarsi.

conference *n* convegno *m*.

confess *vt* confessare.

confession *n* confessione *f*.

confide *vt* confidare.

confidence *n* fiducia *f*.

confident *adj* sicuro.

confidential *adj* riservato.

confirm *vt* confermare; (*relig*) cresimare.

confirmation *n* conferma *f*; (*relig*) cresima *f*.

confirmed *adj* inveterato.

confiscate *vt* confiscare.

confiscation *n* confisca *f*.

conflict *n* conflitto *m*.

conflicting *adj* contraddittorio.

conform *vi* conformarsi.

conformity *n* conformità *f*.

confuse *vt* confondere.

confused *adj* confuso.

confusing *adj* sconcertante.

confusion *n* confusione *f*.

congested *adj* congestionato.

congestion *n* congestione *f*.

congratulate *vt* congratularsi con.

congratulations *npl* congratulazioni *fpl*.

congregation *n* congregazione *f*.

conical *adj* conico.

conifer *n* conifera *f*.

connect *vt* collegare.

connection *n* collegamento *m*.

conquer *vt* conquistare.

conqueror *n* conquistatore *m*.

conquest *n* conquista *f*.

conscience *n* coscienza *f.*

conscious *adj* cosciente.

consecutive *adj* consecutivo.

consent *n* benestare *m:—vi* acconsentire a.

consequence *n* conseguenza *f.*

consequent *adj* conseguente:—*adv* **consequenty** di conseguenza; quindi.

conservation *n* conservazione *f.*

conservationist *n* ambientalista *m/f.*

conservative *adj n* conservatore *m.*

conservatory *n* serra *f*; (*mus*) conservatore *m.*

conserve *vt* conservare.

consider *vt* considerare.

considerable *adj* considerevole.

considerate *adj* premuroso.

consideration *n* considerazione *f.*

considering *conj* visto che:—*adv* tutto sommato.

consign *vt* consegnare.

consignment *n* partita *f.*

consist *vi* consistere.

consistency *n* consistenza *f.*

consistent *adj* coerente:—*adv* **consistently** costantemente.

consolation *n* consolazione *f.*

consommé *n* brodo *m* ristretto.

consonant *n* (*gram*) consonante *f.*

conspiracy *n* congiura *f.*

conspirator *n* cospiratore *m.*

constant *adj* continuo; costante.

constellation *n* costellazione *f.*

constipated *adj* stitico.

constipation *n* stitichezza *f.*

constituency *n* collegio *m* elettorale.

constituent *n* componente *m*; elettore *m.*

constitute *vt* costituire.

constitution *n* costituzione *f.*

constitutional *adj* costituzionale.

construct *vt* costruire.

construction *n* costruzione *f.*

consulate *n* consolato *m.*

consult *vt* consultare.

consume *vt* consumare.

consumer *n* consumatore *m.*

consumption *n* consumo *m*; (*med*) consunzione *f.*

contact *n* contatto:—*vt* contattare.

contact lenses *npl* lenti *fpl* a contatto.

contagious *adj* contagioso.

contain *vt* contenere.

container *n* contenitore *m.*

contemporary *adj* contemporaneo.

contempt *n* disprezzo *m.*

contemptible *adj* spregevole.

contemptuous *adj* sprezzante.

contender *n* contendente *m/f.*

content *adj* contento:—*n* contentezza:—*vt* soddisfare.

contents *npl* contenuto *m.*

contest *vt* contestare:—*n* gara *f*; concorso *m.*

context *n* contesto *m.*

continent *n* continente *m.*

continental *adj* continentale.

continual *adj* continuo.

continue *vt, vi* continuare.

continuity *n* continuità *f.*

continuous *adj* continuo.

contraception *n* contraccezione *f.*

contraceptive *adj n* anticoncezionale *f.*

contract *vt* contrarre:—*n* contratto *m.*

contraction *n* contrazione *f.*

contradict *vt* contraddire.

contradiction *n* contraddizione *f.*

contradictory *adj* contraddittorio.

contrary *adj* contrario:—*n* contrario *m.*

contrast *n* contrasto:—*vi* contrastare.

contribute *vt, vi* contribuire.

contribution *n* offerta *f*; contribuzione *f.*

contrition *n* mortificazione *f.*

control *n* controllo *m*, comando *m*: — *vt* controllare, frenare, dominare.

controversial *adj* controverso.

controversy *n* controversia *f*.

convalesce *vi* fare la convalescenza.

convalescence *n* convalescenza *f*.

convenience *n* comodità *f*.

convenient *adj* comodo.

convent *n* convento *m*.

convention *n* convenzione *f*.

conversation *n* conversazione *f*.

conversion *n* (*relig*) conversione *f*; ristrutturazione *f*.

convert *vt* convertire; ristrutturare: — *n* convertito *m*.

convex *adj* convesso.

convey *vt* trasportare; trasmettere.

convict *vt* riconoscere colpevole: — *n* carcerato *m*.

conviction *n* condanna *f*; convinzione *f*.

convince *vt* convincere.

convincing *adj* convincente.

cook *n* cuoco *m*: — *vt* cuocere; (*fam*) falsificare.

cooker *n* cucina *f*.

cookery *n* cucina *f*.

cool *adj* fresco; calmo.

cooperate *vi* cooperare.

cooperation *n* cooperazione *f*.

cooperative *adj* cooperativo: — *n* cooperativa *f*.

coordinate *vt* coordinare: — *n* coordinata *f*.

coordination *n* coordinazione *f*.

cop *n* poliziotto *m*.

cope *vi* cavarsela.

copier *n* copiatrice *f*.

copper *n* rame; poliziotto *m*.

copy *n* copia: — *vt* imitare, copiare.

copyright *n* diritti *mpl* d'autore.

coral *n* corallo *m*.

coral reef *n* corallino *m*.

cord *n* corda *f*.

cork *n* sughero *m*: — *vt* tappare.

corkscrew *n* cavatappi *m*.

corn *n* grano *m*; frumento *m*; callo *m*.

corner *n* angolo *m*: — *vt* intrappolare.

cornet *n* (*mus*) cornetta *f*; cornetto *m*.

coroner *n* coroner *m*.

corporal *adj* corporale: — *n* caporale *m*.

corporate *adj* collettivo.

corporation *n* società *f*; ente *m*.

correct *vt* correggere: — *adj* corretto.

correction *n* correzione *f*.

correspond *vi* corrispondere.

correspondence *n* corrispondenza *f*.

corridor *n* corridoio *m*.

corrosion *n* corrosione *f*.

corrupt *vt* corrompere: — *adj* corrotto.

corruption *n* corruzione *f*.

cosmetic *adj n* cosmetico *m*.

cosmic *adj* cosmico.

cosmos *n* cosmo *m*.

cost *n* costo: — *vt* costare.

costly *adj* costoso.

costume *n* costume *m*.

cosy *adj* accogliente.

cot *n* lettino *m*.

cottage *n* cottage *m*.

cotton *n* cotone *m*.

cotton wool *n* cotone *m* idrofilo.

couch *n* divano *m*.

couchette *n* cuccetta *f*.

cough *n* tosse *f*: — *vi* tossire.

council *n* consiglio *m*.

councillor *n* consigliere *m*.

counsel *n* consiglio; avvocato *m*.

counsellor *n* consigliere *m*.

count *vt*, *vi* contare: — *n* conteggio *m*; conte *m*.

counter *n* banco *m*: — *vt* rispondere.

counteract *vt* neutralizzare.

counterfeit *vt* contraffare: —*adj* contraffatto.

counterpart *n* equivalente *m/f*.

country *n* paese *m*; campagna *f*.

county *n* contea *f*.

coup *n* colpo *m*.

couple *n* coppia *f*: —*vt* associare.

coupon *n* buono *m*.

courage *n* coraggio *m*.

courageous *adj* coraggioso.

courgette *n* zucchino *m*.

courier *n* corriere *m*.

course *n* corso *m*; rotta *f*; portata *f*: — **of course** naturalmente.

court *n* corte *f*.

courteous *adj* cortese.

courtesy *n* cortesia *f*.

courtroom *n* sala *f* d'udienza.

courtyard *n* cortile *m*.

cousin *n* cugino/a *m*.

cove *n* baia *f*.

cover *n* copertura; coperchio *m*; riparo *m*: —*vt* coprire; nascondere.

cow *n* mucca *f*; vacca *f*.

coward *n* vigliacco *m*.

cowardice *n* vigliaccheria *f*.

cowardly *adj* vigliacco.

cowboy *n* cowboy *m*.

crab *n* granchio *m*.

crack *n* crepa *f*: —*vt* incrinare.

cradle *n* culla *f*.

craft *n* mestiere *m*; arte *f*.

craftsman *n* artigiano *m*.

crafty *adj* furbo.

cram *vt* infilare; stipare: —*vi* affollarsi.

cranberry *n* bacca *f* del muschio.

crane *n* gru *f*.

crash *vt* avere un'incidente con: —*vi* precipitare; scontrarsi: —*n* fracasso *m*; incidente *m*.

crate *n* cassa *f*.

crater *n* cratere *m*.

crawl *vi* andare a gattone; procedere lentamente; adulare.

crayfish *n* gambero *m*.

crayon *n* pastello *m*.

craze *n* mania *f*.

crazy *adj* matto; folle.

cream *n* crema *f*; panna *f*.

creamy *adj* cremoso.

crease *n* piega *f*: —*vt* sgualcire.

create *vt* creare.

creation *n* creazione *f*.

creator *n* creatore *m*.

creature *n* creatura *f*.

crèche *n* asilo *m* nido.

credit *n* credito *m*; onore *m*: —*vt* credere; accreditare.

credit card *n* carta *f* di credito.

creed *n* credo *m*.

creek *n* insenatura *f*.

creep *vi* strisciare; andare furtivamente: —*n* tipo *m* viscido.

cremate *vt* cremare.

cremation *n* cremazione *f*.

crescent *n* mezzaluna *f*; via *f*.

cress *n* crescione *m*.

crest *n* cresta *f*.

crew *n* equipaggio *m*.

crib *n* culla *f*; mangiatoia *f*: —*vt* copiare.

cricket *n* grillo *m*; cricket *m*.

crime *n* criminalità *f*; delitto *m*.

criminal *adj n* criminale *m/f*.

crimson *adj* cremisi.

cripple *n* zoppo *m*; mutilato *m*: —*vt* lasciare mutilato.

crisis *n* crisi *f*.

crisp *adj* croccante; fresco; conciso: — *n* patatina *f*.

criticise *vt* criticare.

crocodile *n* coccodrillo *m*.

crocus *n* croco *m*.

crook *n* bastone *m*; pastolare *m*; (*fam*) ladro *m*.

crop *n* coltivazione *f*; raccolto *m*.

cross *n* croce *f*; incrocio *m*:—*adj* seccato:—*vt* attraversare; sbarrare; incrociare.

crossword *n* cruciverba *m*.

crowd *n* folla *f*:—*vt* affollare.

crown *n* corona *f*; cima *f*:—*vt* incoronare.

crucifix *n* crocefisso *m*.

crucifixion *n* crocifissione *f*.

crucify *vt* crocifiggere.

crude *adj* grezzo; grossolano.

cruel *adj* crudele.

cruelty *n* crudeltà *f*.

crumb *n* briciola *f*.

crust *n* crosta *f*.

cry *vi* gridare; piangere:—*vt* gridare:—*n* grido *m*; pianto *m*.

crystal *n* cristallo *m*.

cub *n* cucciolo *m*.

cube *n* cubo *m*.

cubicle *n* cabina *f*.

cucumber *n* cetriolo *m*.

cuddle *n* abbraccio *m*:—*vt* coccolare.

culminate *vi* culminare.

culmination *n* culmine *m*.

cult *n* culto *m*.

cultivate *vt* coltivare.

cultural *adj* culturale.

culture *n* cultura *f*, (*agric*) coltura *f*.

cup *n* tazza *f*.

cupboard *n* armadio *m*.

curable *adj* guaribile.

curate *n* curato *m*.

cure *n* cura *f*; guarigione *m*:—*vt* guarire; salare; conciare.

curiosity *n* curiosità *f*.

curious *adj* curioso.

curl *n* ricciolo *m*:—*vt* arricciare.

currant *n* uva *f* passa; ribes *m*.

currency *n* moneta *f*; valuta *f* estera.

current *adj* attuale; corrente:—*n* corrente *f*.

currently *adv* attualmente.

curry *n* curry *m*.

curse *vt* maledire:—*vi* bestemmiare:—*n* maledizione *f*.

curt *adj* brusco.

curtain *n* tenda *f*.

curtsy *n* inchino:—*vi* fare un inchino.

curve *vt* curvare:—*vi* curvarsi:—*n* curva *f*.

cushion *n* cuscino *m*:—*vt* attutire.

custard *n* crema *f* pasticcera.

custody *n* custodia *f*; detenzione *f*.

custom *n* costume *m*; consuetudine *f*; abitudine *f*; clientela *f*.

customer *n* cliente *m/f*.

customs *npl* dogana *f*.

customs officer *n* doganiere *m*.

cut *vt* tagliare; ridurre:—*n* taglio *m*; incisione *f*; riduzione *f*.

cute *adj* carino.

cutlery *n* posate *fpl*.

cutlet *n* cotoletta *f*.

cuttlefish *n* seppia *f*.

cyanide *n* cianuro *m*.

cycle *n* bicicletta *f*; ciclo *m*:—*vi* andare in bicicletta.

cycling *n* ciclismo *m*.

cyclist ciclista *m/f*.

cyclone *n* ciclone *m*.

cygnet *n* giovane cigno *m*.

cylinder *n* cilindro *m*.

cymbal *n* cembalo *m*.

cynic(al) *adj* cinico:—*n* cinico *m*.

cynicism *n* cinismo *m*.

cypress *n* cipresso *m*.

cyst *n* cisti *f*.

D

dachshund *n* bassotto *m*.

dad(dy) *n* papà *m*, babbo *m*.

daffodil *n* trombone *m*.

daily *adj* quotidiano; giornaliero.

dairy *n* latteria *f*.

daisy *n* margherita *f*.

dam *n* diga *f*: — *vt* arginare.

damage *n* danno *m*.

dame *n* (*nob*) gentildonna *f*; (*teat*) vecchia signora *f*.

damp *adj* umido: — *n* umidità *f*: — *vt* inumidire.

dance *n* ballo *m*; danza *f*: — *vt* ballare: — *vi* danzare.

dancer *n* ballerino *m*.

dandelion *n* dente *m* di leone.

dandruff *n* forfora *f*.

danger *n* pericolo *m*.

dangerous *adj* pericoloso.

dare *vt* sfidare; *vi* osare: — *n* sfida *f*.

dark *adj* scuro; buio: — *n* buio *m*; oscurità *f*.

darling *adj* caro: — *n* tesoro *m*.

dart *n* dardo *m*; pince *f*: — *vi* lanciarsi.

data *npl* dati *mpl*.

database *n* database *m*.

date *n* data *f*; appuntamento *m*; dattero *m*: — *vt* datare.

dated *adj* antiquato.

daughter *n* figlia *f*.

daughter-in-law *n* nuora *f*.

dawn *n* alba *f*: — *vi* spuntare.

day *n* giorno *m*; giornata *f*; epoca *f*: — **by day** di giorno: — **day by day** giorno per giorno.

daybreak *n* alba *f*.

deacon *n* diacono *m*.

dead *adj* morto; intorpidito; scarico; assoluto.

deaden *vt* attutire.

deadline *n* scadenza *f*.

deaf *adj* sordo.

deal *n* affare *m*; accordo *m*: — *vt* dare le carte.

dear *adj* caro.

death *n* morte *f*.

debate *n* dibattito *m*: — *vt* dibattere.

debit *n* addebito: — *vt* addebitare.

debt *n* debito *m*.

debtor *n* debitore *m*.

debut *n* debutto *m*.

decade *n* decennio *m*.

decadence *n* decadenza *f*.

decadent *adj* decadente.

decaffeinated *adj* decaffeinato.

decanter *n* caraffa *f*.

decay *vi* putrefarsi; deteriorarsi: — *n* decomposizione *f*.

deceit *n* inganno *m*.

deceive *vt* ingannare.

December *n* dicembre *m*.

decency *n* decenza *f*.

decent *adj* decente.

decide *vt* decidere.

deciduous *adj* deciduo.

decimal *adj n* decimale *m*.

decision *n* decisione *f*.

decisive *adj* decisivo.

deckchair *n* sedia *f* a sdraio.

declaration *n* dichiarazione *f*.

declare *vt* dichiarare.

decline *vt vi* declinare: — *n* declino *m*.

decor *n* arredamento *m*.

decorate *vt* decorare.

decrease *vt vi* diminuire: — *n* diminuzione *f*.

decree *n* decreto *m*: — *vt* decretare.

dedicate *vt* dedicare.

dedication *n* dedizione *f*; dedica *f*.

deduce *vt* dedurre.

deduct *vt* dedurre.

deduction *n* deduzione *f*.

deed *n* azione *f*.

deem *vt* giudicare.

deep *adj* profondo.

deepen *vt* approfondire.

deer *n* cervo *m*.

defeat *n* sconfitta *f*: — *vt* sconfiggere.

defect *n* difetto *m*: — *vi* defezionare.

defection *n* defezione *f*.

defective *adj* difettoso.

defector *n* rifugiato *m* politico.

defence *n* difesa *f*.

defenceless *adj* indifeso.

defend *vt* difendere.

defensive *adj* difensivo.

defer *vt* rimandare.

defiance *n* sfida *f*.

defiant *adj* ribelle.

deficiency *n* mancanza *f*; insufficienza *f*.

deficient *adj* mancante.

deficit *n* deficit *m*.

definable *adj* definibile.

define *vt* definire.

definite *adj* definitivo: — **definitely** *adv* certamente.

defy *vt* sfidare.

degenerate *vi* degenerare: — *adj n* degenerato *m*.

degree *n* grado *m*; laurea *f*.

dehydrate *vt* disidratare.

deign *vt* degnarsi.

delay *vt* rimandare: — *vi* ritardare: — *n* ritardo *m*.

delegate *vt* delegare: — *n* delegato *m*.

delegation *n* delegazione *f*.

delete *vt* cancellare.

deliberate *vi* deliberare: — *adj* premeditato: — **deliberately**: — *adv* apposta.

deliberation *n* deliberazione *f*.

delicacy *n* delicatezza *f*; ghiottoneria *f*.

delicate *adj* delicato.

delicatessen *n* salumeria *f*.

delicious *adj* delizioso.

delight *n* delizia *f*: — *vt* riempire di gioia.

delighted *adj* contentissimo.

deliver *vt* consegnare.

delta *n* delta *m*.

delusion *n* illusione *f*.

demand *n* richiesta *f*: — *vt* esigere.

demanding *adj* esigente.

demented *adj* pazzo.

demise *n* decesso *m*.

democracy *n* democrazia *f*.

democrat *n* democratico *m*.

demolish *vt* demolire.

demolition *n* demolizione *f*.

demon *n* demonio *m*.

demonstration *n* manifestazione *f*.

demote *vt* degradare.

denial *n* rifiuto *m*; diniego *m*.

denim *n* tessuto *m* jeans.

dense *adj* denso.

density *n* densità *f*.

dentist *n* dentista *m/f*.

deny *vt* negare; smentire.

depart *vi* partire.

department *n* reparto *m*; sezione *f*.

departure *n* partenza *f*.

depend *vi* dipendere: — **depend on** contare su.

dependable *adj* affidabile.

dependant *n* persona *f* a carico.

depict *vt* rappresentare.

deplore *vt* deplorare.

deploy *vt* schierare.

deport *vt* deportare.

deposit *vt* depositare: — *n* deposito *m*.

depot *n* deposito *m*.

depreciation *n* deprezzamento *m*.

depress *vt* deprimere.

depression *n* depressione *f*.

deprive *vt* privare.

depth *n* profondità *f*.

deputy *n* sostituto *m*.

derive *vt* derivare.

descend *vt* scendere.

descendant *n* discendente *m/f*.

descent *n* discesa *f*.

describe *vt* descrivere.

description *n* descrizione *f*.

desecration *n* profanazione *f*.

desert *n* deserto: — *adj* desertico: — *vt* abbandonare.

deserve *vt* meritare.

design *vt* progettare: — *n* progetto *m*; disegno *m*.

designer *n* disegnatore *m*.

desirable *adj* desiderabile.

desire *n* desiderio *m*: — *vt* desiderare.

desist *vi* desistere.

desk *n* scrivania *f*.

despair *n* disperazione *f*: — *vi* disperare.

desperate *adj* disperato.

despise *vt* disprezzare.

despite *prep* malgrado.

dessert *n* dessert *m*.

destination *n* destinazione *f*.

destiny *n* destino *m*.

destroy *vt* distruggere.

destruction *n* distruzione *f*.

detail *n* particolare *m*; dettaglio *m*: — *vt* dettagliare.

detect *vt* individuare.

detective *n* detective *m*, investigatore *m*.

detention *n* detenzione *f*.

deter *vt* dissuadere.

detergent *n* detersivo *m*.

deteriorate *vi* deteriorarsi.

determination *n* determinazione *f*.

determine *vt* determinare.

deterrent *n* deterrente *m*.

detest *vt* detestare.

detestable *adj* detestabile.

detonate *vi* detonare.

detour *n* deviazione *f*.

devaluation *n* svalutazione *f*.

devastate *vt* devastare.

develop *vt* sviluppare.

development *n* sviluppo *m*.

device *n* congegno *m*; dispositivo *m*.

devil *n* diavolo *m*.

devilish *adj* diabolico.

devious *adj* subdolo.

devise *vt* escogitare.

devolution *n* decentramento *m*.

devolve *vt* devolvere.

devote *vt* dedicare.

devoted *adj* devoto.

devotion *n* devozione *f*.

diabetes *n* diabete *m*.

diabetic *adj n* diabetico *m*.

diagnose *vt* diagnosticare.

diagnosis *n* diagnosi *f*.

diagonal *adj* diagonale.

diagram *n* diagramma *m*.

dial *n* quadrante *m*.

dialect *n* dialetto *m*.

dialogue *n* dialogo *m*.

dialysis n dialisi f.
diameter n diametro m.
diamond n diamante m.
diaphragm n diaframma m.
diarrhoea n diarrea f.
diary n diario m; agenda f.
dice npl dado m.
dictate vt vi dettare.
dictator n dittatore m.
dictionary n dizionario m.
die[1] vi morire.
die[2] n (sing of **dice**) dado m.
diesel n gasolio m.
diet n dieta f; alimentazione f:—vi seguire una dieta.
dietary adj dietetico.
differ vi differire; discordare.
difference n differenza f.
different adj diverso.
difficult adj difficile.
difficulty n difficoltà f.
dig vt vangare; scavare.
digest vt digerire.
digestion n digestione f.
dignity n dignità f.
dilemma n dilemma m.
diligence n diligenza f.
diligent adj diligente.
dilute vt diluire.
dim adj fioco:—vt abbassare.
dimension n dimenzione f.
diminish vt diminuire.
diminished adj ridotto.
diminutive adj minuto.
dimple n fossetta f.
dine vi pranzare.
dinghy n gommone m.
dingy adj squallido.
dinner n cena f.
dinosaur n dinosauro m.
diocese n diocesi f.

dip vt immergere:—vi essere in pendenza:—n nuotatina f.
diploma n diploma m.
diplomacy n diplomazia f.
diplomat n diplomatico m.
direct adj diretto:—vt dirigere a.
direction n direzione f.
directly adj direttamente.
director n dirigente m/f.
directory n elenco m.
dirt n sporco m.
disabled adj invalido.
disadvantage n svantaggio m.
disagree vi essere in disaccordo.
disagreement n discordanza f.
disappear vi scomparire.
disappearance n scomparsa f.
disappoint vt deludere.
disappointed adj deluso.
disappointment n delusione f.
disapprove vi disapprovare.
disaster n disastro m.
disc n disco m.
discard vt scartare.
discern vt discernere.
discharge vt scaricare; licenziare; assolvere:—n scarica f; licenziamento m; secrezione f.
disciple n discepolo m.
discipline n disciplina f:—vt castigare; punire.
disclose vt rivelare.
disco n discoteca f.
discomfort n disaggio m.
disconnect vt staccare.
discord n disaccordo m.
discount n sconto:—vt non badare a.
discover vt scoprire.
discovery n scoperta f.
discreet adj discreto.
discrepancy n discrezione f.

discriminate *vi* distinguere; fare discriminazione tra.

discuss *vt* discutere.

discussion *n* discussione *f.*

disease *n* malattia *f.*

diseased *adj* malato.

disembark *vi* sbarcare.

disgrace *n* vergogna *f;* disonore *m:* — *vt* disonorare.

disgraceful *adj* vergognoso.

disguise *vt* travestire; mascherare: — *n* travestimento *m.*

disgust *n* disgusto *m:* — *vt* disgustare.

dish *n* piatto *m;* pietanza *f:* — *vt* **dish out** servire.

dishonest *adj* disonesto.

dishonesty *n* disonestà *f.*

disillusion *vt* disingannare: — *n* disinganno *m.*

disinfect *vt* disinfettare.

disinfectant *n* disinfettante *m.*

disintegrate *vi* disintegrarsi.

disk *n* dischetto *m.*

dislike *n* antipatia *f:* — *vt* non piacere.

dismal *adj* tetro.

dismantle *vt* smontare.

dismay *n* sgomento: — *vt* sgomentare.

dismiss *vt* congedare; licenziare.

dismissal *n* licenziamento *m;* congedo *m:*

disorder *n* disordine *m.*

dispatch *vt* spedire; inviare: — *n* invio *m,* spedizione *f.*

dispel *vt* dissipare.

dispense *vt* dispensare.

disperse *vt* disperdere.

display *vt* esporre: — *n* mostra *f;* esposizione *f.*

disposable *adj* disponibile

disposal *n* eliminazione *f.*

dispose *vt* disporre.

dispute *n* disputa *f;* controversia *f:* — *vt* contestare; disputarsi.

disrupt *vt* scombussolare.

dissect *vt* sezionare.

dissent *vi* dissentire: — *n* dissenso *m.*

dissolve *vt* sciogliere; dissolvere.

distance *n* distanza *f;* lontananza *f:* — *vt* distanziare.

distant *adj* lontano; distante.

distaste *n* ripugnanza *f.*

distil *vt* distillare.

distinct *adj* distinto.

distinction *n* distinzione *f.*

distinctive *adj* particolare.

distinguish *vt* distinguere.

distinguished *adj* eminente; noto.

distort *vt* distorcere.

distract *vt* distrarre.

distraction *n* distrazione *f.*

distraught *adj* stravolto.

distress *n* angoscia *f;* pericolo *m:* — *vt* addolorare.

distribute *vt* distribuire.

district *n* distretto *m.*

distrust *n* diffidenza *f:* — *vt* diffidare.

distrustful *adj* diffidente.

disturb *vt* disturbare.

ditto *adv* idem.

dive *vi* tuffarsi; lanciarsi: — *n* tuffo *m;* bettola *f.*

diver *n* tuffatore *m.*

diverse *adj* svariato.

divide *vt* dividere.

divided *adj* diviso.

divine *adj* divino: — *vt* intuire.

division *n* divisione *f.*

divorce *n* divorzio *m:* — *vi* divorziare.

dizzy *adj* vertiginoso.

do *vt* fare; compiere; eseguire.

dock *n* (*bot*) romice *m;* bacino *m;* darsena *f;* banco degli imputati: — *vt* mozzare; decurtare:—*vi* entrare in bacino.

doctor *n* dottore *m*; medico *m*:—*vt* adulterare.

document *n* documento *m*:—*vt* documentare.

dog *n* cane *m*:—*vt* perseguitare.

dogma *n* dogma *m*.

dogmatic *adj* dogmatico.

doll *n* bambola *f*.

dollar *n* dollaro *m*.

dome *n* cupola *f*.

dominant *a* dominante.

dominate *vt* dominare.

don *n* docente *m* universitario:—*vi* mettersi.

donate *vt* donare.

donation *n* donazione *f*.

done *adj* fatto; cotto.

donkey *n* asino *m*.

donor *n* donatore *m*.

door *n* porta *f*.

doorbell *n* campanello *m*.

dose *n* dose *f*:—*vt* somministrare; dosare.

dot *n* punto *m*:—*vi* punteggiare.

double *adj* doppio:—*vt* raddoppiare:—*n* sosia *m*.

doubly *adj* doppiamente.

doubt *n* dubbio *m*:—*vt* dubitare di.

doubtful *adj* indeciso.

doubtless *adv* indubbiamente.

dough *n* impasto *m*.

dove *n* colombo *m*.

down *n* (feathers) piume *fpl*:—*adv* giù:— ~ **there** laggiù; ~ **here** quaggiù:—*adj* **upside down** capovolto.

dozen *n* dozzina *f*.

drab *adj* grigio; monotono.

draft *n* abbozzo *m*; tratta *f*:—*vt* abbozzare.

dragon *n* drago *m*.

dragonfly *n* libellula *f*.

drain *vt* prosciugare; drenare; svuotare:—*n* scarico *m*; drenaggio *m*.

drainpipe *n* tubo *m* di scarico.

drama *n* dramma *m*.

drape *vt* drappeggiare.

draper *n* negoziante *m/f* di stoffe.

drastic *adj* drastico.

draught *n* spiffero *m*; sorsata *f*:—*adj* **on draught** alla spina.

draughtsman *n* disegnatore *m* tecnico.

draw *vt* disegnare; tirare; attirare; pareggiare; estrarre:—*n* sorteggio *m*; lotteria *f*; estrazione *f*; pareggio *m*.

drawer *n* cassetto *m*.

drawing *n* disegno *m*.

dream *n* sogno *m*:—*vt vi* sognare.

dress *vt* vestire; condire:—*n* vestito *m*, abito *m*; abbigliamento *m*.

dresser *n* credenza *f*.

dressing table *n* toilette *f*.

drift *n* deriva *f*:—*vi* andare alla deriva.

drill *n* trapano *m*:—*vt* trapanare.

drink *vt vi* bere:—*n* bevanda *f*; bibita *f*.

drip *vi* sgocciolare:—*n* goccia *f*, (*med*) fleboclisi *f*.

drive *vt* spingere; guidare; azionare: —*n* giro *m* in macchina; viale *m*; grinta *f*.

driver *n* guidatore *m*; autista *m/f*; conducente *m/f*.

driving licence *n* patente *m* di guida.

drop *n* goccia *f*; calo *m*:—*vi* lasciar cadere; abbandonare; piantare; calare.

drought *n* siccità *f*.

drown *vt vi* affogare, annegare.

drug *n* medicina *f*; medicinale *f*; droga *f*:—*vt* drogare.

drug addict *n* tossicodipendente *m/f*.

drum n tamburo m:—vt vi tamburellare.

drunk adj n ubriaco m.

dry adj secco:—vt seccare.

dual adj doppio; duplice.

duchess n duchessa f.

duck n anatra f.

due adj pagabile; dovuto; atteso.

duel n duello m.

duet n duetto m.

duke n duca m.

dull adj ottuso.

dumb adj muto.

dump vt scaricare:—n discarica f.

dumpling n gnocco m di pasta.

dunce n somaro m.

dune n duna f.

dungeon n segreta f.

durable adj durevole.

duration n durata f.

during prep durante.

dusk n crepuscolo m.

dust n polvere f:—vt vi spolverare.

dustbin n bidone m.

duster n straccio m.

dutiful adj deferente; rispettoso.

duty n dovere m; tassa f; dazio m.

duvet n piumone m.

dwarf n nano m.

dwell vi dimorare.

dwindle vi diminuire; affievolirsi.

dye vt tingere:—n colorante m; tintura f.

dying adj morente:—n morte f.

dyke n diga f; (fam) lesbica f.

dynamic adj dinamico.

dynamite n dinamite f.

dynamo n dinamo f.

dynasty n dinastia f.

E

each adj ogni; ciascuno:—pn ognuno; ciascuno:—adv ciascuno.

eager adj appassionato.

eagle n aquila f.

ear n orecchio m.

earl n conte m.

early adj primo; precoce; prematuro:—adv presto.

earn vt guadagnare.

earring n orecchino m.

earth n terra f:—vt collegare a terra.

earthquake n terremoto m.

earthworm n lombrico m.

earwig n forbicina f.

ease n disinvoltura f; tranquillità:—vt facilitare; alleviare.

easily adv facilmente.

east n est m; oriente m.

Easter n Pasqua f.

easy adj facile.

eat vt mangiare.

ebony n ebano m.

eccentric adj n eccentrico m.

echo n eco m/f:—vi echeggiare.

eclectic adj eclettico.

eclipse n ecclissi f:—vt eclissare.

ecology n ecologia f.

economic(al) adj economico.

economics npl economia f.

economy n economia f.

ecstasy n estasi f.

eczema n eczema m.

edge *n* orlo *m*; bordo *m*:—*vt* bordare.
edible *adj* mangiabile; commestibile.
edit *vt* dirigere; redigere.
edition *n* edizione *f.*
editor *n* direttore *m.*
educate *vt* istruire; educare.
educated *adj* colto.
education *n* istruzione *f*, educazione *f*,formazione *f.*
eel *n* anguilla *f.*
effect *n* effetto *m.*
effective *adj* efficace.
efficiency *n* efficenza *f.*
effort *n* sforzo *m.*
egg *n* uovo *m.*
ego *n* ego *m.*
egoist *n* egoista *m/f.*
egotism *n* egotismo *m.*
egotist *n* egotista *m/f.*
eight *num* otto.
eighteen *num* diciotto.
eighth *adj n* ottavo *m.*
eighty *num* ottanta.
either *pron*, *adj* l'uno o l'altro:—*adj* entrambi:—*conj* **either ... or** o ... o:—*adv* neanche.
eject *vt* espellere.
ejection *n* espulsione *f.*
eke *vt*:—**eke out** integrare; far bastare.
elaborate *vt* elaborare:—*adj* complicato; ricercato.
elastic *adj n* elastico *m.*
elbow *n* gomito *m.*
elderly *adj* anziano.
eldest *adj* maggiore.
elect *vt* eleggere; decidere:—*adj* futuro.
election *n* elezione *f.*
electoral *adj* elettorale.
electrician *n* elettricista *m/f.*

electricity *n* elettricità *f.*
electronic *adj* elettronico:—**electronics** *npl* elettronica *f.*
elegance *n* eleganza *f.*
elegant *adj* elegante.
element *n* elemento *m.*
elephant *n* elefante *m.*
elevate *vt* elevare.
elevation *n* elevazione *f.*
elevator *n* montacarichi *m.*
eleven *num* undici.
eleventh *adj n* undicesimo *m.*
eligibility *n* eleggibilità *f.*
eligible *adj* eleggibile.
eliminate *vt* eliminare.
elimination *n* eliminazione *f.*
elm *n* olmo *m.*
eloquence *n* eloquenza *f.*
eloquent *adj* eloquente.
else *adv* altro; altrimenti.
elsewhere *adv* altrove.
embankment *n* argine *m.*
embargo *n* embargo *m.*
embark *vt* imbarcarsi.
embarrass *vi* mettere in imbarazzo.
embassy *n* ambasciata *f.*
embitter *vt* inasprire.
emblem *n* emblema *f.*
embody *vt* incarnare.
embrace *vt* abbracciare:—*n* abbraccio *m.*
embroider *vt* ricamare.
embroidery *n* ricamo *m.*
embryo *n* embrione *m.*
emerald *n* smeraldo *m.*
emergency *n* emergenza *f.*
eminent *adj* eminente.
emission *n* emissione *f.*
emit *vt* emettere.
emotion *n* emozione *f.*
emotional *adj* emotivo.

emotive *adj* emotivo; commovente.

emperor *n* imperatore *m*.

emphasis *n* accento *m*; enfasi *f*.

emphasise *vt* sottolineare.

emphatic *adj* enfatico.

empire *n* impero *m*.

employ *vt* impiegare; assumere.

employee *n* dipendente *m/f*.

employer *n* datore *m* di lavoro.

employment *n* occupazione *f*.

empress *n* imperatrice *f*.

emptiness *n* vuoto *m*.

empty *adj* vuoto:—*vt* vuotare.

emu *n* emù *m*.

enamel *n* smalto:—*vt* smaltare.

enchant *vt* incantare.

enclose *vt* allegare; recintare.

enclosure *n* allegato *m*; recinto *m*.

encompass *vt* comprendere.

encore *excl*, *n* bis *m*.

encounter *n* incontro *m*:—*vt* incontrare.

encourage *vt* incoraggiare.

encouragement *n* incoraggiamento *m*.

encroach *vi* usurpare; invadere.

encrust *vt* incrostare.

encyclopedia *n* enciclopedia *f*.

end *n* fine *f*; estremità *f*:—*vi* finire; terminare:—*vt* porre fine a.

endive *n* indivia *f*.

endorse *vt* girare; approvare.

endurance *n* resistenza *f*.

endure *vt* sopportare.

enemy *n* nemico *m*.

energy *n* energia *f*.

enforce *vt* applicare; far rispettare.

engage *vt* assumere; innestare; ingaggiare.

engaged *adj* fidanzato.

engagement *n* fidanzamento *m*; impegno *m*.

engine *n* motore *m*; locomotivo *m*.

engineer *n* ingegnere *m*.

engineering *n* ingegneria *f*.

engrave *vt* incidere.

engraving *n* incisione *f*.

enhance *vt* valorizzare.

enigma *n* enigma *m*.

enjoy *vt* godere; divertirsi.

enlarge *vt* ingrandire; ampliare.

enlist *vt* arruolare.

enlistment *n* arruolamento *m*.

enormous *adj* enorme.

enough *adj* sufficiente:—*adv* abbastanza.

enquire *vt* = **inquire**.

enrol *vt* iscrivere; immatricolare.

enrolment *n* iscrizione *f*; immatricolazione *f*.

enslave *vt* rendere schiavo.

enter *vt* registrare:—*vi* entrare.

enterprise *n* impresa *f*; iniziativa *f*.

enterprising *adj* intraprendente.

entertain *vt* intrattenere.

entertaining *adj* divertente.

enthuse *vi* entusiasmarsi.

enthusiasm *n* entusiasmo *m*.

enthusiastic *adj* appassionato.

entice *vt* allettare.

entire *adj* intero.

entitle *vt* intitolare; dare diritto a.

entity *n* entità *f*.

entrance *n* entrata *f*, ingresso *m*, ammissione *f*:—*vt* mandare in estasi.

entreat *vt* implorare.

entrepreneur *n* imprenditore *m*.

entry *n* ingresso *m*, entrata *f*, accesso *m*; voce *f*.

envelope *n* busta *f*.

enviable *adj* invidiabile.

envious *adj* invidioso.

environment *n* ambiente *m*.

envoy *n* inviato *m*.
envy *n* invidia *f*.
epic *adj* epico:—*n* epopea *f*.
epidemic *n* epidemia *f*.
Epiphany *n* Epifania *f*.
episcopal *adj* episcopale.
episode *n* episodio *m*.
equal *adj* uguale:—*n* pari *m*:—*vt* uguagliare.
equality *n* uguaglianza *f*.
equally *adv* ugualmente.
equator *n* equatore *m*.
equestrian *adj* equestre.
equilibrium *n* equilibrio *m*.
equipment *n* attrezzatura *f*.
equity *n* equità *f*.
equivalent *adj* equivalente.
era *n* era *f*.
eradicate *vt* sradicare.
erase *vt* cancellare.
erect *vt* erigere:—*adj* diritto.
erotic *adj* erotico.
errand *n* commissione *f*.
error *n* errore *m*.
erupt *vi* essere in eruzione; erompere.
eruption *n* eruzione *f*.
escalator *n* scala *f* mobile.
escape *vt* sfuggire a; scampare:—*vi* scappare; evadere:—*n* fuga *f*; evasione *f*.
escort *n* scorta *f*:—*vt* scortare.
especial *adj* particolare.
essay *n* saggio *m*.
essential *adj* essenziale.
establish *vt* stabilire; istituire; fondare.
establishment *n* istituzione *f*; azienda *f*.
estimate *vt* valutare; preventivare:—*n* preventivo *m*; valutazione *f*.
estuary *n* estuario *m*.

etching *n* incisione *f* all'acquaforte.
eternal *adj* eterno.
eternity *n* eternità *f*.
ethics *npl* etica *f*.
ethnic *adj* etnico.
eucalyptus *n* eucalipto *m*.
Eucharist *n* eucarestia *f*.
evacuate *vt* evacuare.
evacuation *n* evacuazione *f*.
evangelical *adj* evangelico.
evangelist *n* evangelista *m*.
evaporate *vi* evaporare.
evaporation *n* evaporazione *f*.
evasion *n* evasione *f*.
evasive *adj* evasivo.
even *adj* liscio; regolare; pari:—*adv* perfino; addirittura; ancora.
evening *n* sera *f*, serata *f*.
evenly *adv* uniformemente.
event *n* avvenimento *m*.
ever *adv* sempre; mai.
every *adj* ogni, tutti:—*pron* **everybody** ognuno, tutti:—**everything** tutto:—*adv* **everywhere** dappertutto.
evidence *n* testimonianza *f*, prove *fpl*.
evident *adj* evidente.
evil *adj* cattivo; malvagio:—*n* male *m*.
evolution *n* evoluzione *f*.
evolve *vt* elaborare:—*vi* evolversi.
exact *adj* esatto:—*vt* esigere.
exactly *adj* esattamente.
exaggerate *vt* esagerare.
exaggeration *n* esagerazione *f*.
examination *n* esame *m*; visita *f*.
examine *vt* esaminare; visitare.
examiner *n* esaminatore *m*.
example *n* esempio *m*.
excavate *vt* scavare.
exceed *vt* eccedere; superare.
excel *vt* superare.

excellent *adj* eccellente.
except *prep* tranne, eccetto.
exception *n* eccezione *f*.
exceptional *adj* eccezionale.
excess *n* eccesso *m*.
exchange *vt* scambiare: — *n* scambio *m*.
excite *vt* eccitare.
exciting *adj* emozionante.
exclaim *vt* esclamare.
exclamation *n* esclamazione *f*.
exclamation mark *n* punto *m* esclamativo.
exclude *vt* escludere.
exclusion *n* esclusione *f*.
exclusive *adj* esclusivo.
excursion *n* gita *f*, escursione *f*.
excuse *vt* scusare; esonerare: — *n* scusa *f*.
execute *vt* giustiziare; eseguire.
execution *n* esecuzione *f*.
executive *adj* esecutivo: — *n* dirigente *m/f*.
exempt *adj* esente: — *vt* esentare.
exercise *n* esercizio *m*: — *vt* esercitare.
exhale *vt vi* espirare.
exhaust *n* gas *m* di scarico: — *vt* stremare; esaurire.
exhaustion *n* esaurimento *m*.
exhibit *vt* esporre: — *n* oggetto *m* esposto; reperto *m*.
exhibition *n* mostra *f*.
exhilarate *vt* rinvigorire.
exile *n* esilio *m*; esule *m/f*: — *vt* esiliare.
exist *vi* esistere.
existence *n* esistenza *f*.
existent *adj* esistente.
exit *n* uscita *f*.
exotic *adj* esotico.
expand *vt* espandere.
expansion *n* espansione *f*.

expect *vt* aspettare; pensare; pretendere; esigere.
expel *vt* espellere.
expenditure *n* dispendio *m*.
expense *n* spesa *f*.
expensive *adj* costoso, caro.
experience *n* esperienza *f*.: — *vt* sperimentare.
experiment *n* esperimento *m*.
expert *adj n* esperto *m*.
expertise *n* perizia *f*.
expire *vi* scadere; spirare.
expiry *n* scadenza *f*.
explain *vt* spiegare.
explanatory *adj* esplicativo.
explicable *adj* spiegabile.
explode *vi* esplodere.
exploit *vt* sfruttare: — *n* impresa *f*.
explore *vt* esplorare.
explorer *n* esploratore *m*.
explosion *n* esplosione *f*.
explosive *adj n* esplosivo *m*.
export *vt* esportare: — *n* esportazione *f*.
expose *vt* esporre; smascherare.
exposure *n* esposizione *f*.
express *vt* esprimere: — *adj* espresso.
expression *n* espressione *f*.
expressive *adj* espressivo.
extend *vt* tendere; prolungare.
extension *n* prolunga *f*; (numero) interno.
extensive *adj* esteso.
extent *n* estensione *f*; portata *f*.
exterior *adj n* esterno *m*.
external *adj* esterno.
extinct *adj* estinto.
extinguisher *n* estintore *m*.
extortion *n* estorsione *f*.
extra *adj* in più; supplementare; maggiore: — *adv* extra; eccezionalmente.
extract *vt* estrarre: — *n* spezzone *m*.

extraordinary *adj* straordinario.
extravagant *adj* dispendioso; stravagante.
extreme *adj* *n* estremo *m*.
extrovert *adj* *n* estroverso *m*.
eye *n* occhio *m*: — *vt* scrutare.

eyeball *n* bulbo *m* oculare.
eyebrow *n* sopracciglio *m*.
eyelash *n* ciglio *m*.
eyelid *n* palpebra *f*.
eyesight *n* vista *f*.
eyewitness *n* testimone *m*/*f* oculare.

F

fabric *n* stoffa *f*, tessuto *m*.
fabulous *adj* favoloso.
face *n* faccia *f*, viso *m*; muso *m*; quadrante *m*: — *vt* affrontare; essere di fronte a.
facet *n* sfaccettatura *f*; aspetto *m*.
fact *n* fatto *m*: — **in fact** in realtà.
factor *n* fattore *m*.
factory *n* fabbrica *f*.
faculty *n* facoltà *f*.
fade *vi* appassire; sbiadirsi.
fail *vi* fallire; mancare: — *vt* bocciare.
failure *n* fallimento *m*; insuccesso *m*.
faint *vi* svenire: — *n* svenimento: — *adj* leggero; fievole; vago.
fair *adj* giusto; imparziale; discreto; chiaro: — *n* fiera *f*.
fairly *adv* in modo imparziale; abbastanza.
fairy *n* fata *f*.
fairy tale *n* fiaba *f*.
faith *n* fede *f*.
faithful *adj* fedele.
fake *n* falso *m*; imitazione *f*. — *adj* fasullo: — *vt* falsificare: — *vi* fingere.
falcon *n* falco *m*.
fall *vi* cadere: — *n* caduta *f*; calo *m*.
fallacy *n* errore *m*.
fallible *adj* fallibile.

fallout *n* pioggia *f* radioattiva.
false *adj* falso.
falsify *vt* falsificare.
fame *n* fama *f*, celebrità *f*.
famed *adj* famoso.
familiar *adj* conosciuto, fami liare.
familiarity *n* familiarità *f*.
family *n* famiglia *f*.
famine *n* carestia *f*.
famous *adj* famoso.
fan *n* ventaglio *m*; ventilatore *m*; fan *m*/*f*, tifoso *m*: — *vt* fare vento.
fancy *n* voglia *f*, capriccio *m*: — *adj* elaborato.
fang *n* zanna *f*.
far *adv* lontano: — **so far** finora: — *adj* lontano; di gran lunga; estremo.
fare *n* tariffa *f*; cibo *m*.
farm *n* fattoria *f*: — *vt* coltivare.
farmer *n* agricoltore *m*.
farming *n* agricoltura *f*.
farmyard *n* aia *f*.
fascism *n* fascismo *m*.
fascist *n* fascista *m*/*f*.
fashion *n* moda *f*; modo *m*: — *vt* modellare.
fast *vi* digiunare: — *adj* veloce, rapido: — *adv* velocemente; saldamente: — *n* digiuno *m*.

fasten *vt* legare.

fat *adj*, *n* grasso *m*.

fatal *adj* fatale; nefasto.

fatality *n* vittima *f*.

fate *n* destino *m*; sorte *f*.

father *n* padre *m*.

father-in-law *n* suocero *m*.

fault *n* difetto *m*; colpa *f*; faglia *f*:—*vt* criticare.

fauna *n* fauna *f*.

favour *n* favore *m*:—*vt* favorire.

favourite *n* preferito *m*.

fax *n* fax *m*.

fear *vi* temere, avere paura di:—*n* paura *f*.

feasible *adj* realizzabile.

feast *n* pranzo *m*; banchetto *m*; festa *f*:—*vi* banchettare.

feat *n* impresa *f*; prodezza *f*.

feather *n* penna *f*, piuma *f*.

feature *n* caratteristica *f*:—*vt* dare risalto a.

February *n* febbraio *m*.

federal *adj* federale.

federation *n* federazione *f*.

fee *n* onorario *m*.

feeble *adj* debole.

feed *vt* nutrire; alimentare; dar da mangiare a:—*n* pappa *f*; mangiata *f*; mangime *m*; foraggio *m*.

feel *vt* tastare, sentire; credere; provare:—*n* tatto *m*; sensazione *f*.

feeling *n* senso *m*, sensazione *f*; sentimento *m*; impressione *f*.

fell *vt* abbattere.

felt *n* feltro *m*.

female *adj*, *n* femmina *f*.

feminine *adj* femminile.

feminist *n* femminista *m*/*f*.

fence *n* recinto *m*:—*vt* recintare.

fencing *n* scherma *f*.

fennel *n* finocchio *m*.

fern *n* felce *f*.

ferocious *adj* feroce.

ferry *n* traghetto *m*.

fertile *adj* fertile.

fertilise *vt* fecondare; (*agric*) fertilizzare.

festival *n* festa *f*, festival *m*.

festive *adj* di festa.

fetch *vt* andare a prendere.

feud *n* faida *f*.

feudal *adj* feudale.

feudalism *n* feudalismo *m*.

fever *n* febbre *f*.

feverish *adj* febbrile.

few *adj* pochi.

fewer *adj* meno.

fewest *adj* il minor numero di.

fiancé *n* fidanzato *m*.

fiancée *n* fidanzata *f*.

fiasco *n* fiasco *m*.

fibber *n* bugiardo *m*.

fibre *n* fibra *f*.

fiction *n* narrativa *f*; finzione *f*.

fiddle *n* violino *m*; imbroglio *m*:—*vi* giocherellare:—*vt* falsificare.

fidelity *n* fedeltà *f*.

fidget *n* persona *f* irrequieta:—*vi* agitarsi.

field *n* campo *m*.

fierce *adj* feroce; accanito.

fierceness *n* ferocia *f*

fiery *adj* infocato.

fifteen *num* quindici.

fifteenth *num* quindicesimo.

fifth *num* quinto.

fifty *num* cinquanta.

fig *n* fico *m*.

fight *vt* combattere; lottare:—*n* combattimento *m*; lotta *f*.

fighting *n* combattimento *m*.

figure 152 **flood**

figure n figura f; cifra f; linea f: — vi figurare.

figurehead n (naut) polena f; figura f rappresentativa.

filament n filamento m.

file n lima f; cartella f; archivio m; fila f: — vt limare; archiviare.

fill vt riempire; òrturare.

fillet n filetto m: — vt disossare.

film n film m, pellicola f; rullino m; strato m sottile: — vi filmare.

filter n filtro m: — vt filtrare.

filth n sudiciume f.

filthy adj sudicio.

fin n pinna f.

final adj ultimo, finale: — n finale f.

finalist n finalista m/f.

finance n finanza f: — vt finanziare.

financial adj finanziario.

financier n finanziatore m.

find vt trovare: — **find out** scoprire: — n scoperta f.

fine adj fine, sottile, fino; ottimo: — excl bene: — n multa f: — vt multare.

finger n dito m: — vt tastare.

fingernail n unghia f.

finish vt, vi finire: — n fine f; traguardo m.

finite adj finito.

fir n abete m.

fire n fuoco m; incendio m; stufa f: — vt sparare; licenziare.

fireplace n caminetto m.

firm adj saldo; fermo; definitivo: — n ditta f.

first adj, n primo m: — adv prima: — **at first** sulle prime; **firstly** innanzi tutto.

first aid n pronto soccorso m.

fish n pesce m: — vi pescare.

fisherman n pescatore m.

fishing n pesca f.

fist n pugno m.

fit n attacco m; accesso m: — adj adatto; in forma: — vt andare bene a.

fitness n idoneità f; forma f.

five num cinque.

fix vt fissare; riparare; sistemare: — n guaio m.

flag n bandiera f: — vi stancarsi.

flagpole n pennone m.

flair n disposizione f naturale.

flake n scaglia f: — vi scrostarsi.

flame n fiamma f: — vi divampare

flamingo n fenicottero m.

flap n linguetta f; ribalta f; panico m: — vt, vi sbattere.

flare vi sfolgorare: — n chiarore m.

flash n lampo m; flash m: — vi lampeggiare.

flask n fiaschetta f; termos m.

flat adj piatto; sgonfio; stonato; categorico; bemolle: — n appartamento m; (auto) gomma f a terra.

flatter vt lusingare.

flautist n flautista m/f.

flavour n gusto m; sapore m.

flaw n difetto m.

flea n pulce f.

flesh n carne f.

flex n filo m: — vt stirare.

flexible adj flessibile.

flick n colpetto m: — vt dare un colpetto.

flight n volo m; rampa f; fuga f.

flint n silice f.

flip vi: — **flip through** sfogliare: — n colpetto m.

flirt n civetta f.

flirtation n flirt m.

flog vt frustare.

flood n inondazione f: — vt inondare: — vi straripare.

floor n pavimento m; piano m: —vt pavimentare; sconcertare.

flop n fiasco m.

floppy adj floscio.

flora n flora f.

flour n farina f.

flow vi fluire: —n corrente f; flusso m.

flower n fiore m: —vi fiorire.

flowerbed n aiuola f.

flowerpot n vaso m da fiori.

fluency n scioltezza f.

fluent adj scorrevole; corrente.

fluid adj, n fluido m.

flush vi arrossire: —vt tirare l'acqua: —n sciacquone m; rossore m.

flute n flauto m.

fly vi volare: —n mosca f.

flying saucer n disco m volante.

foal n puledro m.

focus n fuoco m.

foe n nemico m.

foetus n feto m.

fog n nebbia f.

foggy adj nebbioso.

foliage n fogliame m.

folk n gente f.

folk song n canzone m folk.

follow vt seguire: —**follow up** esaminare a fondo.

font n fonte f battesimale.

food n cibo m.

fool n sciocco m; buffone m: —vt ingannare.

foot n piede m: —**to put one's foot down** imporsi.

football n calcio m.

for prep per; a favore di; da: —**as for me** quanto a me: —**what for?** perché?: —conj poiché.

forbid vt proibire.

force n forza f: —**forces** le forze f armate: —vt forzare.

forceps n forcipe m.

fore n prua f; davanti m: —adj anteriore.

forearm n avambraccio m.

forecast vt prevedere: —n previsione f.

forehead n fronte f.

foreign adj straniero; estero; estraneo.

foremost adj più importante.

forename n nome m.

forerunner n precursore m.

foresee vt prevedere.

foreseeable adj prevedibile.

foresight n previdenza f.

forest n foresta f.

forever adv eternamente, per sempre.

forfeit n penitenza f: —vt perdere.

forge n fornace f: —vt forgiare; contraffare.

forget vt dimenticare.

forgive vt perdonare.

forgo vt rinunciare a.

fork n forchetta f; biforcazione f: —vi biforcarsi: —vt **fork out** sborsare.

formal adj formale.

format n formato m: —vt formattare.

formation n formazione f.

former adj precedente: —pron **the former** il primo.

formula n formula f.

fort n forte m.

fortieth adj, n quarantesimo m.

fortify vt fortificare; rafforzare.

fortnight n quindici giorni mpl.

fortress n fortezza f.

forty adj, n quaranta m.

forward adj in avanti; precoce: —**forwards** adv avanti: —n attaccante m: —vt inoltrare.

fossil *adj n* fossile *m*.

foul *adj* disgustoso: — *n* fallo *m*: — *vt* impestare; sporcare.

found *vt* fondare.

foundation *n* fondazione *f*.

foundry *n* fonderia *f*.

fountain *n* fontana *f*.

four *adj, n* quattro *m*.

fourfold *adj* quadruplo.

fourteen *adj, n* quattordici *m*.

fourteenth *adj, n* quattordicesimo *m*.

fourth *adj, n* quarto *m*.

fraction *n* frazione *f*.

fracture *n* frattura *f*.

fragile *adj* fragile.

frame *n* corporatura *f*; montatura *f*; telaio *m*; cornicia *f*: — *vt* incorniciare.

franc *n* franco *m*.

franchise *n* concessione *f*; franchigia *f*.

frank *adj* franco: — *vt* affrancare.

fraud *n* truffa *f*.

fraught *adj* teso.

fray *n* zuffa *f*: — *vi* consumarsi.

freak *n* eccentrico *m*; capriccio *m*: — *adj* anormale.

freckle *n* lentiggine *f*.

free *adj* libero; gratuito: — *vt* liberare.

freedom *n* libertà *f*.

freely *adv* liberamente.

freeze *vt* gelare, congelare, surgelare: — *vi* gelare, congelarsi: — *n* gelata *f*.

freezer *n* congelatore *m*.

freight *n* nolo *m*.

frenzied *adj* forsennato, frenetico.

frenzy *n* frenesia *f*.

frequency *n* frequenza *f*.

frequent *adj* frequente: — *vt* frequentare.

fresh *adj* fresco; sfacciato: — **fresh water** acqua dolce: — *adv* appena.

freshen *vt, vi* rinfrescare.

freshly *adv* appena.

friction *n* frizione *f*.

Friday *n* venerdì *m*: — **Good Friday** Venerdì *m* Santo.

fridge *n* frigo *m*.

friend *n* amico *m*: — **Society of Friends** Quaccheri *mpl*.

friendship *n* amicizia *f*.

frieze *n* fregio *m*.

fright *n* spavento *m*.

frighten *vt* spaventare.

frightened *adj* spaventato, impaurito.

frightening *adj* spaventoso.

frightful *adj* terribile.

frigid *adj* frigido.

fringe *n* frangia *f*.

frisk *vt* perquisire.

frisky *adj* vispo.

fritter *n* frittella *f*: — *vt* sprecare.

frivolity *n* frivolezza *f*.

frivolous *adj* frivolo.

frizzy *adj* crespo.

frock *n* vestito *m*; tonaca *f*.

frog *n* rana *f*.

frolic *vi* sgambettare.

frolicsome *adj* giocoso.

from prep da; per.

frond *n* fronda *f*.

front *n* davanti *m*; fronte *m*; lungomare *m*; *adj* davanti.

frontal *adj* frontale.

front door *n* porta *f* d'ingresso.

frontier *n* frontiera *f*, confine *m*.

front page *n* prima pagina *f*.

frost *n* brina *f*, gelo *m*.

frostbite *n* congelamento *m*.

frostbitten *adj* congelato.

frosted glass *n* vetro *m* smerigliato.

frosty *adj* gelido; glaciale.

froth *n* schiuma *f*: — *vi* schiumare.

frothy *adj* schiumoso.

frown *vi* aggrottare le sopracciglia: — *n* cipiglio *m*.

frozen *adj* congelato, surgelato.

frugal *adj* frugale.

fruit *n* frutta *f*; frutto *m*.

fruiterer *n* fruttivendolo *m*.

fruitful *adj* fruttifero; fruttuoso.

fruition *n*: — **come to fruition** *vi* realizzarsi.

fruit juice *n* succo *m* di frutta.

fruitless *adj* vano.

fruit salad *n* macedonia *f*.

fruit tree *n* albero *m* da frutto.

frustrate *vt* frustrare.

frustated *adj* frustrato.

frustration *n* frustrazione *f*.

fry *vt* friggere.

frying pan *n* padella *f*.

fuchsia *n* fucsia *f*.

fuck *vt* fottere.

fuel *n* combustibile *m*.

fuel tank *n* serbatoio *m* del carburante.

fugitive *adj*, *n* fuggitivo *m*.

fulcrum *n* fulcro *m*.

fulfil *vt* compiere.

fulfilment *n* compimento *m*; soddisfazione *f*.

full *adj* pieno.

full moon *n* luna *f* piena.

fullness *n* abbondanza *f*; ampiezza *f*.

full-scale *adj* su vasta scala.

full-time *adj* tempo pieno.

fully *adv* completamente.

fulsome *adj* insincero.

fumble *vi* brancolare; andare a tentoni.

fume *n* esalazione *f*: — *vi* emettere fumo (o vapore); essere arrabbiatissimo.

fumigate *vt* suffumicare.

fun *n* divertimento *m*.

function *n* funzione *f*.

functional *adj* funzionale.

fund *n* fondo *m*: — *vt* finanziare.

fundamental *adj* fondamentale.

funeral *n* funerale *m*.

funereal *adj* funereo.

fun fair *n* luna park

fungus *n* muffa *f*.

funnel *n* imbuto *m*.

funny *adj* buffo.

fur *n* pelo *m*.

fur coat *n* pelliccia *f*.

furious *adj* furioso.

furlong *n* 201 metri.

furnace *n* fornace *f*.

furnish *vt* arredare; fornire.

furnishings *npl* mobili *mpl*

furniture *n* mobili *mpl*.

furore *n* scalpore *m*.

furrier *n* pellicciaio *m*.

furrow *n* solco *m*: — *vt* solcare.

furry *adj* peloso.

further *adv* più avanti; oltre: — **further to** con riferimento a: — *adj* ulteriore: — *vt* favorire.

furthermore *adv* inoltre.

furthest *adv*, *adj* più lontano.

furtive *adj* furtivo.

fury *n* furia *f*.

fuse *n* fusibile *m*: — *vt* fondere.

fuse box *n* scatola *f* dei fusibili.

fuselage *n* fusoliera *f*.

fusion *n* fusione *f*.

fuss *adj* agitazione *f*; storie *fpl*.

fussy *adj* pignolo; schizzinoso.

futile *adj* futile.

futility *n* futilità *f*.

future *adj*, *n* futuro *m*.

fuzz *n* peluria *f*; (*fam*) polizia *f*.

fuzzy *adj* crespo; sfocato.

G

gadget *n* aggeggio *m*.

gag *n* bavaglio *m*; gag *f*:—*vt* imbava-
gliare.

gaiety *n* allegria *f*.

gain *n* aumento *m*; guadagno *m*:—*vt*
ottenere; guadagnare; aumentare.

gala *n* festa *f*; gala *m*.

galaxy *n* galassia *f*.

gale *n* bufera *f*.

gallery *n* galleria *f*; tribuna *f*; museo
m.

galley *n* galea *f*.

gallon *n* gallone *m*.

gallop *n* galoppo *m*:—*vi* galoppare.

gamble *vt vi* giocare d'azzardo:—*n*
azzardo *m*.

gambler *n* giocatore *m* d'azzardo.

game *n* gioco *m*; partita *f*; selvaggina
f.

gammon *n* prosciutto *m* affumicato.

gander *n* maschio dell'oca.

gang *n* banda *f*.

gangster *n* gangster *m*.

gap *n* spazio *m*; vuoto *m*; intervallo *m*.

gape *vi* spalancarsi.

garage *n* autorimessa *f*, garage *m*; officina *f*.

garden *n* giardino *m*.

gardening *n* giardinaggio *m*.

garlic *n* aglio *m*.

garment *n* indumento *m*.

garnish *vt* guarnire:—*n* decorazione *f*.

garter *n* giarrettiera *f*.

gas *n* gas *m*.

gate *n* cancello *m*.

gather *vt* radunare; raccogliere; dedurre.

gauge *n* calibro *m*:—*vt* misurare.

gauze *n* garza *f*.

gay *adj* allegro; omosessuale.

gaze *vi* fissare:—*n* sguardo *m*.

gazelle *n* gazzella *f*.

gazette *n* gazzetta *f*.

gear *n* cambio *m*, marcia *f*; attrezzatura *f*.

gel *n* gel *m*.

gelatine *n* gelatina *f*.

gem *n* gemma *f*.

Gemini *n* Gemelli *mpl*.

gender *n* genere *m*.

gene *n* gene *m*.

general *adj* generale:—*adv* in general
generalmente:—*n* generale *m*.

generate *vt* generare.

generation *n* produzione *f*; generazio-
ne *f*.

generator *n* generatore *m*.

generic *adj* generico.

generosity *n* generosità *f*.

generous *adj* generoso.

genetics *npl* genetica *f*.

genial *adj* cordiale.

genitals *npl* genitali *mpl*.

genius *n* genio *m*.

genteel *adj* snob.

gentile *n* gentile *m*.

gentle *adj* dolce.

gentleman *n* signore *m*; gentiluomo *m*.

gently *adv* dolcemente.

gentry *n* piccola nobiltà *f*.

genuine *adj* genuino.
geography *n* geografia *f.*
geology *n* geologia *f.*
geometry *n* geometria *f.*
geranium *n* geranio *m.*
geriatric *adj* geriatrico.
germ *n* microbo *m.*
gesture *n* gesto *m.*
get *vt* ottenere; ricevere; prendere; portare; afferrare:—*vi* arrivare a; diventare; cominciare a; farsi.
ghost *n* fantasma *m.*
giant *n* gigante *m.*
gift *n* dono *m*; regalo *m.*
gifted *adj* dotato.
gigantic *adj* gigantesco.
gin *n* gin *m.*
ginger *n* zenzero *m*; rossiccio *m.*
giraffe *n* giraffa *f.*
girder *n* trave *f.*
girdle *n* busto *m.*
girl *n* ragazza *f.*
girlfriend *n* amica *f.*
giro *n* postagiro *m.*
give *vt vi* dare.
glacier *n* ghiacciaio *m.*
glad *adj* contento; lieto.
gladiator *n* gladiatore *m.*
glamorous *adj* affascinante; seducente.
glamour *n* fascino *m.*
glance *n* occhiata *f:—vi* dare un' occhiata a.
gland *n* ghiandola *f.*
glare *n* bagliore *m:—vi* sfolgorare.
glaring *adj* accecante; palese.
glass *n* vetro *m*; bicchiere *m*; calice *m*:—glasses *npl* occhiali *mpl.*
glassware *n* cristalleria *f.*
glaze *n* smalto *m.*
gleam *n* lucichio *m:—vi* luccicare.

glean *vt* racimolare.
glimmer *n* barlume *m:—vi* baluginare.
glimpse *n* sguardo passeggero:—*vt* intravedere.
gloat *vi* gongolare.
global *adj* globale.
globe *n* globo *m*; mappamondo *m.*
gloom *n* buio *m.*
gloomy *adj* cupo; deprimente.
glorification *n* glorificazione *f.*
glorify *vt* glorificare.
glorious *adj* glorioso.
glory *n* gloria *f.*
gloss *n* glossa *f*; lucentezza *f:—vt* chiosare.
glossary *n* glossario *m.*
glove *n* guanto *m.*
glow *vi* ardere; rosseggiare:—*n* incandescenza *f.*
glue *n* colla *f:—vt* incollare.
glutton *n* ghiottone *m.*
gluttony *n* ghiottoneria *f.*
glycerine *n* glicerina *f.*
gnat *n* zanzara *f.*
go *vi* andare; andarsene; arrivare.
goal *n* goal *m*; scopo *m.*
goat *n* capra *f.*
God *n* Dio *m.*
goddess *n* dea *f.*
godless *adj* empio.
godlike *adj* divino.
goggles *npl* occhiali *mpl.*
gold *n* oro *m.*
golden *adj* d'oro.
golf *n* golf *m.*
gondola *n* gondola *f.*
gondolier *n* gondoliere *m.*
gong *n* gong *m.*
good *adj* buono:—*n* bene *m.*
goodbye *excl* arrivederci.
goodness *n* bontà *f.*

goodwill n buona f volontà; avviamento m.

goose n oca f.

gooseberry n uva f spina.

gorgeous adj sontuoso, splendido.

gorilla n gorilla m.

gory adj sanguinoso.

goshawk n astore m.

gospel n vangelo m.

gossip n pettegolezzi mpl; pettegolo m: — vi chiacchierare.

gothic adj gotico.

goulash n gulasch m.

gourmet n buongustaio m.

govern vt governare.

government n governo m.

governor n governatore m.

grab vt afferrare.

grace n grazia f; garbo m; proroga f: — vt onorare.

graceful adj aggraziato, garbato.

grade n categoria f; voto m; grado m: — vt classificare; graduare.

gradual adj graduale.

graffiti n graffiti mpl.

graft n innesto m; duro lavoro m: — vt innestare.

grammar n grammatica f.

gramophone n grammofono m.

granary n granaio m.

grandfather n nonno m.

grandmother n nonna f.

grandparents npl nonni mpl.

grant vt accordare; ammettere: — n sovvenzione f; borsa f di studio.

granule n granello m.

grape n chicco m d'uva.

grapefruit n pompelmo m.

grapevine n vite f.

graph n grafico m.

graphics npl grafica f.

grasp vt afferrare: — presa f; padronanza f.

grasping adj avido.

grass n erba f.

grasshopper n cavalletta f.

grass snake n biscia f.

grate n grata f: — vt grattare: — vi cigolare.

grateful adj grato.

gratefulness n riconoscenza f.

gratification n soddisfazione f.

gratify vt soddisfare.

gratitude n gratitudine f.

gratuitous adj gratuito.

gratuity n mancia f.

grave n tomba f: — adj grave.

gravel n ghiaia f.

gravestone n lapide f.

graveyard n cimitero m.

gravity n gravità f.

gravy n sugo m dell'arrosto.

grease n grasso m, unto m: — vt ungere, lubrificare.

greasy adj untuoso, unto.

great adj grande; meraviglioso; eminente.

greed n avidità f.

Greek n greco m.

green adj, n verde m: — **greens** npl verdura f.

greengrocer n fruttivendolo m.

greet vt salutare.

greeting n saluto m.

grenadier n granatiere m.

grey adj, n grigio m.

grid n grata f; rete f.

grief n dolore m.

grieve vt addolorare.

grill n griglia f: — vt cuocere alla griglia.

grim adj torvo; macabro.

grimy *adj* sudicio.

grin *n* largo sorriso *m*: — *vi* fare un largo sorriso.

grip *n* presa *f*; borsone *m*: — *vt* stringere.

gripping *adj* appassionante.

grit *n* pietrisco *m*.

groan *vi* gemere: — *n* gemito *m*.

grocer *n* negoziante *m/f* di alimentari.

groin *n* inguine *m*.

groom *n* palafreniere *m*; sposo *m*: — *vt* governare; aver cura di.

groove *n* solco *m*.

grotto *n* grotta *f*.

ground *n* terra *f*, terreno *m*; campo *m*; motivo *m*: — **grounds** fondi *mpl*: — *vi* incagliarsi.

group *n* gruppo *m*; complesso *m*: — *vt* raggruppare.

grow *vi* crescere; aumentare; diventare: — **grow up** diventare grande: — *vt* coltivare; aumentare.

growth *n* crescita *f*; tumore *m*.

grub *n* larva *f*; (*fam*) cibo *m*.

grubby *adj* sudicio.

grudge *n* rancore *m*: — *vt* invidiare; dare a malincuore.

grudgingly *adv* malvolentieri.

gruelling *adj* estenuante.

gruesome *adj* agghiacciante.

grumpy *adj* scorbutico.

grunt *vi* grugnire: — *n* grugnito *m*.

guarantee *n* garanzia *f*: — *vt* garantire.

guard *n* guardia *f*; protezione *f*: — *vt* fare la guardia a.

guardian *n* tutore *m*.

guerrilla *n* guerrigliero *m*.

guess *vt vi* indovinare; supporre: — *n* supposizione *f*.

guest *n* ospite *m/f*, invitato *m*.

guidance *n* guida *f*; consigli *mpl*.

guidebook *n* guida *f*.

guilt *n* colpa *f*, colpevolezza *f*.

guilty *adj* colpevole.

guitar *n* chitarra *f*.

gulf *n* golfo *m*; abisso *m*.

gum *n* gengiva *f*; colla *f*: — *vt* incollare.

gun *n* fucile *m*, pistola *f*, rivoltella *f*.

guru *n* guru *m*.

gush *vi* sgorgare: — *n* ondata *f*.

gust *n* folata *f*, raffica *f*.

gut *n* intestino *m*; budello *m*: — **guts** *npl* budella *f*: — *vt* sventrare.

gutter *n* grondaia *f*, cunetta *f*.

guzzle *vt* ingozzare.

gym(nasium) *n* palestra *f*.

gymnast *n* ginnasta *m/f*.

gymnastic *adj* ginnastico: — *n* **gymnastics** ginnastica *f*.

gynaecologist *n* ginecologo *m*.

gypsy *n* zingaro *m*.

gyrate *vi* roteare.

H

habit *n* abitudine *f*; tonaca *f*.

habitat *n* habitat *m*.

habitual *adj* abituale.

haddock *n* eglefino *m*.

hail *n* grandine *f*: — *vi* grandinare: — *vt* acclamare.

hailstone *n* chicco *m* di grandine.

hair *n* capelli *mpl*; chioma *f*; pelo *m*.

hairbrush n spazzola f per capelli.

haircut n taglio m dei capelli.

hairdresser n parrucchiere m.

hairstyle n acconciatura f.

hake n nasello m.

half n metà f:—adj metà, mezzo.

halibut n ippoglosso m.

hall n entrata f; salone m; villa f.

hallucination n allucinazione f.

halt vt fermare:—vi fermarsi:—n fermata f; sosta f.

halve vt dimezzare.

ham n prosciutto m; radioamatore m.

hamlet n paesino m.

hammer n martello m:—vt martellare.

hammock n amaca f.

hamper n cesto m:—vt ostacolare.

hamster n criceto m.

hand n mano f:—vt passare; consegnare.

handbag n borsa f.

handbrake n freno m a mano.

handkerchief n fazzoletto m.

handle n manico m:—vt maneggiare; trattare.

handshake n stretto m di mano.

handsome adj bello; considerevole.

handwriting n scrittura f.

handy adj sottomano; comodo.

handyman n tuttofare m.

hang vt appendere; impiccare:—vi pendere.

hanger n gruccia f.

hangover n postumi mpl di una sbornia.

hanker vi avere molto desiderio di.

haphazard adj casuale.

happen vi succedere; capitare; accadere.

happily adv tranquillamente.

happiness n felicità f.

happy adj contento, felice.

harass vt assillare.

harbour n porto m:—vt covare.

hard adj duro; rigido; forte; difficile.

hardy adj robusto.

hare n lepre f.

harm n male m; danno m:—vt nuocere a; danneggiare.

harmful adj nocivo.

harmless adj innocuo.

harmonica n armonica f.

harmonise vt vi armonizzare.

harmony n armonia f.

harp n arpa f.

harsh adj severo.

harvest n raccolto m:—vt fare il raccolto di.

hassock n inginocchiatoio m.

haste n fretta f.

hat n cappello m.

hate n odio m:—vt odiare.

hateful adj odioso.

hatred n odio m.

haughty adj superbo.

haul vt trascinare:—n tragitto m; retata f.

haulage n autotrasporto m.

haunt vt frequentare; abitare:—n covo m.

haunted adj abitato dai fantasmi.

have vt avere; possedere; fare; tenere.

haven n rifugio m.

hawk n falco m:—vt vendere per strada.

hay n fieno m.

haystack n pagliaio m.

hazard n rischio m:—vt rischiare.

haze n foschia f.

hazelnut n nocciola f.

hazy adj sfocato.

he pn egli, lui.

head *n* testa *f*; capo *m*:—*vt* essere in testa a.

headache *n* mal *f* di testa; grattacapo *m*.

headmaster *n* preside *m*.

heal *vt* guarire.

health *n* salute *f*.

healthy *adj* sano.

heap *n* mucchio *m*:—*vt* ammucchiare.

hear *vt vi* sentire.

hearing *n* udito *m*.

hearse *n* carro *m* funebre.

heart *n* cuore *m*.

hearth *n* focolare *m*.

heartless *adj* spietato.

heat *n* calore *m*:—*vt* scaldare.

heater *n* stufa *f*.

heathen *n* pagano *m*.

heating *n* riscaldamento *m*.

heave *vt* strascinare a fatica:—*n* sforzo *m*.

heaven *n* cielo *m*, paradiso *m*.

heavily *adv* pesantemente.

heavy *adj* pesante; intenso; opprimente.

Hebrew *adj* ebreo, ebraico:—*n* ebreo *m*, ebraico *m*.

hectic *adj* movimentato.

hedge *n* siepe *f*:—*vi* premunirsi; tergiversare.

hedgehog *n* riccio *m*.

heed *vt* badare a:—*n* attenzione *f*.

heedless *adj* non curante.

heel *n* calcagno *m*; tacco *m*.

hefty *adj* pesante.

height *n* altezza *f*.

heighten *vt* alzare; aumentare:—*vi* aumentare.

heir, heiress *n* erede *m/f*.

heirloom *n* ricordo *m* di famiglia.

helicopter *n* elicottero *m*.

hell *n* inferno *m*.

helmet *n* casco *m*.

help *vt* aiutare; assistere; soccorrere: —*n* aiuto *m*; aiutante *m/f*; soccorso *m*; assistenza *f*.

helper *n* assistente *m/f*.

hem *n* orlo *m*.

hemisphere *n* emisfero *m*.

hen *n* gallina *f*.

hepatitis *n* epatite *f*.

her *pron* la, lei.

herb *n* erba *f* aromatica.

herbaceous *adj* erbaceo.

here *adv* qui, qua.

heresy *n* eresia *f*.

heretic *adj n* eretico *m*.

heritage *n* eredità *f*; patrimonio *m*.

hermit *n* eremita *m*.

hernia *n* ernia *f*.

hero *n* eroe *m*.

heroin *n* eroina *f*.

heroine *n* eroina *f*.

heroism *adj* eroismo.

herring *n* aringa *f*.

hers *poss pn* suo, di lei.

herself *pn* se stessa, lei stessa.

hesitant *adj* esitante.

hesitate *vi* esitare.

hesitation *n* esitazione *f*.

heterosexual *adj n* eterosessuale *m/f*.

hexagon *n* esagono *m*.

hexagonal *adj* esagonale.

hibernate *vi* cadere in letargo.

hiccup *n* singhiozzo *m*:—*vi* avere il singhiozzo.

hidden *adj* nascosto.

hide *vt* nascondere:—*n* cuoio *m*.

hideous *adj* orribile.

hierarchy *n* gerarchia *f*.

hi-fi *n* stereo *m*:—*adj* hi-fi.

high *adj* alto.

hijack *n* dirottamento *m*:—*vt* dirottare.

hike n escursione f a piedi.
hilarious adj spassosissimo.
hill n collina f, colle m.
hilly adj collinoso.
him pron lo, lui.
himself pron lui stesso.
hind adj posteriore:—n cerva f.
hinge n cardine m, cerniera f.
hint n allusione f:—vt alludere.
hip n anca f.
hippopotamus n ippopotamo m.
hire vt noleggiare:—n noleggio m.
his pron suo, di lui.
hiss vt sibilare:—n sibilo m.
historian n storico m.
historic(al) adj storico.
history n storia f.
hit vt colpire; picchiare; sbattere; raggiungere:—n colpo m; successo m.
hitchhike vi fare l'autostop.
hive n alveare m.
hoarse adj rauco.
hoax n scherzo m:—vt ingannare.
hobby n hobby m, passatempo m.
hockey n hockey m.
hoe n zappa f:—vt zappare.
hog n porco m:—vt accaparrarsi.
hold vt tenere; mantenere:—n presa f; stiva f;
hole n buca f, buco m, falla f; tana f:—vt bucare.
holiday n vacanza f.
hollow adj cavo; falso:—n cavità:—vt scavare.
holly n agrifoglio m.
hollyhock n malvone m.
holocaust n olocausto m.
holy adj santo, religioso.
home n casa f; patria f; habitat m; istituto m.
homely adj semplice, familiare.

homoeopath adj n omeopatico m.
homoeopathy n omeopatia f.
homesick n nostalgia f (di casa).
homicide n omicidio m.
homosexual adj n omosessuale m/f.
honest adj onesto.
honey n miele m.
honeymoon n luna f di miele.
honorary adj onorario.
honour n onore m:—vt onorare.
hoof n zoccolo m.
hook n gancio m:—vt agganciare.
hooked adj (naso) aquilino; fanatico.
hooligan n teppista m/f.
hop n saltello m; (bot) luppolo:—vi saltellare.
hope n speranza f:—vi sperare.
hopeful adj fiducioso.
hopeless adj impossibile; incorreggibile; disperato.
horizon n orizzonte m.
horn n corno m; clacson m.
horoscope n oroscopo m.
horrible adj orribile.
horrific adj spaventoso.
horror n orrore m.
horse n cavallo m.
horseradish n raffano m.
hosepipe n tubo m di gomma.
hospital n ospedale m.
hospitality n ospitalità f.
host n ospite m; presentatore m; moltitudine f; (relig) ostia f.
hostage n ostaggio m.
hostel n ostello m.
hostile adj ostile.
hot adj caldo; piccante; focoso.
hotel n albergo m.
hound n segugio m:—vt perseguitare.
hour n ora f.
hourly adv ogni ora.

house n casa f:—vt sistemare, alloggiare.

housewife n casalinga f.

hover vi librarsi.

how adv come.

however adv comunque, tuttavia.

howl vi ululare; urlare; piangere:—n ululato m.

hub n mozzo m; (fig) fulcro m.

hubcap n coprimozzo m.

hue n tinta f.

hug vt abbracciare:—n abbraccio m.

huge adj enorme.

hull n scafo m.

hullo excl ciao!; pronto.

human adj umano:—n essere m umano.

humane adj umanitario.

humanitarian adj umanitario.

humanity n umanità f.

humanly adv umanamente.

humble adj umile:—vt umiliare.

humbly adv umilmente.

humid adj umido.

humidity n umidità f.

humiliate vt umiliare.

humiliation n umiliazione f.

humility n umiltà f.

humorist n umorista m/f.

humorous adj spiritoso.

humour n umorismo m; umore m:—vt accontentare.

hunch n impressione f.

hunchback n gobbo m:—adj **hunch-backed** gobbo.

hundred adj n cento m.

hundredth adj n centesimo m.

hunger n fame f.

hunger strike n sciopero m della fame.

hungrily adv avidamente.

hungry adj affamato:—**be hungry** aver fame.

hunt vi cacciare; cercare:—n caccia f; ricerca f.

hunter n cacciatore m.

hunting n caccia f.

hurdle n ostacolo m.

hurricane n uragano m.

hurried adj frettoloso.

hurry vi affrettarsi, fare in fretta:—n fretta f.

hurt vt ferire; danneggiare; far male:—n ferita f, lesione f.

hurtful adj ingiurioso.

husband n marito m.

hush n silenzio m:—vt quietare.

hut n baracca f.

hutch n gabbia f.

hyacinth n giacinto m.

hybrid adj n ibrido m.

hydrangea n ortensia f.

hydroelectric adj idroelettrico.

hydrofoil n aliscafo m.

hydrogen n idrogeno m.

hyena n iena f.

hygiene n igiene f.

hygienic adj igienico.

hymn n inno m.

hypermarket n ipermercato m.

hyphen n trattino m.

hypnosis n ipnosi f.

hypnotic adj ipnotico.

hypnotism n ipnotismo m.

hypochondria n ipocondria f.

hypochondriac n ipocondriaco m.

hypocrisy n ipocrisia f.

hypocrite n ipocrita m/f.

hypodermic adj ipodermico.

hypothesis n ipotesi f.

hypothetical adj ipotetico.

hysteria n isterismo m.

hysterical adj isterico.

I

I *pron* io
ice *n* ghiaccio *m*; gelato *m*.
iceberg *n* iceberg *m*.
ice cream *n* gelato *m*.
icing *n* glassa *f*.
icon *n* icona *f*.
icy *adj* ghiacciato.
idea *n* idea *f*.
ideal *adj n* ideale *m*.
identical *adj* identico.
identification *n* identificazione *f*.
identify *vt* identificare.
identity *n* identità *f*.
ideology *n* ideologia *f*.
idiosyncrasy *n* peculiarità *f*.
idiot *n* idiota *m/f*.
idiotic *adj* stupido.
idle *adj* pigro; inattivo; infondato.
idol *n* idolo *m*.
if *conj* se, qualora.
ignite *vt* accendere.
ignition *n* iniezione *f*; accensione *f*.
ignoble *adj* ignobile.
ignorance *n* ignoranza *f*.
ignorant *adj* ignorante.
ignore *vt* ignorare; fingere di non vedere.
ill *adj* malato; indisposto; cattivo.
illegal *adj* illegale.
illegality *n* illegalità *f*.
illegible *adj* illeggibile.
illegitimate *adj* illegittimo.
illiterate *adj n* analfabeta *m/f*.
illness *n* malattia *f*.
illogical *adj* illogico.
illuminate *vt* illuminare.

illusion *n* illusione *f*.
illustrate *vt* illustrare.
illustration *n* illustrazione *f*.
illustrative *adj* illustrativo.
illustrious *adj* illustre.
image *n* immagine *f*.
imagination *n* immaginazione *f*.
imagine *vt* immaginare.
imbalance *n* squilibrio *m*.
imitate *vt* imitare.
imitation *n* imitazione *f*.
immaculate *adj* impeccabile.
immaterial *adj* irrilevante.
immature *adj* immaturo.
immediate *adj* immediato.
immense *adj* immenso.
immerse *vt* immergere.
immigrant *n* immigrato *m*.
immigration *n* immigrazione *f*.
imminent *adj* imminente.
immobile *adj* immobile.
immodest *adj* impudico.
immoral *adj* immorale.
immortal *adj* immortale.
immune *adj* immune.
immunise *vt* immunizzare.
immunity *n* immunità *f*.
impartial *adj* imparziale.
impartiality *n* imparzialità *f*.
impatience *n* impazienza *f*.
impatient *adj* impaziente.
impeccable *adj* impeccabile.
impediment *n* impedimento *m*.
impending *adj* incombente.
imperceptible *adj* impercettibile.
imperfect *adj* difettoso; imperfetto.

imperfection n imperfezione f.
imperial adj imperiale.
impermeable adj impermeabile.
impersonal adj impersonale.
impertinence n impertinenza f.
impetus n spinta f.
implant vt innestare.
implement n utensile m: — vt attuare.
implication n implicazione f.
imply vt implicare.
impolite adj scortese.
import vt importare: — n importazione f.
importance n importanza f.
important adj importante.
importation n importazione f.
importer n importatore m.
impose vt imporre.
impossible adj impossibile.
impostor n impostore m.
imprecise adj impreciso.
impregnable adj inattaccabile.
impregnate vt impregnare.
impress vt colpire, fare impressione a.
impression n impressione f.
impressive adj imponente, che colpisce.
imprison vt imprigionare.
imprisonment n reclusione f.
improbable adj improbabile.
improper adj scorretto.
improve vt vi migliorare.
improvement n miglioramento m.
improvise vt vi improvvisare.
impulse n impulso m.
impulsive adj impulsivo.
impurity n impurità f.
in prep in; a.
inability n inabilità f.
inaccurate adj inesatto.

inaction n inazione f.
inactive adj inattivo.
inadequate adj inadeguato.
inaugural adj inaugurale.
inauguration n inaugurazione f.
incalculable adj incalcolabile.
incapable adj incapace.
incapacitate vt rendere incapace.
incapacity n incapacità f.
incendiary adj incendiario.
incense n incenso m: — vt rendere furibondo.
incentive n incentivo m.
inception n principio m.
incest n incesto m.
inch n pollice m.
incidence n incidenza f.
incident n avvenimento m; episodio m.
incidental adj secondario; fortuito.
incinerator n inceneritore m.
inclination n tendenza f; inclinazione f; voglia f.
incline vi tendere a: — n pendenza f.
include vt includere.
including adj incluso.
inclusion n inclusione f.
inclusive adj incluso.
incognito adj in incognito.
income n reddito m.
incomparable adj incomparabile.
incompetence n incompetenza f.
incomplete adj incompleto.
incomprehensible adj incomprensibile.
inconceivable adj inimmaginabile.
inconclusive adj inconcludente.
incongruous adj incongruo.
inconsequential adj insignificante.
inconsiderate adj irriguardoso.
inconsistency n incoerenza f.
inconsistent adj contraddittorio.

inconsolable *adj* inconsolabile.
inconspicuous *adj* poco appariscente.
incontinence *n* incontinenza *f*.
incontinent *adj* incontinente.
inconvenience *n* scomodità *f*: — *vt* incomodare.
incorporate *vt* incorporare.
incorrect *adj* scorretto.
increase *vt vi* aumentare: — *n* aumento *m*.
incredible *adj* incredibile.
increment *n* incremento *m*.
incriminate *vt* incriminare.
incubator *n* incubatrice *f*.
incur *vt* contrarre.
indebted *adj* obbligato.
indecency *n* indecenza *f*.
indecent *adj* indecente.
indecision *n* indecisione *f*.
indecisive *adj* indeciso.
indeed *adv* infatti.
indefinite *adj* indefinito.
indemnity *n* indennizzo *m*.
indent *vt* rientrare dal margine.
independence *n* indipendenza *f*.
independent *adj* indipendente.
index *n* indice *m*.
indicate *vt* indicare: — *vi* mettere la freccia.
indication *n* indicazione *f*.
indifference *n* indifferenza *f*.
indigestion *n* indigestione *f*.
indignant *adj* indignato.
indirect *adj* indiretto.
indiscreet *adj* indiscreto.
indiscretion *n* indiscrezione *f*.
indiscriminate *adj* indiscriminato.
individual *adj* individuale: — *n* individuo *m*.
individuality *n* individualità *f*.
indoors *adv* all'interno.

induction *n* induzione *f*.
indulge *vt* accontentare; viziare.
indulgence *n* indulgenza *f*.
indulgent *adj* indulgente.
industrial *adj* industriale.
industry *n* industria *f*.
inedible *adj* immangiabile.
inefficient *adj* inefficiente.
inequality *n* ineguaglianza *f*.
inert *adj* inerte.
inertia *n* inerzia *f*.
inescapable *adj* inevitabile.
inevitable *adj* inevitabile.
inexpensive *adj* economico.
inexplicable *adj* inspiegabile.
infamous *adj* infame.
infamy *n* infamia *f*.
infancy *n* infanzia *f*.
infant *n* bambino *m*.
infantry *n* fanteria *f*.
infatuated *adj* infatuato.
infatuation *n* infatuazione *f*.
infect *vt* infettare.
infection *n* infezione *f*.
infectious *adj* infettivo.
infer *vt* dedurre.
inference *n* deduzione *f*.
inferior *adj* inferiore.
inferiority *n* inferiorità *f*.
infernal *adj* infernale.
infest *vt* infestare.
infidel *adj n* infedele *m*.
infinite *adj* infinito.
infinitive *n* (*gr*) infinito *m*.
infinity *n* infinità *f*.
infirm *adj* infermo.
inflate *vt* gonfiare.
inflation *n* inflazione *f*.
inflexible *adj* inflessibile.
inflict *vt* infliggere.
influence *n* influenza *f*: — *vt* influenzare.

influential *adj* influente.
influenza *n* influenza *f*.
inform *vt* informare.
informal *adj* informale.
information *n* informazioni *fpl*.
infrequent *adj* infrequente.
infuriate *vt* rendere furioso.
infusion *n* infusione *f*.
ingenuity *adj* ingegnosità *f*.
ingratitude *n* ingratitudine *f*.
ingredient *n* ingrediente *m*.
inhabit *vt* abitare.
inhabitant *n* abitante *m/f*.
inhale *vt* inalare.
inherit *vt* ereditare.
inheritance *n* eredità *f*.
inhibit *vt* inibire.
inhuman *adj* inumano.
inimical *adj* ostile.
inimitable *adj* inimitabile.
initial *adj n* iniziale *f*.
initially *adv* all'inizio.
initiate *vt* iniziare.
initiation *n* iniziazione *f*.
initiative *n* iniziativa *f*.
inject *vt* iniettare.
injection *n* iniezione *f*.
injure *vt* ferire.
injury *n* ferita *f*.
injustice *n* ingiustizia *f*.
ink *n* inchiostro *m*.
inlay *vt* intarsiare.
inlet *n* insenatura *f*.
inn *n* locanda *f*.
innocence *n* innocenza *f*.
innocent *adj* innocente.
innovate *vi* fare innovazioni.
inoculate *vt* inoculare.
inoculation *n* inoculazione *f*.
inoffensive *adj* inoffensivo.
inpatient *n* ricoverato *m*.

input *n* alimentazione *f*; input *m*.
inquest *n* inchiesta *f*.
inquire *vi* indagare; informarsi.
inquiry *n* domanda *f*; inchiesta *f*.
inquisition *n* inquisizione *f*.
inquisitive *adj* curioso.
insane *adj* pazzo, folle.
insanity *n* follia *f*; infermità *f* mentale.
insatiable *adj* insaziabile.
inscribe *vt* incidere.
inscription *n* iscrizione *f*; dedica *f*.
insect *n* insetto *m*.
insecticide *n* insetticida *m*.
insecure *adj* malsicuro.
insecurity *n* insicurezza *f*.
insensitive *adj* insensibile.
inseparable *adj* inseparabile.
insert *vt* inserire:—*n* inserto *m*.
insertion *n* inserzione *f*.
inside *n* interno *m*:—*adv*, *prep* dentro.
inside out *adv* alla rovescia.
insignificant *adj* insignificante.
insincere *adj* insincero.
insincerity *n* insincerità *f*.
insist *vt vi* insistere.
insistence *n* insistenza *f*.
insistent *adj* insistente.
insoluble *adj* insolubile.
insolvency *n* insolvenza *f*.
insolvent *adj* insolvente.
insomnia *n* insonnia *f*.
inspect *vt* controllare.
inspection *n* controllo *m*; ispezione *f*.
instability *n* instabilità *f*.
instal *vt* installare.
installation *n* installazione *f*.
instalment *n* rata *f*; puntata *f*.
instance *n* esempio *m*.
instant *adj* immediato; solubile:—*n* istante *m*.
instantaneous *adj* istantaneo.

instead *adv* invece.
instinct *n* istinto *m*.
institution *n* istituzione *f*.
instruct *vt* istruire.
instruction *n* istruzione *f*.
instructive *adj* istruttivo.
instrument *n* strumento *m*.
insufficient *adj* insufficiente.
insulate *vt* isolare.
insulation *n* isolamento *m*.
insulin *n* insulina *f*.
insult *vt* insultare:—*n* insulto *m*.
insurance *n* assicurazione *f*.
insure *vt* assicurare.
insurer *n* assicuratore *m*.
intact *adj* intatto.
intake *n* immissione *f*.
integral *adj* integrante.
integrate *vt* integrare.
integration *n* integrazione *f*.
intellect *n* intelletto *m*.
intellectual *adj n* intellettuale *m/f*.
intelligence *n* intelligenza *f*.
intelligent *adj* intelligente.
intend *vt* avere intenzione, intendere; destinare.
intense *adj* intenso.
intensive *adj* intensivo.
intent *adj* assorto, intento:—*n* intenzione *f*, intento *m*.
intention *n* intenzione *f*.
intentional *adj* intenzionale.
inter *vt* seppellire.
interaction *n* interazione *f*.
intercept *vt* intercettare.
interest *vt* interessare:—*n* interesse *m*.
interfere *vi* interferire; intromettersi.
interior *adj n* interno *m*.
intermediary *n* intermediario *m*.
intermediate *adj* intermedio.
interment *n* seppellimento *m*.

intermission *n* interruzione *f*.
internal *adj* interno.
international *adj* internazionale.
interpret *vt* interpretare.
interpretation *n* interpretazione *f*.
interpreter *n* interprete *m/f*.
interrelated *adj* correlato.
interrogate *vt* interrogare.
interrogation *n* interrogatorio *m*.
interrogative *adj* interrogativo.
interrupt *vt vi* interrompere.
interruption *n* interruzione *f*.
interval *n* intervallo *m*.
intervene *vi* sopraggiungere; intervenire.
intervention *n* intervento *m*.
interview *n* colloquio *m*, intervista *f*.
interviewer *n* intervistatore *m*.
intestine *n* intestino *m*.
intimacy *n* intimità *f*.
intimate *adj* intimo:—*vt* fare capire.
intimidate *vt* intimidire.
into *prep* in, dentro.
intolerant *adj* intollerante.
intoxicate *vt* inebriare.
intoxication *n* ebbrezza *f*.
intravenous *adj* endovenoso.
intrepid *adj* intrepido.
intricate *adj* intricato.
intrigue *n* intrigo *m*; tresca *f*:—*vt* incuriosire.
introduce *vt* introdurre; presentare.
introduction *n* introduzione *f*; presentazione *f*.
introductory *adj* introduttivo.
intrude *vi* intromettersi.
intruder *n* intruso *m*.
intrusion *n* intrusione *f*.
intuition *n* intuito *m*.
invade *vt* invadere.
invader *n* invasore *m*.

invalid *adj* invalido; nullo:—*n* invalido *m*.

invaluable *adj* inestimabile.

invasion *n* invasione *f*.

invent *vt* inventare.

invention *n* invenzione *f*.

inventive *adj* inventivo.

inventor *n* inventore *m*.

inventory *n* inventario *m*.

invest *vt* investire.

investigate *vt* indagare.

investigation *n* indagine *f*.

investigator *n* investigatore *m*.

investment *n* investimento *m*.

invincible *adj* invincibile.

invisible *adj* invisibile.

invitation *n* invito *m*.

invite *vt* invitare; sollecitare.

invoice *n* fattura *f*:—*vt* fatturare.

involve *vt* coinvolgere.

inward *adj* interiore.

iodine *n* iodio *m*.

iris *n* iride *f*; (*bot*) iris *f*.

iron *n* ferro *m*:—*vt vi* stirare.

ironic *adj* ironico.

irony *n* ironia *f*.

irrational *adj* irragionevole.

irregular *adj* irregolare.

irrelevant *adj* non pertinente.

irresistible *adj* irresistibile.

irresponsible *adj* irresponsabile.

irrigate *vt* irrigare.

irritable *adj* irritabile.

irritate *vt* irritare.

irritating *adj* irritante.

irritation *n* irritazione *f*.

Islam *n* Islam *m*.

island *n* isola *f*.

isle *n* isola *f*.

isolate *vt* isolare.

issue *n* questione *f*; emissione *f*; rilascio *m*; numero *m*; prole *f*:—*vt* rilasciare; pubblicare; emettere.

it *pron* esso.

itch *n* prurito *m*:—*vi* prudere.

item *n* voce *f*, articolo *m*.

itinerary *n* itinerario *m*.

its *poss pn* suo.

itself *pn* si, se stesso.

ivy *n* edera *f*.

J

jackal *n* sciacallo *m*.

jackdaw *n* taccola *f*.

jacket *n* giacca *f*.

jade *n* giada *f*.

jaguar *n* giaguaro *m*.

jail *n* carcere *m*, prigione *f*.

jailer *n* carceriere *m*.

jam *n* marmellata *f*; ingorgo *m*; pasticcio *m*:—*vt* bloccare; ficcare:—*vi* incepparsi.

janitor *n* portinaio *m*; bidello *m*.

January *n* gennaio *m*.

jar *vi* urtare; stonare:—*n* barattolo *m*.

jasmine *n* gelsomino *m*.

jaundice *n* itterizia *f*.

javelin *n* giavellotto *m*.

jaw *n* mascella *f*.

jay *n* ghiandaia *f*.

jazz *n* jazz *m*

jealousy *n* gelosia *f*.

jeans *npl* jeans *mpl*
jelly *n* gelatina *f*.
jelly-fish *n* medusa *f*.
jeopardise *vt* mettere in pericolo.
jersey *n* maglia *f*.
jester *n* buffone *m*.
Jesuit *n* gesuita *f*.
Jesus *n* Gesù *m*.
jet *n* (*min*) giaietto *m*; getto *m*; jet *m*.
jetty *n* molo *m*.
Jew *n* ebreo *m*.
jewel *n* gioiello *m*.
jewellery *n* gioielli *mpl*.
jib *n* (*mar*) braccio *m*.
jig *n* giga *f*.
jigsaw *n* puzzle *m*.
job *n* lavoro *m*; compito *m*; impiego *m*.
jockey *n* fantino *m*.
jogging *n* jogging *m*.
join *vt* unire, collegare:—*vi* unirsi a; confluire:—*n* giuntura *f*.
joint *n* articolazione *f*; pezzo *m* di carne; spinello *m*:—*adj* comune.
joke *n* battuta *f*; scherzo *m*:—*vi* scherzare.
joker *n* burlone *m*; (cards) jolly *m*.
journal *n* periodico *m*.

journey *n* viaggio *m*.
jovial *adj* gioviale.
joy *n* gioia *f*.
jubilee *n* giubileo *m*.
judge *n* giudice *m*:—*vt* giudicare.
judgement *n* giudizio *m*.
judo *n* judo *m*.
jug *n* brocca *f*.
juice *n* succo *m*.
juke-box *n* juke-box *m*.
July *n* luglio *m*.
jump *vt, vi* saltare:—*n* salto *m*.
jumper *n* saltatore *m*; maglione *m*.
jumpy *adj* nervoso.
junction *n* incrocio *m*.
June *n* giugno *m*.
jungle *n* giungla *f*.
juniper *n* (*bot*) ginepro *m*.
junk *n* giunca *f*; cianfrusaglie *fpl*.
jury *n* giuria *f*.
just *adj* giusto:—*adv* proprio; appena; soltanto:—**just as** altrettanto: —**just now** attualmente.
justice *n* giustizia *f*.
justify *vt* giustificare.
juvenile *adj* giovanile; minorile:—*n* minorenne *m/f*.

K

kaleidoscope *n* caleidoscopio *m*.
kangaroo *n* canguro *m*.
karate *n* karatè *m*.
keen *adj* entusiasta; tagliente; acuto.
keep *vt* tenere; mantenere; trattenere; osservare:—*n* vito e alloggio; torrione *m*.
keepsake *n* ricordo *m*.

ketchup *n* ketchup *m*.
kettle *n* bollitore *m*.
key *n* chiave *f*; (*mus*) tasto *m*.
key-ring *n* portachiavi *m*.
kick *vt* dare un calcio:—*n* calcio *m*.
kid *n* capretto *m*; ragazzino *m*:—*vt* scherzare.
kidnap *vt* rapire.

kidney n rene m; (*cul*) rognone m.
kill vt uccidere, ammazzare.
killer n assassino m.
kilo n chilo m.
kilogram n chilogrammo m.
kilometre n chilometro m.
kind adj gentile:—n genere m.
kindergarten n asilo m.
kindness n gentilezza f.
king n re m.
kingdom n regno m.
kiosk n chiosco m.
kiss n bacio m:—vt baciare.
kit n equipaggiamento m.
kitchen n cucina f.
kite n aquilone m.
kitten n gattino m.
knapsack n zaino m.
knead vt impastare.

knee n ginocchio m.
kneel vi inginocchiarsi.
knickers npl mutande fpl.
knife n coltello m.
knight n cavaliere m; (*chess*) cavallo m.
knit vt lavorare a maglia; aggrottare: —**knit one's brow** aggrottare le sopracciglie.
knock vt vi bussare; colpire; ~ **down** demolire:—n colpo m.
knocker n battente m.
knot n nodo m:—vt annodare.
know vt, vi sapere; conoscere; riconoscere.
know-all n sapientone m.
knowledge n conoscenza f; sapere m.
knowledgeable adj informato.
knuckle n nocca f.

L

label n etichetta f.
laboratory n laboratorio m.
labour n lavoro m; mano d'opera f:— adj (*pol*) laburista:—**be in labour** avere le doglie:—vt faticare.
lace n pizzo m; laccio m:—vt allacciare.
lack vt, vi mancare:—n mancanza f.
lad n ragazzo m.
ladder n scala f:—vt smagliare.
lady n signora f.
ladybird n coccinella f.
lager n birra f bionda.
lagoon n laguna f.
lake n lago m.
lamb n agnello m.

lame adj zoppo.
laminated adj laminato.
lamp n lampada f.
lampshade n paralume m.
land n terra f, terreno m; paese m:—vt atterrare; sbarcare.
landing n pianerottolo m; atterraggio m; sbarco m.
landlord n proprietario m.
landmark n punto m di riferimento.
landscape n paesaggio m.
lane n stradina f.
language n linguaggio m, lingua f.
lantern n lanterna f.
lap n grembo m; giro m:—vt lambire:— vi lappare.

lapel *n* risvolto *m*.

lapse *n* svista *f*; intervallo *m*:—*vi* scadere; sgarrare.

larch *n* larice *m*.

larder *n* dispensa *f*.

large *adj* grande:—**at large** in libertà:—*adv* **largely** in gran parte.

lark *n* allodola *f*; scherzo *m*.

larva *n* larva *f*.

laryngitis *n* laringite *f*.

larynx *n* laringe *f*.

laser *n* laser *m*.

lash *n* ciglio *m*; frustata *f*:—*vt* frustare; legare.

lasso *n* lasso *m*.

last *adj* ultimo; scorso:—*adv* **at last** finalmente:—**lastly** in fine:—*vi* durare.

latch *n* chiavistello *m*.

late *adj* in ritardo, tardi; defunto:—*adv* **lately** ultimamente.

lateral *adj* laterale.

latitude *n* latitudine *f*.

latter *adj* ultimo:—**latterly** negli ultimi tempi.

lattice *n* reticolato *m*.

laugh *vi* ridere:—*n* risata *f*.

laughter *n* risata *f*.

launch *vt* varare:—*n* varo; motolancia *f*.

laundrette *n* lavanderia *f* (automatica).

laundry *n* lavanderia *f*; biancheria *f*.

laurel *n* alloro *m*.

lava *n* lava *f*.

lavatory *n* gabinetto *m*.

lavender *n* lavanda *f*.

lavish *adj* sontuoso:—*vt* colmare di.

law *n* legge *f*.

law court *n* tribunale *m*.

lawn *n* prato *m*.

lawnmower *n* tagliaerba *m*.

lawyer *n* avvocato *m*.

laxative *n* lassativo *m*.

lay *vt* porre; posare; stendere; apparecchiare:—*adj* laico.

layer *n* strato *m*.

laze *vi* oziare.

laziness *n* pigrizia *f*.

lazy *adj* pigro.

lead *n* piombo *m*; indizio *m*; ruolo principale; guinzaglio *m*; filo *m*:—*vt* condurre, guidare:—**to be in the lead** essere in testa:—*vi* andare avanti.

leader *n* capo *m*; leader *m*; guida *f*.

leadership *n* direzione *f*.

leading *adj* in testa; preminente:—**leading question** *n* domanda *f* tendenziosa.

leaf *n* (*bot*) foglia *f*; foglio *m*.

leaflet *n* volantino *m*.

league *n* lega *f*; campionato *m*.

leak *n* perdita *f*:—*vt* perdere; divulgare:—*vi* perdere.

lean *vi* pendere; appoggiarsi:—*vt* appoggiare:—*adj* magro.

leap *vi* saltare; balzare:—*n* salto *m*; balzare.

leap year *n* anno *m* bisestile.

learn *vt* imparare.

lease *n* contratto *m* di affitto:—*vt* affittare.

leasehold *n* proprietà *f* in affitto.

least *adj*, *n* minimo *m*:—*adv* meno:—**at least** almeno:—**not in the least** niente affatto.

leather *n* pelle *f*, cuoio *m*.

leave *n* autorizzazione *f*, permesso *m*; licenza *f*:—*vt* lasciare; restare:—*vi* partire.

lecture *n* conferenza *f*:—*vi* tenere una conferenza.

ledge *n* sporgenza *f*; cengia *f*.

leech *n* sanguisuga *f*.

leek n (bot) porro m.

left adj sinistro: —on the left a sinistra.

left-handed adj mancino.

leg n gamba f; coscia f; tappa f.

legacy n eredità f.

legal adj legale: —adv legally legalmente.

legality n legalità f.

legend n leggenda f.

legendary adj leggendario.

legible adj leggibile.

legion n legione f.

legislate vt legiferare.

legislation n legislazione f.

legitimate adj legittimo: —vt legittimare.

leisure n svago m, tempo m libero: —leisurely adj tranquillo.

lemon n limone m.

lemonade n limonata f.

lend vt prestare.

length n lunghezza f; durata: —at length esaurientemente.

lenient adj indulgente.

lens n lente f, obiettivo m.

Lent n quaresima f.

lentil n lenticchia f.

leopard n leopardo m.

leotard n body m.

leper n lebbroso m.

leprosy n lebbra f.

lesbian adj lesbico: —n lesbica f.

less adj, pron meno: —adv meno: —prep meno.

lesser adj minore.

lesson n lezione f.

let vt lasciare; affittare.

lethal adj letale.

letter n lettera f.

lettuce n lattuga f.

leukaemia n leucemia f.

level adj piano, piatto, alla pari: —n livello m: —vt livellare, spianare.

lever n leva f.

liability n responsabilità f.

liable adj responsabile; soggetto: —adv probabile.

liar n bugiardo m.

liberal adj liberale.

liberate vt liberare.

liberation n liberazione f.

liberty n libertà f.

libido n libido f.

Libra n Bilancia f.

library n biblioteca f.

libretto n libretto m.

licence n autorizzazione f; canone m; patente f.

lick vt leccare: —n leccata f.

lid n coperchio m.

lie n menzogna f: —vi mentire; sdraiarsi.

lieutenant n tenente m.

life n vita f.

lifeboat n lancia f di salvataggio.

lifelike adj realistico.

lift vt sollevare; revocare: —n ascensore m; montacarichi mpl; passaggio m.

ligament n legamento m.

light n luce f: —adj chiaro; leggero: —vt accendere; illuminare.

lighthouse n faro m.

lightning n fulmine m.

like adj simile: —prep come: —vt piacere: —I like coffee il caffè mi piace: —he likes chocolates gli piacciono i cioccolatini: —which do you like best? quale preferisci?

likely adj probabile.

lilac n lilla m.

lily n giglio m: —lily of the valley n mughetto m.

limb n arto m.

lime n calce f; tiglio m; laim f, limetta f.

limit n limite m: — vt limitare.

limp vi zoppicare: — n zoppicamento m: — adj floscio, molle.

line n linea f; tratto m; ruga f; lenza f; fila f; riga f: — vt foderare.

linen n lino m.

liner n transatlantico m.

linesman n guardalinee m.

lingerie n biancheria f intima.

linguist n linguista m/f.

linguistics n linguistica f.

link n legame m; anello m: — vt collegare.

linseed n: — **linseed oil** olio di lino.

lint n garza f.

lintel n architrave f.

lion n leone m.

lioness n leonessa f.

lip n labbro m.

liqueur n liquore m.

liquid adj, n liquido m.

liquor n bevande fpl alcoliche.

list n lista f, elenco m: — vt elencare.

listen vi ascoltare.

literature n letteratura f.

litre n litro m.

litter n rifiuti mpl; (zool) cucciolata f.

little adj piccolo: — pron poco: — adv **little by little** gradualmente: — n poco m.

live[1] vi vivere, abitare.

live[2] adj vivo; inesploso.

lively adj vivace.

liver n fegato m.

livid adj furibondo; livido.

living adj vivente, vita.

living room n soggiorno m.

lizard n lucertola f.

load vt caricare: — n carico m.

loaded adj carico.

loaf n pane m: — **meat loaf** polpettone m.

loafer n bighellone m.

loan n prestito m: — vt prestare.

lobster n aragosta f.

local adj locale.

locate vt collocare.

location n posizione f.

lock n serratura f; chiusa f; sterzo m; (of hair) ciocca f: — vt chiudere a chiave.

locker n armadietto m.

locket n medaglione m.

locomotive n locomotiva f.

locust n locusta f.

loft n soffitta f.

log n tronco m.

logbook n (mar) giornale m di bordo; libretto m di circolazione.

logic n logica f.

logical adj logico.

loll vi ciondolare.

loneliness n solitudine f.

lonely adj solitario.

long adj lungo: — vi desiderare.

longitude n longitudine f.

look vt guardare: — vi guardare; sembrare; assomigliare: — **look after** occuparsi di: — **look for** cercare: — n occhiata f; aria f; aspetto m.

looking glass n specchio m.

loop n cappio m.

loose adj allentato; sciolto; staccato; dissoluto.

lord n signore m.

lorry n camion m.

lose vt, vi perdere.

loss n perdita f: — **to be at a loss** non saper come fare.

lost property office n ufficio m oggetti smarriti.

lot *n* destino *m*, sorte *f*; partita *f*; lotto *m*; molto *m*.

lotion *n* lozione *f*.

lottery *n* lotteria *f*.

loud *adj* forte.

loudspeaker *n* altoparlante *m*.

lounge *n* salone *m*, sala *f* d'attesa.

love *n* amore *m*: —**to fall in love** innamorarsi: —*vt* amare, voler bene a.

lover *n* amante *m/f*.

low *adj* basso; scadente; malfamato: —*n* depressione *f*: —*vi* muggire.

lower *adj* inferiore: —*vt* calare; ridurre.

loyal *adj* leale.

lozenge *n* pastiglia *f*; (*geom*) losanga *f*.

lubricant *n* lubrificante *m*.

lubricate *vt* lubrificare.

luck *n* fortuna *f*.

lucky *adj* fortunato.

luggage *n* bagagli *mpl*.

lukewarm *adj* tiepido.

lump *n* zolletta *f*; grumo *m*; nodulo *m*.

lunacy *n* pazzia *f*.

lunatic *adj*, *n* matto *m*, pazzo *m*.

lunch, luncheon *n* pranzo *m*, (seconda) colazione *f*.

lung *n* polmone *m*.

lurk *vi* girare furtivamente.

luscious *adj* appetitoso.

lust *n* libidine *f*: —*vi* desiderare.

lustful *adj* libidinoso.

lusty *adj* vigoroso.

luxurious *adj* lussuoso.

luxury *n* lusso *m*.

lynx *n* lince *f*.

lyrics *npl* parole *fpl*.

M

macaroni *n* maccheroni *mpl*.

mace *n* mazza *f*; macis *m/f*.

machination *n* macchinazione *f*.

machine *n* macchina *f*.

machinery *n* macchinari *mpl*.

mackerel *n* sgombro *m*.

mackintosh *n* impermeabile *m*.

mad *adj* pazzo.

madam *n* signora *f*.

madness *n* follia *f*.

magazine *n* rivista *f*; caricatore *m*.

magic *n* magia *f*: —*adj* magico.

magician *n* mago *m*.

magistrate *n* magistrato *m*.

magnet *n* calamita *f*.

magnetism *n* magnetismo.

magnificent *adj* magnifico.

magnify *vt* ingrandire.

magnifying glass *n* lente *f* d'ingrandimento.

magnitude *n* vastità *f*.

magpie *n* gazza *f*.

maid *n* cameriera *f*.

mail *n* posta *f*: —*vt* spedire (per posta).

main *adj* principale: —*n* conduttura *f* principale.

mainly *adv* principalmente.

maintain *vt* mantenere.

maize *n* granturco *m*.

majesty *n* maestà *f*.

major *adj* maggiore: —*n* (*mil*) maggiore *m*.

majority *n* maggioranza *f.*
make *vt* fare; fabbricare:—*n* marca *f.*
malaise *n* malessere *m.*
malaria *n* malaria *f.*
male *adj* maschile:—*n* maschio *m.*
malfunction *n* cattivo funzionamento *m.*
malice *n* malizia *f.*
malicious *adj* cattivo.
malignant *adj* maligno.
mall *n* viale *m.*
mallet *n* mazzuolo *m.*
mallow *n* (*bot*) malva *f.*
malnutrition *n* denutrizione *f.*
malt *n* malto *m.*
mammal *n* mammifero *m.*
mammoth *n* mammut *m:*—*adj* colossale.
man *n* uomo *m:*—*vt* fornire di uomini.
manage *vt* gestire.
manager *n* gestore *m*, manager *m.*
mane *n* criniera *f.*
mango *n* mango *m.*
manhood *n* virilità *f.*
mania *n* mania *f.*
maniac *n* maniaco *m.*
manicure *n* manicure *f.*
mankind *n* umanità *f.*
manliness *n* virilità *f.*
manly *adj* virile.
man-made *adj* artificiale.
manner *n* maniera *f:*—*npl* **manners** educazione *f.*
manoeuvre *n* manovra *f:*—*vt, vi* manovrare.
mansion *n* palazzo *m.*
manual *adj*, *n* manuale *m.*
manufacture *n* fabbricazione *f:*—*vt* fabbricare.
manufacturer *n* fabbricante *m.*
many *adj* molti, tanti:—**many a time**

più volte:—**how many?** quanti?:—
as many as tanti quanti.
map *n* carta *f*, pianta *f:*—*vt* tracciare una mappa.
maple *n* acero *m.*
marathon *n* maratona *f.*
marble *n* marmo *m*; bilia *f:*—*adj* di marmo.
March *n* marzo *m.*
march *n* marcia *f:*—*vi* marciare.
mare *n* giumenta *f.*
margarine *n* margarina *f.*
margin *n* margine *m.*
marigold *n* calendola *f.*
marina *n* marina *f.*
marine *adj* marino:—*n* marina *f.*
marjoram *n* maggiorana *f.*
mark *n* segno *m*; voto *m*; marco *m:* — *vt* macchiare; segnare; correggere.
market *n* mercato *m.*
marmalade *n* marmellata *f* d'arance.
marquee *n* grande tenda *f.*
marriage *n* matrimonio *m.*
married *adj* sposato, coniugato.
marrow *n* midollo *m*; (*bot*) zucca *f.*
marry *vt* sposare:—*vi* sposarsi.
marshal *n* maresciallo *m:*—*vt* schierare.
marsupial *adj*, *n* marsupiale *m.*
martial *adj* marziale:—**martial law** stato d'assedio.
martyr *n* martire *m.*
marvel *n* meraviglia *f:*—*vi* stupirsi.
marvellous *adj* meraviglioso.
mascot *n* portafortuna *m.*
masculine *adj*, *n* maschile *m.*
mask *n* maschera *f:*—*vt* mascherare.
masochist *n* masochista *m/f.*
masonry *n* muratura *f*; massoneria *f.*
masquerade *n* mascherata *f.*
mass *n* messa *f*, massa *f:*—*vt* adunare:—*vi* adunarsi.

massacre *n* massacro *m*: — *vt* massacrare.

massage *n* massaggio *m*: — *vt* massaggiare.

masseur *n* massaggiatore *m*.

masseuse *n* massaggiatrice *f*.

massive *adj* massiccio.

mast *n* albero *m*.

master *n* padrone *m*; insegnante *m*: — *vt* dominare; (*fig*) impadronirsi.

mat *n* tappetino *m*, zerbino *m*.

match *n* fiammifero *m*; partita *f*, incontro *m*; pari *m/f*, uguale *m/f*: — *vt* uguagliare: — *vi* intonarsi; corrispondere.

mate *n* compagno *m*: — *vt* accoppiare: — *vi* accoppiarsi.

material *adj* materiale: — *n* stoffa *f*, tessuto *m*; materiale *m*.

maternal *adj* materno.

mathematical *adj* matematico.

mathematics *npl* matematica *f*.

maths *npl* matematica *f*.

matt *adj* opaco.

matted *adj* infeltrito.

matter *n* materia *f*; faccenda *f*: — **what is the matter?** cosa c'è?: — **a matter of fact** per la verità: — *vi* importare.

mattress *n* materasso *m*.

mature *adj* maturo: — *vi* maturarsi.

mauve *adj* malva.

maximum *adj*, *n* massimo *m*.

May *n* maggio *m*: — **May Day** il primo maggio *m*: — **mayday** S.O.S. *m*.

maybe *adv* forse, può darsi.

mayonnaise *n* maionese *f*.

mayor *n* sindaco *m*.

maze *n* labirinto *m*.

me *pron* mi, me.

meadow *n* prato *m*.

meal *n* farina *f*; pasto *m*.

mean *adj* avaro; meschino; medio: —

n mezzo *m*: — *npl* **means** mezzi *mpl*: — **in the meantime, meanwhile** nel frattempo: — *vt* significare; intendere.

measles *n* morbillo *m*.

measure *n* misura *f*; provvedimento *m*: — *vt* misurare.

meat *n* carne *f*.

mechanic *n* meccanico *m*.

mechanism *n* meccanismo *m*.

medal *n* medaglia *f*.

media *npl* media *mpl*.

mediate *vi* mediare.

medical *adj* medico: — *n* visita *f* medica.

medicine *n* medicina *f*.

medieval *adj* medievale.

mediocre *adj* mediocre.

meditate *vi* meditare.

meditation *n* meditazione *f*.

Mediterranean *adj* mediterraneo: — *n* Mediterraneo *m*.

medium *n* mezzo *m*: — *adj* medio.

meet *vt* incontrare; soddisfare: — **they met with an accident** hanno avuto un incidente.

meeting *n* incontro *m*; riunione *f*; raduno *m*.

melody *n* melodia *f*.

melon *n* melone *m*.

melt *vt* fondere, sciogliere.

member *n* membro *m*; socio *m*.

memento *n* ricordo *m*.

memo *n* promemoria *m*.

memoir *n* saggio *m* monografico.

memorable *adj* memorabile.

memorandum *n* memorandum *m*.

memorial *n* monumento *m*: — *adj* commemorativo.

memorise *vt* imparare a memoria.

memory *n* memoria *f*; ricordo *m*.

mend *vt* aggiustare, accomodare.

mending *n* rammendo *m*.

meningitis *n* meningite *f*.

menopause *n* menopausa *f*.

menstruation *n* mestruazione *f*.

mental *adj* mentale.

mentality *n* mentalità *f*.

mentally *adv* mentalmente.

mention *n* menzione *f*:—*vt* accennare a.

mentor *n* mentore *m*.

menu *n* menu *m*.

merchant *n* commerciante *m/f*.

mercury *n* mercurio *m*.

mercy *n* misericordia *f*.

mere *adj* puro:—**merely** semplicemente.

merit *n* merito *m*:—*vt* meritare.

mermaid *n* sirena *f*.

merry *adj* allegro; brillo.

mesh *n* maglia *f*.

mesmerise *vt* ipnotizzare.

mess *n* disordine *m*; pasticcio *m*:—*vt* **mess up** scompigliare.

message *n* messaggio *m*.

messenger *n* messaggero *m*.

metal *n* metallo *m*.

metamorphosis *n* metamorfosi *f*.

metaphor *n* metafora *f*.

mete (out) *vi* ripartire.

meteor *n* meteora *f*.

meteorite *n* meteorite *m*.

meteorological *adj* meteorologico.

meter *n* contattore *m*.

method *n* metodo *m*.

metric *adj* metrico.

metropolis *n* metropoli *f*.

metropolitan *adj* metropolitano.

mew *n* miagolio *m*:—*vi* miagolare.

microbe *n* microbo *m*.

microchip *n* chip *m*.

microphone *n* microfono *m*.

microscope *n* microscopio *m*.

microwave *n* microonda *f*.

mid *adj* metà.

middle *adj* centrale:—*n* mezzo *m*, centro *m*.

midge *n* moscerino *m*.

midget *n* nano *m*.

midnight *n* mezzanotte *f*.

midway *adv* a metà strada.

midwife *n* ostetrica *f*.

midwinter *n* pieno inverno *m*.

might *n* forza *f*.

mighty *adj* possente.

migraine *n* emicrania *f*.

migrate *vi* migrare.

mild *adj* mite.

mile *n* miglio *m*.

military *adj* militare:—*n* esercito *m*.

milk *n* latte *m*.

milkshake *n* frappé *m*.

milky *adj* latteo:—**Milky Way** *n* Via Lattea *f*.

mill *n* mulino *m*; fabbrica *f*:—*vt* macinare.

milligramme *n* milligrammo *m*.

millilitre *n* millilitro *m*.

millimetre *n* millimetro *m*.

million *n* milione *m*.

millionaire *n* milionario *m*.

millionth *adj, n* milionesimo *m*.

millipede *n* millepiedi *m*.

millstone *n* macina *f*.

mime *n* mimmo *m*:—*vt, vi* mimare.

mimic *n* imitatore:—*vt* imitare.

mince *vt* tritare:—*n* carne *f* macinata.

mind *n* mente *f*:—*vt* badare a:—*vi* preoccuparsi.

minded *adj*:—**open-minded** di mente aperta.

mine *pron* mio:—*n* miniera *f*; mina *f*:—*vt* estrarre, minare.

miner n minatore m.
mineral adj, n minerale m.
minimal adj minimo.
minimise vt minimizzare.
minimum n minima f.
mining n estrazione f mineraria.
minister n ministro m: — vi assistere.
ministry n ministero m.
mink n visone m.
minor adj minore: — n minorenne m/f.
minority n minoranza f.
mint n (bot) menta; zecca f: — vt coniare.
minus adv meno.
minute n minuto m: — npl **minutes** verbale m.
minute adj minuscolo.
miracle n miracolo m.
mirage n miraggio m.
mirror n specchio m: — vt riflettere.
misbehave vi comportarsi male.
miscalculate vt calcolare male.
miscarry vi abortire.
miscellaneous adj vario.
mischief n birichinata f; cattiveria f.
misconception n idea f sbagliata.
miscreant adj scellerato.
misdemeanour n trasgressione f.
misdirect vt indirizzare male.
miser n avaro m.
miserable adj infelice.
misery n tristezza f, miseria f.
misfortune n disgrazia f.
misinterpret vt interpretare male.
mislay vt smarrire.
mislead vt trarre in inganno.
misogynist n misogino m.
misplace vt smarrire.
Miss n signorina f.
miss vt perdere; mancare; evitare: — n colpo m mancato.

missile n missile m.
mission n missione f.
missionary n missionario m.
mist n foschia f.
mistake vt sbagliare: — vi sbagliarsi: — n errore m, sbaglio m.
Mister n signore m.
mistreat vt maltrattare.
mistress n amante f; padrona f.
misty adj brumoso.
misunderstand vt fraintendere.
misunderstanding n malinteso m.
misuse vt abusare di: — n abuso m.
mix vt mescolare: — n mescolanza f.
mixer n frullatore m; betoniera f.
mixture n mistura f; miscela f.
moan n gemito m: — vi gemere.
mobile adj mobile.
mode n modo m.
model n modello m; indossatore m: — vt modellare; indossare: — vi posare.
moderate adj, n moderato m: — vi attenuarsi.
moderation n moderazione f.
modern adj moderno.
modest adj modesto.
modesty n modestia f.
modify vt modificare.
module n modulo m.
moist adj umido.
moisture n umidità f.
molar n molare m.
mole n neo m; talpa f.
molest vt molestare.
moment n momento m.
momentous adj importante.
monarch n monarca m.
monastery n monastero m.
Monday n lunedì m.
money n denaro m, soldi mpl.
mongol n mongoloide m/f.

mongrel *n* bastardo *m*.

monk *n* monaco *m*.

monkey *n* scimmia *f*.

monopoly *n* monopolio *m*.

monster *n* mostro *m*: —*adj* gigantesco.

monstrous *adj* colossale; mostruoso.

month *n* mese *m*.

monthly *adj* mensile.

monument *n* monumento *m*.

moo *vi* muggire: —*n* muggito *m*.

mood *n* (*gr*) modo *m*; umore *m*.

moon *n* luna *f*.

mop *n* scopa *f* di filacce: —*vt* passare lo straccio.

moped *n* ciclomotore *m*.

moral *adj* morale: —*npl* **morals** principi morali *mpl*.

morale *n* morale *m*.

morality *n* moralità *f*.

morbid *adj* morboso.

more *adj* più, ancora, altro: —**once more** un'altra volta: —*adv* **more and more** sempre di più.

morgue *n* orbitorio *m*.

morning *n* mattina *f*: —**good morning** buon giorno.

morphine *n* morfina *f*.

Morse Code *n* alfabeto *m* Morse.

mortal *adj*, *n* mortale *m*.

mortgage *n* ipoteca *f*: —*vt* ipotecare.

mortuary *n* orbitorio *m*.

mosaic *n* mosaico *m*.

mosque *n* moschea *f*.

mosquito *n* zanzara *f*.

most *adj* più: —*pron* quasi tutto.

mother *n* madre *f*.

mother-in-law *n* suocera *f*.

motif *n* motivo *m*.

motion *n* moto *m*, movimento *m*; cenno *m*.

motive *n* motivo *m*.

motor *n* motore *m*.

motorbike *n* moto *f*.

motorcycle *n* motocicletta *f*.

motorist *n* automobilista *m/f*.

motorway *n* autostrada *f*.

motto *n* motto *m*.

mound *n* mucchio *m*.

mountain *n* montagna *f*.

mountainous *adj* montagnoso.

mourn *vt*, *vi* piangere.

mouse *n* topo *m*.

moustache *n* baffi *mpl*.

mouth *n* bocca *f*.

mouthful *n* boccone *m*.

moveable *adj* movibile.

move: —*vt* spostare, muovere; commuovere: —*vi* traslocare: —*n* mossa *f*, movimento *m*, trasloco *m*.

movement *n* movimento *m*.

movie *n* film *m*.

mow *vt* falciare.

Mrs *n* signora *f*.

much *adj*, *pron*, *adv* molto.

mud *n* fango *m*.

muddle *n* confusione *f*.

muddy *adj* fangoso.

mug *n* tazzone *m*; boccale *m*: —*vt* aggredire.

mugger *n* rapinatore *m*.

multiple *adj*, *n* multiplo *m*.

multiplication *n* moltiplicazione *f*: —**multiplication table** tavola *f* pitagorica.

multiply *vt* moltiplicare.

mummy *n* mummia *f*; mamma *f*.

mumps *npl* orecchioni *mpl*.

municipality *n* comune *m*.

mural *n* pittura *f* murale: —*adj* murale.

murder *n* omicidio *m*, assassinio *m*: —*vt* assassinare.

murderer *n* assassino *m*.

muscle *n* muscolo *m*.
museum *n* museo *m*.
mushroom *n* fungo *m*: — *vi* svilupparsi rapidamente.
music *n* musica *f*.
mussel *n* cozza *f*.
must *mod.aux.vb* dovere: — *n* necessità *f*.
mustard *n* senape *f*.

mutate *vt*, *vi* cambiare, mutare.
mute *adj* muto.
my *pron* mio.
myself *pron* io stesso, me stesso.
mysterious *adj* misterioso.
mystery *n* mistero *m*.
mystique *n* fascino *m*.
myth *n* mito *m*.
mythology *n* mitologia *f*.

N

nail *n* unghia *f*; chiodo *m*: — *vt* inchiodare.
naïve *adj* ingenuo.
naked *adj* nudo.
name *n* nome *m*: — *vt* chiamare; nominare; stabilire.
namely *adv* cioè.
nanny *n* bambinaia *f*.
napkin *n* tovagliolo *m*.
narcissus *n* (bot) narciso *m*.
narrate *vt* narrare.
narrative *adj* narrativo: — *n* narrazione *f*.
narrow *adj* stretto: — *vt* restringere: — *vi* stringersi.
nasal *adj* nasale.
nasturtium *n* nasturzio *m*.
nasty *adj* cattivo, sgradevole, maligno.
nation *n* nazione *f*.
nationalist *adj*, *n* nazionalista *m/f*.
nationality *n* nazionalità *f*.
nationwide *adj* a livello nazionale.
native *adj* natale; indigeno: — *n* nativo *m*; indigeno *m*.
Nativity *n* Natività *f*.
natural *adj* naturale.

naturalist *n* naturalista *m/f*.
nature *n* natura *f*.
naughty *adj* disubbidiente; spinto.
nausea *n* nausea *f*.
nautical *adj* nautico.
navel *n* ombelico *m*.
navy *n* marina *f*.
Nazi *adj*, *n* nazista *m/f*.
near *prep*, *adj*, *adv* vicino: — *vi* avvicinarsi a.
nearly *adv* quasi.
near-sighted *adj* miope.
neat *adj* ordinato.
necessarily *adv* necessariamente.
necessary *adj* necessario.
neck *n* collo *m*.
necklace *n* collana *f*.
nectar *n* nettare *m*.
need *n* bisogno *m*: — *vt* aver bisogno di.
needle *n* ago *m*: — *vt* punzecchiare.
needy *adj* bisognoso.
negative *adj* negativo: — *n* (*gr*) negazione *f*; (*phot*) negativa *f*.
neglect *vt* trascurare.
negligence *n* negligenza *f*.
negotiate *vt* trattare; superare.

Negress *n* negra *f.*
Negro *adj, n* negro *m.*
neighbour *n* vicino *m.*
neither *adv, pron, adj* né: — *conj* nemmeno, neanche, neppure.
neon *n* neon *m.*
nephew *n* nipote *m.*
nerve *n* nervo *m.*
nest *n* nido *m:* — *vi* nidificare.
net *n* rete *f:* — *adj* netto.
netball *n* specie di pallacanestro.
nettle *n* ortica *f.*
neuter *adj (gr)* neutro: — *vt* castrare.
never *adv* mai: — **never mind** non fa niente.
nevertheless *adv* ciò nonostante.
new *adj* nuovo.
news *npl* notizie *fpl;* notiziario *m*, telegiornale *m;* giornale radio *m.*
newsagent *n* giornalaio *m.*
New Year *n* Anno *m* Nuovo: — **New Year's Day** capodanno: — **New Year's Eve** la notte di San Silvestro.
newt *n* tritone *m.*
next *adj* prossimo, successivo: — *adv* dopo: — *n* prossimo *m:* — *prep* accanto a.
nibble *vt* rosicchiare.
nice *adj* simpatico, piacevole, gentile, bello.
nick *n* taglietto *m:* — *vt (sl)* fregare: — **in the nick of time** appena in tempo.
nicotine *n* nicotina *f.*
niece *n* nipote *f.*
night *n* notte *f:* — **by night** di notte: — **good night** buona notte.
nightingale *n* usignolo *m.*
nightmare *n* incubo *m.*
nil *n* nulla *m*, zero *m.*
nimble *adj* agile.
nine *adj, n* nove *m.*

nineteen *adj, n* diciannove.
nineteenth *adj, n* diciannovesimo *m.*
ninetieth *adj, n* novantesimo *m.*
ninth *adj, n* nono *m.*
nipple *n* capezzolo *m.*
nitrogen *n* azoto *m.*
no *adv* no: — *adj* nessuno.
nobility *n* nobiltà *f.*
noble *adj, n* nobile *m.*
nobody *n* nullità *f:* — *pron* nessuno.
noise *n* rumore *m;* fracasso *m.*
nomad *n* nomade *m/f.*
none *pron* nessuno, niente.
nonentity *n* nullità *f.*
nonetheless *adv* nondimeno.
nonsense *n* sciocchezze *fpl.*
noodles *npl* tagliatelle *fpl.*
nook *n* angolino *m.*
noon *n* mezzogiorno *m.*
noose *n* cappio *m.*
nor *conj* né.
normal *adj* normale.
north *n* nord *m*, settentrione *m:* — *adj* nord.
North America *n* America *f* del nord.
north-east *n* nordest *m.*
northerly *adj* del nord; verso nord.
northern *adj* settentrionale, del nord.
north pole *n* polo *m* nord.
northwards *adv* verso nord.
north-west *n* nordovest *m.*
nose *n* naso *m.*
nostalgia *n* nostalgia *f.*
nostril *n* narice *f.*
not *adv* non.
notable *adj* notevole.
notably *adv* notevolmente.
notary *n* notaio *m.*
notation *n* notazione *f.*
notch *n* tacca *f:* — *vt* intaccare.
note *n* nota *f;* biglietto *m:* — *vt* notare.

notebook *n* taccuino *m*.
noted *adj* famoso.
nothing *n* niente:—*adv* per niente: — **think nothing of it!** s'immagini!
notice *n* avviso *m*; preavviso *m*; recensione *f*:—*vt* accorgersi di.
notify *vt* notificare.
notion *n* idea *f*; nozione *f*.
notorious *adj* famigerato.
notwithstanding *conj* benché:—*adv* ciononostante:—*prep* nonostante.
nougat *n* torrone *m*.
nought *n* zero *m*.
noun *n* (*gr*) sostantivo *m*.
nourish *vt* nutrire.
nourishment *n* nutrimento *m*.
novel *n* romanzo:—*adj* originale.
novelist *n* romanziere *m*.
novelty *n* novità *f*.
November *n* novembre *m*.
novice *n* novizio *m*.
now *adv* adesso, ora:—*conj* adesso che, ora che:—**now and then** ogni tanto.
nowhere *adv* in nessun posto.
nuclear *adj* nucleare.
nucleus *adj* nucleo.
nude *adj*, *n* nudo *m*.
nudist *adj*, *n* nudista *m*/*f*.
nuisance *n* seccatura *f*.
numb *adj* intorpidito:—*vt* intorpidire.
number *n* numero *m*:—*vt* numerare; contare.
nun *n* suora *f*.
nurse *n* infermiere *m*.
nursery *n* camera *f* dei bambini; vivaio *m*.
nursery school *n* asilo *m* infantile.
nurture *vt* nutrire.
nut *n* noce (walnut), mandorla (almond), nocciola (hazelnut); (*mech*) dado; (*sl*) matto *m*:—*adj* (*sl*) svitato.
nutmeg *n* noce *f* moscata.
nutritious *adj* nutriente.
nylon *n* nailon *m*.

O

oak *n* quercia *f*.
oasis *n* oasi *f*.
oath *n* giuramento *m*.
obedience *n* ubbidienza *f*.
obedient *adj* ubbidiente.
obese *adj* obeso.
obey *vt* ubbidire.
obituary *n* necrologio *m*.
object *n* oggetto *m*:—*vt* obbiettare.
objective *n* obiettivo *m*.
obligatory *adj* obbligatorio.
oblivion *n* oblio *m*.
oblivious *adj* ignaro.
oblong *adj* oblungo:—*n* rettangolo *m*.
obscene *adj* osceno.
obscure *adj* oscuro:—*vt* oscurare.
observation *n* osservazione *f*.
obsess *vt* ossessionare.
obsolete *adj* obsoleto.
obstacle *n* ostacolo *m*.
obstruct *vt* ostruire.

obstruction n ostruzione f.

obtain vt ottenere.

obtainable adj ottenibile.

obvious adj ovvio.

occasion n occasione f: —vt causare.

occupant, occupier n inquilino m, titolare m.

occur vi accadere.

ocean n oceano m.

ochre n ocra f.

octagon n ottagono m.

October n ottobre m.

octopus n piovra f.

odd adj strano; dispari; scompagnato.

odour n odore m.

oesophagus n esofago m.

of prep di.

off adv distante: —adj spento; andato a male: —prep da.

offence n infrazione f; offesa f.

offend vt offendere.

offensive adj offensivo.

offer n offerta f: —vt offrire.

office n ufficio m.

officer n ufficiale m.

official adj ufficiale: —n funzionario m.

often adv spesso, di frequente.

oil n olio m; petrolio m: —vt oleare.

oil painting n quadro m a olio.

oil well n pozzo m petrolifero.

ointment n unguento m.

OK, okay excl OK, va bene: —vt approvare.

old adj vecchio, anziano; precedente.

oleander n oleandro m.

olive n oliva f: —**olive tree** n ulivo m.

omelette n frittata f.

omen n auspicio m.

omit vt omettere.

on prep su, a, sopra: —adj acceso.

once adv una volta: —**at once** subito:

—**all at once** improvvisamente: —**once more** ancora una volta.

one adj uno, unico, stesso: —n uno m.

oneself pron se stesso.

onion n cipolla f.

only adj solo: —adv solo, solamente.

onset n inizio m.

onwards adj in avanti.

opal n opale m/f

opaque adj opaco.

open adj aperto: —vt aprire.

opening n apertura f; inaugurazione f; breccia f.

opera n opera f.

operation n operazione f; intervento m.

opinion n opinione f, parere m.

opium n oppio m.

opponent n avversario m.

opportunity n occasione f.

oppose vt opporsi a.

opposite adv di fronte: —n contrario m.

oppression n oppressione f.

opt vi optare.

optician n ottico m.

optimist n ottimista m/f.

optional adj facoltativo.

or conj o.

oral adj, n orale m: —**orally** adv oralmente.

orange n arancia f: —**orange tree** n arancio m; (colour) arancio m.

orangeade n aranciata f.

orchard n frutteto m.

orchestra n orchestra f.

orchid n orchidea f.

order n ordine m, comando m, ordinazione f: —vt, vi ordinare.

ordinary adj abituale, comune; ordinario.

ore n minerale m grezzo.

oregano *n* origano *m.*
organ *n* organo *m.*
organic(al) *adj* organico.
organise *vt* organizzare.
organism *n* organismo *m.*
orgasm *n* orgasmo *m.*
oriental *adj* orientale.
origin *n* origine *f.*
original *adj*, *n* originale *m.*
ornament *n* ornamento *m*: — *vt* ornare.
orphan *adj*, *n* orfano *m.*
orthodox *adj* ortodosso.
osprey *n* falco *m* pescatore.
osteopathy *n* osteopatia *f.*
other *adj*, *pron* altro: — *adv* other than diversamente.
otter *n* lontra *f.*
ouch! *excl* ahi!
ought *vb aux* dovere.
ounce *n* oncia *f.*
our *adj* nostro.
ourselves *pron* noi stessi.
out *adv* fuori: — *prep* fuori, per, da, senza.
outback *n* entroterra *m.*
outcast *n* emarginato *m.*
outing *n* escursione *f.*
outlaw *n* fuorilegge *m*: — *vt* bandire.
outlay *n* spesa *f.*
outlet *n* scarico *m*; punto *m* vendita.
outline *n* contorno *m*: — *vt* riassumere.
outlook *n* veduta *f.*
outrage *n* atrocità *f*; sdegno *m*: — *vt* oltraggiare.
outrageous *adj* scandaloso.
outset *n* inizio *m.*

outshine *vt* eclissare.
outside *n* esterno *m*: — *adj* esterno: — *adv* fuori: — *prep* fuori di.
outskirts *npl* periferia *f.*
outspoken *adj* franco.
outward *adj* esterno; apparente.
ovary *n* ovaia *f.*
oven *n* forno *m.*
over *prep* su, sopra: — *adj* finito: — over again da capo: — over and over mille volte.
overall *adj* generale: — *npl* overalls tuta *f.*
overboard *adv* fuori bordo.
overcharge *vt* far pagare troppo.
overcoat *n* soprabito *m.*
overestimate *vt* sopravvalutare.
overjoyed *adj* felicissimo.
overleaf *adv* a tergo.
overseas *adv* all'estero: — *adj* estero.
oversee *vt* sorvegliare.
overseer *n* sorvegliante *m.*
overshadow *vt* eclissare.
overtake *vt* superare.
owe *vt* dovere.
owing *adj* da pagare: — *prep* owing to a causa di.
owl *n* civetta *f*, gufo *m.*
own *adj* proprio: — *vt* possedere.
owner *n* proprietario *m.*
ownership *n* proprietà *f.*
ox *n* bue *m*: — oxen *npl* buoi *mpl.*
oxidise *vt* ossidare.
oxygen *n* ossigeno *m.*
oyster *n* ostrica *f.*
ozone *n* ozono *m.*

P

pace *n* passo *m*:—*vi* camminare su e giù.

pacemaker *n* pace-maker *m*.

pacific *adj* pacifico:—*n* pacifico *m*.

pack *n* pacco *m*; branco *m*:—*vt* imballare; stipare di:—*vi* fare le valigie.

package *n* pacchetto *m*:—*vt* confezionare.

packet *n* pacchetto *m*.

pact *n* patto *m*.

pad *n* cuscinetto *m*; blocchetto *m*; rampa *f* di lancio; (*sl*) casa *f*:—*vt* imbottire.

paddle *vi* sguazzare:—*n* pala *f*.

paddock *n* recinto *m*.

padlock *n* lucchetto *m*.

pagan *adj*, *n* pagano *m*.

page *n* paggio *m*; pagina *f*.

pail *n* secchio *m*.

pain *n* dolore *m*:—*vt* addolorare.

paint *n* tinta *f*; vernice:—*vt* dipingere; verniciare.

painter *n* pittore *m*; imbianchino *m*.

painting *n* quadro *m*; pittura *f*.

pair *n* paio *m*, copia *f*.

palate *n* palato *m*.

pale *adj* pallido.

palette *n* tavolozza *f*.

palm *n* palma *f*.

Palm Sunday *n* domenica delle Palme.

pamphlet *n* opuscolo *m*.

pan *n* pentola *f*.

pancake *n* frittella *f*.

pancreas *n* pancreas *m*.

panda *n* panda *m*.

pane *n* vetro *m*.

panel *n* pannello *m*; giuria *f*.

panic *adj*, *n* panico *m*.

pansy *n* (*bot*) pensée *f*.

panties *npl* mutandine fpl.

pantihose *n* collant *m*.

pants *npl* mutande fpl, slip *m*.

papacy *n* papato *m*.

paper *n* carta *f*; relazione *f*; giornale *m*:—**papers** *pl* documenti *mpl*:—*vt* tappezzare.

paprika *n* paprica *f*.

parachute *n* paracaduta *m*.

parade *n* sfilata *f*, parata *f*.

paradise *n* paradiso *m*.

paragraph *n* paragrafo *m*.

parallel *adj* parallelo:—*n* parallela *f*.

paralysis *n* paralisi *f*.

paralyse *vt* paralizzare.

parasite *n* parassita *m*.

parasol *n* parasole *m*.

parcel *n* pacco *m*:—*vt* impacchettare.

parchment *n* pergamena *f*.

pardon *n* perdone *m*:—*vt* perdonare.

parent *n* genitore *m/f*.

perentage *n* natali mpl.

park *n* parco *m*:—*vt vi* parcheggiare.

parliament *n* parlamento *m*.

Parmesan *n* parmigiano *m*.

parrot *n* pappagallo *m*.

parsley *n* prezzemolo *m*.

parsnip *n* pastinaca *f*.

part *n* parte *f*:—*vt* separare:—*vi* lasciarsi:—**part with** disfarsi di.

partial *adj* parziale.

participant *n* partecipante *m/f*.

participle *n* (*gr*) participio *m*.

particle *n* particella *f*.

particular *adj* particolare; pignolo:—*n* particolare *m*.

partition *n* parete *f* divisoria.

partner *n* partner *m/f*, socio *m*.

partnership *n* associazione *f*.

partridge *n* pernice *f*.

party *n* partito *m*; festa *f*.

pass *vt vi* passare:—*n* passo *m*; lasciapassare *m*; sufficienza *f*:—**make a pass at** fare delle avances a.

passage *n* passaggio *m*.

passenger *n* passeggero *m*.

passion *n* passione *f*.

passion flower *n* passiflora *f*.

Passover *n* Pasqua *f* ebraica.

passport *n* passaporto *m*.

password *n* parola *f* d'ordine.

past *adj* passato:—*n* passato *m*:—*prep* davanti; oltre; passato.

pasta *n* pasta *f*.

pat *vi* dare dei colpetti leggeri:—*n* colpetto *m*.

patent *adj* palese; brevettato:—*n* brevetto *m*:—*vt* brevettare.

paternal *adj* paterno.

path *n* sentiero *m*.

pathetic *adj* patetico.

patience *n* pazienza *f*.

patient *adj*, *n* paziente *m*.

patio *n* terrazza *f*.

patriotic *adj* patriottico.

patriotism *n* patriottismo *m*.

patrol *n* pattuglia *f*:—*vt* perlustrare.

pattern *n* disegno *m*, modello *m*.

pause *n* pausa *f*:—*vi* fare una pausa.

pave *vt* lastricare.

pavement *n* marciapiede *m*.

paw *n* zampa *f*:—*vt* scalpitare, dare una zampata.

pay *vt*, *vi* pagare:—*n* paga *f*.

pea *n* pisello *m*.

peace *n* pace *f*.

peach *n* pesca *f*:—**peach tree** pesco *m*.

peacock *n* pavone *m*.

peal *n* scampanio *m*.

peanut *n* arachide *f*.

pear *n* pera *f*:—**pear tree** *n* pero *m*.

pearl *n* perla *f*.

pebble *n* ciottolo *m*.

peculiar *adj* strano.

pedal *n* pedale *m*:—*vi* pedalare.

pedant *n* pedante *m/f*.

pedantic *adj* pedante.

peddle *vt* spacciare.

pedestal *n* piedistallo *m*.

pedestrian *n* pedone *m*:—*adj* mediocre.

peel *vt* sbucciare:—*vi* spellarsi:—*n* buccia *f*.

pelican *n* pellicano *m*.

pelvis *n* bacino *m*.

pen *n* penna *f*; recinto *m*:—*vt* scrivere; rinchiudere.

pencil *n* matita *f*, lapis *m*.

pendant *n* pendaglio *m*.

penetrate *vt*, *vi* penetrare.

penguin *n* pinguino *m*.

penicillin *n* penicillina *f*.

peninsula *n* penisola *f*.

penis *n* pene *m*.

penny *n* penny *m*.

pension *n* pensione *f*.

Pentecost *n* Pentecoste *f*.

peony *n* peonea *f*.

people *n* gente *f*, popolo *m*, persone *fpl*:—*vt* popolare.

pepper (spice) pepe *m*; (vegetable) peperone *m*:—*vt* pepare.

peppermint *n* menta *f* peperita.

perceive *vt* percepire.

percentage n percentuale f.

perch n pesce m persico; posatoio m:
— vi appollaiarsi.

percolator n caffettiera f a filtro.

perfect adj perfetto: — vt perfezionare.

perfection n perfezione f.

perform vt svolgere; rappresentare;
eseguire: — vi esibirsi.

performance n rappresentazione f; interpretazione f; rendimento m.

performer n artista m/f.

perfume n profumo m: — vt profumare.

perhaps adv forse.

peril n pericolo m.

perimeter n perimetro m.

period n periodo m; ora f; punto m;
mestruazioni fpl.

periphery n periferia f.

perish vi perire.

perishable adj deperibile.

peritonitis n peritonite f.

perk n vantaggio m.

perm n permanente f.

permanent adj permanente.

permission n permesso m.

permit vt, vi permettere: — n autorizzazione f.

perpetual adj perpetuo.

perplex vt lasciare perplesso.

persecute vt perseguitare.

persecution n persecuzione f.

persevere vi perseverare.

persist vi persistere.

persistence n perseveranza f.

persistent adj persistente.

person n persona f.

personal adj personale.

personality n personalità f.

perspiration n traspirazione f.

perspire vi traspirare.

persuade vt persuadere.

pessimist n pessimista m/f.

pet n animale m domestico; beniamino
m: — vt accarezzare.

petal n petalo m.

petrol n benzina f.

petroleum n petrolio m.

petty adj insignificante.

pewter n peltro m.

phantom adj, n fantasma m.

Pharaoh n faraone m.

pharmacist n farmacista m/f.

pharmacy n farmacia f.

phase n fase f.

philosopher n filosofo m.

philosophy n filosofia f.

phlegm n flemma f.

phobia n fobia f.

phone n telefono m: — vt telefonare.

phoney adj falso.

photocopier n fotocopiatrice f.

photograph n fotografia f: — vt fotografare.

photographer n fotografo m.

phrase n frase f: — vt esprimere.

phrase book n frasario m.

physical adj fisico.

physics n fisica f.

piano n pianoforte m.

pick n piccone m; scelta f: — vt scegliere; cogliere.

picket n picchetto m: — vt, vi picchet-
tare.

pickle n pasticcio m: — **pickles** sottaceti mpl: — vt mettere sottaceto.

picnic n picnic m.

picture n quadro m; fotografia f; disegno m: — vt immaginare.

picturesque adj pittoresco.

pie n torta f; pasticcio m.

piece n pezzo m.

pier n pontile m.

pierce *vt* forare.

piercing *adj* lacerante.

pig *n* maiale *m*, porco *m*; (*fam*) stronzo *m*.

pigeon *n* piccione *m*.

pilchard *n* sardina *f*.

pile *n* mucchio *m*; pila *f*: — **piles** emorroidi *fpl*: — *vt* impilare; ammucchiare.

pilgrim *n* pellegrino *m*.

pilgrimage *n* pellegrinaggio *m*.

pill *n* pillola *f*.

pilot *n* pilota *m/f*: — *vt* pilotare.

pimple *n* foruncolo *m*.

pin *n* spillo *m*: — **pins and needles** formicolio *m*: — *vt* attaccare con uno spillo.

pinch *vt* pizzicare; fregare: — *n* pizzicotto *m*; pizzico *m*.

pine *n* (*bot*) pino *m*: — *vi* languire.

pineapple *n* ananas *m*.

pink *n* rosa *m*.

pint *n* pinta *f*.

pioneer *n* pioniere *m*.

pipe *n* tubo *m*; pipa *f*: — **pipes** *npl* cornamusa *m*.

piping *n* tubature *fpl*.

pirate *n* pirata *m*.

Pisces *n* Pesci *mpl*.

piss *vi* (*fam*) pisciare.

pistol *n* pistola *f*.

pit *n* buca *f*; cava *f*.

pitch *n* pece *f*; campo *m*; intonazione *f*: — *vt* lanciare; piantare.

pity *n* compassione *f*; peccato *m*: — *vt* compatire.

pivot *n* perno *m*.

pixie *n* folletto *m*.

pizza *n* pizza *f*.

place *n* luogo *m*, posto *m*: — *vt* posare, mettere; situare; piazzare.

plague *n* peste *f*: — *vt* tormentare.

plaice *n* passera *f* di mare.

plain *adj* evidente; semplice; in tinta unita: — *n* pianura *f*.

plan *n* piano *m*: — *vt* pianificare; organizzare.

plane *n* (*bot*) platano *m*; pialla *f*: — aeroplano *m*, *adj* piano: — *vt* piallare: — *vi* planare.

planet *n* pianeta *m*.

planetarium *n* planetario *m*.

plank *n* tavola *f*.

planning *n* pianificazione *f*.

plant *n* pianta *f*; impianto *m*; stabilimento *m*: — *vt* piantare.

plantation *n* piantagione *f*.

plaque *n* placca *f*.

plaster *n* intonaco *m*; gesso *m*; cerotto *m*: — *vt* intonacare.

plastic *adj* plastico: — *n* plastica.

plastic surgery *n* chirurgia *f* plastica.

plate *n* piatto *m*; targa *f*; piastra *f*: — *vt* placcare.

platform *n* piattaforma *f*; binario *m*.

platinum *n* platino *m*.

platonic *adj* platonico.

platoon *n* plotone *m*.

platter *n* piatto *m* da portata.

play *n* gioco *m*; commedia *f*: — *vt* giocare; suonare; interpretare: — *vi* giocare; suonare.

player *n* giocatore *m*; suonatore *m*.

plea *n* supplica *f*.

pleasant *adj* piacevole.

please *vi* piacere: — *vt* accontentare: — *excl* per piacere.

pleat *n* piega: — *vt* pieghettare.

plenty *n* abbondanza *f*.

plot *n* appezzamento *m*; complotto *m*; trama *f*: — *vt* tracciare: — *vi* complottare.

plough n aratro m: — vt vi arare.

plug n tappo m; spina f: — vt tappare.

plughole n scarico m.

plum n prugna f, susina f: — **plum tree** prugno m, susino m.

pluperfect n (gr) piuccheperfetto m.

plural adj, n plurale m.

plus n vantaggio m; più m: — prep più: — adj positivo.

plutonium n plutonio m.

ply vt maneggiare; esercitare; incalzare: — vi fare la spola tra: — n strato m; velo m.

pneumonia n polmonite f.

poach vi cacciare di frodo: — vt cuocere in bianco.

pocket n tasca f: — vt intascare.

pod n baccello m.

podgy adj grassottello.

podium n podio m.

poem n poesia f.

poet n poeta m.

poetry n poesia f.

point n punto m; virgola f; punta f; scopo m: — **point of view** punto m di vista: — vt puntare; indicare.

poise n portamento m.

poison n veleno m: — vt avvelenare.

polar adj polare.

pole n palo m; asta f; polo m.

police n polizia f: — vt presidiare.

polish vt lucidare; lustrare: — n lucido m, cera f; lucidata f; raffinatezza f.

polite adj educato.

politician n politico m.

politics npl politica f.

polka n polca f: — **polka dot** n pois m.

poll n votazione f; sondaggio m.

pollution n inquinamento m.

pomegranate n melagrana f.

pomp n fasto m.

pompous adj pomposo.

pond n laghetto m.

pony n pony m.

ponytail n coda f di cavallo.

poof n (fam) finocchio m.

pool n pozza f; piscina f; cassa f comune; riserva f; biliardo m: — vt mettere insieme.

poor adj povero; misero: — n **the poor** i poveri mpl.

poorly adj indisposto.

pop n schiocco m; bevanda f gassata: — adj pop: — vt fare scoppiare.

Pope n papa m.

poplar n pioppo m.

poppy n papavero m.

populace n popolo m.

popular adj popolare; benvoluto.

popularity n popolarità f.

populate vt popolare.

population n popolazione f.

porcelain n porcellana f.

porch n veranda f.

porcupine n porcospino m.

pork n maiale m.

porpoise n focena f.

porridge n porridge m.

port n porto m; (mar) babordo m.

portion n porzione f.

portrait n ritratto m.

portray vt ritrarre.

pose n posa f: — vi posare: — vt porre.

position n posizione f; impiego m: — vt sistemare.

positive adj positivo.

possess vt possedere.

possession n possesso m.

possibility n possibilità f.

possible adj possibile.

post n palo m; posta f; posto m: — vt spedire per posta; affiggere.

postage n affrancatura f.
poster n manifesto m, poster m.
posterior n deretano m, posteriore m.
posterity n posterità f.
posthumous adj postumo.
postman n postino m.
post-mortem n autopsia f.
postpone vt rimandare.
postulate vt postulare.
posture n portamento m.
pot n pentola f; vasetto m; erba f:—vt invasare.
potassium n potassio m.
potato n patata f.
potted adj conservato (in vaso); condensato.
pottery n ceramica f.
poultry n pollame m.
pounce n balzo m:—vt balzare.
pound n libra f; (lira) sterlina; canile municipale; deposito auto:—vt picchiare, pestare.
pour vt versare.
poverty n miseria f; povertà f.
powder n polvere f:—vt ridurre in polvere:—vi incipriarsi.
power n forza f, potenza f; capacità f; potere m:—vt azionare.
powerful adj potente; possente..
pragmatic adj pragmatico.
praise n elogio m:—vt lodare.
prawn n gambero m.
pray vi pregare.
prayer n preghiera f.
preach vt, vi predicare.
preacher n predicatore m.
precaution n precauzione f.
precede vt precedere.
precious adj prezioso.
precise adj preciso.
predator n predatore m.

predecessor n predecessore m.
predict vt predire.
predictable adj prevedibile.
prediction n predizione f.
preface n prefazione f.
prefer vt preferire.
prefix n prefisso m.
pregnancy n gravidanza f.
pregnant adj in cinta, gravida f.
preparation n preparazione f.
preparatory adj preparatorio.
prepare vt preparare.
preposition n preposizione f.
prerequisite n presupposto m necessario.
prescribe vi prescrivere.
prescription n ricetta f.
presence n presenza f.
present n presente m:—adj presente; attuale:—vt presentare.
presentable adj presentabile.
presentation n presentazione f.
presenter n presentatore m.
preservation n conservazione f.
preservative n conservante m.
presidency n presidenza f.
president n presidente m.
press vt, vi premere; stirare:—n pressa f; torchio m; stampa f.
pressure n pressione f.
prestige n prestigio m.
presume vt supporre.
presumption n presunzione f.
presuppose vt presupporre.
pretend vi fingere.
preterite n passato m.
pretty adj grazioso:—adv piuttosto.
prevent vt prevenire.
prevention n prevenzione f.
preventive adj preventivo.
preview n anteprima f.

previous *adj* precedente.
prey *n* preda *f.*
price *n* prezzo *m.*
priceless *adj* di valore inestimabile.
price list *n* listino *m* prezzi.
prick *vt* bucare; pungere:—*n* puntura *f*; (*fam*) cazzo *m.*
prickle *n* spina *f.*
pride *n* orgoglio *m*; branco *m.*
priest *n* prete *m.*
priestess *n* sacerdotessa *f.*
prime *n* apice *m*:—*adj* principale:—*vt* preparare.
Prime Minister *n* Primo Ministro *m.*
primrose *n* (*bot*) primula *f.*
prince *n* principe *m.*
princess *n* principessa *f.*
principality *n* principato *m.*
principle *n* principio *m.*
print *vt* stampare:—*n* impronta *f*; stampato *m*; stampa *f*:—**out of print** esaurito.
printer *n* tipografo *m*; stampante *f.*
prior *adj* precedente:—*n* priore *m.*
priority *n* priorità *f.*
priory *n* prioria *f.*
prise *vt* aprire facendo leva.
prism *n* prisma *m.*
prison *n* prigione *f.*
prisoner *n* prigioniero *m.*
pristine *adj* immacolato.
privacy *n* privacy *f.*
private *adj* privato; confidenziale:—*n* soldato *m* semplice.
private detective *n* detective *m* privato.
privet *n* ligustro *m.*
privilege *n* privilegio *m.*
prize *n* premio *m*:—*vt* valutare.
prizewinner *n* premiato *m.*
probability *n* probabilità *f.*

probable *adj* probabile.
probation *n* periodo *m* di prova; libertà *f* condizionale.
probe *n* sonda *f*:—*vt* sondare.
problem *n* problema *m.*
procedure *n* procedura *f.*
proceed *vi* procedere:—**proceeds** *npl* ricavato *m.*
proceedings *n* provvedimenti *mpl.*
process *n* processo *m*, procedimento *m*; *vt* trattare.
procession *n* processione *f.*
proclaim *vt* proclamare.
proclamation *n* proclama *m.*
procure *vt* procurare.
procurement *n* approvvigionamento *m.*
prodigal *adj* prodigo.
prodigy *n* prodigio *m.*
produce *vt* produrre:—*n* prodotto *m.*
producer *n* produttore *m*; regista *m/f.*
product *n* prodotto *m.*
production *n* produzione *f.*
productive *adj* produttivo.
productivity *n* produttività *f.*
profess *vt* professare.
profession *n* professione *f.*
professional *adj* professionale:—*n* professionista *m/f.*
professor *n* professore *m.*
proficiency *n* competenza *f.*
profile *n* profilo *m.*
profit *n* profitto *m*:—*vi* approfittare.
profitability *n* redditività *f.*
profitable *adj* redditizio.
profiteer *vt* specolare:—*n* speculatore *m.*
profusion *n* profusione *f.*
programme *n* programma *m.*
programmer *n* programmatore *m.*
progress *n* progresso *m*:—*vi* procedere.

progression *n* progressione *f.*
prohibit *vt* proibire; vietare.
prohibition *n* proibizione *f.*
project *vt* proiettare:—*n* progetto *m.*
projection *n* proiezione *f.*
projector *n* proiettore *m.*
proletarian *adj*, *n* proletario *m.*
proletariat *n* proletariato *m.*
prolific *adj* prolifico.
prologue *n* prologo *m.*
prolong *vt* prolungare.
promenade *n* passeggiata *f.*
prominence *n* prominenza *f.*
prominent *adj* prominente.
promise *n* promessa *f.*:—*vt* promettere.
promising *adj* promettente.
promontory *n* promontorio *m.*
promote *vt* promuovere.
promoter *n* promotore *m.*
promotion *n* promozione *f.*
prompt *adj* tempestivo:—*vt* suggerire.
prompter *n* suggeritore *m.*
prone *adj* a faccia in giù; soggetto a.
prong *n* rebbio *m.*
pronoun *n* pronome *m.*
pronounce *vt* pronunciare.
pronounced *adj* netto.
pronunciation *n* pronuncia *f.*
proof *n* prova *f*; bozza *f.*
prop *vt* appoggiare:—*n* sostegno *m.*
propaganda *n* propaganda *f.*
propel *vt* spingere.
propeller *n* elica *f.*
proper *adj* appropriato; giusto; decente.
property *n* proprietà *f.*
prophecy *n* profezia *f.*
prophesy *vt* profetizzare.
prophet *n* profeta *m.*
prophetic *adj* profetico.
proportion *n* proporzione *f.*

proportional *adj* proporzionale.
proportionate *adj* proporzionato.
proposal *n* proposta *f.*
propose *vt* proporre.
proposition *n* proposizione *f.*
proprietor *n* proprietario *m.*
propriety *n* decoro *m.*
propulsion *n* propulsione *f.*
prosaic *adj* prosaico.
prose *n* prosa *f.*
prosecute *vt* proseguire:—*vi* ricorrere in giudizio.
prosecution *n* azione *f* giudiziaria.
prosecutor *n* procuratore *m.*
prospect *n* prospettiva *f.*:—*vt* esplorare.
prospective *adj* futuro.
prospector *n* prospettore *m.*
prospectus *n* prospetto *m.*
prosper *vi* prosperare.
prosperity *n* prosperità *f.*
prosperous *adj* prospero.
prostitute *n* prostituta *f.*
prostitution *n* prostituzione *f.*
protagonist *n* protagonista *m/f.*
protect *vt* proteggere.
protection *n* protezione *f.*
protective *adj* protettivo.
protector *n* protettore *m.*
protein *n* proteina *f.*
protest *vt*, *vi* protestare:—*n* protesta *f.*
Protestant *n* protestante *m.*
protester *n* contestatore *m.*
protocol *n* protocollo *m.*
prototype *n* prototipo *m.*
protracted *adj* protratto.
protrude *vi* sporgere.
proud *adj* orgoglioso.
prove *vt* dimostrare, provare; *vi* rivelarsi.
proverb *n* proverbio *m.*

proverbial *adj* proverbiale.

provide *vt* fornire.

provided *conj*:—**provided that** a patto che.

providence *n* provvidenza *f*.

province *n* provincia *f*.

provincial *adj* provinciale.

provision *n* fornitura *f*.

provisional *adj* provvisorio.

provocation *n* provocazione *f*.

provocative *adj* provocatorio.

provoke *vi* provocare.

prow *n* (*mar*) prua *f*.

prowess *n* prodezza *f*.

prowl *vi* aggirarsi.

prowler *n* chi si aggira furtivamente.

proxy *n* procura *f*.

prudence *n* prudenza *f*.

prudent *adj* prudente.

prudish *adj* puritano.

prune *vt* potare:—*n* prugna.

psalm *n* salmo *m*.

pseudonym *n* pseudonimo *m*.

psyche *n* psiche *f*.

psychiatric *adj* psichiatrico.

psychiatrist *n* psichiatra *m/f*.

psychiatry *n* psichiatria *f*.

psychic *adj* psichico.

psychoanalysis *n* psicanalisi *f*.

psychoanalyst *n* psicanalista *m/f*.

psychological *adj* psicologico.

psychologist *n* psicologo *m*.

psychology *n* psicologia *f*.

psychopath *n* psicopatico *m*.

psychosomatic *adj* psicosomatico.

pub *n* pub *m*.

puberty *n* pubertà *f*.

pubic *adj* pubico.

public *adj*, *n* pubblico *m*.

public address system *n* impianto di amplificazione *m*.

publican *n* gestore di un pub *m*.

publication *n* pubblicazione *f*.

publicise *vt* reclamizzare.

publicity *n* pubblicità *f*.

publish *vt* pubblicare.

publisher *n* editore *m*.

publishing *n* editoria *f*.

pucker *vt* increspare.

pudding *n* dolce *m*; budino *m*; dessert *m*.

puddle *n* pozzanghera *f*.

puerile *adj* puerile.

puff *n* soffio *m*:—*vi* ansimare, soffiare.

puff pastry *n* pasta *f* sfoglia.

puffin *n* pulcinella *f* di mare.

puffy *adj* gonfio.

pug *n* carlino *m*.

puke *vt*, *vi* vomitare.

pull *vi* tirare.

pulley *n* puleggia *f*.

pullover *n* pullover *m*.

pulp *n* pasta (di legno) *f*; polpa *f*.

pulpit *n* pulpito *m*.

pulsate *vi* pulsare.

pulse *n* polso *m*.

pulverise *vt* polverizzare.

puma *n* puma *m*.

pumice *n* pomice *f*.

pummel *vt* prendere a pugni.

pump *n* pompa *f*:—*vt* pompare.

pumpkin *n* zucca *f*.

pun *n* gioco *m* di parole.

punch *n* pugno *m*; perforatrice *f*; punzonatrice *f*:—*vt* dare un pugno; forare.

punctual *adj* puntuale.

punctuate *vt* punteggiare.

punctuation *n* punteggiatura *f*.

pundit *n* esperto *m*.

pungent *adj* pungente.

punish *vt* punire.

punishment *n* punizione *f*.
punk *n* punk *m*.
punt *n* barchino *m*.
puny *adj* gracile; striminzito.
pup *n* cucciolo *m*.
pupil *n* allievo *m*; pupilla *f*.
puppet *n* burattino *m*.
puppy *n* cagnolino *m*.
purchase *vt* acquistare: — *n* acquisto *m*; presa *f*.
purchaser *n* acquirente *m/f*.
pure *adj* puro.
purée *n* purè *m*.
purge *n* purga *f*: — *vt* purgare.
purification *n* depurazione *f*.
purify *vt* depurare.
purist *n* purista *m/f*.
puritan *adj*, *n* puritano *m*.
purity *n* purezza *f*.
purl *n* rovescio *m*.
purple *adj*, *n* viola *m*.
purport *vt* voler sembrare: — *n* significato *m*.

purpose *n* scopo *m*: — **on purpose** apposta.
purposeful *adj* risoluto.
purr *vi* fare le fusa.
purse *n* borsellino *m*; portamonete *m*.
purser *n* commissario *m* di bordo.
pursue *vt* inseguire; proseguire.
pursuit *n* inseguimento *m*; attività *f*.
purveyor *n* fornitore *m*.
pus *n* pus *m*.
push *vt* spingere: — *n* spinta *f*.
pusher *n* spiacciatore *m*.
pussy *n* micio *m*.
put *vt* mettere, posare; esprimere.
putrid *adj* putrido.
putt *n* putting *m*.
putty *n* stucco *m*.
puzzle *n* rompicapo *m*, rebus *m*.
puzzling *adj* sconcertante.
pylon *n* pilone *m*.
pyramid *n* piramide *f*.
pyromaniac *n* piromane *m/f*.
python *n* pitone *m*.

Q

quack *vi* fare qua qua: — *n* qua qua *m*.
quadrangle *n* quadrangolo *m*; cortile *m*.
quadrant *n* quadrante *m*.
quadrilateral *adj* quadrilatero.
quadruple *adj* quadruplo.
quail *n* quaglia *f*.
quaint *adj* pittoresco; singolare.
quake *vi* tremare.
Quaker *n* quacchero *m*.
qualification *n* qualifica *f*; riserva *f*.
qualified *adj* qualificato; condizionato.

qualify *vt* qualificare.
quality *n* qualità *f*.
quantitative *adj* quantitativo.
quantity *n* quantità *f*.
quarrel *n* lite *f*, litigio *m*: — *vi* litigare.
quarry *n* preda *f*; cava *f*.
quarter *n* quarto *m*: — **quarter of an hour** quarto d'ora; quartiere *m*: — *vt* dividere in quattro.
quartet *n* (*mus*) quartetto *m*.
quartz *n* (*min*) quarzo *m*.
quay *n* molo *m*.

queen n regina f.

queer adj strano; (fam) omosessuale:—n (fam) finocchio m.

query n domanda f:—vt contestare.

quest n ricerca f.

question n domanda f; questione f: — vt interrogare.

questionable adj discutibile.

question mark n punto m interrogativo.

questionnaire n questionario m.

queue n coda f.

quick adj veloce:—n vivo m.

quicken vt affrettare.

quid n (fam) sterlina f.

quiet adj silenzioso, tranquillo:—n silenzio m.

quieten vt placare.

quill n (ornith) penna f.

quilt n trapunta f.

quince n cotogna f; (tree) cotogno m.

quintet n (mus) quintetto m.

quit vt lasciare; smettere:—vi dimettersi.

quite adv proprio, piuttosto.

quiver vi tremare:—n faretra f.

quiz n quiz m:—vt interrogare.

quizzical adj canzonatorio; interrogativo.

quorum n quorum m.

quota n quota f.

quotation n citazione f; preventivo m.

quote vt citare; indicare.

R

rabbi n rabbino m.

rabbit n coniglio m.

rabies n rabbia f.

raccoon n procione m.

race n corsa f; razza f:—vt gareggiare contro:—vi correre.

racial adj razziale.

racing n corsa f.

racism n razzismo m.

radar n radar m.

radial adj radiale.

radiation n radiazione f.

radiator n radiatore m; termosifone m.

radical adj, n radicale m.

radio n radio f.

radioactive adj radioattivo.

radioactivity n radioattività f.

radiographer n radiologo m.

radish n ravanello m.

raffle n riffa:—vt mettere in palio.

raft n zattera f.

rag n straccio m, cencio m.

rage n colera f, furia f:—vi infuriarsi.

raid n irruzione f; rapina f:—vt fare irruzione in; saccheggiare.

rail n sbarra f; corrimano m; rotaia f: —vi **rail against** inveire.

railway n ferrovia f.

rain n pioggia f:—vi piovere.

rainbow n arcobaleno m.

raincoat n impermeabile m.

raise vt sollevare; erigere; alzare:—n aumento m.

raisin n uvetta f.

rally n raduno m; rally m:—vi radunare; riunire.

ram *n* montone *m*, ariete:—*vt* speronare; ficcare.

ramp *n* rampa *f*.

random *adj* a caso.

range *n* portata *f*; autonomia *f*; gamma *f*; catena *f*:—*vi* variare, estendersi.

ranger *n* (forest) guardia *f* forestale.

rank *adj* puzzolente, rancido:—*n* grado; posteggio *m*:—*vt* ritenere.

rape *n* stupro *m*:—*vt* violentare, stuprare.

rapid *adj* rapido:—**rapids** *npl* rapida *f*.

rapist *n* violentatore *m*, stupratore *m*.

rare *adj* raro; al sangue.

rarity *n* rarità *f*.

rash *adj* avventato:—*n* sfogo, orticaria *f*.

raspberry *n* lampone *m*:—**raspberry bush** lampone *m*.

rat *n* ratto *m*.

rate *n* tasso *m*; tariffa *f*:—*vt* valutare.

rather *adv* piuttosto.

ratio *n* rapporto *m*.

ration *n* razione *f*:—*vt* razionare.

rattle *vt* innervosire; acciottolare:—*vi* sferragliare; blaterare:—*n* rumore *m* secco; acciottolio *m*; raganella *f*; rantolo *m*; sonaglio *m*.

rattlesnake *n* crotalo *m*.

raven *n* corvo *m*.

raw *adj* crudo, greggio; gelido.

ray *n* raggio *m*; razza *f*.

razor *n* rasoio *m*.

reach *vt* raggiungere:—*vi* estendersi:—*n* portata *f*; tratto *m*.

reaction *n* reazione *f*.

read *vt* leggere:—*vi* studiare.

reader *n* lettore *m*; antologia *f*.

readily *adv* prontamente.

readjust *vt* regolare:—*vi* riadattarsi.

ready *adj* pronto.

reappear *vi* ricomparire.

rear *n* parte *f* posteriore:—*adj* posteriore:—*vt* allevare:—*vi* impennarsi.

reason *n* ragione *f*, motivo *m*:—*vi* ragionare.

rebel *adj*, *n* ribelle *m/f*:—*vi* ribellarsi.

rebellion *n* ribellione *f*.

recede *vi* ritrarsi.

receipt *n* ricevuta *f*.

receive *vt* ricevere.

recent *adj* recente.

reception *n* ricevimento *m*; reception *f*; accettazione *f*.

recession *n* recessione *f*.

recipe *n* ricetta *f*.

recline *vi* essere sdraiato.

recognise *vt* riconoscere.

recognition *n* riconoscimento *m*.

recoil *vi* indietreggiare.

recollect *vt* rammentare.

recollection *n* ricordo *m*.

recommend *vt* raccomandare; consigliare.

record *vt* annotare; registrare:—*n* registro *m*; precedenti penali *mpl*; record *m*; disco *m*:—**records** annali *mpl*; archivi *mpl*.

recover *vt* ricuperare; ricoprire:—*vi* riprendersi.

recovery *n* ricupero *m*; ripresa *f*.

recreation *n* ricreazione *f*.

recruit *vt* reclutare:—*n* recluta *f*.

recruitment *n* reclutamento.

rectangle *n* rettangolo *m*.

rectum *n* retto *m*.

recuperate *vi* ristabilirsi.

red *adj*, *n* rosso *m*.

redeem *vt* redimere.

Redeemer *n* Redentore *m*.

reduce *vt* ridurre:—*vi* diminuire.

reduction *n* riduzione *f*.

redundancy *n* ridondanza *f*; licenziamento *m*.

redundant *adj* ridondante; licenziato.

refectory *n* refettorio *m*.

refer *vi* riferirsi a; consultare:—*vt* rimandare.

referee *n* arbitro *m*.

reference *n* riferimento *m*.

referendum *n* referendum *m*.

refill *n* ricambio:—*vt* riempire.

refine *vt* raffinare.

refinery *n* raffineria *f*.

reflect *vt*, *vi* riflettere:—*vt* rispecchiare.

reflection *n* riflessione *f*; riflesso *m*.

reflex *adj*, *n* riflesso *m*.

reform *vt* riformare:—*n* riforma *f*.

Reformation *n* Riforma *f*.

refreshment *n* ristoro *m*.

refrigerate *vt* refrigerare.

refrigerator *n* frigorifero *m*.

refuge *n* riparo *m*, rifugio *m*.

refugee *n* profugo *m*.

refusal *n* rifiuto *m*.

refuse *vt* rifiutare:—*n* rifiuti *mpl*.

regal *adj* regale.

regard *vt* considerare; riguardare:—*n* riguardo *m*.

regarding *prep* riguardo a.

régime *n* regime *m*.

region *n* regione *f*.

regional *adj* regionale.

register *n* registro *m*:—*vt* registrare; immatricolare:—*vi* iscriversi.

registered letter *n* raccomandata *f*.

registrar *n* ufficiale *m* di stato civile.

registration *n* registrazione *f*.

registry *n*:—**registry office** anagrafe *f*.

regress *vi* regredire.

regret *n* rimpianto *m*; rammarico *m*: —*vt* rimpiangere; dispiacersi di.

regrettable *adj* deplorevole.

regular *adj* regolare; fedele.

regularity *n* regolarità *f*.

regulate *vt* regolare.

regulation *n* regolamento *m*.

regulator *n* regolatore *m*.

rehabilitate *vt* riabilitare.

rehabilitation *n* riabilitazione *f*.

rehearse *vt* provare.

reign *n* regno *m*:—*vi* regnare.

reincarnation *n* reincarnazione *f*.

reinforce *vt* rinforzare.

reject *vt* scartare:—*n* scarto *m*.

rejection *n* rigetto *m*.

rejoice *vi* rallegrarsi.

relapse *vi* ricadere:—*n* ricaduta *f*.

relate *vt* collegare; raccontare.

relation *n* relazione *f*; rapporto *m*; parente *m/f*.

relationship *n* nesso *m*; relazione *f*; legami *mpl* di parentela.

relax *vt* rilassare.

relaxation *n* relax *m*.

relay *n* ricambio *m*; relé *m*:—*vt* ritrasmettere; passare.

release *vt* rilasciare; mollare; emettere:—*n* rilascio *m*; emissione *f*; uscita *f*.

relevance *n* pertinenza *f*.

relevant *adj* pertinente.

reliable *adj* affidabile.

reliance *n* dipendenza *f*.

relic *n* reliquia *f*.

relief *n* sollievo *m*; rilievo *m*.

relieve *vt* alleviare.

religion *n* religione *f*.

religious *adj* religioso.

relish *n* gusto *m*; condimento *m*:—*vt* gustare.

reluctance *n* riluttanza *f*.
rely *vi* contare su.
remain *vi* rimanere.
remains *npl* resti *mpl*; avanzi *mpl*.
remark *n* osservazione *f*:—*vt* osservare.
remarkable *adj* notevole.
remedial *adj* correttivo.
remedy *n* rimedio *m*:—*vt* rimediare.
remember *vt* ricordare.
remind *n* ricordare.
remote *adj* remoto; vago.
remunerate *vt* rimunerare.
remuneration *n* rimunerazione *f*.
Renaissance *n* Rinascimento *m*.
renal *adj* renale.
rendezvous *n* appuntamento *m*:—*vi* ritrovarsi.
renew *vt* rinnovare.
renewal *n* rinnovo *m*.
renounce *vt* rinunciare.
renovate *vt* rinnovare.
renovation *n* restauro *m*.
renown *n* rinomanza *f*.
renowned *adj* rinomato.
rent *n* affitto *m*, pigione *m*:—*vt* affittare.
rental *n* nolo *m*.
repair *vt* aggiustare, riparare:—*n* riparazione *f*.
repeat *vt* ripetere:—*n* replica *f*.
repeatedly *adv* ripetutamente.
replace *vt* rimpiazzare; sostituire.
replacement *n* sostituto *m*.
replete *adj* sazio.
replica *n* replica *f*.
reply *n* risposta *f*:—*vt*, *vi* rispondere.
report *vt* riportare; denunciare:—*n* rapporto *m*; pagella *f*; reportage *m*.
reporter *n* cronista *m/f*.
representative *adj* rappresentativo: — *n* rappresentante *m*..

reproduce *vt* riprodurre.
reproduction *n* riproduzione *f*.
reptile *n* rettile *m*.
republic *n* repubblica *f*.
republican *n* repubblicano *m*.
repulse *vt* respingere.
repulsive *adj* ripugnante.
reputation *n* reputazione *f*.
request *n* richiesta *f*: — *vt* richiedere.
require *vt* richiedere.
requirement *n* esigenza *f*.
rescue *vt* salvare:—*n* salvataggio *m*.
research *vi* fare ricerca:—*n* ricerca *f*.
resemblance *n* somiglianza *f*.
resemble *vt* somigliare.
resent *vt* risentirsi per.
reservation *n* prenotazione *f*; riserva *f*.
reserve *vt* prenotare; riservare:—*n* riserva *f*; riservo *m*.
reservoir *n* bacino *m* idrico.
reside *vi* risiedere.
residence *n* residenza *f*.
resign *vi* dimettersi.
resignation *n* dimissioni *fpl*.
resist *vt*, *vi* resistere.
resistance *n* resistenza *f*.
resolve *vt* decidere; risolvere:—*n* risolutezza *f*.
resort *vi* fare ricorso a:—*n* ricorso *m*; località *f* di villeggiatura.
resound *vi* risonare.
resource *n* risorsa *f*.
respect *n* rispetto *m*:—**in some respects** sotto certi aspetti:—*vt* rispettare.
respectability *n* rispettabilità *f*.
respectable *adj* rispettabile.
respond *vi* rispondere.
respondent *n* (*law*) convenuto *m*.
response *n* risposta *f*.

responsibility n responsabilità f.

responsible adj responsabile.

rest n riposo m; pausa f; appoggio m; resto m:—vt riposare:—vi riposarsi; poggiare.

restaurant n ristorante m.

restoration n restauro m:—**the Restoration** la Restaurazione f.

restore vt restaurare; restituire.

restrict vt limitare.

restriction n restrizione f.

restrictive adj restrittivo.

result vi avere come risultato:—n risultato m.

resume vt, vi riprendere.

resuscitate vt risuscitare.

retail vt vendere al dettaglio:—adj al dettaglio.

retailer n dettagliante m/f.

retain vt tenere; conservare.

retina n retina f.

retire vt mandare in pensione:—vi ritirarsi, andare in pensione.

retort vt ribattere:—n risposta f; storta f.

retreat n rifugio m:—vi ritirarsi.

retrieve vt ricuperare; richiamare.

return vt restituire:—vi tornare:—n ritorno m; resa f; guadagno m; (ticket) andata e ritorno.

reunion n riunione f.

reveal vt rivelare.

revelation n rivelazione f.

revenge vt vendicare:—n vendetta f.

revenue n reddito m.

Reverend n reverendo m.

reverse vt invertire:—vi fare marcia indietro:—n opposto m; rovescio m; retromarcia f:—adj inverso; marcia indietro.

review vt fare una revisione di; recensire:—n revisione f; rivista f.

revise vt ripassare; rivedere.

revision n ripasso m; revisione f.

revival n risveglio m; ripristino m.

revive vt rianimare.

revolution n rivoluzione f.

revolutionary adj, n rivoluzionario m.

revolve vt, vi girare.

revolver n rivoltella f.

reward vt premiare:—n ricompensa f.

rheumatism n reumatismo m.

rhinoceros n rinoceronte m.

rhododendron n rododendro m.

rhubarb n rabarbaro m.

rhyme n rima f:—vi fare rima con.

rib n costola f.

ribbon n nastro m.

rice n riso m.

rich adj ricco.

rid vt sbarazzare.

ride vi cavalcare; andare:—n cavalcata f; giro m.

ridicule n ridicolo m:—vt mettere in ridicolo.

ridiculous adj ridicolo.

rifle vt svaligiare:—vi frugare:—n fucile m; carabina f.

rift n spaccatura f.

right adj giusto, retto; adatto; destro; diritto; corretto:—adv completamente; bene; giustamente:—n diritto m; destra f:—vt raddrizzare; correggere: —**to be right** avere ragione.

righteous adj virtuoso.

rigid adj rigido.

rim n orlo m.

rind n buccia f; cotenna f.

ring n anello m; cerchio m; ring m; squillo m; scampanellata:—vt accerchiare; suonare:—vi telefonare; suonare; risuonare.

rinse vt sciacquare:—n sciacquatura f.

rip *vt* strappare:—*n* strappo *m*:—**to let rip** scatenarsi.

ripe *adj* maturo, stagionato.

ripen *vt*, *vi* maturare.

rip off *vt* pelare.

rise *vi* alzarsi; sorgere; lievitare; aumentare:—*n* sorgere *m*; ascesa *f*; aumento *m*; salita *f*.

risk *n* rischio *m*:—*vt* rischiare.

rite *n* rito *m*.

ritual *adj*, *n* rituale *m*.

rival *adj*, *n* rivale *m*:—*vt* rivaleggiare.

road *n* strada *f*, via *f*.

roadsign *n* cartello *m* stradale.

roadworks *npl* lavori *mpl* stradali.

roam *vi* gironzolare.

roan *n* roano *m*.

roar *vi* ruggire:—*n* ruggito *m*.

roaring *adj* strepitoso.

roast *vt* arrostire; torrefare:—*n* arrosto *m*.

roast beef *n* rosbif *m*.

rob *vt* derubare.

robber *n* rapinatore *m*.

robbery *n* rapina *f*.

robe *n* tunica *f*; accappatoio *m*.

robin pettirosso *m*.

robot *n* robot *m*.

robust *adj* robusto.

rock *n* roccia *f*, (*mus*) rock *m*:—*vt* cullare:—*vi* dondolare; oscillare.

rocket *n* razzo *m*

rocky *adj* roccioso; vacillante.

rod *n* bacchetta *f*; bastone *m*.

rodent *n* roditore *m*.

roe *n* uova *fpl* di pese.

rogue *n* mascalzone *m*.

role *n* ruolo *m*.

roll *vt*, *vi* rotolare:—*n* rotolo *m*; rullino *m*; panino *m*; lista *f*.

roller *n* rullo *m*; rotella *f*; bigodino *m*.

roller skate *n* patino *m* a rotelle.

rolling pin *n* matterello *m*.

Roman Catholic *adj*, *n* cattolico *m*.

romance *n* storia *f* d'amore.

romantic *adj* romantico.

romp *vi* giocare chiassosamente:—*n* gioco *m* chiassoso.

roof *n* tetto *m*:—*vt* mettere il tetto.

rook *n* corvo *m*; (*chess*) torre *f*.

room *n* stanza *f*; spazio *m*; posto *m*.

roomy *adj* spazioso.

rooster *n* gallo *m*.

root *n* radice *f*:—*vt* far radicare:—*vi* attecchire:—**root out** eradicare.

rope *n* fune *f*; corda *f*:—*vt* legare.

rosary *n* rosario *m*.

rose *n* rosa *f*; rosone *m* di stucco; (*watering can*) cipolla *f*.

rosebed *n* rosaio *m*.

rosebud *n* bocciolo *m* di rosa.

rosemary *n* rosmarino *m*.

rosy *adj* roseo.

rot *vi* marcire:—*n* marciume *m*.

rotate *vi* rotare.

rotten *adj* marcio; schifoso.

rotund *adj* grassoccio.

rough *adj* ruvido, rozzo; rauco; approssimativo; burrascoso.

roughen *vt* irruvidire.

roughly *adv* brutalmente; grossolanamente.

roughness *n* ruvidità *f*.

roulette *n* roulette *f*.

round *adj* rotondo:—*n* cerchio *m*; giro *m*; round *m*:—*prep* intorno a:—*vt* arrotondare.

roundabout *adj* indiretto:—*n* giostra *f*; rotatoria *f*.

roundup *n* retata *f*.

rouse *vt* svegliare; scuotere.

route *n* itinerario *m*, percorso *m*; rotta *f*.

routine n routine f, tran tran m:—adj comune, abituale.

row n baccano m; lite f:—vi litigare.

row n fila f:—vt remare.

rowdy adj turbolento.

royal adj reale.

royalty n reali mpl; royalty m.

rub vt strofinare, sfregare:—n strofinamento m.

rubber n gomma f, caucciù m.

rubbish n spazzatura f, immondizie fpl.

rubble n macerie fpl.

ruby adj, n rubino m.

rucksack n zaino m.

rudder n timone m.

rudeness n maleducazione f.

rudiment n rudimento m.

rug n tappeto m; plaid m.

rugby n rugby m.

rugged adj accidentato; frastagliato; marcato.

ruin n rudere m, rovina f:—vt rovinare.

rule n regola f; regolamento m:—vt governare; decretare; rigare:—vi regnare.

ruler n sovrano m; righello m.

rum n rum m:—adj strambo.

rumble vi brontolare:—vt scoprire:—n rombo m.

rumour n voce f.

run vt correre; dirigere; gestire; organizzare:—vi correre; funzionare; scorrere; collare:—n corsa f; giro m; tragitto m; serie f; recinto m; smagliatura f.

rung n piolo m; traversa f.

running adj corrente:—n gestione f.

runny adj sciolto.

runway n pista f.

rupture n rottura f:—vt rompere.

rural adj rurale.

rush n giunco m; ressa f; premura f; fretta f:—vt fare fretta a:—vi precipitarsi.

rusk n fetta f biscottata.

rust n ruggine f:—vt, vi arrugginire.

rustic adj rustico:—n contadino m.

rustle vi frusciare:—n fruscio m.

rusty adj rugginoso.

ruthless adj spietato.

rye n segale f.

S

Sabbath n domenica f.

sabotage n sabotaggio m:—vt sabotare.

saccharin n saccarina f.

sack n sacco m; saccheggio m:—vt licenziare; saccheggiare.

sacred adj sacro.

sacrifice n sacrificio m:—vt sacrificare.

sad adj triste; deplorevole.

sadism n sadismo m.

sadist n sadico m.

sadness n tristezza f.

safe adj salvo; sicuro:—**safe and sound** sano e salvo:—n cassaforte f.

safeguard n salvaguardia f:—vt salvaguardare.

safety n sicurezza f.

sage *n* (*bot*) salvia *f*; saggio *m*:—*n* saggio *m*.

Sagittarius *n* Sagittario *m*.

sail *n* vela *f*; pala *f*:—*vt* condurre:—*vi* salpare, navigare.

sailor *n* marinaio *m*.

saint *n* santa *f*.

salad *n* insalata *f*.

salami *n* salame *m*.

salary *n* stipendio *m*.

sale *n* vendita *f*; svendita *f*.

saliva *n* saliva *f*.

salmon *n* salmone *m*.

salmon trout *n* trota *f* salmonata.

saloon *n* salone *m*; saloon *m*.

salt *n* sale *m*:—*vt* salare.

salvage *vt* ricuperare:—*n* salvataggio *m*.

same *adj*, *pron* stesso.

sample *n* campione *m*:—*vt* assaggiare.

sanctuary *n* santuario *m*.

sand *n* sabbia *f*:—*vt* cartavetrare; cospargere di sabbia.

sandal *n* sandalo *m*.

sandwich *n* tramezzino *m*, sandwich *m*.

sane *adj* sano di mente.

sanity *n* sanità *f* mentale.

sapphire *n* zaffiro *m*.

sarcasm *n* sarcasmo *m*.

sardine *n* sardina *f*.

Satan *n* Satana *m*.

satellite *n* satellite *m*.

satin *n* raso *m*.

satisfaction *n* soddisfazione *f*.

satisfy *vt* soddisfare.

Saturday *n* sabato *m*.

sauce *n* salsa *f*.

saucepan *n* pentola *f*.

sausage *n* salsiccia *f*; salame *m*.

savage *adj*, *n* selvaggio *m*:—*vt* sbranare.

save *vt* salvare; risparmiare; parare: — *n* parata *f*:—*prep* salvo.

saving *n* risparmio *m*:—**savings** risparmi *mpl*.

Saviour *n* salvatore *n*.

savoury *adj* salato; *n* piatto *m* salato.

saw *n* sega *f*:—*vt* segare.

saxophone *n* sassofono *m*.

say *vt*, *vi* dire; indicare.

saying *n* detto *m*.

scab *n* crosta *f*; crumiro *m*.

scale *n* scaglia *f*; squama *f*; scala *f*:—*vt* squamare; scalare.

scales *n* bilancia *f*.

scallop *n* (*zool*) pettine *m*; smerlo *m*: —*vt* smerlare.

scalp *n* cuoio *m* capelluto:—*vt* scotennare.

scalpel *n* bisturi *m*.

scampi *npl* gamberoni *mpl*.

scandal *n* scandalo *m*.

scar *n* cicatrice *f*:—*vt* sfregiare:—*vi* cicatrizzarsi.

scare *vt* spaventare; impaurire:—*n* spavento *m*.

scarf *n* sciarpa *f*, foulard *m*.

scarlet *adj*, *n* scarlatto *m*.

scene *n* scena *f*; luogo *m*.

scenery *n* paesaggio *m*.

scenic *adj* pittoresco.

scent *n* profumo *m*; pista *f*:—*vt* profumare; fiutare.

sceptic *n* scettico *m*.

sceptical *adj* scettico.

scepticism *n* scetticismo *m*.

schedule *n* programma *m*; orario *m*; tabella *f*.

scheme *n* piano *m*:—*vi* tramare..

schizophrenia *n* schizofrenia *f*.

scholar n studioso m.

school n scuola f; facoltà f; banco m: —vt addestrare.

schoolteacher n maestro m, insegnante m/f.

science n scienza f.

scientist n scienziato m.

scooter n monopattino m; scooter m.

scope n possibilità fpl, ambito m, capacità f.

scorch vt bruciacchiare: —n bruciacchiatura f.

score n punteggio m; motivo m; scalfittura f; (mus) partitura f: —vt segnare; incidere; (mus) orchestrare.

Scorpio n Scorpione m.

scorpion n scorpione m.

scramble vi inerpicarsi: —vt (culin) strapazzare; ingarbugliare: —n parapiglia f; gara f di motocross.

scrap n pezzetto m; briciolo m; ferraglia f; baruffa f: —vt demolire.

scratch vt graffiare; grattare; cancellare: —n graffio m.

scrawl vt scribacchiare: —n graffia n illeggibile.

scream vt, vi urlare: —n urlo m, strillo m.

screen n paravento m; schermo m: —vt nascondere; proiettare; (fig) vagliare.

screw n vite f; elica f; (sl) secondino m: —vt avvitare; spiegazzare.

script n copione m, scrittura f.

Scripture n Sacre Scritture fpl.

scrotum n scroto m..

scull vt remare.

scullery n retrocucina m.

sculpt vt, vi scolpire.

sculptor n scultore m.

sculpture n scultura f.

scythe n falce f: —vt falciare.

sea n mare m.

seal n foca f; sigillo m: —vt sigillare.

sealing wax n ceralacca f.

seam n cucitura f; vena f.

seaman n marinaio m.

seamstress n sarta f.

search vt perquisire; perlustrare: —vi cercare: —n ricerca f; perquisizione f.

season n stagione f: —vt stagionare; condire.

seat n sedia f; posto m; sedile m; sellino m; seggio m; sede f: —vt far sedere.

seclusion n isolamento m.

second adj secondo: —n secondo m: —vt appoggiare; distaccare.

secondary adj secondario.

secrecy n segretezza f.

secret adj, n segreto m.

secretary n segretario m.

section n sezione f, tratto m.

secure adj sicuro: —vt assicurare; garantire.

security n sicurezza f.

seduce vt sedurre.

seducer n seduttore m.

seduction n seduzione f.

see vt vedere; capire; accompagnare: —n sede f vescovile.

seed n seme m: —vt seminare.

seek vt cercare.

seem vi sembrare, parere.

see-through adj trasparente.

segment n segmento m; spicchio m.

segregation n segregazione f.

seize vt afferrare; cogliere.

seldom adj raramente.

select vt selezionare, scegliere: —adj scelto; esclusivo.

selection n scelta f, selezione f.

self *n* io *m*, se *m* stesso.

selfish *adj* egoista.

selfless *adj* altruista.

sell *vt* vendere.

seller *n* venditore *m*.

sellotape *n* scotch *m*.

semantics *npl* semantica *f*.

semblance *n* apparenza *f*.

semen *n* sperma *m*.

semicircle *n* semicerchio *m*.

semicolon *n* punto e virgola *m*.

semifinal *n* semifinale *f*.

seminar *n* seminario *m*.

semiprecious *adj* semiprezioso.

semolina *n* semolino *m*.

senate *n* senato *m*.

senator *n* senatore *m*.

send *vt* mandare, inviare; spedire.

senile *adj* senile.

senior *adj* maggiore, superiore.

sensation *n* sensazione *f*, scalpore *m*.

sense *n* senso *m*; ragione *f*; senno *m*: — *vt* intuire, avvertire.

sensibility *n* suscettibilità *f*.

sensible *adj* assennato; pratico.

sensitive *adj* sensibile.

sensual *adj* sensuale.

sensuality *n* sensualità *f*.

sensuous *adj* voluttuoso.

sentence *n* frase *f*; sentenza *f*: — *vt* condannare.

sentiment *n* sentimento *m*.

separate *vt* separare: — *adj* separato: — **separately** *adv* separatamente.

September *n* settembre *m*.

septic *adj* settico.

sequel *n* seguito *m*.

sequin *n* lustrino *m*.

serenade *n* serenata *f*: — *vt* fare la serenata a.

sergeant *n* sergente *m*.

serial *n* opera *f* a puntate.

series *n* serie *f*.

serious *adj* serio; grave.

sermon *n* sermone *m*.

serpent *n* serpente *m*.

serpentine *n* serpentina *f*.

serrated *adj* seghettato.

serum *n* siero *m*.

servant *n* domestico *m*.

serve *vt*, *vi* servire: — *vt* **serve a warrant** notificare.

service *n* servizio *m*; funzione *f*; revisione: — *vt* revisionare.

serviette *n* tovagliolo *m*.

session *n* seduta *f*; anno *m*.

set *vt* porre; regolare; stabilire; assegnare: — *vi* tramontare; saldarsi; indurirsi: — *n* serie *f*, raccolta *f*, batteria *f*; set *m*; apparecchio *m*: — *adj* fisso; obbligatorio; stabilito; deciso.

settee *n* divano *m*.

settle *vt* sistemare; definire; saldare; appianare; colonizzare: — *vi* depositarsi; insediarsi; concordare.

settlement *n* regolamento *m*; accordo *m*; insediamento *m*.

settler *n* colono *m*.

seven *num* sette.

seventeen *num* diciasette.

seventeenth *num* diciassettesimo.

seventh *num* settimo.

seventieth *num* settantesimo.

seventy *num* settanta.

sever *vt* tagliare, troncare.

several *adj* parecchi.

severe *adj* severo.

sew *vt*, *vi* cucire.

sewage *n* acque *fpl* di fogna.

sewer *n* fogna *f*.

sewing machine *n* macchina *f* da cucire.

sex *n* sesso *m*; rapporti *mpl* sessuali.

sexual *adj* sessuale.

sexuality *n* sessualità *f*.

sexy *adj* sexy.

shade *n* ombra *f*; paralume *m*; tonalità *f*: —*vt* riparare.

shadow *n* ombra *f*: —*vt* pedinare.

shady *adj* ombroso.

shake *vt* scuotere: —*vi* tremare: — **shake hands** dare la mano: —*n* scossa *f*.

shallow *adj* poco profondo.

shame *n* vergogna *f*; peccato *m*: —*vt* disonorare; far vergognare.

shamefaced *adj* vergognoso.

shameful *adj* vergognoso.

shameless *adj* spudorato.

shammy *n* pelle *f* di camoscio.

shampoo *n* shampoo *m*.

shamrock *n* trifoglio *m*.

shank *n* stinco *m*; gambo *m*.

shanty *n* canzone *f* marinaresca; baracca *f*.

shanty town *n* bidonville *f*

shape *vt* formare: —*n* forma *f*.

share *n* parte *f*; azione *f*: —*vt* dividere; condividere.

shark *n* squalo *m*, pesce *m* cane.

sharp *adj* affilato, aguzzo; brusco; nitido; acuto; in diesis.

shatter *vt* frantumare.

shave *vt* radere: —*vi* radersi.

shaver *n* rasoio *m* elettrico.

she *pron* ella, lei.

sheep *n* pecora *f*.

sheet *n* lenzuolo *m*; foglio *m*.

sheik *n* sceicco *m*.

shelf *n* ripiano *m*.

shell *n* conchiglia *f*; guscio *m*; struttura *f*: —*vt* sgranare; bombardare.

shellfish *n* crostaceo *m*.

shelter *n* riparo *m*; rifugio *m*: —*vt* riparare.

sheriff *n* sceriffo *m*.

sherry *n* sherry *m*.

shine *vt* lustrare: —*vi* brillare: —*n* lucentezza *f*.

ship *n* nave *f*: —*vt* imbarcare; spedire.

shirt *n* camicia *f*.

shit *n* (*vulg*) merda *f*.

shiver *n* brivido *m*: —*vi* rabbrividire.

shock *n* scossa *f*; shock: —*vt* scioccare: —*vi* scandalizzare.

shoe *n* scarpa *f*: — **horse shoe** ferro di cavallo: —*vt* ferrare.

shoot *vt* sparare; fucilare; lanciare; (*film*) girare: —*vi* sparare: —*n* germoglio *m*; partita *f* di caccia.

shop *n* negozio *m*; officina *f*: —*vi* fare la spesa: —*vt* tradire.

shore *n* sponda *f*.

short *adj* basso; corto; breve: — **shortly** *adv* tra poco.

shorthand *n* stenografia *f*.

shorts *npl* calzoncini *mpl*.

short-sightedness *n* miopia *f*.

shot *n* sparo *m*; tiratore *m*; iniezione *f*; foto *f*.

shotgun *n* fucile *m* da caccia.

shoulder *n* spalla *f*: —*vt* accollarsi.

shout *vt*, *vi* gridare: —*n* grido *m*.

shovel *n* pala *f*: —*vt* spalare.

show *vt* mostrare; esporre; presentare; segnare: —*vt* vedersi: —*n* manifestazione *f*, esposizione *f*; spettacolo *m*; fiera *f*; figura *f*.

shower *n* acquazzone *m*; doccia *f*: —*vt* coprire: —*vi* fare la doccia.

shrimp *n* gamberetto *m*.

shrine *n* santuario *m*.

shrink *vi* restringersi.

shroud *n* sudario *m*: —*vt* avvolgere.

Shrove Tuesday n martedì m grasso.

shrub n cespuglio m.

shut vt chiudere: — vi chiudersi.

shutter n persiana f; saracinesca f; otturatore m.

shy adj timido.

shyness n timidezza f.

sick adj malato; macabro: — vi **to be sick** vomitare.

sickness n malattia f.

side n fianco m, lato m; faccia f; ciglio m; parte f, squadra f: — adj laterale: — vi parteggiare per.

sideboard n credenza f.

siege n assedio m.

sieve n setaccio: — vt setacciare.

sigh vi sospirare: — n sospiro m.

sight n vista f; spettacolo m; mirino m: — **sights** attrazioni fpl turistiche.

sightseeing n turismo m.

sign n segno m; gesto m; indizio m; segnale m: — vt, vi firmare.

signal n segnale m: — vt, vi segnalare.

signature n firma f; (mus) segnatura f.

significant adj significativo.

signify vt significare.

signpost n indicazione f stradale.

silence n silenzio m: — vt fare tacere.

silent adj silenzioso.

silk n seta f.

silly adj sciocco.

silver n argento m; argenteria f.

similar adj simile.

similarity n somiglianza f.

simple adj semplice; ingenuo.

simply adv semplicemente.

sin n peccato m: — vi peccare.

since adv da allora: — prep da: — conj siccome.

sincere adj sincero: — **yours sincerely** adv distinti saluti.

sincerity n sincerità f.

sing vt, vi cantare.

singer n cantante m/f.

single adj solo, unico, celibe, nubile: — n singolo m; di andata.

sinister adj sinistro.

sink vi affondare; cedere; abbassarsi; sommergersi: — vt scavare: — n lavandino m, acquaio m.

sinner n peccatore m.

sinus n seno m.

sip vt sorseggiare: — n sorso m.

sir n signore m.

siren n sirena f.

sister n sorella f; suora f.

sister-in-law n cognata f.

sit vi sedersi; riunirsi.

site n ubicazione f: — vt collocare.

sitting room n salotto m.

situation n posizione f, situazione f.

six num sei.

sixteen num sedici.

sixteenth num sedicesimo.

sixth num sesto.

sixtieth num sessantesimo.

sixty num sessanta.

size n dimensioni fpl; taglia f; misura f; numero m.

skeleton n scheletro m.

skill n capacità f, abilità f, tecnica f.

skilled adj abile, specializzato.

skilful adj abile.

skim vt schiumare; scremare.

skimmed milk n latte m scremato.

skin n pelle f; buccia f; pellicola f: — vt spellare; sbucciare.

skin diving n immersione con autorespiratore.

skinned adj scoiato.

skirt n gonna f: — vt aggirare.

sky n cielo m.

skyscraper n grattacielo m.

slab n lastra f.

slander vt calunniare:—n calunnia f.

slang n slang m, gergo m.

slap n schiaffo m, ceffone m:—adv in pieno:—vt dare uno schiaffo.

slat n stecca f.

slaughter n macellazione f; massacro m; strage f:—vt macellare; massacrare; trucidare.

slave n schiavo m:—vi sgobbare.

sleek adj lucente, liscio.

sleep vi dormire:—n sonno m.

sleeve n manica f.

slender adj snello; scarso.

slenderness n snellezza f.

slice n fetta f; paletta f:—vt affettare.

slight adj minuto:—n affronto m:—vt snobbare.

slightly adv leggermente.

slim adj esile; insufficiente.

sling n fionda f; fascia f:—vt scagliare.

slink vi svignarsela.

slip vi scivolare; sfuggire; sbagliarsi:—n smottamento m; scivolata f; sbaglio m; sottoveste f; federa f; foglietto m.

slipper n pantofola f.

slipway n scalo m.

slope n versante m, pendio m:—vi essere inclinato.

slow adj lento:—**slowly** adv piano:—vt, vi rallentare.

slug n lumaca f.

sly adj astuto; scaltro.

smack n schiaffo m; schiocco m:—vt sculacciare, schiaffeggiare.

small adj piccolo.

smallpox n violo m.

smart adj elegante, chic; sveglio; svelto:—vi bruciare.

smash vt rompere; frantumare:—n fracasso m; scontro m; successone m.

smashing adj meraviglioso.

smear n traccia f, (med) striscio m:—vt spalmare; sporcare; diffamare.

smell n olfatto m, fiuto m; odore; profumo m; puzzo m:—vt sentire odore di:—vi sapere; puzzare.

smile vi sorridere:—n sorriso m.

smog n smog m.

smoke vt fumare; affumicare:—vi fumare:—n fumo m.

smoker n fumatore m.

smooth adj liscio; omogeneo:—vt lisciare, spianare.

snack n spuntino m.

snail n chiocciola f.

snake n serpente m.

snap vt rompere; schioccare; fotografare:—n schiocco; rubamazzo:—adj improvviso.

snatch vt strappare; afferrare; cogliere:—n furto m, rapimento m; pezzo m.

sneeze vi starnutire:—n starnuto m.

sniff vt annusare; sniffare.

sniper n franco tiratore m.

snob n snob m/f.

snooty adj altezzoso.

snooze n sonnellino m:—vi sonnecchiare.

snore vi russare.

snow n neve f:—vi nevicare.

snuff n tabacco m da fiuto.

so adv così, in questo modo:—conj affinché.

soak vt inzuppare; mettere a mollo.

soap n sapone m:—vt insaponare.

soar vi librarsi.

sob vi singhiozzare; n singhiozzo m.

sober adj sobrio.

soccer *n* calcio *m*.

sociable *adj* socievole.

socialism *n* socialismo *m*.

socialist *n* socialista *m/f*.

society *n* società *f*, compagnia *f*.

sock *n* calzino *m*, calzettone *m*; pugno *m*:—*vt* picchiare.

sofa *n* sofà *m*.

soft *adj* morbido, soffice; dolce; indulgente:—**softly** *adv* silenziosamente.

soil *vt* sporcare; infangare:—*n* terreno *m*.

solar *adj* solare.

solarium *n* solarium *m*.

soldier *n* soldato *m*.

solicitor *n* avvocato *m*.

solid *adj*, *n* solido *m*.

solitude *n* solitudine *f*.

solo *n* (*mus*) assolo.

solution *n* soluzione *f*.

solve *vt* risolvere.

sombre *adj* tetro.

some *adj* di, qualche, alcuno, certo: — *pron* alcuni, certi:—*adv* circa.

somebody *pron* qualcuno.

somehow *adv* in qualche modo.

something *pron* qualcosa.

sometimes *adv* qualche volta.

somewhat *adv* piuttosto, alquanto.

somewhere *adv* in qualche parte; circa.

son *n* figlio *m*.

song *n* (*mus*) canzone *f*, canto *m*.

sonic *adj* sonico.

son-in-law *n* genero *m*.

soon *adv* presto:—**as soon as possible** appena possibile.

sooner *adv* prima; piuttosto.

soot *n* fuliggine *f*.

soothe *vt* calmare.

soothing *adj* calmante; rassicurante.

sophisticated *adj* sofisticato, raffinato.

sophistication *n* complessità *f*.

sore *n* piaga *f*:—*adj* indolenzito; doloroso.

sorrel *n* (*bot*) acetosa *f*.

sorrow *n* dolore *m*.

sorry *adj* dispiacente; pietoso:—*vi* dispiacersi:—*excl* scusa, scusi.

sort *n* genere *n*, tipo *m*, specie *f*:—*vt* classificare; smistare; risolvere.

soul *n* anima *f*.

sound *adj* sano; valido; profondo:—*n* suono *m*, rumore *m*; volume *m*; (*geog*) stretto *m*:—*vt* suonare; sondare:—*vi* suonare.

soup *n* minestra *f*, zuppa *f*.

south *n* sud *m*, meridione *m*:—*adj* sud, meridionale.

southerly, southern *adj* del sud.

souvenir *n* souvenir *m*, ricordo *m*.

sovereign *adj*, *n* sovrano *m*.

sovereignty *n* sovranità *f*.

soviet *adj* sovietico.

sow *vt* seminare.

sowing *n* semina *f*.

soya *n* soia *f*.

spa *n* stazione *f* termale.

space *n* spazio *m*:—*vt* distanziare.

spacecraft *n* veicolo *m* spaziale.

spaceman/woman *n* astronauta *m/f*, cosmonauta *m/f*.

spacious *adj* spazioso.

spade *n* vanga *f*, paletta *f*:—**spades** picche.

spaghetti *n* spaghetti *mpl*.

spank *vt* sculacciare.

spanner *n* chiave *f* fissa.

spare *vt* risparmiare; prestare:—*adj* di riserva; in più; asciutto:—*n* pezzo *m* di ricambio:—**spare time** tempo libero:—**spare wheel** ruota di scorta.

spark n scintilla f; vi provocare.
sparkling adj frizzante.
sparrow n passero m.
spastic adj, n spastico m.
spatula n spatola f.
speak vt dire; parlare; vi parlare.
special adj speciale; particolare.
speciality n specialità f.
species n specie f.
specific adj specifico.
spectacle n spettacolo m: — **spectacles** npl occhiali mpl.
speech n parola f; parlata f; linguaggio m; discorso m.
speechless adj senza parola.
speed n velocità f, rapidità f; marcia f: — vi procedere velocemente; andare a velocità eccessiva.
spell n incantesimo m; periodo m: — vt dire/scrivere lettera per lettera.
spend vt spendere; trascorrere.
spent adj usato; esaurito.
sperm n sperma m.
sperm whale n capodoglio m.
sphere n sfera f.
sphinx n sfinge f.
spice n droga f; spezie fpl: — vt drogare.
spider n ragno m.
spider-web n ragnatela f.
spill vt rovesciare, versare.
spin vt filare; prolungare: — vi girare: — n giro m; effetto m; giretto m.
spinach n spinaci mpl.
sprin-drier n centrifuga f.
spine n spina f dorsale.
spinster n zitella f.
spirit n spirito m; coraggio m: — **spirits** liquori mpl.
spiritualist n spiritista m/f.
spirituality n spiritualità f.

spit n spiedo m; sputo m: — vt, vi sputare.
spite n dispetto m: — conj **in spite of** nonostante, malgrado: — vt fare dispetto a.
spittle n sputo m.
splash vt, vi schizzare: — n tonfo m; spruzzo m.
splendid adj splendido.
splinter n scheggia f; vi scheggiarsi.
split n fessura f; spacco m; scissione f: — vt spaccare; dividere: — vi spaccarsi.
spoil vt rovinare: — vi guastarsi: — n bottino m.
sponge n spugna f; pan di Spagna: — vt lavare con una spugna; scroccare.
spoon n cucchiaio m.
sport n sport m; divertimento m; persona f di spirito.
spot n macchia f; puntino m; pois m; foruncolo m; posto m: — vt macchiare; notare.
sprain n slogatura f: — vt slogarsi.
sprat n spratto m.
spread vt spiegare; spalmare; cospargere; propagare: — n propagazione f; apertura f; banchetto m.
spring vi saltare; sorgere: — n sorgente f; primavera f; salto m; molla f.
sprout n germoglio m; cavolino m: — vi germogliare.
spruce n abete: — adj azzimato.
spry adj arzillo.
spur n sperone m, sprone m: — vt spronare.
spurn vt rispingere.
spy n spia f: — vt scorgere: — vi spiare.
spying n spionaggio m.
square adj quadrato; onesto: — n quadrato m; quadro; piazza f; (fam)

matusa *m*:—*vt* squadrare:—*vi* quadrare.

squarely *adv* direttamente.

squash *n* concentrato *m* di frutta; calca *f*; squash *m*:—*vt* schiacciare.

squeeze *vt* premere; strizzare, spremere:—*n* stretta *f*; strizzata *f*.

squib *n* petardo *m*.

squid *n* calamaro *m*.

squint *vi* essere strabico:—*n* strabismo *m*.

squirrel *n* scoiatolo *m*.

stab *vt* pugnalare:—*n* coltellata *f*; fitta *f*.

stability *n* stabilità *f*.

stable *n* stalla *f*; scuderia *f*:—**stables** maneggio *m*:—*adj* stabile.

staff *n* personale *m*; bastone *m*; pentagramma *m*.

stag *n* cervo *m*.

stage *n* palco *m*; stadio *m*; tappa *f*.

stain *vt* macchiare; tingere:—*n* macchia *f*; colorante *m*.

stainless *adj* inossidabile.

stair *n* scalino:—**stairs** *npl* scale *fpl*.

staircase *n* scala *f*.

stake *n* palo *m*; puntata *f*:—*vt* (*fig*) rivendicare.

stale *adj* stantio; rafferno.

stalemate *n* stallo *m*.

stalk *vi* inseguire:—*n* gambo *m*, torsolo *m*.

stall *n* stalla *f*; bancarella *f*; stand *m*:—**stalls** platea *f*:—*vi* andare in stallo; bloccarsi.

stallion *n* stallone *m*.

stamina *n* resistenza *f*.

stammer *vt*, *vi* balbettare:—*n* balbuzie *f*.

stamp *vt* pestare; affrancare; timbrare:—*n* francobollo *m*; timbro *m*.

stand *vt* mettere; reggere a; sopportare; offrire:—*vi* stare in piedi; trovarsi; riposare; presentarsi:—*n* posizione *f*; stand *m*; leggio *m*:—**stand up** alzarsi.

standard *n* insegna *f*; standard *m*:—*adj* standard, classico.

staple *n* graffetta *f*; prodotto *m* principale:—*adj* base.

stapler *n* cucitrice *f*.

star *n* stella *f*; asterisco *m*; divo *m*.

stare *vt* fissare:—*n* sguardo *m* fisso.

starfish *n* stella *f* di mare.

stark *adj* austero.

starling *n* storno *m*.

starry *adj* stellato.

start *vt* cominciare; iniziare, avviare:—*vi* cominciare; partire; trasalire:—*n* sobbalzo *m*; inizio *m*; vantaggio *m*.

starvation *n* inedia *f*.

starve *vt* far morire di fame:—*vi* morire di fame.

starving *adj* affamato.

state *n* stato *m*; condizione *f*; agitazione *f*:—*vt* affermare; indicare.

station *n* stazione *f*:—*vt* stanziare; piazzare.

stationary *adj* fermo, stazionario.

statistics *npl* statistica *f*.

statue *n* statua *f*.

stay *n* soggiorno *m*, degenza *f*; sospensione *f* dell'esecuzione:—*vi* rimanere, restare, stare; alloggiare: —*vt* sospendere, fermare.

steady *adj* fermo, saldo; costante; fisso:—*vt* tenere fermo; calmare.

steak *n* bistecca *f*.

steal *vt* rubare.

steam *n* vapore *m*:—*vt* cuocere a vapore:—*vi* fumare.

steel *n* acciaio *m*.

steep *adj* ripido:—*vt* immergere; impregnare.

stem *n* stelo *m*:—*vt* arrestare.

step *n* passo *m*; misura *f*; gradino *m*:—*vi* fare un passo.

stepbrother *n* fratellastro *m*.

stepdaughter *n* figliastra *f*.

stepfather *n* patrigno *m*.

stepmother *n* matrigna *f*.

stepsister *n* sorellastra *f*.

stepson *n* figliastro *m*.

stereo *n* stereo *m*, stereofonia *f*.

sterile *adj* sterile.

sterilise *vt* sterilizzare.

sterling *n* sterlina *f*:—*adj* genuino.

stew *vt* stufare:—*n* stufato *m*.

stick *n* bastone *m*, bastoncino; asticella *f*:—*vt* incollare; conficcare:—*vi* appiccicarsi; bloccarsi; incepparsi; attenersi a.

stigma *n* stigma *m*.

stigmatise *vt* stigmatizzare.

stiletto *m* stiletto *m*.

still *adj* fermo, immobile; non gassato:—*n* alambicco:—*adv* ancora.

still life *n* natura *f* morta.

stimulate *vt* stimolare.

stimulation *n* stimolazione *f*.

stimulus *n* stimolo *m*.

sting *vt* pungere; pizzicare:—*vi* bruciare:—*n* pungiglione *m*, puntura *f*.

stint *n* dovere *m*.

stipulate *vt* stabilire.

stipulation *n* stipulazione *f*.

stir *vt* mescolare; agitare; risvegliare:—*vi* muoversi:—*n* scalpore *m*.

stitch *vt* cucire:—*n* punto *m*; maglia *f*; fitta *f* al fianco.

stoat *n* ermellino *m*.

stock *n* provvista *f*, stock *m*; bestiame *m*; brodo *m*; stirpe *f*:—**stocks** *npl* ti-

toli *mpl*:—*adj* solito:—*vt* tenere; rifornire.

stock exchange *n* borsa *f* valori.

stocking *n* calza *f*.

stomach *n* stomaco *m*, ventre *f*:—*vt* sopportare.

stone *n* pietra *f*:—*vt* lapidare.

stone-deaf *adj* sordo come una campana.

stony *adj* sassoso.

stool *n* sgabello *m*.

stoop *vi* chinarsi, abbassarsi.

stop *vt* arrestare, fermare; impedire; smettere; bloccare:—*vi* cessare, fermarsi:—*n* arresto *m*, pausa *f*, sosta *f*; fermata *f*; punto.

stopover *n* breve sosta *f*.

store *n* provvista *f*; deposito *m*; grande magazzino *m*:—*vt* accumulare; immagazzinare.

stork *n* cicogna *f*.

storm *n* tempesta *f*; temporale *m*:—*vt* prendere d'assalto:—*vi* infuriare.

story *n* storia *f*, trama *f*, racconto *m*; articolo *m*.

stove *n* stufa *f*.

straight *adj* diritto; liscio; onesto; semplice; eterosessuale:—*adv* diritto; direttamente.

strain *vt* tendere, tirare; slogare; affaticare; passare:—*n* tensione *f*; pressione *f*; sforzo *m*; (*med*) strappo *m*; (*biol*) razza *f*.

strange *adj* sconosciuto; strano.

stranger *n* sconosciuto *m*, forestiero *m*.

strangle *vt* strangolare, strozzare.

strap *n* cinturino *m*; spallina *f*; tracollo *m*:—*vt* legare, fasciare.

strategy *n* strategia *f*.

stratum *n* strato *m*.

straw *n* paglia *f*; cannuccia *f*.

strawberry *n* fragola *f.*

stray *vi* smarrirsi:—*adj* randagio.

streak *n* striscia *f;* vena *f:*—*vt* striare; rigare.

stream *n* ruscello *m;* (*fig*) fiume:—*vt* grondare:—*vi* scorrere.

street *n* strada *f.*

strength *n* forza *f;* resistenza *f;* gradazione *f* alcolica.

stress *n* sforzo *m,* stress *m,* tensione *f;* enfasi *f:*—*vt* mettere in rilievo.

stretch *vt* tendere, stendere; far bastare:—*vi* stiracchiarsi; esagerare:—*n* elasticità *f;* distesa *f;* tratto *m.*

stretcher *n* barella *f.*

strict *adj* severo, rigido; stretto:— **strictly speaking** a rigor di termini.

strike *vt* colpire; sbattere contro; accendere; scoprire:—*vi* scioperare; rintoccare:—*n* sciopero *m;* scoperta *f,* attacco *m.*

striking *adj* che fa colpo.

string *n* spago *m;* filo *m,* corda *f:*—*vt* infilare; incordare.

stringy *adj* fibroso.

strip *vt* spogliare; sverniciare; smontare:—*vi* spogliarsi:—*n* striscia *f;* divisa *f.*

stripe *n* riga *f.*

stripper *n* spogliarellista *m/f.*

strive *vi* sforzarsi.

stroke *—n* colpo *m;* carezza *f;* rintocco *m:*—*vt* accarezzare.

stroll *n* passeggiatina *f:*—*vi* gironzolare.

strong *adj* forte; resistente; concentrato.

strongbox *n* cassaforte *f.*

structure *n* struttura *f:*—*vt* struttureare

struggle *vt, vi* lottare:—*n* lotta *f.*

strum *vt* (*mus*) strimpellare.

stub *n* mozzicone *m;* matrice *f.*

stubble *n* stoppia *f;* barba *f* corta.

stud *n* chiodo *m;* stallone *m.*

student *n* studente *m.*

studio *n* studio *m.*

study *n* studio *m:*—*vt, vi* studiare.

stuff *n* roba *f:*—*vt* riempire; imbottire; farcire.

stumble *vi* inciampare.

stump *n* troncone *m:*—*vt* sconcertare.

stun *vt* tramortire.

stunning *adj* splendido.

stuntman *n* stuntman *m.*

stupid *adj* stupido.

sturgeon *n* storione *m.*

style *n* stile *m;* classe *f.*

stylish *adj* elegante.

stylus *n* puntina *f.*

subconscious *adj* subcosciente:—*n* subconscio *m.*

subcontract *vt* subappaltare.

subdue *vt* sottomettere; dominare.

subdued *adj* pacato, tenue.

subject *adj* assoggettato; soggetto a: —*n* suddito *m;* soggetto *m;* argomento *m;* materia *f:*—*vt* sottoporre.

subjection *n* sottomissione *f.*

subjective *adj* soggettivo.

subjunctive *adj, n* congiuntivo *m.*

sublet *vt, vi* subaffittare.

sublime *adj* sublime.

subliminal *adj* subliminale.

submarine *n* sommergibile *m.*

submerge *vt* sommergere.

submission *n* sottomissione *f.*

submit *vt* presentare:—*vi* cedere a.

subnormal *adj* subnormale.

subordinate *adj* subalterno; (*gr*) subordinato:—*n* subalterno *m;* subordinato *m:*—*vt* subordinare.

subordination *n* subordinazione *f.*

subpoena n citazione f:—vt citare in giudizio.

subscribe vi abbonarsi; approvare.

subside vi decrescere; avvallarsi.

subsidence adj avvallamento.

subsidiary n sussidiario m; complimentare.

subsidise vt sovvenzionare.

subsidy n sovvenzione f.

substance n sostanza f.

substantial adj sostanzioso; sostanziale; notevole.

substantiate vt comprovare.

substantive adj, n sostantivo m.

substitute vt, vi sostituire:—n sostituto m.

substitution n sostituzione f.

subterfuge n sotterfugio m.

subterranean adj sotterraneo.

subtitle n sottotitolo m.

subtle adj sottile.

subtlety n sottigliezza f.

subtly adj sottilmente.

subtract vt sottrarre.

subtraction n sottrazione f.

suburb n sobborgo m.

suburban adj suburbano.

suburbia n periferia f.

subversion n sovversione f.

subversive adj, n sovversivo m.

subway n sottopassaggio m.

succeed vi riuscire:—vt succedere.

succeeding adj successivo; futuro.

success n successo m; riuscita f.

successful adj riuscito; affermato.

succession n serie f; successione f.

succulent adj succulento:—n pianta f grassa.

succumb vi soccombere.

such adj tale:—**such as** come:—adv talmente; così.

suck vt, vi succhiare.

suction n aspirazione f.

sudden adj improvviso.

sue vt citare:—vi intentare causa.

suede n pelle f scamosciata.

suffer vt soffrire; tollerare:—vi soffrire.

suffering n sofferenza f.

suffice vt bastare.

sufficient adj sufficiente.

suffocate vt, vi soffocare.

suffocation n soffocazione f.

suffrage n suffragio m.

sugar n zucchero m:—vt zuccherare.

sugar beet n barbabietola f da zucchero.

sugar cane n canna f da zucchero.

suggest vt suggerire.

suggestion n suggerimento m; punta f.

suggestive adj spinto.

suicidal adj suicida.

suicide n suicidio m; suicida m/f.

suit n completo m; tailleur m; causa f; colore m:—vt adattare; andare bene a; contentare.

suitcase n valigia f.

suite n suite f; appartamento m.

suitor n corteggiatore m.

sulk vi tenere il broncio.

sulphate adj solfato.

sulphide n solfuro m.

sulphur n zolfo m.

sulphuric adj solforico.

sultan n sultano m.

sultana n uva f sultanina.

sultry adj afoso; passionale.

sum n somma f:—**sum up** vt, vi riassumere.

summary n riassunto m.

summer n estate f.

summerhouse *n* padiglione *m*.
summit *n* cima *f*, vetta *f*; vertice *m*.
summon *vt* convocare.
sumptuous *adj* sontuoso.
sun *n* sole *m*.
sunbathe *vi* prendere il sole.
sunburn *n* scottatura *f*.
Sunday *n* domenica *f*.
sundial *n* meridiana *f*.
sundry *adj* diversi.
sunflower *n* girasole *m*.
sunglasses *npl* occhiali *mpl* da sole.
sunlight *n* luce *f* del sole.
sunny *adj* assolato, soleggiato; radioso.
sunrise *n* alba *f*.
sunset *n* tramonto *m*.
sunshade *n* parasole *m*.
sunstroke *n* insolazione *f*.
super *adj* (*fam*) fantastico.
superb *adj* superbo.
superficial *adj* superficiale.
superhuman *adj* sovrumano.
superior *adj*, *n* superiore *m/f*.
superiority *n* superiorità *f*.
superlative *adj*, *n* superlativo *m*.
supermarket *n* supermercato *m*.
supernatural *adj*, *n* soprannaturale *m*.
supersede *vt* soppiantare.
superstition *n* superstizione *f*.
supervise *vt* sorvegliare.
supper *n* cena *f*.
supplant *vt* soppiantare.
supple *adj* flessibile.
supplement *n* supplemento *m*: — *vt* integrare.
supplication *n* supplica *f*.
supplier *n* fornitore *m*.
supply *vt* fornire: — *n* fornitura *f*.
support *vt* sostenere; mantenere; appoggiare: — *n* sostegno *m*.

supporter *n* sostenitore *m*; tifoso *m*.
suppose *vt* supporre.
supposition *n* supposizione *f*.
suppress *vt* reprimere; sopprimere.
suppression *n* repressione *f*.
supremacy *n* supremazia *f*.
supreme *adj* supremo; sommo.
surcharge *n* sovrapprezzo *m*.
sure *adj* sicuro, certo: — **be sure to do something** mi raccomando.
surf *n* (*mar*) cavalloni *mpl*.
surface *n* superficie *f*: — *vt* asfaltare: — *vi* risalire in superficie.
surfboard *n* surf *m*.
surge *n* ondata *f*: — *vi* riversarsi.
surgeon *n* chirurgo *m*.
surgery *n* chirurgia *f*; ambulatorio *m*.
surgical *adj* chirurgico.
surly *adj* burbero.
surmise *vt* congetturare: — *n* congettura *f*.
surmount *vt* sormontare.
surname *n* cognome *m*.
surpass *vt* superare.
surplus *n* surplus *m*: — *adj* di sovrappiù.
surprise *vt* sorprendere: — *n* sorpresa *f*.
surprising *adj* sorprendente.
surrealism *n* surrealismo *m*.
surrealistic *adj* surreale.
surrender *vt* rinunciare a: — *vi* arrendersi: — *n* resa *f*.
surrogate *adj*, *n* surrogato *m*.
surround *vt* circondare; *n* borgo *m*.
survey *vt* guardare; esaminare: — *n* indagine *f*; perizia *f*; rilevamento *m*.
survive *vt*, *vi* sopravvivere.
susceptibility *n* suscettibilità *f*.
susceptible *adj* predisposto.
suspect *vt* sospettare: — *adj* sospetto: — *n* persona *f* sospetta.

suspend vt sospendere.
suspense n suspense m; incertezza f.
suspension n sospensione f.
suspicion n sospetto m.
suspicious adj sospettoso.
sustain vt sostenere; subire.
sustenance n nutrimento m.
suture n sutura f.
swallow n deglutizione; rondine f:—
vt, vi inghiottire.
swamp n palude f:—vt inondare.
swan n cigno m.
swap vt scambiare:—n scambio m.
swarm n sciame m:—vi sciamare.
swathe vt avvolgere.
sway vi ondeggiare; oscillare:—vt influenzare:—n ondeggiamento m; influenza f.
swear vt, vi giurare, vi bestemmiare.
swearword n parolaccia f.
sweat n sudore m:—vt, vi sudare.
sweater n maglione m.
sweatshirt n felpa f.
sweep vt, vi scopare; spazzare:—n sco-
pata f, spazzacamino m; ampio gesto m.
sweet adj dolce, carino:—n caramella
f; dolce m.
sweetbreads npl animelle fpl.
sweeten vt zuccherare, addolcire.
sweetener n dolcificante m.
sweetheart n tesoro m.
sweetness n dolcezza f.
swell vi gonfiarsi:—n mare m lungo:—
adj eccezionale.
swelling n gonfiore m.
sweltering adj soffocante.
swerve n sterzata f; vi sterzare.
swift adv rapido; n rondone m.
swiftness n rapidità f.
swill vt risciacquare; tracannare:—n
brodaglia f.

swim vt, vi nuotare:—n nuotata f.
swimming n nuoto m.
swimming pool n piscina f.
swimsuit n costume m da bagno.
swindle vt truffare:—n truffa f.
swindler n imbroglione m.
swine n suini mpl.
swing vt dondolare; brandire; influenzare:—vi dondolare; penzolare:—n
oscillazione f; altalena f; ritmo m;
swing m.
switch n interruttore m; mutamento m:
—vt cambiare; invertire:—**switch off**
spegnere:—**switch on** accendere.
swoon vi svenire:—n svenimento m.
swoop vi scendere in picchiata; fare un
incursione:—n picchiata f; incursione f.
sword n spada f.
swordfish n pesce f spada.
sycamore n sicomoro m.
symbol n simbolo m.
symbolic adj simbolico.
symmetry n simmetria f.
sympathy n comprensione f.
symphony n sinfonia f.
synagogue n sinagoga f.
syndicate n sindacato m.
syndrome n sindrome f.
synod n sinodo m.
synonym n sinonimo m.
synonymous adj sinonimo di.
synopsis n sinossi f.
syntax n sintassi f.
synthesis n sintesi f.
syphilis n sifilide f.
syringe n siringa f:—vt siringare.
system n sistema m.
systematic adj sistematico.

T

tabby *n* soriano *m*.

table *n* tavolo *m*; tavola *f*; tabella *f*: — **table d'hôte** pasto a prezzo fisso: — *vt* presentare.

tablecloth *n* tovaglia *f*.

tablespoon *n* cucchiaio *m* da portata.

tablet *n* lapide *f*; compressa *f*.

taboo *n* tabù *m*.

tacit *adj* tacito.

tack *n* bulletta *f*; (*naut*) bordo *m*; (sewing) punto *m* d'imbastitura: — *vt* fissare con chiodi; imbastire: — *vi* bordeggiare.

tackle *n* paranco *m*; attrezzatura *f*: — *vt* affrontare.

tact *n* tatto *m*.

tactical *adj* tattico.

tactless *adj* indelicato.

tadpole *n* girino *m*.

taffeta *n* taffettà *m*.

tag *n* etichetta *f*.

tail *n* coda *f*: — *vt* pedinare.

tailor *n* sarto *m*: — *vt* confezionare.

taint *vt* infangare: — *n* macchia *f*.

take *vt* prendere; portare; accettare; contenere; sopportare: — *vi* attecchire.

talc, talcum powder *n* talco *m*.

talent *n* talento *m*.

talk *vt*, *vi* parlare: — *n* conversazione *f*; conferenza *f*.

tall *adj* alto.

tame *adj* addomesticato: — *vt* addomesticare; domare.

tamper *vi* manomettere.

tampon *n* tampone *m*.

tan *vi* abbronzarsi: — *n* abbronzatura *f*.

tangerine *n* mandarino *m*.

tangle *vt* aggrovigliare: — *n* groviglio *m*.

tank *n* serbatoio *m*; cisterna *f*; carro armato *m*.

tanker *n* autocisterna *f*; nave *f* cisterna.

tantrum *n* collera *f*.

tap *vt* intercettare; sfruttare: — *vi* bussare: — *n* rubinetto *m*; colpetto *m*.

tape *n* nastro *m*; fettuccia *f*: — *vt* registrare.

tape recorder *n* registratore *m*.

tapestry *n* arazzo *m*.

tar *n* catrame *m*.

tarantula *n* tarantola *f*.

target *n* bersaglio *m*; obiettivo *m*.

tariff *n* tariffa *f*.

tarragon *n* (*bot*) dragoncello *m*.

tart *adj* aspro: — *n* crostata *f*; (*fam*) sgualdrina.

taste *n* gusto *m*; sapore *m*: — *vt* assaggiare; assaporare.

Taurus *n* Toro *m*.

tavern *n* taverna *f*.

tax *n* tassa *f*; imposta *f*: — *vt* tassare; gravare.

taxi *n* taxi *m*: — *vi* rullare.

tea *n* tè *m*.

teach *vt*, *vi* insegnare.

teacher *n* insegnante *m/f*; maestro *m*; professore *m*.

teaching *n* insegnamento *m*.

team *n* équipe *f*, squadra *f*.

teamwork *n* lavoro *m* d'équipe.

teapot *n* teiera *f.*
tear *vt* strappare:—*n* strappo *m.*
tear *n* lacrima *f.*
tease *vt* stuzzicare:—*n* burlone *m.*
teaspoon *n* cucchiaino *m.*
teat *n* tettarella *f.*
technical *adj* tecnico.
technique *n* tecnica *f.*
technology *n* tecnologia *f.*
teddy (bear) *n* orsacchiotto *m.*
teenage *adj* adolescenziale.
teenager *n* adolescente *m/f*; teenager *m/f.*
teeth *npl* denti *mpl.*
telecommunications *npl* telecomunicazioni *fpl.*
telegram *n* telegramma *m.*
telephone *n* telefono *m.*
telescope *n* telescopio *m.*
televise *vt* trasmettere per televisione.
television set *n* televisore *m.*
telex *n* telex *m.*
tell *vt* dire; raccontare; indicare; distinguere:—*vi* parlare; sapere.
temper *vt* moderare:—*n* indole *f*; temperamento *m*; collera *f.*
temperament *n* temperamento *m.*
temperature *n* temperatura *f.*
temple *n* tempio *m*; (*anat*) tempia *f.*
temporarily *adv* temporaneamente.
temporary *adj* provvisorio.
tempt *vt* tentare.
temptation *n* tentazione *f.*
ten *adj, n* dieci *m.*
tenacity *n* tenacia *f.*
tenancy *n* contratto *m* d'affitto.
tenant *n* inquilino *m.*
tendency *n* tendenza *f.*
tender *adj* tenero; sensibile:—*n* tender *m*; offerta *f*:—*vt* presentare; offrire.
tenement *n* casamento *m.*

tennis *n* tennis *m.*
tennis court *n* campo *m* da tennis.
tennis racket *n* racchetta *f* da tennis.
tense *n* (*gr*) tempo *m*:—*adj* teso:—*vt* tendere.
tension *n* tensione *f.*
tent *n* tenda *f.*
tenth *adj, n* decimo *m.*
terminal *adj* incurabile:—*n* terminale *m*; capolinea *m.*
terminate *vt, vi* terminare.
terrace *n* terrazza *f.*
terrible *adj* terribile.
terrier *n* terrier *m.*
terrific *adj* stupendo; enorme.
terrify *vt* terrificare.
terror *n* terrore *m*; peste *f.*
terrorism *n* terrorismo *m.*
test *n* prova *f*; collaudo *m*; esame *m*:—*vt* controllare; collaudare; sperimentare.
testicle *n* testicolo *m.*
tetanus *n* tetano *m.*
text *n* testo *m.*
textbook *n* libro *m* di testo.
textile *adj* tessile:—**textiles** *npl* tessuti *mpl.*
texture *n* consistenza *f.*
than *conj* che; di.
thank *vt* ringraziare.
thankful *adj* grato, riconoscente.
that *adj* quel:—*pron* ciò:—*dem pron* così:—*rel pron* che:—*conj* che:—**so that** affinché.
the *def art* il, lo, ls, i, gli, le.
theatre *n* teatro *m.*
theft *n* furto *m.*
their *poss adj* loro.
them *pron* gli; loro.
theme *n* tema *m.*
themselves *pron* si; se stessi.

then *adv* allora; poi: — **now and then** ogni tanto.

theory *n* teoria *f*.

therapy *n* terapia *f*.

there *adv* la, lì.

thermal *adj* termale.

thermometer *n* termometro *m*.

these *dem adj*, *dem pron* questi.

they *pers pron* essi.

thick *adj* grosso; spesso; ottuso.

thief *n* ladro *m*.

thigh *n* coscia *f*.

thin *adj* sottile; magro: — *vt* diradarsi.

thing *n* cosa *f*: — **things** *npl* roba *f*.

think *vi* pensare; credere: — **think over** riflettere su.

thinker *n* pensatore *m*.

thinking *adj* ragionevole: — *n* pensiero *m*.

third *adj*, *n* terzo *m*.

thirst *n* sete *f*.

thirsty *adj* assettato.

thirteen *num* tredici.

thirteenth *num* tredicesimo.

thirtieth *num* trentesimo.

thirty *num* trenta.

this *dem adj*, *dem pron* questo.

thorn *n* spina *f*.

thorough *adj* minuzioso; approfondito.

those *dem adj* quei: — *dem pron* quelli.

though *conj* benché: — *adv* tuttavia.

thought *n* pensiero *m*.

thoughtful *adj* pensieroso; gentile.

thoughtless *adj* sconsiderato.

thousand *adj*, *m* mille *m*.

thousandth *adj*, *n* millesimo *m*.

thrash *vt* percuotere.

thread *n* filo *m*: — *vt* infilare.

threat *n* minaccia *f*.

three *num* tre.

thrill *vt* entusiasmare: — *vi* fremere: — *n* brivido; fremito *m*.

thriller *n* thriller *m*.

thrive *vi* prosperare.

thriving *adj* fiorente.

throat *n* gola *f*.

throne *n* trono *m*.

through *prep* attraverso; per: — *adj* finito; di passaggio.

throughout *prep* in tutto: — *adv* dappertutto.

throw *n* lancio *m*: — *vt* lanciare; gettare: — **throw away** buttar via: — **throw up** vomitare.

thrush *n* tordo *m*; (*med*) candida *f*.

thug *n* teppista *m/f*.

thumb *n* pollice *m*.

thunder *n* tuono *m*: — *vi* tonare.

Thursday *n* giovedì *m*.

thyme *n* (*bot*) timo *m*.

tick *n* tic tac *m*; segno *m*; zecca *f*: — *vt* spuntare; ticchettare.

ticket *n* biglietto *m*.

tickle *vt* fare il solletico a.

tidal *adj* (*mar*) di marea.

tide *n* marea *f*; ondata *f*.

tidy *adj* ordinato: — *vt* mettere in ordine.

tie *vt* legare; allacciare: — *vi* pareggiare: — *n* cravatta *f*; pareggio *m*.

tiger *n* tigre *f*.

tight *adj* stretto; sbronzo.

tile *n* tegola *f*; mattonella *f*: — *vt* piastrellare.

till *vt* coltivare: — *n* cassa *f*.

time *n* tempo *m*; momento *m*; periodo *m*; ora *f*; era *f*; volta *f*: — *vt* programmare; cronometrare.

timetable *n* orario *m*.

timid *adj* timido.

tin *n* stagno *m*; scattola *f*:—*vt* inscatolare.

tinfoil *n* carta *f* stagnola.

tin opener *n* apriscatole *m*.

tiny *adj* minuscolo.

tip *n* punta *f*; mancia *f*; suggerimento *m*; discarica:—*vt* dare la mancia a; pronosticare; rovesciare:—*vi* rovesciarsi.

tire *vt* stancare.

tissue *n* velina *f*; fazzolettino *m* di carta; (*anat*) tessuto *m*.

tit *n* cincia *f*.

title *n* titolo *m*.

to *prep* a; secondo; per; da.

toad *n* rospo *m*.

toadstool *n* fungo *m* velenoso.

toast *vt* tostare; brindare:—*n* pane *m* tostato; brindisi *m*.

tobacco *n* tabacco *m*.

tobacconist *n* tabaccaio *m*.

today *adv*, *n* oggi *m*.

toe *n* dito *m* del piede.

together *adv* insieme.

toilet *n* gabinetto *m*, toilette *f*.

toilet paper *n* carta *f* igienica.

toiletries *npl* articoli *mpl* da toilette.

token *n* buono *m*; segno *m*:—*adj* simbolico.

toll *n* pedaggio *m*.

tomato *n* pomodoro *m*.

tomb *n* tomba *f*.

tomorrow *adv*, *n* domani *m*.

ton *n* tonnellata *f*.

tone tono *m*:—*vi* intonarsi:—**tone down** attenuare.

tongue *n* lingua *f*.

tonic *n* (*med*) ricostituente *m*; acqua *f* tonica.

tonight *adv* stasera.

tonsil *n* tonsilla *f*.

tonsillitis *n* tonsillite *f*.

too *adv* troppo, anche.

tool *n* arnese *m*, attrezzo *m*, strumento *m*.

tooth *n* dente *m*.

toothache *n* mal *m* di denti.

toothbrush *n* spazzolino *m* da denti.

toothpaste *n* dentifricio *m*.

top *n* cima *f*; superficie *f*; tappo *m*; trottola *f*:—**big top** tendone *m*:—*adj* ultimo; migliore:—*vt* sormontare; superare.

topaz *n* topazio *m*.

topic *n* argomento *m*.

topography *n* topografia *f*.

torch *n* torcia *f*, (*fam*) pila *f*.

torment *vt* tormentare:—*n* tormento *m*.

tornado *n* tornado *m*.

torso *n* torso *m*.

tortoise *n* tartaruga *f*.

torture *n* tortura *f*:—*vt* torturare.

total *adj* totale:—**totally** *adv* completamente:—*n* totale *m*:—*vt* ammontare.

totalitarian *adj* totalitario.

touch *vt* toccare; commuovere; uguagliare:—*n* tatto *m*; tocco *m*; pizzico *m*; contatto *m*.

tough *adj* resistente; faticoso.

tour *n* giro *m*; tournée *f*; visita *f*:—*vt* fare un giro.

tourism *n* turismo *m*.

tourist *n* turista *m*/*f*.

tourist office *n* ufficio *m* del turismo.

toward(s) *prep* verso.

towel *n* asciugamano *m*.

tower *n* torre *f*.

town *n* città *f*.

towrope *n* cavo *m* per rimorchio.

toxic *adj* tossico.

toxin *n* tossina *f*.

toy *n* giocattolo *m*:—*vi* **toy with** giocherellare.

trachea *n* trachea *f*.

track *n* orma *f*; sentiero *m*; pista *f*; binario *m*:—*vt* essere sulle tracce di.

tractor *n* trattore *m*.

trade *n* commercio *m*; industria *f*; mestiere *f*:—*vt* barattare:—*vi* commerciare.

tradition *n* tradizione *f*.

traditional *adj* tradizionale.

traffic *n* traffico *m*:—*vi* trafficare.

traffic lights *npl* semaforo *m*.

tragedy *n* tragedia *f*.

tragic *adj* tragico:—**tragically** *adv* tragicamente.

train *vt* addestrare; allenare:—*vi* fare tirocinio:—*n* treno *m*; codazzo *m*; serie *f*.

traitor *n* traditore *m*.

tram *n* tram *m*.

tramp *n* vagabondo *m*:—*vi* camminare pesantemente.

tranquil *adj* tranquillo.

tranquilliser *n* tranquillante *m*.

transatlantic *adj* transatlantico.

transfer *vt* trasferire:—*n* trasferimento *m*.

transform *vt* trasformare.

transformation *n* trasformazione *f*.

transfusion *n* trasfusione *f*.

translate *vt*, *vi* tradurre.

translation *n* traduzione *f*.

translator *n* traduttore *m*.

transparent *adj* trasparente.

transport *vt* trasportare:—*n* trasporto *m*.

transportation *n* trasporto *m*.

transvestite *n* travestito *m*.

trap *n* trappola *f*; calesse *m*:—*vt* intrappolare.

trauma *n* trauma *m*.

traumatic *adj* traumatizzante.

travel *vi* viaggiare:—*n* viaggi *mpl*.

tray *n* vassoio *m*.

treasure *n* tesoro *m*; *vt* stimare.

treasurer *n* tesoriere *m*.

treat *vt* trattare; considerare; offrire; curare:—*n* sorpresina *f*.

treatment *n* trattamento *m*.

treaty *n* trattato *m*.

treble *adj* triplo; alto:—*vt* triplicare.

tree *n* albero *m*.

trellis *n* graticcio *m*.

tremble *vi* tremare:—*n* tremito *m*.

tremor *n* scossa *f*.

trial *n* processo *m*; prova *f*.

triangle *n* triangolo *m*.

triangular *adj* triangolare.

tribal *adj* tribale.

tribe *n* tribù *f*.

trick *n* scherzo *m*; trucco *m*; inganno *m*:—*vt* ingannare.

trickery *n* astuzia *f*.

tricky *adj* difficile.

trifle *n* sciocchezza *f*; zuppa *f* inglese:—*vi* prendere alla leggera.

trim *adj* snello:—*n* spuntata *f*:—*vt* spuntare.

Trinity *n* Trinità *f*.

trio *n* trio *m*.

trip *vi* inciampare:—*n* viaggio *m*; gita *f*; trip *m*.

tripe *n* trippa *f*.

triple *adj* triplo.

triumph *n* trionfo *m*.

troop *n* squadrone *m*:—**troops** *npl* truppe *fpl*.

trophy *n* trofeo *m*.

tropical *adj* tropicale.

trot *n* trotto *m*:—*vi* trottare.

trouble *vt* preoccupare; disturbare: — *n* problemi *mpl*; guai *mpl*.

trough *n* mangiatoia *f*; cavo *m*.

trousers *npl* pantaloni *mpl*.

trout *n* trota *f*.

trowel *n* cazzuola *f*.

truck *n* camion *m*.

true *adj* vero; sincero; fedele.

trumpet *n* tromba *f*.

trunk *n* tronco *m*; proboscide *f*; baule *m*.

trust *n* fiducia *f*; (*com*) trust *m*:—*vt* fidarsi.

truth *n* verità *f*.

try *vt* provare; cercare; verificare; processare:—*vi* provare:—*n* tentativo *m*; meta *f*.

tsar *n* zar *m*.

T-shirt *n* maglietta *f*.

tuberculosis *n* tubercolosi *f*.

Tuesday *n* martedì *m*.

tuition *n* lezioni *fpl*.

tulip *n* tulipano *m*.

tumbler *n* bicchiere *m*.

tummy *n* pancia *f*.

tumour *n* tumore *m*.

tuna *n* tonno *m*.

tune *n* melodia *f*:—*vt*, *vi* accordare.

tunic *n* tunica *f*.

turkey *n* tacchino *m*.

turmoil *n* confusione *f*.

turn *vt* girare; voltare; trasformare; tornire:—*vi* girare; virare; alzare: —*n* giro *m*; curva *f*; crisi *f*; turno *m*; numero *m*.

turquoise *adj*, *n* turchese *m*.

turtle *n* tartaruga *f* acquatica.

tutor *n* insegnante *m* privato.

twelfth *adj*, *n* dodicesimo *m*.

twelve *adj*, *n* dodici *m*.

twentieth *adj*, *n* ventesimo *m*.

twenty *adj*, *n* venti *m*.

twice *adv* due volte.

twin *adj*, *n* gemello *m*.

twine *vi* attorcigliarsi:—*n* cordicella *f*.

twist *vt* attorcigliare:—*vi* slogarsi; attorcigliarsi:—*n* piega *f*; sviluppo *m*; twist *m*.

two *adj*, *n* due *m*.

tycoon *n* tycoon *m*.

type *n* tipo *m*; carattere *m*:—*vt* battere a macchina.

typhoid *n* tifoidea *f*.

typhoon *n* tifone *m*.

typhus *n* tifo *m*.

typical *adj* tipico.

tyranny *n* tirannia *f*.

tyrant *n* tiranno *m*.

tyre *n* gomma *f*.

U

udder *n* mammella *f*.

ugh *excl* puah!

ugliness *n* bruttezza *f*.

ugly *adj* brutto.

ulcer *n* ulcera *f*.

ultramarine *adj*, *n* oltremarino *m*.

umbrella *n* ombrello *m*.

umpire *n* arbitro *m*.

unable *adj* incapace.

unaccountable *adj* inesplicabile.

unaccustomed *adj* non abituato.

unacknowledged *adj* senza risposta.

unacquainted *adj* non al corrente; ignorare.

unadorned *adj* disadorno.

unadulterated *adj* puro.

unaffected *adj* naturale.

unaided *adj* senza aiuto.

unalterable *adj* inalterabile.

unaltered *adj* inalterato.

unambitious *adj* poco ambizioso.

unanimity *n* unanimità *f*.

unanimous *adj* unanime.

unanswerable *adj* irrefutabile.

unapproachable *adj* inavvicinabile.

unarmed *adj* disarmato.

unashamed *adj* sfrontato.

unassuming *adj* modesto.

unattached *adj* staccato; libero.

unattainable *adj* irraggiungibile.

unattended *adj* incustodito.

unauthorised *adj* non autorizzato.

unavailable *adj* non disponibile.

unavoidable *adj* inevitabile.

unaware *adj* ignaro.

unbalanced *adj* squilibrato.

unbearable *adj* insopportabile.

unbecoming *adj* indecoroso, sconveniente.

unbelievable *adj* incredibile.

unbiased *adj* imparziale.

unblemished *adj* senza macchia.

unblock *vt* sbloccare.

unborn *adj* non ancora nato.

unbounded *adj* sconfinato.

unbreakable *adj* infrangibile.

unbroken *adj* intatto; ininterrotto; insuperato.

unbutton *vt* sbottonare.

uncalled-for *adj* fuori luogo.

uncertain *adj* incerto.

uncertainty *n* incertezza *f*.

unchallenged *adj* incontestato.

unchanged *adj* invariato.

uncharitable *adj* severo.

unchecked *adj* incontrollato.

unchristian *adj* poco cristiano.

uncle *n* zio *m*.

uncombed *adj* spettinato.

uncomfortable *adj* scomodo.

uncomfortably *adv* in modo disagevole.

uncommon *adj* insolito.

uncompromising *adj* assoluto.

unconcerned *adj* tranquillo.

unconditional *adj* incondizionato.

unconfirmed *adj* non confermato.

unconnected *adj* sconnesso.

unconscious *adj* privo di sensi; inconscio:—*n* inconscio *m*

unconstrained *adj* disinvolto.

uncontrollable *adj* incontrollabile.

unconventional *adj* non convenzionale.

unconvincing *adj* non convincente.

uncooked *adj* crudo.

uncorrected *adj* non riveduto.

uncover *vt* scoprire.

uncultivated *adj* incolto.

uncut *adj* non tagliato.

undamaged *adj* intatto.

undaunted *adj* imperterrito.

undecided *adj* indeciso.

undefined *adj* indefinito.

undeniable *adj* innegabile.

under *prep* sotto; secondo:—*adv* sotto.

undercarriage *n* carello *m* d'atterraggio.

undercharge *vt* far pagare di meno.

undercoat *n* prima *f* mano.

undercover *adj* clandestino.

undercurrent *n* vena *f* nascosta.

undercut *vt* vendere a minor prezzo di.

underdeveloped *adj* sottosviluppato.

underestimate *vt* sottovalutare.

underexposed *adj* sottoesposto.

underfed *adj* denutrito.

undergo *vt* subire.

undergraduate *n* studente *m* universitario.

underground *n* (rail) metropolitana *f*; controcultura *f*:—*adj* sotterraneo.

undergrowth *n* sottobosco *m*.

underhand *adj* equivoco.

underline *vt* sottolineare.

undermine *vt* minare.

underneath *prep*, *adv* sotto.

undernourished *adj* denutrito.

underpaid *adj* mal pagato.

underpants *npl* slip *m*.

underpass *n* sottopassaggio *m*.

underplay *vt* minimizzare.

underprivileged *adj* svantaggiato.

underrate *vt* sottovalutare.

undersecretary *n* sottosegretario *m*.

underside *n* parte *f* di sotto.

undersigned *adj*, *n* sottoscritto *m*.

understand *vt* capire; credere:—*vi* capire.

understandable *adj* comprensibile.

understanding *n* comprensione *f*; intesa *f*:—*adj* comprensivo.

understate *vt* sminuire.

understatement *n* minimizzare *m*.

understudy *n* doppio *m*.

undertake *vt* assumersi.

undertaker *n* impresario *m* di pompe funebri.

undertaking *n* impresa *f*; assicurazione *f*.

undervalue *vt* sottovalutare.

underwater *adj* subacqueo; sottomarino.

underwear *n* biancheria *f* intima.

underweight *adj* sottopeso.

underwrite *vt* sottoscrivere.

undeserved *adj* immeritato.

undeserving *adj* indegno.

undesirable *adj* sgradevole.

undetermined *adj* indeterminato.

undiminished *adj* non diminuito.

undisciplined *adj* indisciplinato.

undisguised *adj* palese.

undismayed *adj* imperterrito.

undisputed *adj* incontrastato.

undisturbed *adj* imperturbato.

undivided *adj* completo.

undo *vt* disfare; slacciare.

undoubted *adj* indubbio.

undress *vt* spogliare; *vi* spogliarsi.

undue *adj* esagerato.

undying *adj* imperituro.

unearth *vt* dissotterrare.

unearthly *adj* innaturale.

uneasy *adj* inquieto; precario.

uneducated *adj* incolto.

unemotional *adj* impassibile.

unemployed *adj*, *n* disoccupato *m*.

unemployment *n* disoccupazione *f*.

unending *adj* interminabile.

unendurable *adj* insopportabile.

unenviable *adj* poco invidiabile.

unequal *adj* disuguale.

unequalled *adj* insuperato.

unequivocal *adj* inequivocabile.

uneven *adj* ineguale; accidentato.

unexpected *adj* inatteso.

unexplained *adj* inspiegato.

unexplored *adj* inesplorato.

unfailing *adj* immancabile.

unfair *adj* ingiusto.

unfaithful *adj* infedele.

unfaltering *adj* risoluto.

unfamiliar *adj* sconosciuto.

unfashionable *adj* fuori moda.

unfasten *vt* slacciare.
unfavourable *adj* sfavorevole.
unfeeling *adj* insensibile.
unfinished *adj* incompiuto.
unfit *adj* inadatto.
unflagging *adj* instancabile.
unfold *vt* spiegare: — *vi* schiudersi.
unforeseeable *adj* imprevedibile.
unforeseen *adj* imprevisto.
unforgettable *adj* indimenticabile.
unforgiveable *adj* imperdonabile.
unfortunate *adj* sfortunato.
unfounded *adj* infondato.
unfriendly *adj* ostile.
unfruitful *adj* infruttuoso.
unfurnished *adj* non ammobiliato.
ungainly *adj* goffo.
ungovernable *adj* ingovernabile.
ungrateful *adj* ingrato.
unhappily *adv* sfortunatamente.
unhappiness *n* infelicità *f*.
unhappy *adj* infelice.
unharmed *adj* illeso.
unhealthy *adj* malsano; malaticcio.
unheeding *adj* disattento.
unhinge *vi* scardinare.
unhook *vt* sganciare.
unhoped-for *adj* insperato.
unhurt *adj* sano e salvo.
unhygienic *adj* insalubre.
unicorn *n* unicorno *m*.
unification *n* unificazione *f*.
uniform *adj* uniforme: — *n* divisa *f*.
uniformity *n* uniformità *f*.
unify *vt* unire; unificare.
unilateral *adj* unilaterale.
unimaginable *adj* inimmaginabile.
unimpaired *adj* intatto.
unimpeachable *adj* irreprensibile.
unimportant *adj* trascurabile.
uninformed *adj* non al corrente.

uninhabitable *adj* inabitabile.
uninhabited *adj* disabitato.
uninjured *adj* incolume.
unintelligible *adj* inintelligibile.
unintentional *adj* involontario.
uninterested *adj* indifferente.
uninterrupted *adj* ininterrotto.
uninvited *adj* non invitato.
union *n* unione *f*; sindacato *m*.
unionise *vt* sindacalizzare.
unionist *n* sindacalista *m*.
unique *adj* unico: — **uniquely** *adv* eccezionalmente.
unison *n* unisono *m*.
unit *n* unità *f*; reparto *m*.
unite *vt* unire; unificare.
united *adj* unito.
unity *n* unità *f*; unione *f*.
universal *adj* universale.
universe *n* universo *m*.
university *n* università *f*.
unjust *adj* ingiusto.
unjustified *adj* ingiustificato.
unkempt *adj* scarmigliato.
unkind *adj* scortese; crudele.
unknowingly *adv* inconsapevolmente.
unknown *adj* sconosciuto, ignoto.
unlawful *adj* illecito.
unleash *vt* liberare.
unless *conj* a meno che.
unlicensed *adj* senza licenza.
unlike *adj* dissimile.
unlikely *adj* improbabile; inverosimile.
unlikelihood *n* improbabilità *f*.
unlimited *adj* illimitato.
unlined *adj* sfoderato.
unload *vt, vi* scaricare.
unlock *vt* aprire.
unluckily *adv* purtroppo.
unlucky *adj* sfortunato; disgraziato.

unmanageable *adj* intrattabile; poco maneggevole.

unmarried *adj* scapolo (man); nubile (woman).

unmask *vt* smascherare.

unmentionable *adj* innominabile.

unmerited *adj* immeritato.

unmistakable *adj* inconfondibile.

unmotivated *adj* immotivato.

unmoved *adj* indifferente.

unnamed *adj* anonimo.

unnatural *adj* innaturale.

unnecessary *adj* non necessario.

unneighbourly *adj* non da buon vicino.

unnoticed *adj* inosservato.

unobserved *adj* inosservato.

unobtainable *adj* introvabile.

unobtrusive *adj* discreto.

unoccupied *adj* libero; vuoto.

unoffending *adj* inoffensivo.

unofficial *adj* ufficioso.

unorganised *adj* disorganizzato.

unorthodox *adj* eterodosso.

unpack *vt* disfare.

unpaid *adj* non retribuito.

unpalatable *adj* immangiabile.

unparalleled *adj* senza pari.

unpleasant *adj* spiacevole.

unpleasantness *n* sgradevolezza *f*.

unpolished *adj* non lucidato.

unpopular *adj* impopolare.

unpractised *adj* inesercitato.

unprecedented *adj* senza precedenti.

unpredictable *adj* imprevedibile.

unprejudiced *adj* obiettivo.

unprepared *adj* impreparato.

unproductive *adj* improduttivo.

unprofitable *adj* non redditizio.

unpronounceable *adj* impronunciabile.

unprotected *adj* indifeso.

unpublished *adj* inedito.

unpunished *adj* impunito.

unqualified *adj* non qualificato; incondizionato.

unquestionable *adj* indiscutibile.

unquestioned *adj* indiscusso.

unravel *vt* dipanare.

unreadable *adj* illeggibile.

unreal *adj* irreale.

unrealistic *adj* illusorio.

unreasonable *adj* irrazionale; irragionevole.

unrecognisable *adj* irriconoscibile.

unrefined *adj* greggio.

unrelated *adj* senza nesso; non imparentato.

unrelenting *adj* implacabile.

unreliable *adj* non attendibile.

unrepeatable *adj* irrepetibile.

unrepentant *adj* impenitente.

unreserved *adj* incondizionato.

unripe *adj* acerbo.

unsafe *adj* pericoloso.

unsatisfactory *adj* poco soddisfacente; insufficiente.

unsatisfying *adj* insoddisfacente.

unsavoury *adj* poco raccomandabile.

unscathed *adj* indenne.

unscrew *vt* svitare.

unseemly *adj* indecoroso.

unseen *adj* inosservato.

unsettle *vt* scombussolare.

unsettled *adj* instabile.

unshaken *adj* non scosso.

unsightly *adj* non bello a vedersi.

unskilful *adj* inesperto.

unskilled *adj* non specializzato.

unsociable *adj* poco socievole.

unsound *adj* cagionevole.

unspeakable *adj* indicibile.

unstable *adj* instabile.

unsteady *adj* vacillante.

unsuccessful *adj* non riuscito.

unsuitable *adj* inadatto; inopportuno.

unsure *adj* incerto.

unsympathetic *adj* non comprensivo.

untamed *adj* indomato.

untangle *vt* sbrogliare.

untenable *adj* insostenibile.

unthinkable *adj* impensabile.

unthinking *adj* irriguardoso.

untidy *adj* disordinato.

until *prep* fino a:—*conj* finché.

untimely *adj* prematuro.

untiring *adj* infaticabile.

untold *adj* mai rivelato.

untouchable *n* paria *m*.

untried *adj* non messo alla prova.

untrue *adj* falso.

untrustworthy *adj* indegno di fiducia.

unused *adj* inutilizzato.

unusual *adj* insolito.

unvaried *adj* monotono.

unwavering *adj* incrollabile.

unwelcome *adj* non gradito.

unwell *adj* indisposto.

unwieldy *adj* poco maneggevole.

unwilling *adj* riluttante:—**unwillingly** *adv* malvolentieri.

unwind *vt* srotolare:—*vi* distendersi.

unwise *adj* avventato.

unwitting *adj* involontario.

unworkable *adj* inattuabile.

unwrap *vt* scartare.

unwritten *adj* tacito.

up *adv* su.

upbringing *n* educazione *f*.

update *vt* aggiornare.

upheaval *n* sconvolgimento *m*.

uphill *adj* in salita; faticoso.

upholstery *n* tappezzeria *f*.

upkeep *n* manutenzione *f*.

uplift *vt* sollevare.

upper *adj* superiore:—*n* tomaia *f*.

upper-class *adj* dell'alta borghesia.

upright *adj* ritto; retto:—*adv* diritto:—*n* montante *m*.

uprising *n* insurrezione *f*.

uproar *n* trambusto *m*.

upset *vt* rovesciare; turbare; scombussolare:—*n* contrattempo *m*:—*adj* turbato; scombussolato; offeso.

upshot *n* risultato *m*.

upside-down *adv* sottosopra:—*adj* capovolto.

upstairs *adv* di sopra:—*n* piano *m* di sopra.

upstanding *adj* aitante.

upstart *n* parvenu *m*.

uptight *adj* teso.

up-to-date *adj* aggiornato; attuale.

upturn *n* ripresa *f*.

upward *adj* verso l'alto:—**upwards** *adv* verso l'alto; in su.

uranium *n* uranio *m*.

urban *adj* urbano.

urbane *adj* civile.

urchin *n* monello *m*.

urge *vt* insistere:—**urge on** spronare:—*n* impulso *m*.

urgency *n* urgenza *f*.

urgent *adj* urgente; pressante.

urinal *n* vespasiano *m*.

urinate *vi* orinare.

urine *n* orina *f*.

urn *n* urna *f*.

us *pron* noi; ci.

usable *adj* utilizzabile.

usage *n* usanza *f*; uso *m*.

use *n* uso *m*; impiego *m*:—*vt* usare; adoperare.

used *adj* usato.

useful *adj* utile.
useless *adj* inutile.
uselessness *n* inutilità *f*.
usher *n* usciere *m*.
usherette *n* maschera *f*.
usual *adj* solito: — **usually** *adv* di solito
utensil *n* utensile *m*.

uterus *n* utero *m*.
utility *n* utilità *f*.
utilise *vt* utilizzare.
utmost *n* massimo *m*; estremo *m*: — *adj* totale.
utter *vt* pronunciare.
utterly *adv* completamente.

V

vacancy *n* vuoto *m*; stanza *f* libera.
vacant *adj* libero; vacuo.
vacate *vt* lasciare.
vacation *n* vacanza *f*.
vaccinate *vt* vaccinare.
vaccination *n* vaccinazione *f*.
vaccine *n* vaccino *m*.
vacuum *n* vuoto *m*.
vacuum flask *n* termos *m*.
vagina *n* vagina *f*.
vague *adj* vago.
vain *adj* vano; vanitoso.
valid *adj* valido.
validity *n* validità *f*.
valley *n* valle *f*.
valour *n* coraggio *m*.
valuable *adj* prezioso: — **valuables** *npl* preziosi *mpl*.
valuation *n* valutazione *f*; stima *f*.
value *n* valore *m*: — *vt* valutare.
vampire *n* vampiro *m*.
van *n* furgone *m*.
vandalism *n* vandalismo *m*.
vanilla *n* vaniglia *f*.
vanish *vi* svanire.
vanity *n* vanità *f*.
vapour *n* vapore *m*.

variable *adj* variabile.
variation *n* variazione *f*.
varicose vein *n* vena *f* varicosa.
varied *adj* vario.
variety *n* varietà *f*.
varnish *n* vernice *f* trasparente.
vary *vt, vi* variare.
vase *n* vaso *m*.
vasectomy *n* vasectomia *f*.
vaseline *n* vaselina *f*.
vast *adj* vasto.
VAT *n* IVA *f*.
vat *n* tino *m*.
vault *n* volta *f*: — *vt* saltare con un balzo.
veal *n* vitello *m*.
veer *vi* virare.
vegetable *n* ortaggio *m*: — **vegetables** *npl* verdure *fpl*.
vegetable garden *n* orto *m*.
vegetarian *adj, n* vegetariano *m*.
vegetate *vi* vegetare.
vehicle *n* veicolo *m*.
vein *n* vena *f*.
velocity *n* velocità *f*.
velvet *n* velluto *m*.
vendor *n* venditore *m*.

veneer *n* impiallacciatura *f.*
venerate *vt* venerare.
vengeance *n* vendetta *f.*
venom *n* veleno *m.*
venomous *adj* velenoso.
ventilator *n* ventilatore *m.*
venture *n* impresa *f*; *vt* rischiare.
venue *n* luogo *m* d'incontro.
veranda(h) *n* veranda *f.*
verb *n* verbo *m.*
verbal *adj* verbale.
verdict *n* verdetto *m.*
verge *n* bordo *m*; orlo *m.*
verify *vt* verificare.
vermin *n* animali *mpl* nocivi.
vermouth *n* vermut *m.*
versatile *adj* versatile.
verse *n* verso *m*; poesia *f.*
version *n* versione *f.*
versus *prep* contro.
vertebra *n* vertebra *f.*
vertebrate *adj*, *n* vertebrato *m.*
vertical *adj*, *n* verticale *f.*
vertigo *n* vertigine *f.*
very *adj* stesso; solo:—*adv* molto.
vessel *n* vascello *m*; recipiente *m.*
vest *n* canottiera *f.*
vet *vt* esaminare:—*n* veterinario *m.*
veteran *n* veterano *m.*
veterinary *adj* veterinario.
veterinary surgeon *n* veterinario *m.*
veto *n* veto *m*:—*vt* porre il veto.
via *prep* attraverso; via.
viaduct *n* viadotto *m.*
vibrant *adj* vibrante.
vibrate *vi* vibrare.
vibration *n* vibrazione *f.*
vicar *n* pastore *m.*
vice *n* vizio *m*; morsa *f.*
vice versa *adv* viceversa.
vicinity *n* vicinanze *fpl.*

vicious *adj* maligno.
victim *n* vittima *f.*
victory *n* vittoria *f.*
video *n* video *m.*
view *n* vista *f*; veduta *f*; punta *f* di vista:—*vt* guardare; vedere.
vigil *n* veglia *f.*
vigilance *n* vigilanza *f.*
vigilant *adj* vigile.
vigour *n* vigore *m.*
vile *adj* detestabile.
villa *n* villa *f.*
village *n* paese *m.*
villain *n* mascalzone *m.*
vine *n* vite *f.*
vinegar *n* aceto *m.*
vineyard *n* vigneto *m*, vigna *f.*
viola *n* (*mus*) viola *f.*
violate *vt* violare.
violation *n* violazione *f.*
violence *n* violenza *f.*
violent *adj* violento.
violet *n* (*bot*) viola *f*; violetto *m.*
violin *n* violino *m.*
viper *n* vipera *f.*
virgin *adj*, *n* vergine *f.*
Virgo *n* Vergine *f.*
virile *adj* virile.
virtual *adj* effettivo:—**virtually** *adv* praticamente.
virtue *n* virtù *f.*
virus *n* virus *m.*
visa *n* visto *m.*
visibility *n* visibilità *f.*
visible *adj* visibile.
vision *n* vista *f*; visione *f.*
visit *vt* visitare:—*n* visita *f.*
vista *n* vista *f.*
visual *adj* visivo.
visual aid *n* sussidi *mpl* visivi.
vital *adj* vitale; fattale.

vitamin *n* vitamina *f.*
vivacious *adj* vivace.
vivisection *n* vivisezione *f.*
vocabulary *n* vocabolario *m.*
vocal *adj* vocale.
vociferous *adj* rumoroso.
vodka *n* vodka *f.*
vogue *n* moda *f.*
voice *n* voce *f:—vt* esprimere.
volcanic *adj* vulcanico.
volcano *n* vulcano *m.*
volleyball *n* pallavolo *f.*
volt *n* volt *m.*

voltage *n* voltaggio *m.*
volume *n* volume *m.*
voluntary *adj* volontario.
vomit *vt, vi* vomitare:*—n* vomito *m.*
vote *n* votazione *f*; voto *m:—vt, vi* votare.
voucher *n* buono *m.*
vow *n* voto *m:—vi* giurare.
vowel *n* vocale *f.*
voyage *n* viaggio *m* per mare.
vulgar *adj* volgare.
vulnerable *adj* vulnerabile.
vulture *n* avvoltoio *m.*

W

wad *n* batuffolo *m*; tampone *m.*
waffle *vi* ciarlare:*—n* cialda *f.*
wag *vi* scodinzolare:*—vt* dimenare.
wage *vt* intraprendere:*—npl* **wages** stipendio *m.*
wagon *n* carro *m*; vagone *m.*
waist *n* vita *f.*
waistline *n* vita *f.*
wait *vt, vi* aspettare; *vi* aspettare; servire:*—n* attesa *f.*
waiter *n* cameriere *m.*
waive *vt* rinunciare a.
wake *vi* svegliarsi:*—vt* svegliare:*—n* (*mar*) scia *f*; veglia *f.*
walk *vt* percorrere:*—vi* camminare; passeggiare:*—n* passeggiata *f*; andatura *f.*
wall *n* muro *m*; parete *f.*
wallet *n* portafoglio *m.*
wallflower *n* (*bot*) violacciocca *f.*
wallpaper *n* carta *f* da pareti.
walnut *n* noce *f*; (*tree*) noce *m.*

waltz *n* valzer *m:—vi* ballare il valzer.
wander *vi* gironzolare:*—vt* girovagare per.
wane *vi* calare.
wanker *n* uomo *m* insulso; masturbatore *m.*
want *vt* volere; desiderare:*—vi* mancare:*—n* mancanza *f*; miseria *f*; bisogno *m.*
war *n* guerra *f.*
ward *n* corsia *f.*
wardrobe *n* guardaroba *m.*
warily *adj* cautamente.
wariness *n* cautela *f.*
warm *adj* caldo; sentito:*—vt* scaldare:*—vi* **warm up** scaldarsi.
warmth *n* calore *m.*
warn *vt* avvertire.
warning *n* avvertimento *m.*
warrant *n* mandato *m*; giustificazione *f.*
warrior *n* guerriero *m.*

wart *n* porro *m*.

wash *vt* lavare:—*vi* lambire; trascinare; lavarsi:—*n* lavata *f*.

washbasin *n* lavabo *m*.

washing machine *n* lavatrice *f*.

wasp *n* vespa *f*.

waste *vt* sprecare; perdere:—*n* spreco *m*; perdita *f*:—*adj* di scarto;

watch *n* orologio *m*; sorveglianza *f*; guardia *f*:—*vt, vi* guardare.

water *n* acqua *f*:—*vt* innaffiare.

watercolour *n* acquerello *m*.

waterfall *n* cascata *f*.

waterlily *n* ninfea *f*.

watermelon *n* anguria *f*, cocomero *m*.

watt *n* watt *m*.

wave *n* onda *f*, ondata *f*; cenno *m*:—*vt* sventolare; salutare con un cenno della mano:—*vi* gesticolare.

wax *n* cera *f*:—*vt* dare la cera a.

way *n* strada *f*; direzione *f*; modo *m*; abitudine *f*:—*vt* **to give way** dare la precedenza.

we *pron* noi.

weak *adj* debole.

weaken *vt* indebolire; allentare:—*vi* indebolirsi.

wealth *n* ricchezza *f*.

wealthy *adj* ricco.

weapon *n* arma *f*.

wear *vt* portare; indossare; consumare:—*n* uso *m*; logoramento *m*; usura *f*; abbigliamento *m*.

weather *n* tempo *m*:—*vt* superare.

weave *vt, vi* tessere; intrecciare:—*n* trama *f*.

weaving *n* tessitura *f*.

web *n* tela *f*; ragnatela *f*.

wed *vt* sposare.

wedding *n* matrimonio *m*; nozze *fpl*.

wedding ring *n* fede *f*.

wedge *n* zeppa *f*; cuneo *m*.

Wednesday *n* mercoledì *m*.

week *n* settimana *f*:—**a week today** oggi a otto.

weekday *n* giorno *m* feriale.

weekend *n* weekend *m*; fine settimana *m*.

weekly *adj, n* settimanale *m*.

weeping willow *n* salice *m* piangente.

weigh *vt, vi* pesare.

weight *n* peso *m*.

weighty *adj* importante.

welcome *adj* gradito, benvenuto:—*n* accoglienza *f*; benvenuto *m*:—*vt* accogliere.

welfare *n* bene *m*; benessere *m*.

well *n* pozzo *m*:—*vi* sgorgare:—*adj*, *adv* bene:—**as well** anche.

west *adj* ovest, occidentale:—*n* ovest *m*:—*adv* verso ovest.

westerly *adj* di ponente.

western *adj* occidentale:—*n* (film) western *m*.

wet *adj* bagnato; umido; piovoso:—*n* umidità *f*:—*vt* bagnare.

whale *n* balena *f*.

what *pron* cosa:—*adj* che, quale.

whatever *pron* qualsiasi cosa.

wheat *n* grano *m*, frumento *m*.

wheel *n* ruota *f*:—*vi* roteare.

wheelchair *n* sedia *f* a rotelle.

when *adv, conj* quando.

whenever *adv* in qualsiasi momento.

where *adv, conj* dove.

whereabouts *adv* dove.

whereas *conj* mentre.

whereby *adv* per cui.

wherever *conj* dovunque.

whet *vt* stimolare.

whether *conj* se.

which *adj, pron* quale:—*rel pron* che.

while *n* tempo *m*:—*conj* mentre.
whim *n* capriccio *m*.
whimper *vi* piagnucolare:—*n* piagnucolio *m*.
whine *vi* guaire:—*n* guaito *m*.
whinny *vi* nitrire.
whip *n* frusta *f*:—*vt* frustare.
whisky *n* whisky *m*.
whisper *vt*, *vi* bisbigliare:—*n* bisbiglio *m*.
whistle *vi* fischiare:—*vt* fischiettare: —*n* fischio *m*.
Whitsun *n* Pentecoste *f*.
white *adj*, *n* bianco *m*.
who *pron* chi:—*rel pron* che.
whoever *pron* chiunque.
whole *adj* intero; tutto; completo:—*n* tutto *m*.
whom *pron* chi:—*rel*, *dir*, *obj* che.
whooping cough *n* pertosse *f*.
whore *n* puttana *f*.
whose *pron* di chi:—*rel pron* il cui.
why *adv*, *conj* perché.
wicked *adj* cattivo, malvagio, perfido.
wicker *n* vimine *m*:—*adj* di vimine.
wide *adj* largo:—**widely** *adv* molto.
widow *n* vedova *f*.
widower *n* vedovo *m*.
width *n* larghezza *f*.
wife *n* moglie *f*.
wig *n* parrucca *f*.
wiggle *vt* ancheggiare.
wild *adj* selvatico; selvaggio; furibondo.
wilful *adj* ostinato.
will *n* volontà *f*; testamento *m*:—*vt* volere; pregare:—*vi* volere.
willing *adj* volenteroso; disposto.
willow *n* salice *m*.
wilt *vt* appassire.

win *vt* vincere; conquistare:—*vi* vincere:—*n* vittoria *f*.
wind *n* vento *m*; flatulenza *f*; fiato *m*.
wind *vt* avvolgere; caricare.
winding *adj* serpeggiante.
windmill *n* mulino *m* a vento.
window *n* finestra *f*; vetrina *f*; finestrino *m*.
windpipe *n* trachea *f*.
wine *n* vino *m*.
wing *n* ala *f*.
wink *vi* ammiccare:—*n* strizzatina *f*.
winner *n* vincitore *m*.
winter *n* inverno *m*:—*adj* invernale.
wipe *vt* pulire:—*n* passata *f*.
wire *n* filo *m*.
wisdom *n* saggezza *f*.
wise *adj* saggio.
wish *vt* volere; desiderare; augurare:— *vi* desiderare:—*n* desiderio *m*; augurio *m*.
wishbone *n* forcella *f*.
wishful *adj* desideroso.
wit *n* intelligenza *f*; arguzia *f*.
witch *n* strega *f*.
with *prep* con.
withhold *vt* trattenere.
within *prep* dentro:—*adv* all'interno.
without *prep* senza.
witness *n* testimone *m*:—*vt* autenticare:—*vi* testimoniare.
witness box *n* banco *m* dei testimoni.
wizard *n* mago *m*.
wolf *n* lupo *m*; mandrillo *m*:—*vt* divorare.
woman *n* donna *f*.
womanly *adj* femminile.
womb *n* utero *m*; grembo *m*.
won't *abbr* = **will not**.
wood *n* legno *m*; bosco *m*.
woodcutter *n* tagliaboschi *m*.

woodpecker n picchio m.
wool n lana f.
word n parola f; notizia f: —vt formulare.
wordblind adj dislessico.
word processor n word processor m.
work vt azionare: —vi lavorare; funzionare: —n lavoro m; opera f: —**works** npl meccanismo m; fabbrica f.
world n mondo m: —adj mondiale.
worldly adj mondano.
worry vt preoccupare; importunare: —vi preoccuparsi: —n preoccupazione f.
worse adj peggiore: —adv peggio: —n peggio m.
worship n adorazione f: —**your worship** Vostro Onore: —vt adorare.
worst adj peggiore: —adv peggio: —n peggio m.

worth n valore m.
worthless adj inutile.
worthwhile adj valido.
worthy adj lodevole.
wound n ferita f: —vt ferire.
wreath n ghirlanda f.
wreck n naufragio m; relitto m: —vt distruggere.
wrinkle n ruga f: —vt stropicciare.
wrist n polso m.
wristwatch n orologio m da polso.
write vt vi scrivere.
writer n autore m; scrittore m.
writing desk n scrivania f.
wrong n torto m; male m: —adj sbagliato; ingiusto m: —vt fare torto a.
wrongly adv erroneamente.

X Y Z

Xmas n Natale m
X-ray n radiografia f.
xylophone n xilofono m
yacht n yacht m.
yachting n velismo m.
Yankee n yankee m.
yard n yard f; cortile m; cantiere m.
yardstick n criterio m.
yarn n filato m; racconto m.
yawn vi sbadigliare: —n sbadiglio m.
yawning n spalancato.
yeah adv sì.
year n anno m; annata f.
yearbook n annuario m.

yearling n yearling m.
yearly adj annuale.
yearn vi bramare.
yearning n desiderio m intenso: —adj bramoso.
yeast n lievito m.
yell vt, vi urlare: —n urlo m.
yellow adj, n giallo m.
yen n yen m.
yes adv, n sì m.
yesterday adv ieri.
yet conj ma; tuttavia: —adv già; ancora.
yew n tasso m.

yield *vt* fruttare; cedere:— *vi* cedere:— *n* resa *f.*

yoga *n* yoga *m.*

yoghurt *n* yogurt *m.*

yoke *n* giogo *m*; sprone *m.*

you *pron* tu, lei, voi, loro.

young *adj* giovane:—*n* prole *f*; **~er** *adj* minore.

youngster *n* giovane *m.*

your(s) *pron* tuo, suo, vostro, loro; **~ sincerely** distinti saluti.

yourself *pron* ti, si, vi, si.

youth *n* gioventù *f*; giovane *m.*

youthful *adj* giovanile.

yuppie *n* yuppy *m/f.*

zeal *n* zelo *m.*

zealous *adj* zelante.

zebra *n* zebra *f.*

zenith *n* zenit *m.*

zero *n* zero *m.*

zest *n* entusiasmo *m*; buccia *f.*

zigzag *n* zigzag *m.*

zinc *n* zinco *m.*

zip *n* cerniera *f*; zip *m.*

zither *n* cetra *f.*

zodiac *n* zodiaco *m.*

zone *n* zona *f.*

zoo *n* zoo *m.*

zoological *adj* zoologico.

zoologist *n* zoologo *m.*

zoology *n* zoologia *f.*

zoom *vi* zumare; sfrecciare via:—*n* zoom *m.*

Verbi Irregulari en Inglese

Presente	Preterito	Participio passato	Presente	Preterito	Participio passato
arise	arose	arisen	buy	bought	bought
awake	awoke	awaked, awoken	can	could	(been able)
			cast	cast	cast
be	[I am, you/we/they are, he/she/it is, *gerundio* being] was, were been		catch	caught	caught
			choose	chose	chosen
			cling	clung	clung
bear	bore	borne	come	came	come
beat	beat	beaten	cost	cost	cost
become	became	become	creep	crept	crept
begin	began	begun	cut	cut	cut
behold	beheld	beheld	deal	dealt	dealt
bend	bent	bent	dig	dug	dug
beseech	besought, beseeched	besought, beseeched	do	[he/she/it does] did	done
beset	beset	beset	draw	drew	drawn
bet	bet, betted	bet, betted	dream	dreamed, dreamt	dreamed, dreamt
bid	bade, bid	bidden			
bite	bit	bitten	drink	drank	drunk
bleed	bled	bled	drive	drove	driven
bless	blessed	blessed, blest	dwell	dwelt, dwelled	dwelt, dwelled
blow	blew	blown	eat	ate	eaten
break	broke	broken	fall	fell	fallen
breed	bred	bred	feed	fed	fed
bring	brought	brought	feel	felt	felt
build	built	built	mistake	mistook	mistaken
burn	burnt, burned	burnt, burned	fight	fought	fought
			find	found	found
burst	burst	burst	flee	fled	fled

Presente	Preterito	Participio passato	Presente	Preterito	Participio passato
fling	flung	flung	leave	left	left
fly	[he/she/it flies]		lend	lent	lent
	flew	flown	let	let	let
forbid	forbade	forbidden	lie	[gerund lying]	
forecast	forecast	forecast	lay		lain
forget	forgot	forgotten	light	lighted, lit	lighted, lit
forgive	forgave	forgiven			
forsake	forsook	forsaken	lose	lost	lost
foresee	foresaw	foreseen	make	made	made
freeze	froze	frozen	may	might	—
get	got	got, gotten	mean	meant	meant
give	gave	given	meet	met	met
go	[he/she/it goes]		mow	mowed	mowed,
	went	gone		mown	
grind	ground	ground	must	(had to)	(had to)
grow	grew	grown	overcome	overcame	overcome
hang	hung,	hung,	pay	paid	paid
hanged	hanged		put	put	put
have	[I/you/we/they have,		quit	quitted	quitted
he/she/it has, gerundio having]				quit	quit
	had	had	read	read	read
hear	heard	heard	rid	rid	rid
hide	hid	hidden	ride	rode	ridden
hit	hit	hit	ring	rang	rung
hold	held	held	rise	rose	risen
hurt	hurt	hurt	run	ran	run
keep	kept	kept	saw	sawed	sawn
kneel	knelt,	knelt	say	said	said
	kneeled	kneeled	see	saw	seen
know	knew	known	seek	sought	sought
lay	laid	laid	sell	sold	sold
lead	led	led	send	sent	sent
lean	leant,	leant,	set	set	set
	leaned	leaned	sew	sewed	sewn
leap	leapt,	leapt,	shake	shook	shaken
	leaped	leaped	shall	should	—
learn	learnt,	learnt	shear	sheared	sheared,
	learned	learned			shorn

Presente	Preterito	Participio passato	Presente	Preterito	Participio passato
shed	shed	shed	sting	stung	stung
shine	shone	shone	stink	stank	stunk
shoot	shot	shot	stride	strode	stridden
show	showed	shown, showed	strike	struck	struck
			strive	strove	striven
shrink	shrank	shrunk	swear	swore	sworn
shut	shut	shut	sweep	swept	swept
sing	sang	sung	swell	swelled	swelled, swollen
sink	sank	sunk			
sit	sat	sat	swim	swam	swum
slay	slew	slain	swing	swung	swung
sleep	slept	slept	take	took	taken
slide	slid	slid	teach	taught	taught
sling	slung	slung	tear	tore	torn
smell	smelt, smelled	smelt, smelled	tell	told	told
			think	thought	thought
sow	sowed	sown, sowed	throw	threw	thrown
			thrust	thrust	thrust
speak	spoke	spoken	tread	trod	trodden
speed	sped, speeded	sped, speeded	understand	understood	understood
			upset	upset	upset
spell	spelt, spelled	spelt, spelled	wake	woke	woken
			wear	wore	worn
spend	spent	spent	weave	wove, weaved	wove, weaved
spill	spilt, spilled	spilt, spilled			
			wed	wed, wedded	wed, wedded
spin	span	spun			
spit	spat	spat	weep	wept	wept
split	split	split	win	won	won
spoil	spoilt, spoiled	spoilt, spoiled	wind	wound	wound
spread	spread	spread	withdraw	withdrew	withdrawn
spring	sprang	sprung	withhold	withheld	withheld
stand	stood	stood	withstand	withstood	withstood
steal	stole	stolen	wring	wrung	wrung
stick	stuck	stuck	write	wrote	written

Regular Italian Verbs

infinitive

amare	temere	partire (capire)
to love	to fear	to depart (to understand)*

gerund amando temendo partendo

past participle

amato	temuto	partito

present indicative

amo	temo	parto (capisco)
ami	temi	parti (capisci)
ama	teme	parte (capisce)
amiamo	temiamo	partiamo
amate	temete	partite
amano	temono	partono (capiscono)

imperfect indicative

amavo	temevo	partivo
amavi	temevi	partivi
amava	temeva	partiva
amavamo	temevamo	partivamo
amavate	temevate	partivate
amavano	temevano	partivano

past absolute or preterit

amai	temei (temetti)	partii
amasti	temesti	partisti
amo	teme (temette)	parte
amammo	tememmo	partimmo
amaste	temeste	partiste
amarono	temerono (temettero)	partirono

---

* Third conjugation verbs with -isc- suffix include: agire, ammonire, capire, finire, obbedire, percepire, scolpire, sparire, unire.
  Some third conjugation verbs can take either form, with or without the -isc-suffix. These include applaudire, assorbire, inghiottire, mentire, nutrire, tossire.

future

amerò	temerò	partirò
amerai	temerai	partirai
amerà	temerà	partirà
ameremo	temeremo	partiremo
amerete	temerete	partirete
ameranno	temeranno	partiranno

conditional

amerei	temerei	partirei
ameresti	temeresti	partiresti
amerebbe	temerebbe	partirebbe
ameremmo	temeremmo	partiremmo
amereste	temereste	partireste
amerebbero	temerebbero	partirebbero

imperative

ama	temi	parti (capisci)
ami	tema	parta (capisca)
amiamo	temiamo	partiamo
amate	temete	partite
amino	temano	partano (capiscano)

present subjunctive

ami	tema	parta (capisca)
ami	tema	parta (capisca)
ami	tema	parta (capisca)
amiamo	temiamo	partiamo
amiate	temiate	partiate
amino	temano	partano (capiscano)

imperfect subjunctive

amassi	temessi	partissi
amassi	temessi	partissi
amasse	temesse	partisse
amassimo	temessimo	partissimo
amaste	temeste	partiste
amassero	temessero	partissero

Auxiliary Verbs

infinitive	avere	essere
	to have	to be
gerund	avendo	essendo

past participle

	avuto	stato

present indicative

	ho	sono
	hai	sei
	ha	è
	abbiamo	siamo
	avete	siete
	hanno	sono

imperfect indicative

	avevo	ero
	avevi	eri
	aveva	era
	avevamo	eravamo
	avevate	eravate
	avevano	erano

past absolute or preterit

	ebbi	fui
	avesti	fosti
	ebbe	fu
	avemmo	fummo
	aveste	foste
	ebbero	furono

future

	avrò	sarò
	avrai	sarai
	avrà	sarà
	avremo	saremo
	avrete	sarete
	avranno	saranno

conditional

	avrei	saremmo
	avresti	sareste
	avrebbe	sarebbero
	avremmo	sarei
	avreste	saresti
	avrebbero	sarebbero

imperative

	abbi	sii
	abbia	sia
	abbiamo	siamo
	abbiate	siate
	abbiano	siano

present subjunctive

	abbia	sia
	abbia	sia
	abbia	sia
	abbiamo	siamo
	abbiate	siate
	abbiano	sano

imperfect subjunctive

	avessi	fossi
	avessi	fossi
	avesse	fosse
	avessimo	fossimo
	aveste	foste
	avessero	fossero